A330   Myth in the Greek and Roman worlds

Textual Sources 2

This publication forms part of the Open University module A330 *Myth in the Greek and Roman worlds*. Details of this and other Open University modules can be obtained from the Student Registration and Enquiry Service, The Open University, PO Box 197, Milton Keynes MK7 6BJ, United Kingdom (tel. +44 (0)845 300 60 90; email general-enquiries@open.ac.uk).

Alternatively, you may visit the Open University website at www.open.ac.uk where you can learn more about the wide range of modules offered at all levels by The Open University.

To purchase a selection of Open University materials visit www.ouw.co.uk, or contact Open University Worldwide, Walton Hall, Milton Keynes MK7 6AA, United Kingdom for a brochure (tel. +44 (0)1908 858793; fax +44 (0)1908 858787; email ouw-customer-services@open.ac.uk).

The Open University
Walton Hall, Milton Keynes
MK7 6AA

First published 2010

Edited and designed by The Open University.

Typeset in India by Alden Prepress Services, Chennai.

Printed in the United Kingdom by Charlesworth Press, Wakefield.

ISBN 978 1 8487 3197 4

1.1

Contents

Primary Sources

Block 3   Ovid and the reception of myth

Block 3,
p. 31

Primary Source 3.1   Parthenius, 'The Story of Daphne'

(Source: Edmunds, J.M. and Gaselee, S. (eds) (1924) *Daphnis and Chloe: The Love Romances of Parthenius and Other Fragments*, London, Heinemann, pp. 305–7)

From the elegiac poems of Diodorus[1] of Elaea and the twenty-fifth book of Phylarchus[2]

1. This is how the story of Daphne, the daughter of Amyclas, is related. She used never to come down into the town, nor consort with the other maidens; but she got together a large pack of hounds and used to hunt, either in Laconia, or sometimes going into the further mountains of the Peloponnese. For this reason she was very dear to Artemis, who gave her the gift of shooting straight.

2. On one occasion she was traversing the country of Elis, and there Leucippus, the son of Oenomaus, fell in love with her; he resolved not to woo her in any common way, but assumed women's clothes, and, in the guise of a maiden, joined her hunt. And it so happened that she very soon became extremely fond of him, nor would she let him quit her side, embracing him and clinging to him at all times.

3. But Apollo was also fired with love for the girl, and it was with feelings of anger and jealousy that he saw Leucippus always with her; he therefore put it into her mind to visit a stream with her attendant maidens, and there to bathe. On their arrival there, they all began to strip; and when they saw that Leucippus was unwilling to follow their example, they tore his clothes from him: but when they thus became aware of the deceit he had practised and the plot he had devised against them, they all plunged their spears into his body.

4. He, by the will of the gods, disappeared; but Daphne, seeing Apollo advancing upon her, took vigorously to flight; then, as he pursued her, she implored Zeus that she might be translated away from mortal sight, and she is supposed to have become the bay-tree which is called *daphne* after her.

Primary Source 3.2   Extract from *Piramus et Tisbé*

(Source: Eley, P. (trans. and ed.) (2001) *Piramus et Tisbé*, The Liverpool Online Series: Critical Editions of French Texts, University of Liverpool, pp. 35–71)

> In the city of Babylon
>   There were two men of great renown,
> Of great valour and high rank,
>   Wealthy men from noble families
> These wealthy men had two children   5
>   Alike in beauty and appearance;
> One was a boy, the other a girl:
>   No king or queen had such beautiful offspring.
> Two children were born to these wealthy men,
>   Whom Ovid names in his book   10

---

[1]   Otherwise unknown.

[2]   A historian, variously described as being of Athens or Egypt. Besides his historical works, he wrote a μυθικὴ ἐπιτομή (Epitome of Myths), from which this story may be taken.

And says that they called
    The boy Piramus and the girl Tisbé.
Before they were seven years old
    Love laid his hand on the two children
And inflicted a deeper wound on them   15
    Than would be normal for their age.
Their being of the same age and disposition,
    Their great beauty, their noble birth,
Their conversations, laughter and games,
    And their delightful surroundings,   20
And being able to see one another frequently
    All predisposed them to love.
Ah, Love, no one, young or old,
    Can withstand your gaze;
Neither youth nor old age   25
    Can avoid being wounded by your arrow.
Against your arrow neither
    A double hauberk nor a double byrnie can prevail.
Your arrow cannot miss its mark:
    No man can protect himself against it;   30
It makes him sigh without causing any pain,
    It makes him turn pale without shedding any blood.
Your arrowhead carries burning desire,
    The shaft in the middle sighs,
The feathers wiles and entreaties   35
    And the nock behind the sweetness of love.
The arrowhead inflicts its wound through the eyes,
    The shaft slips into one's thoughts,
The feathers prepare the way,
    The nock makes two people of one mind.   40
With such an arrow and such a dart
    Did Love wound
The boy and girl when they were children,
    And bring them to the brink of death.
As yet they know nothing of love,   45
    Yet they have been profoundly disturbed by it.
Already each finds pleasure in rising in the morning
    And thinking about the other,
And they go without food more than they should
    and more than is normal at their age.   50
Early in the morning each one slips away,
    And they spend the day playing together,
Enjoying themselves with other children
    Of the same age as themselves.
During the day, they are engrossed in gazing at one another,   55
    And they can never have their fill of it;
It is late when they return to their homes
    Because parting is painful for them.
They take pleasure in doing all kinds of things
    For which they are often threatened and scolded.   60
Just as jasper is superior to glass
    And gold is superior to silver, and the primrose
Has proved superior to the mayweed,
    So these two were superior in virtue

And in valour and in beauty   65
   To all the others in the city.
It was after great deliberation and with great care
   And great wisdom that Nature created them.
For as long as their age prevented them
   From doing what Love demands,   70
And they were under the age of ten,
   They had considerable freedom
To be together and talk to one another,
   To enjoy themselves and play together.
Their loving looks and guileless minds,   75
   And their inappropriate age,
And the fact that nothing good fails to arouse envy,
   And that no low-born servant is ever free of treachery,
Caused them to be separated and kept under watch,
   So that they could not be together.   80
A servant noticed the way they behaved
   And said: Now there is no doubt in my mind
That these children are deeply in love,
   And if they were a little older
And had the opportunity,   85
   It would be very hard to keep them away from one another.
The servant took this news
   To the young girl's mother,
And she said to him: Now say no more about it,
   For they shall never be together again!   90
Then she said to a chambermaid:
   If you have any regard for me,
Make sure that Tisbé does not leave the house
   And that she does not see Piramus.
At that time great ill-feeling arose   95
   Between the children's fathers,
A quarrel and a source of hatred
   That lasted for the rest of their lives.
This business prevented
   The two children from being united   100
And brought together in marriage,
   And from sending messages to one another.
The two young people are in dire straits;
   Neither can see or hear the other:
The separation that their parents have imposed on them   105
   Seems very harsh to them.
However, the fact that they are more closely guarded –
   Tisbé dare not leave her house
And Piramus dare not look in her direction –
   Makes their love burn more fiercely.   110
Both of them grow up as their age dictates;
   As they grow older, so they grow more knowledgeable,
As their desire grows, so their suffering increases,
   And the fire that nothing quenches grows too,
Their love grows as they get older,   115
   And soon they reached the age of fifteen.
And when they entered adolescence
   And reached the age of reason

And their lives entered the period
   When nature becomes aware of love,   120
Then they no longer had any escape
   From lengthy rêveries, bitter sighs,
Great suffering, loud laments;
   Cruel torment never leaves their hearts.
They lament night and day;   125
   Their whole lives are filled with suffering;
Both of them weep and groan to themselves,
   They can see no way out of their predicament
Nor can they find relief
   Through either medicine or doctor.   130
The fire burns deep in their bones,
   That will not let them rest,
But torments them day and night
   And consumes them with a fatal flame.
This fire, this flame alone   135
   Shrivels the nerves, burns the very marrow,
Saps strength, mars beauty
   And puts all cheerfulness to flight.
Piramus is full of sorrow,
   Full of sighs and full of tears,   140
Full of sadness and full of care.
   This is how he laments:
'Alas', he says, 'poor sorrowful wretch,
   Am I to suffer this torment for long?
I am always grieving, never joyful,   145
   And the more I grieve, the more I am inflamed
By Love.
   I lie, indeed, it is not love but a fire
That recurs in this way day after day,
   Drains the colour from my face and my complexion   150
As frost drains the colour from a leaf.
   Alas!
Ah, Piramus, what will you do?
   How will you behave?
Oh, father who sired me,   155
   Why
Do you not take pity on me now?
   If you do not change your mind,
Then either by cunning or by recklessness
   I will make sure,   160
Lovely Tisbé, that I see you,
   Or if not, I will die for you.
Know that if I do not have you by consent
   I will take you away by force.
Death   165
   Will be my refuge and my comfort
If this terrible sickness afflicts me for much longer
   Or if I suffer this injustice for long.
Injustice?
   Ah, God, why is some agreement not made   170
Whereby our parents might be at peace with each other?
   We would have fewer people spying on us.

Spying?
   I cannot even manage
To find a messenger   175
   Whom I could send to her.
What matter?
   It is no use, so help me God.
Ah, father who dwells above,
   Put out the fire that besets me so,   180
The fire
   That has deprived me of laughter and enjoyment.
I cannot find a cure anywhere.
   My love,
Because of you the colour has left my cheeks,   185
   My body is wounded and my flesh has turned pale.
Fair one, because of you I spend my life
   In tears.
May the God of Love yet allow me
   To hold her in my arms by night or day,   190
Either in joy or in sorrow!
   Faint,
I cannot help but do so now; I cannot speak.
   One moment I am cheerful, the next I weep,
One moment I am burning hot, the next I feel like shivering.'195
   Before he could finish his lament
The blood began to drain from his face;
   Weeping and crying
He fell in a dead faint upon the paved floor.
   After a long while he rose to his feet,   200
All sad and wan,
   He takes himself off to the temple of Venus,
Prostrates himself on the grey marble
   And began to pray
That she might grant him an opportunity   205
   To talk to his beloved Tisbé.
Tisbé for her part is confined indoors:
   She dare not leave the palace.
Often she recalls her love,
   Often her colour comes and goes each day,   210
Often she laments and often weeps:
   'Alas!' she says. 'On what an ill-starred day
I was born!
   Ah, God, what a wretched fate,
What a harsh life has been assigned to me!   215
   Never before was there a girl kept under guard
Alive
   Who could not devise some ruse
Through intelligence or cunning,
   But me.   220
But when the more I think the less I see,
   How shall I find a way,
Sweet love, of speaking to you?
   Speaking?
Tisbé, you fool, are you losing your mind?   225
   Do you want to compromise your virginity

And bring shame upon your family?
  No, indeed!
Heed Reason, who opposes you in this!
  May you never be tempted to entertain   230
Any desire
  Which might make you commit such madness.
No woman from your family
  Was ever accused of wantonness.
Accused?   235
  I shall not be, in any shape or form.
I would rather suffer a hundred deaths.
  Tisbé,
Where did you come up with that idea?
  You have forgotten Piramus soon enough!   240
My love,
  I never meant what I said.
Now, it seems to me, you can say
  Rightly
That there is no constancy in a woman's love.   245
  Fair sweet love, duly accept
The pledge:
  Here, my lord, for this transgression
I now grant you my virginity.
  I was too proud-hearted just now.   250
Too proud?
  I should bow my head before you.
I would hold the censure dear
  If I heard myself being blamed for this.
No one,   255
  So it seems to me, and as I see it,
Should pass censure on me
  Or denounce me in this matter.
Insane!
  Be quiet, you foolish, shameless girl!   260
What impulse has brought about this change in you?
  Now you are completely taking leave of your senses!
Away
  With all these thoughts I have now;
With my father's counsel I shall have   265
  Another lover just as fair as him, I know.
As fair?
  I shudder to think that Piramus may hear me.
Yes, I am trembling, I can feel it.
  I was wrong to say it, and now I regret it.   270
Fair one!
  Rose bud and newly-opened lily,
Flower of all other youths,
  Have mercy!
Take no notice of whatever I say;   275
  My heart is led astray by fear.
I shall never have any other love
  But you,
But your parents are hostile towards me
  And mine guard me jealously.   280

What matter?
  It does not matter, so help me God.
One moment I feel my heart pounding, the next I am too hot;
  I am on the brink of taking the plunge for you.
Alas!   285
  What have I said? This sickness spares me nothing
Which so often saps my strength.
  Poor wretch!
May the God of Love grant me,
  Whether I rejoice in it or regret it,   290
That I may hold him in my arms again
  Soon.
Here I shall end my lament in tears.
  I cannot help fainting; now is the time.
And this   295
  Is what I have to do each day,
This is the fief I hold from my love.'
  The maiden fainted three times,
And when she rose to her feet again
  She holds out both her hands towards the heavens: 300
She implores the gods with great humility
  To grant that she may find a way
To be able to speak to her beloved.
  The two palaces were next to one another
And constructed in such a manner   305
  That only one partition, one wall
Separated the two of them.
  In the inner chamber
Where fewest people went,
  Where the maiden was confined,   310
The wall was slightly cracked.
  The crack was not very large
And had lain hidden for many years,
  Until Love brought it to light,
Love, from which nothing can be concealed.   315
  What is there that Love does not become aware of?
The two lovers were the first ones
  To notice this hole:
First Tisbé, then Piramus.
  Tisbé discovered the crack,   320
Took the pendant on her belt
  And pushed the metal part of it through
So that her beloved could see it.
  Piramus returned from taking exercise,
Intended to bring comfort from his grief,   325
  He enters the chamber, makes himself inconspicuous,
Turns his eyes towards the wall,
  Looks and sees the token
That shows him where the crack is.
  He goes over, takes the pendant   330
And sees the hole it reveals:
  'Tisbé', he says, 'fair creature,
Flower of all other women,
  By the token of this belt,

I have come here to make amends   335
　　For not discovering this crack;
To you belongs the good fortune
　　Of having noticed this opening.
If you really care for me
　　No lock or bolt will stop you   340
From coming here with confidence:
　　Without messengers, quite openly,
Quietly and in a whisper,
　　We can speak about the wrong that has been done to us;
Then you will know how Love   345
　　Has set me on fire, though I have done him no wrong.
Ah, God, how harsh life is
　　For anyone who suffers such torment for long!'
The maiden on the other side
　　Is listening and watching;   350
She hears the sound of his words,
　　Moves closer to the wall,
Puts her eye to the crack
　　And recognises her beloved's face.
She tries to speak, but cannot,   355
　　Because of the love that shakes her to the core.
The moment she sees him
　　She shivers and sighs and burns with love,
Quakes and trembles and perspires all over,
　　Her colour changes, comes and goes,   360
She thinks about what she should say to him,
　　Is lost in thought for a while;
Love oppresses her in so many ways,
　　Love which conquers all.
Eventually, she has gathered her thoughts   365
　　And taken heart somewhat;
She puts her mouth to the crack,
　　Then this is what she says:
'My love – I dare to call you that:
　　They cannot forbid me to do so –   370
I cannot hide my feelings from you.
　　I am going to make fun of your valour:
I was the one who first found a way
　　For us to be together here,
Because the one who loves most deeply sees most clearly.   375
　　I hear you lamenting bitterly,
But you have little idea what love is:
　　You can still make a game of it;
You leave me to endure sorrow,
　　I to whom nothing can bring comfort.   380
I have exchanged joy for weeping,
　　For pouring out sorrowful laments,
And merriment for grieving,
　　Sweet sleep for desolate thoughts,
Joy and pleasure for sighing.   385
　　My love, I cannot stay here any more:
Tears cloud my eyes,
　　Sighs prevent me from speaking.

Be sure to come back tomorrow;
   We shall be able to talk at greater length   390
And comfort one another.'
   She could not say any more to him,
And so the two of them parted.
   The day passes, the night comes to an end.
In the morning both of them return   395
   And come back to their crevice.
Piramus is the first to speak:
   'My love, I am in agony,
For I am mortally wounded because of you,
   Whom I love.   400
Now I come back to the call,
   Like a falcon when it is hungry;
I am more securely hooked than a fish on a line,
   I am trapped
Because of you, it seems to me: 405
   I do not know what joy and laughter are.
If I am held much longer, I shall not escape alive.
   I am dying!
The God of Love does not keep faith with us,
   For his justice has passed us by: 410
We are entangled in one net
   Together.
I do not know whom to implore, you or him.
   Fair one, I take refuge with you.
If I die because of you, so much the worse for me!   415
   My love,
You would be guilty of great treachery
   If I were to lose my life because of you,
When you can save me.
   Unhappy me!   420
Well may I suffer grief and torment,
   I who have loved so long
And cannot do what I desire.
   Poor wretch!
Ah, fair one, how I am afflicted,   425
   How I am overcome by love of you!
Sorrow
   Never leaves me, night or day:
One moment I am lost in thought, I sigh and then I weep;
   The colour has all vanished from my cheeks.   430
Sleeping,
   Eating and drinking are things I must leave behind.
I cannot speak without sighing.
   I have certainly learned how to suffer pain.
Pleasure   435
   And all that I desire have fled from me.
Ah, God of Love, against whose sickness I struggle!
   I shall never be cured unless I leave.
Leave?
   Love is not going to abandon me: 440
I shall have to die because of Love.
   Die?

If it please God and you, no,
    Rather, I shall entreat you:
I shall not beg, I believe,   445
    In vain,
But I shall hold my hand out so straight
    That you will cure me of this sickness
And assure me of your love.
    Ah, wall,   450
You are so harsh and unyielding,
    But if I felt a little safer here
The crack
    Would be made so wide by my hands
That without the guard noticing   455
    I would have drawn you through it.
O wall,
    Have mercy on these sufferers!
O crack, you are so very narrow!
    Stone, if you would only open up   460
Enough
    For us to be together as we speak
And to kiss one another!
    My love,
If I were at your side,   465
    I would be cured of my great pain,
But everything is against us.
    O lodging,
We should still love you
    For allowing us to speak through you.   470
O crack,
    Hide yourself well, so that none of those
Who threaten us can find you.
    I can half-see the face
Through you   475
    Of the one who has drawn
My heart and soul to her.
    O wall,
You are so pitiless and cruel,
    Who do not open up at my entreaty   480
Even enough for me to kiss her face,
    Her mouth,
Whose sweetness stirs my heart.
    Ah, fair wall,
Do just this much for me without delay,   485
    No more.
Let us pray now to the heavens above
    That lady Venus may help us
So that no one finds this hole.'
    The young man laments and sighs,   490
Then he trembled and could say no more,
    And when his tale breaks off,
Tisbé begins her lament:
    'My love, you are in great distress;
No wonder, for you love me so deeply: 495
    I know that you have received a mortal wound

For me,
   And I for you, by my faith.
I do not know what to do with my life,
   I am no less troubled   500
Than you.
   You are very sad and tearful,
And my heart is full of anguish.
   Bitterly
You lament this torment,   505
   But, I believe, I lament more bitterly still.
My love,
   You who say that you are overcome,
My heart has been ambushed by love
   In truth;   510
It burns more fiercely than fire in straw.
   Love is killing me and torturing me.
Great God,
   What anger, what ill-will is this
That you have harboured against me for so long?   515
   Divine father,
Who caused me to be brought into this world,
   You see my grief and my suffering,
My torment.
   Ill-treatment and ill fortune   520
Were mine,
   My love, when first I came to know you.
Never since, day or night, have I been free of
   Love's wound.
No wonder then if she is distressed,   525
   The girl
Who suffers such anguish for you:
   Nothing can make her joyful.
Unjustly
   Have I lost joy and pleasure;   530
Nothing can bring me comfort;
   In agony I await death.
By day
   I am in tears and fearful,
Anxious and doleful,   535
   Suffering and sorrowful;
By night
   I have neither pleasure nor enjoyment.
When I lie in my bed, there is
   Silence,   540
And it fills me with pain and distress;
   It seems as though I can see you,
But you cannot speak to me,
   Which makes things even worse for me than they were.
I shake,   545
   I sweat with anguish and torment;
Then I stretch out my hands to reach you,
   And when I am about to hold you, it comes to nothing.
My love,
   When I go back to sleep, then it seems   550

That you are there before my face,
    All stricken and downcast.
God grant
    That some good may come to me from this dream!
Then it seems that I am hailed   555
    Time and again
By some voice, I know not which, lamenting,
    That speaks clearly to me
Like this:
    Tisbé, do you recognise your love?   560
Wake up, let us go away from here.
    'Tisbé,
The gods have commanded us
    To go out from the city,
Beneath the mulberry tree,   565
    Straight to the spring by the gravel bank:
There we can enjoy ourselves together.
    My love,
Tell me what you think of this.
    I want you to be quite sure of my love,   570
In truth.
    I shall steal away during the first part of the night,
At midnight I shall go and see,
    Beyond the walls,
If I can find you there.   575
    My love, your life is my treasure:
Take care
    Not to be late, and do not tarry;
Rise from your first sleep,
    Look for me at the spring,   580
Under the mulberry tree in the middle of the fields,
    Where Ninus was buried,
You will surely find me there.'
    So they make their compact
And then the two lovers part   585
    And took their leave of the crack
That they never saw again,
    But first each of them kisses the wall
As they leave.
    The two lovers are very anxious;   590
It seems to them that the day is too long;
    They keep reproaching the sun,
And frequently call it, traitor.
    For being so slow to set,
And holding back the night for so long: 595
    They say that it is doing it on purpose
In order to disrupt their plans.
    The daylight wanes, night returns
And with it comes the hour for their venture.
    The watchmen climb up on the city walls;   600
People who are peace with themselves fall asleep,
    But neither of these two can rest,
They have something else on their minds;
    Each of them is privately preoccupied

With getting their undertaking off to a good start.   605
   Now their hearts are filled with hope,
And yet they are still uncertain
   As to whether they should do it or not,
But desire overcomes reason.
   They rejoice in the pleasant thought   610
That they are about to be together,
   And they also go over in their minds
The grief, the suffering and death that could be theirs.
   Both of them experience joy and pain,
But Love triumphs nonetheless;   615
   Neither sense nor reason can dissuade them
From doing what they have embarked upon.
   Everyone was already asleep
When Tisbé made the first move:
   She rises from the bed where she is lying,   620
And leaves the chamber very quietly.
   Neither door nor lock held her back;
She leaves the chamber with confidence,
   Alone in the night but without fear:
Such was the boldness Love gave her.   625
   When she had left the palace
And was going undisturbed down the steps,
   She put her left foot forward;
Then she looked towards her right,
   Felt the whole palace tremble,   630
And saw the moon turn dim.
   When she had looked all around,
She felt no hint of fear
   That she would not carry out her plan,
Whatever fate might await her as a result.   635
   She had already reached the city walls
When a watchman saw her,
   And, seeing her at that hour of the night,
He believes that she is a goddess,
   Draws back and does not challenge her;   640
And so the maiden goes her way
   Under the very eyes of the watchman.
She went her way through a breach in the wall
   And came without delay to the place
Where they had agreed to meet.   645
   She was already sitting on the marble slab
By the spring under the tree
   Where they were to be together,
And she begins to think
   About how she would tease   650
The young man for not arriving on time,
   When a lion from the mountains
Which had killed a flock
   Of sheep came through the fields.
It was still covered   655
   In entrails and wool;
It came down to drink at the spring.
   The maiden cowered

When she saw the ferocious animal coming,
   The blood drains from her face, she turns pale: 660
No wonder she was afraid.
   She runs away along a track,
Fearing that the lion will see her,
   But she is so agitated that, unwittingly,
She drops her wimple as she goes.   665
   She swiftly goes and conceals herself
In the shadow of an almond tree.
   The lion approached roaring loudly,
Quenches its thirst at the spring,
   And when it has drunk its fill,   670
It gambols off through the fields.
   It finds the wimple on a path,
Tramples it and covers it with blood;
   And when it has left the fields
And Piramus has arrived,   675
   O, God, what a calamity!
What a heart-breaking discovery he makes!
   For in the moonlight,
As fate would have it,
   He looked in the shadow of the mulberry tree   680
And saw the white gleam of the wimple,
   And on the dust all around
He recognised the lion's tracks;
   He sees the sand scattered around,
The water in the spring muddied,   685
   He finds the wimple trampled to pieces
And covered in fresh blood:
   He believes it is his beloved's blood,
Looks around and sees no sign of her.
   Alas! Tragically, she stays where she is!   690
She did not come forward at this point:
   She is so afraid of the ferocious animal
That she did not yet dare to come back.
   When Piramus does not see his beloved,
He is convinced that she has perished.   695
   He turned greener than an ivy-leaf
And was fixed to the spot like a stone.
   His blood runs cold, his heart turns over;
Then he burns with anguish and rage,
   And afterwards he speaks such words as anguish   700
And wrath will allow him to utter:
   'Night of sorrow, night of torment,
Mulberry, tree of tears,
   Fields, bloody with her blood,
O spring,   705
   Why have you not kept her safe for me,
The girl whose blood lies on the sand?
   Suddenly they all come to nothing,
My plans,
   My hopes, my love, my expectations.   710
Ah, God, what grief it represents for me,
   This wimple I see covered in blood!

My love,
   How was the wild animal bold enough
To launch such an attack on you?   715
   What a calamity, what a tragedy, what a crime
That you should have died this way!
   My dear,
It is a bitter blow that I am still alive,
   I who gave you the confidence to come   720
Alone to such a place at night, in the darkness.
   Alone!
Ah, to think of the vile maw
   That is sated with your flesh!
Alas!   725
   I see blood here and I see clothing.
Lion, you who devoured her,
   I marvel that you did not leave more of her,
And you, pitiless moon, who watched it happen,
   That you did not cover your face at that moment.   730
It is unjust
   That she is dead and I am not:
I do not know which grieves me more.
   Death is my best comfort.
Poor wretch,   735
   When she is dead and I am still alive!
For God's sake, earth, swallow me up,
   Or you, lion, who killed her,
Return:
   I am ready and shall put up no resistance,   740
You can do what you will with me.
   Come back,
You who devoured the sweet creature;
   You drank her blood, now drink mine!
Forlorn!   745
   My sweet love, I am too slow,
For I was not present at your death.
   Death, return and take me now!
Ah, Death,
   Why are you waiting? It is a crime   750
That I am not dead here and now.
   Dear sister,
I killed you, by arriving last
   At the rendez-vous, while you were first.
Now I beg my right hand to strike well: 755
   This is how I shall avenge you.
Avenge?
   But first I shall pray to the gods
To display in this mulberry tree
   A sign of death and tribulation   760
And grief:
   May they make its fruit turn a colour
Which befits sorrow.'
   When he had given vent to his grief and made his prayer,
Then he drew his sword,   765
   And lifted up the wimple

On the tip of the sword.
   He kisses the wimple and the blood;
He runs himself through the flank,
   So that the sword emerges   770
On the other side of his body.
   As he lies dying he kisses the wimple.
Such is the love that caused this hapless youth's death!
   His blood spurts on to the branches
And turns the white fruit black: 775
   Mulberries had always been
White until that time;
   Then black became their colour
As a testament to sorrow.
   Meanwhile Tisbé returned,   780
So as not to dash her lover's hopes;
   She is very eager to tell him
What danger she has escaped from.
   She believes she is going to achieve her goal
And she will have what she had desired so much,   785
   But now the time is rapidly approaching
When their love will run its course!
   It seems to her that she is already with him,
That they are embracing one another
   And talking of their love,   790
But soon sorrow will be hers.
   Quietly she retraces her steps,
And when she approaches the mulberry tree,
   She thought that she had lost her way
Because of the change in colour she could see,   795
   For to begin with the fruit she had seen was white,
Which now is black with blood.
   While she is puzzling over this
She has kept going straight ahead.
   She hears the young man sobbing,   800
Moaning, groaning, gasping for breath;
   She saw how he was pressing the wimple
Time and again to his lips,
   And when she notices the wound,
No wonder she is horrified.   805
   When she sees the sword through his body,
The blood drains from her face and she fainted.
   She comes round, disconsolate, distraught,
Tears her hair, claws her face with her nails,
   Rips at her flesh, weeps and cries aloud,   810
Death is sweeter to her than life.
   Then she bends over the body
And pulled the sword out of it.
   She raised it up high
And speaks like a woman in despair: 815
   'O sword that I have in my hand,
That has brought my joy to an end in grief,
   Show me now how bold you are.
O sword
   That has put an end to our love,   820

Be warmed again in my breast
   And bloodied with my blood and his.
Bloodied!
   Ah, God, what an ending, what a dream,
How soon our youth is destroyed!   825
   Dear lord,
Grief has not spared you anything
   When you decided to die by your own hand.
Wretch, how can I speak a word
   When I see him gasping for breath?   830
I see
   That he is in his death-throes, because of me.
What a shallow love, what worthless loyalty
   Mine would be,
My love, if I did not follow you   835
   And kill myself straightaway.
Dear one,
   Such a tragedy, such a disaster!
Your heart was too ruthless!
   Moon, spring, fields, mulberry tree,   840
Pale night,
   Who sent me a baleful omen
When I had left the hall,
   Hear me!
I invoke you as witnesses to my death.   845
   Oh, God, my heart, how distraught it is!
Tisbé, faint-heart, why do you delay?
   Faint-heart,
All you need is the desire to die,
   For time and opportunity are not lacking!   850
To die?
   I desire nothing more
Than to put an end to my sorrows.
   It is wrong for me to stay my hand.
Wrong!   855
   Love, make my hand strong enough
For a single blow to kill me,
   And his soul will be greatly comforted:
We shall both die the same death.
   My love,   860
I know that Love has killed you.
   If we cannot be together in life,
Death will unite us, so it seems to me.
   Parents,
Who planned to keep us confined indoors,   865
   You will soon be broken-hearted.
What a terrible tragedy
   You will see,
When you find the two of us
   Together, dead in one another's arms!   870
I beg you to grant me this boon:
   As we were parted in our joy
And are separated by death,
   At least

Let a single grave enclose us;   875
   Let one tomb receive us both.'
Then the maiden bends forward,
   Kisses her lover's lips and addresses him:
'Piramus, see, your beloved is here.
   Look at her and she will be saved.'   880
As he lay dying, the youth
   Half opens his eyes and sees
That it was his beloved Tisbé
   Who was addressing him, distraught.
He tries to speak to her, but cannot,   885
   For death, which has him in its clutches, will not let him.
But he managed to say: 'Tisbé, my love,
   In God's name, who brought you back to life?'
At this he falls silent, he can say no more,
   Then he looks at her and sighs;   890
His heart stops beating and he dies,
   Leaving Tisbé distraught.
He is dead and she has fainted.
   Oh, God, what a love has ended here!
The maiden raised herself up;   895
   She grasped the sword in both hands;
Through the chest, underneath her breast,
   The young girl runs herself through with it.
The blood spurts out on both sides,
   And she falls across her lover's body.   900
She puts her arms around the body and embraces it,
   Kisses his eyes and mouth and face;
She kisses his lips passionately:
   For as long as she is conscious and alive,
She proves herself to be a true lover.   905
   Now he is dead and she is dead.
There she died; this is how
   The two lovers came to be together.
Say 'Amen' aloud, each of you,
   And may God grant them true forgiveness,   910
And grant us redemption,
   And give us His blessing.

Primary Source 3.3 'Pasiphae' (Book 8, lines 623–986)

(Source: Translated, with footnotes, by Dr Jeremy Dimmick (2009), from C. de Boer, Martina G. de Boer and Jeannette Th. M. van't Sant (eds) (1915–38) *Ovide moralisé: poème du commencement du quatorzième siècle*, 5 vols, Amsterdam, Koninklije Akademie van Wetenschappen. Reprinted 1966, Wiesbaden, M. Sändig)

'Pasiphae' (Book 8, lines 623–986)

(623) Minos, the righteous judge, the mighty king, the good justice, had a wife who came from a very good family and noble lineage, supported by wealth and friends.[1] (628) Nature had done her utmost to make such a creature. She had a

---

[1]   Here and in a couple of other places I borrow turns of phrase from Renate Blumenfeld-Kosinski's renderings in her 1996 article 'The scandal of Pasiphae: narration and interpretation in the *Ovide moralisé*' (*Modern Philology*, vol. 93, pp. 307–26).

body of beautiful proportions, tall and straight, slender and shapely. (632) She did not cover her face in cosmetics, nor was there any need for them, for God had taken care to place in her everything that belongs to a beautiful lady. (636) She was the daughter of the sun, and her face and her body were very attractive. (638) If I wanted to describe her beauty completely it would prolong my subject-matter too much. All the same I'll speak of it a little and describe her briefly. (643) She was most beautiful and attractive: she had grey, captivating eyes, black eyebrows in a semicircle; nor was her forehead covered in scabs or warts, but broad and flat and white without blemish. (649) Her nose was well-formed and artfully turned, her teeth white, delicate and small and well-arranged in her mouth. On her chin she had a little dimple which Nature had placed just right. (654) Her face was well-drawn and painted in a single colour, a delicate vermilion which lit up the whiteness of her skin. Her hair was brighter than fine gold. There was no end to her beauties. Her neck was white, round and smooth. (660) If I wanted to describe all the rest in complete detail there would be too much of it to take in; so I choose to fall silent now, except to say that Nature had never been able to create anyone more lovely than her.

(666) Pasiphae pleased and charmed the king very much because of her beauty. But she showed him not the slightest fidelity or loyalty, the faithless woman. (670) Her heart was treacherous and false, full of madness and folly. Badly was that beauty placed which Nature had set in her, for there never was and never will be a woman more vile or base. She was full of every kind of wickedness, along with wild madness and vileness. Vileness? Truly, no one has ever seen the like, so base and abominable. She was utterly devilish and had a mad passion in her heart: such great madness came to her in both will and desire— (684) yet I don't know how I can speak such vile reproaches of a woman. I'll never defile my mouth by telling of such a vile shame. (688) She had no shame about her actions, for she had lost all sense of shame. Her mind and her attention were on crime and sin: she had fixed her heart on wrongdoing and left all virtue behind. (694) She never paid any attention to courtesy or honour, or set any store by them: she hated honour, and dishonour she held to be honourable and good. Her thoughts were entirely wicked; her hands, her tongue and her thoughts she used to prevent all good and to do evil and encourage evil. She was wicked in deeds and words.

(706) Then what blame will there be if you speak evil of evil, disloyalty of the disloyal? It would cause much greater shame and blame if one wanted to praise the wicked wrongfully. (711) Then I can say this without being blamed (and I could not speak ill without being blamed for it). It's not at all scandalous or blameworthy to speak of the ignoble in ignoble terms. Then I'll speak without hesitation – yet it causes me shame and great embarrassment ever to speak so ill of a woman. (718) She loved a bull against nature. – Loved? Not so! This wasn't love at all. What then? A madness that intoxicated her heart as soon as she set eyes on the bull, a sight that utterly delighted her.

(724) One day she was sitting at her window and gazing out over the meadows when she saw amid a herd of cows an amazingly fierce bull. Pasiphae gazed at the bull's beauty intently. She set her eyes, her heart, her face to look at the bull out of the window where she was sitting; it utterly enthralled her. (734) The more she gazed at it, the more she burned with desire, this unfortunate and crazy woman. The more she studied it, the more crazed she grew, more and more the mad passion seized and drove her. (738) A violent passion had seized her heart, oppressing and tormenting her severely: she sighed, lamented, gaped, shuddered, trembled, perspired. She kept turning pale; many times a day her colour changed. In many ways the poor woman had been caught unawares by love for the bull. The frenzy so drove her that she couldn't control herself.

(748) She has forgotten all about Minos, the good and faithful king – this wicked woman faithless of heart – he who cherished and loved her so much. Surely she has and ought to have great shame and dishonour when she thought to herself about such an outrage, but if her desire was to cause him such disgrace, why didn't she love some handsome young man who would serve her as she pleased? (758) She could have had plenty of choice, for she was rich, beautiful and noble – but she had set her sights on the bull. She didn't spare a thought for King Minos; neither he nor anyone else suited her. She cared for nothing but the mute beast: her heart and her thoughts didn't shift from the fierce bull. (765) It was unfortunate that she saw its beauty, certainly, but more so its penis: she would surely have never loved it for its beauty if it hadn't had such a large penis. (769) Ah, God! What a shameful, disgraceful thing to say! How can it have come out of my mouth? I'm appalled that it came out – truly I didn't speak it, it escaped me. From now on I must make sure I guard against saying anything I should be blamed for, for the man who acts foolishly just once ought to be punished straight away. Henceforth I'll guard against such madness. – (779) But if I do so, so ought Pasiphae, that disloyal woman, in this whorish affair. She behaved utterly madly as soon as she allowed her heart to fall into thinking about something so crazy. (784) She ought to draw her heart and her thoughts back from such vile madness – but love for the bull so bound her that she had no intention to repent of it, but rather set all her thoughts and attention on bringing about her wicked purpose. Her heart would never be at rest unless she achieved what she desired. (792) Love for the bull made her suffer, melt into tears, burn with desire; she would gladly strive to have its love, be it by trickery or by cunning. Without it she could not endure or live on.

(798) Like someone mad or drunk, forgetting entirely about her nature, her rank, the noble family she came from, this faithless woman, full of mad passion, without delay, without holding back, set out into the meadows to gaze, close to the one she desired in her heart. (806) She gathered grass with her white hands to give it to the bull to eat. (808) Now the bull could easily have kissed her without meeting any resistance, if it had wanted to. It would have been able to carry out its will and its desire in all the rest too, but it knew nothing about any of this: it didn't fit with its nature to do what she asked of it. It left Pasiphae alone, wandered off, and went to make love to the cows.

(817) Then Pasiphae was furious, so upset that she couldn't speak. She was anguished and humiliated when the bull, in which all her comfort lay, scorned her in favour of the cows. The fire that goaded her so fiercely could not be healed except by the bull. (824) She often gazed at herself and studied herself in her mirror, kept adorning and dressing herself up to be more attractive to it (so she thought). (828) Her face had lost its colour and turned pale. 'I'm sure that it will help when he sees my face so pallid, my complexion so pale and thin for his sake. If his heart isn't entirely cruel and harsh, he'll feel some pity because of it.' – (834) (I'm sure it will never happen that he feels any pity because of it!) – (836) Often, seeing the bull, she combed her hair because her beautiful tresses were tangled; time and again she spoke to it, beseeched it: 'My love, for God's sake help me!'

(840) Ah Pasiphae, think about it! Leave these unhappy thoughts, which such an insane passion makes you think! You know perfectly well, if you have the slightest bit of understanding (but you possess neither reason nor moderation) – you ought to realise that he doesn't pay any attention to you; he never realises that you're talking to him. You're wasting your prayers and your speeches. (849) What does he care about your costume, your attractive body, your figure, or your lovely golden hair? If your face is discoloured, and if you love him,

what good does it do you? He doesn't know, he doesn't care, for he has no reason or intelligence. (856) Your heart is truly full of madness to be in such turmoil for love. You dishonour your husband, yourself and your family with your mad desires. (861) For sure, the tales and condemnations of malicious scandalmongers will be a reproach to all women: all women will be slandered because of what you have done. (865) Slandered? It would be a great shame for someone to slander good women because of something done by a wicked woman. Blame and scandal obliterate the good reputation which good women have. (870) Never should such ladies be defamed by malicious and wicked tongues so that their reputation can be ruined by something people go about saying. (874) They condemn no one but themselves, for when someone condemns unjustly, the condemnation rebounds on their own head. (877) No one should be blamed for a crime except the man or woman who commits it, or who gives consent to it; for 'he flays well enough who holds the foot',[2] and so it is ignoble and a great injury to blame good women for others' madness. (883) But anyone who did want to blame every woman because of one woman's error, it seems to me, ought also to praise all women for the sake of one [good] woman. (887) But the good woman will never be condemned, less honoured or loved, because of the evil done by the bad, nor will the bad woman gain any favour from the good deeds done by the good lady. Each must carry her own burden, some of praise, some of blame. (894) Then anyone who condemns someone else because of Pasiphae's crime is acting wrongly.

(896) She is entirely in the grip of the devil. Love for the bull is so deep-rooted in her that she cannot endure or have any happiness without it. (900) She neglects her chambers and runs across fields and mountains, pasture and plains, where the dumb beasts dwell, to have her pleasure with the bull. The poor, wretched woman is determined and set upon deceiving herself.

(908) When she saw that she could never have the one she pursued as her lover, she resorted to trickery to put her lust into action. She had a cow made of wood, with the advice of a carpenter who was a great expert in this craft. (915) Daedalus was this master-craftsman's name; his name is still famous because of his great intelligence and mastery. He was the one who found the trick by which Pasiphae finally achieved her devilry and sin. (921) When the cow was finished, Pasiphae hid herself inside it. She had a cow flayed, one which she had seen the bull chasing. The bull thought it was a cow when he saw the wood covered with cow's hide. Ah, what shame! I'm embarrassed to speak of it. The bull committed adultery with Pasiphae because the cow's form deceived it.

(930) Pasiphae became pregnant from the bull. The seed did not die in her, but she gave birth when her time came, to a half-man half-bull. It was named Minotaurus, after Minos and the bull.[3]

(936) Minos will be utterly distraught, he will have ample reason to grieve, when he discovers the child back home. (939) Where was he, the good lord Minos? In Athens, avenging his son: he had been put to death by the Athenians who resented and hated him. (943) Minos was a brave and skilful warrior, and he destroyed the land and laid it waste. He exerted himself so well that he compelled the Athenians by force of arms to submit and put themselves on his mercy, and they all consented to hold their lands and all their possessions from him. (950) By a peace treaty they all agreed to offer him homage and also promised to pay tribute: for ever more, without asking for any respite or delay, they would choose one of their noblemen and send him to Crete. The one on

---

[2]   Proverbial.

[3]   Latin *taurus* (*toriau* in the French).

whom the lot fell would not be able to refuse – so Minos stipulated. (960) When guarantees had been given, Minos swore the oaths he had promised. He immediately set off for his own land, full of joy and delight at what he had won. (964) But soon such great harm will come to him that he'll have grief and anger over it, when he learns the truth of the adultery, treachery and crime his wife has committed against him.

(969) In his chambers he found the monster. With its double form, just as Nature had formed it, the monster demonstrated[4] the shame and the adultery. (973) To lock the monster away, Minos had a strong prison built. No one has ever seen another like it. (976) The house was designed and fortified by Daedalus, the good carpenter. He put in so many routes and paths, so many corners and nooks and crannies, and made the routes so twisting that when someone thought they were right next to the exit they were furthest from it. Minos had the monster locked and hidden away in this secret prison.

Primary Source 3.4   Commentary on 'Pyramus and Thisbe' (Book 4, lines 1170–1267)

(Source: Translated, with footnotes, by Jeremy Dimmick (2009) from C. de Boer, Martina G. de Boer and Jeannette Th. M. van't Sant (eds) (1915–38) *Ovide moralisé: poème du commencement du quatorzième siècle*, 5 vols, Amsterdam, Koninklije Akademie van Wetenschappen. Reprinted 1966, Wiesbaden, M. Sändig)

Commentary on 'Pyramus and Thisbe' (Book 4, lines 1170–1267)

(1170) Now I want to give you an explanation of the metamorphosis of the mulberry, which had been white and then turned black hanging from the branch. When a mulberry is young it's white, and later when it is dying it turns black.[1]

(1176) Now I'll tell you the allegory which this fable signifies. In this wretched world full of filth and iniquity, full of vice and disorder, God wanted to become incarnate out of love for humanity. (1183) He lowered himself so much as to take up lodging with humanity, and to save the human race the Deity was stretched out, hanged with humanity on that holy and glorious tree which was stained a bloody colour by his holy, precious blood. (1191) Then true God and true man entered a single tomb together.

(1193) He showed us a good example, it seems to me, that we ought to do penance for him, endure suffering and mortify our flesh. He allowed Himself to be crucified for love of us and suffered death. (1199) The Good Lord Himself has suffered death out of pity for us: then we ought to endure tribulation and penance for His love, and accept in true patience whatever trouble we endure for Him. It's right that we should offer ourselves up to all kinds of suffering for His love. (1207) This is what the holy martyrs used to do in times gone by: they despised the world and gave themselves up to endure all kinds of torments for God. Some were imprisoned, locked up with strong chains; others were stoned; some were beaten and abused, scorned and insulted by the world. (1216) Some were tempted, some put to death, yet they welcomed their deaths and the

---

[4]   *monstre / Li monstres* ('the monster displays'): the paronomasia is a characteristic piece of wordplay in the original French, which is hard to replicate in translation.

[1]   This kind of brief 'natural' explanation before the allegorical commentary is fairly common in the *Ovide Moralisé*. The poet also sometimes claims that a true story underlies the fable, shorn of its mythological aspects, and in his conclusion to 'Piramus e Tisbé' he has stated that 'la fable ... a voire istoire s'acorde' ('the fable agrees with actual history', 4.1158–9)

torments they endured, and bore witness to the God of love and charity. The martyrs were put to the test by many persecutions and were found firm in the faith.

(1224) This was how the holy men of old used to win paradise – but nowadays there's no one who'll seek death or suffer martyrdom for Jesus Christ or for His name. No one now is after anything but physical comfort and worldly pleasures. Where are the pure, where are the innocent who, for the love of God and to pay Him back for His love, are willing to suffer death or give up their bodies to the torments of the martyrs? (1236) But when the Son of God comes back, the Judge who will faithfully reward everyone according to their deserts, how will they expect to be redeemed? How will those who chose to use their time living a life of pleasure excuse themselves, when they knew very well that God was willing to give Himself up to death to redeem them and deliver them from death and from the hands of the devil?

(1247) The devil is the terrifying lion, the cruel and furious beast which devoured the entrails of the animals it had disembowelled. He has devoured the souls of all the dead. This is the lion who will never be weary of keeping watch in case he can find anything to devour. (1256) This is the one whose custom is to swallow up every soul, who tramples and bloodies the life and the wimple of the beautiful innocent young woman – that is, the lady the Creator loves, for whom the Son of God fearlessly chose to suffer death and Passion to rescue her from the lion. Well may the lion flee from the field of the world when the Son of God approaches. This is the lion, the worst of the wicked. May our Lord protect us from him!

Primary Source 3.5 Apuleius, 'The Exemplar of Thelyphron'
(Source: Walsh, P.G. (trans. and ed.) (1994) Apuleius: *The Golden Ass*, Oxford, Oxford University Press, pp. 18–21)

1   As soon as the darkness was dispelled and a new sun ushered in the day, I rose from my couch the moment I awoke from sleep, for I was generally buoyed up, and most eager to discover the weird and wonderful features of the place. I recalled that I was in the heart of Thessaly, the source of those spells of the magic art which are famed by common consent through the entire world. I remembered too that the tale recounted by Aristomenes, that best of companions, had its origin in this city. So in expectation and enthusiasm alike I was quite alert, and I studied each feature with some care. I did not believe that anything which I gazed on in the city was merely what it was, but that every single object had been transformed into a different shape by some muttered and deadly incantation. I thought that the stones which caused me to trip were petrified persons, that the birds which I could hear were feathered humans, that the tree enclosing the city-limits were people who had likewise sprouted foliage, that the waters of the fountains were issuing from human bodies. I imagined that at any moment the statues and portraits would parade about, that the walls would speak, that oxen and other cattle would prophesy, that the very sky and the sun's orb would suddenly proclaim an oracular message.

2   In this trance, or rather hypnosis, induced by such tortured longing, I went round examining everything, but without finding a suggestion or even a trace of what I passionately sought. I wandered from door to door like a man seeking some extravagant and dissolute diversion, and all unknowing I suddenly found myself at the food-market. I caught sight of a woman walking through it, surrounded by a sizeable retinue, and I quickened my

step and overtook her. Her jewellery was gold-inlaid and her clothes gold-embroidered, undoubtedly signalling that she was an upper-class matron. Walking close to her side was a man of advanced years. As soon as he set eyes on me he exclaimed: 'Heavens, it's Lucius!' and he gave me a kiss of greeting. At once he whispered something in the lady's ear which I could not overhear. 'This is your aunt,' he said. 'You must approach her yourself, and greet her.' 'I'm shy of doing that', I said, 'for I do not know her.' Whereupon I blushed all over, and kept my distance with my head bowed.

The lady then turned to stare at me. 'My goodness,' she said, 'he has the manners of a gentleman. He gets them from his mother Salvia who is a model of goodness. And damn me if his appearance generally isn't just right! He is tall, but not lofty; he's slim, but there is spunk there; his colour is moderately ruddy, his hair is blonde but not foppish; his green eyes have a watchful look, quick to focus, sharp as an eagle's. His face looks healthy from every angle, and his walk is pleasing and natural.'

3 Then she added: 'Lucius, these hands of mine reared you. That was as it should be, for not only am I your mother's blood relation, but we were brought up together. We are both descended from Plutarch's household, we had the same wet-nurse, and we grew up together as inseparable sisters. The one thing that distinguishes us is our social standing. She contracted marriage with a prominent public figure, whereas I married a private citizen. I'm called Byrrhena; you may recall the name through mention of it among those who brought you up. So don't be shy of accepting our hospitality; in fact our house is yours.'

These remarks of hers had given me time to disguise my blushes, and I spoke up in reply. 'Dear aunt,' I said, 'I could hardly bid my host Milo goodbye without his feeling aggrieved. I shall make every effort to do what I can, short of breaching my obligation to him. Whenever any occasion for a journey this way arises in future, I shall always lodge with you.' In the course of these and similar exchanges, the short journey we had made on foot brought us to Byrrhena's house.

4 The reception-area was very fine. Pillars stood at each corner, supporting statues representing the goddess Victory. In these representations, her wings were outspread but motionless, and her dewy feet stood on tiptoe on the slippery surface of a revolving sphere, momentarily joined to it but giving the impression of imminent flight. But the notable feature was Parian marble chiselled into the likeness of Diana, which occupied the centre of the whole atrium, and was raised off the ground. The statue gleamed spectacularly; with her garment breeze-blown, her lively figure was hastening forward as if to confront the incomer with the august majesty of her godhead. Hounds, likewise executed in marble, escorted the goddess on both flanks. Their eyes were threatening, their ears pricked up, their nostrils flaring, their maws savage. If barking sounded loudly from anywhere near at hand, you would think that it issued from those mouths of marble. But the highest feat of craftsmanship achieved by that genius of a sculptor was that the hounds were rearing breast-high, and their hind legs were braking while their forelegs were in rapid motion.

To the rear of the goddess rose a rock forming a cave. Out of the stone sprouted moss, green plants, foliage and brushwood; vines on one side were set off against miniature trees on the other. Within the cave the reflection of the statue shone out because of the smooth brightness of the marble. Apples and grapes hung from the lower edge of the rock; their highly artistic finish, depicted with a skill rivalling nature's, made them lifelike, so that you could imagine that some of them could be plucked for eating once the maturing autumn endowed them with the colour of ripeness. If you bent low and gazed into the water which skirted the goddess's feet as it lapped in gentle waves, you would think that the bunches of grapes hanging from the rock possessed the faculty of movement as well as other lifelike qualities. In the middle of the marble foliage a statue of Actaeon was visible, fashioned in marble and reflected in the water; his neck craned forward as he gazed with curiosity towards the goddess. He was already animal-like, on the point of becoming a stag as he waited for Diana to take her bath.

5   As I repeatedly ran my eye over this scene with intense delight, Byrrhena remarked: 'All that you see is yours.'

Block 4   Myth and reason in classical Greece

Primary Source 4.1   Hesiod, *Theogony* 116–128

(Source: Wender, D. (trans.) (1986) 'Hesiod: *Theogony*', in *Hesiod and Theognis*, Harmondsworth, Penguin, p. 27)

> Chaos was first of all, but next appeared
> Broad-bosomed Earth, sure standing-place for all
> The gods who live on snowy Olympus' peak,
> Any misty Tartarus, in a recess
> Of broad-pathed earth, and Love, most beautiful
> Of all the deathless gods. He makes men weak,
> He overpowers the clever mind, and tames
> The spirit in the breasts of men and gods.
> From Chaos came black Night and Erebos.
> And Night in turn gave birth to Day and Space
> Whom she conceived in love to Erebos.
> And Earth bore starry Heaven, first, to be
> An equal to herself, to cover her
> All over, and to be a resting-place,
> Always secure, for all the blessed gods.

Primary Source 4.2   Genesis 1: 1–5

(Source: The New English Bible)

IN THE BEGINNING OF CREATION, when God made heaven and earth, the earth was without form and void, with darkness over the face of the abyss, and a mighty wind that swept over the surface of the waters. God said, 'Let there be light', and there was light; and God saw that the light was good, and he separated light from darkness. He called the light day, and the darkness night. So evening came, and morning came, the first day.

Primary Source 4.3   The Babylonian hymn of creation

(Source: Jacobsen, T. (trans.) in Frankfort, H. and H.A., Wilson, J.A. and Jacobsen, T. (1963) *Before Philosophy: The Intellectual Adventure of Ancient Man*, Harmondsworth, Penguin, p. 184)

> When a sky above had not (yet even) been mentioned
> (And) the name of firm ground below had not (yet even) been thought of;
> (When) only primeval Apsu, their begetter,
> And Mummu and Ti'amat – she who gave birth to them all –
> Were mingling their waters in one;
> When no bog had formed (and) no island could be found;
> When no god whosoever had appeared,
> Had been named by name, had been determined as to (his) lot,
> Then were gods formed within them.

Primary Source 4.4   Herodotus, *The Histories* 2.53

(Source: de Sélincourt, A. (trans.) revised by J. Marincola (2003) *Herodotus: The Histories*, 2.53, London, Penguin, pp. 117–8)

But it was only – if I may so put it – the day before yesterday that the Greeks came to know the origin and form of the various gods, and whether or not all of them had always existed; for Homer and Hesiod are the poets who composed theogonies and described the gods for the Greeks, giving them all their appropriate titles, offices, and powers, and they lived, as I believe, not more than four hundred years ago. The poets who are said to have preceded them were, I think, in point of fact later.

Primary Source 4.5   Hesiod, *Theogony* 156–206 and 459–91

(Source: Wender, D. (trans.) (1986) 'Hesiod: *Theogony*' in *Hesiod and Theognis*, Harmondsworth, Penguin, pp. 28–9 and 38–9)

Theogony 156–206

And these most awful sons of Earth and Heaven
Were hated by their father from the first.
As soon as each was born, Ouranos hid
The child in a secret hiding-place in Earth
And would not let it come to see the light,
And he enjoyed this wickedness. But she,   160
Vast Earth, being strained and stretched inside her, groaned.
And then she thought of a clever, evil plan.
Quickly she made grey adamant, and formed
A mighty sickle, and addressed her sons,
Urging them on, with sorrow in her heart,
'My sons, whose father is a reckless fool,
If you will do as I ask, we shall repay
Your father's wicked crime. For it was he
Who first began devising shameful acts.'

She spoke, but fear seized all of them, and none   170
Replied. Then crooked Kronos, growing bold,
Answered his well-loved mother with these words:
'Mother, I undertake to do the deed;
I do not care for my unspeakable
Father, for he first thought of shameful acts.'
He spoke, and giant Earth was glad at heart.
She set him in a hiding-place, and put
Into his hands the saw-toothed scimitar,
And told him all the plot she had devised.

Great Heaven came, and with him brought the night.
Longing for love, he lay around the Earth,
Spreading out fully. But the hidden boy
Stretched forth his left hand; in his right he took
The great long jagged sickle; eagerly   180
He harvested his father's genitals
And threw them off behind. They did not fall
From his hands in vain, for all the bloody drops
That leaped out were received by Earth; and when
The year's time was accomplished, she gave birth
To the Furies, and the Giants, strong and huge,
Who fought in shining armour, with long spears,
And the nymphs called Meliae on the broad earth.

The genitals, cut off with adamant
And thrown from land into the stormy sea,
Were carried for a long time on the waves.
White foam surrounded the immortal flesh,   190
And in it grew a girl. At first it touched
On holy Cytherea, from there it came
To Cyprus, circled by the waves. And there
The goddess came forth, lovely, much revered,
And grass grew up beneath her delicate feet.
Her name is Aphrodite among men
And gods, because she grew up in the foam,
And Cytherea, for she reached that land,
And Cyprogenes from the stormy place
Where she was born, and Philommedes from   200
The genitals, by which she was conceived.
Eros is her companion; fair Desire
Followed her from the first, both at her birth
And when she joined the company of the gods.
From the beginning, both among gods and men,
She had this honour and received this power:
Fond murmuring of girls, and smiles, and tricks,
And sweet delight, and friendliness, and charm.

Theogony 459–91

Then,
As each child issued from the holy womb
And lay upon its mother's knees, each one   460
Was seized by mightly Kronos, and gulped down.
He had in mind that no proud son of Heaven
Should hold the royal rank among the gods
Except himself. For he had learned from Earth
And starry Heaven, that his destiny
Was to be overcome, great though he was,
By one of his own sons, and through the plans
Of mighty Zeus. Therefore he never dropped
His guard, but lay in wait, and swallowed down
His children. Rhea suffered endless grief;   470
But when she was about to bring forth Zeus,
Father of gods and men, she begged the Earth
And starry Heaven, her parents, to devise
A plan to hide the birth of her dear son
And bring the Fury down on Kronos, for
His treatment of his father and his sons
Whom mighty, crooked Kronos swallowed down.
They heard their daughter and agreed, and told
Her all that fate would bring upon the king
Kronos, and to his mighty-hearted son.
They sent her to the fertile land of Crete,
To Lyctus, when she was about to bear
Her youngest child, great Zeus. And in broad Crete
Vast Earth received the child from her, to raise   480
And cherish. And she carried him, with speed,
Through the black night, and came to Lyctus first.
She took him in her arms and hid him, deep

Under the holy earth, in a vast cave,
On thickly-wooded Mount Aegeum. Then,
To the great lord, the son of Heaven, the past
King of the gods, she handed, solemnly,
All wrapped in swaddling-clothes, a giant stone.
He seized it in his hands and thrust it down
Into his belly, fool! He did not know
His son, no stone, was left behind, unhurt
And undefeated, who would conquer him
With violence and force, and drive him out   490
From all his honours, and would rule the gods.

Primary Source 4.6   Homer, *The Iliad* 1.568–611

(Source: Lattimore, R. (trans.) (1951) *The Iliad of Homer*, Chicago and London, The University of Chicago Press, pp. 74–5)

He spoke, and the goddess the ox-eyed lady Hera was frightened
and went and sat down in silence wrenching her heart to obedience,
and all the Uranian gods in the house of Zeus were troubled.   570
Hephaistos the renowned smith rose up to speak among them,
to bring comfort to his beloved mother, Hera of the white arms:
'This will be a disastrous matter and not endurable
if you two are to quarrel thus for the sake of mortals
and bring brawling among the gods. There will be no pleasure
in the stately feast at all, since vile things will be uppermost.
And I entreat my mother, though she herself understands it,
to be ingratiating toward our father Zeus, that no longer
our father may scold her and break up the quiet of our feasting.
For if the Olympian who handles the lightning should be minded   580
to hurl us out of our places, he is far too strong for any.
Do you therefore approach him again with words made gentle,
and at once the Olympian will be gracious again to us.'
He spoke, and springing to his feet put a two-handled goblet
into his mother's hands and spoke again to her once more:
'Have patience, my mother, and endure it, though you be saddened,
for fear that, dear as you are, I see you before my own eyes
struck down, and then sorry though I be I shall not be able
to do anything. It is too hard to fight against the Olympian.
There was a time once before now I was minded to help you,   590
and he caught me by the foot and threw me from the magic threshold,
and all day long I dropped helpless, and about sunset
I landed in Lemnos, and there was not much life left in me.
After that fall it was the Sintian men who took care of me.'
He spoke, and the goddess of the white arms Hera smiled at him,
and smiling she accepted the goblet out of her son's hand.
Thereafter beginning from the left he poured drinks for the other
gods, dipping up from the mixing bowl the sweet nectar.
But among the blessed immortals uncontrollable laughter
went up as they saw Hephaistos bustling about the palace.   600
Thus thereafter the whole day long until the sun went under
they feasted, nor was anyone's hunger denied a fair portion,

nor denied the beautifully wrought lyre in the hands of Apollo
nor the antiphonal sweet sound of the Muses singing.
    Afterwards when the light of the flaming sun went under
they went away each one to sleep in his home where
for each one the far-renowned strong-handed Hephaistos
had built a house by means of his craftsmanship and cunning.
Zeus the Olympian and lord of the lightning went to
his own bed, where always he lay when sweet sleep came on him.   610
Going up to the bed he slept and Hera of the gold throne beside him.

Primary Source 4.7   Homer, *The Odyssey* 13.287–310

(Source: Lattimore, R. (trans.) (1965) *The Odyssey of Homer*, New York, HarperCollins, pp. 205–6)

    So he spoke. The goddess, gray-eyed Athene, smiled on him,
and stroked him with her hand, and took on the shape of a woman
both beautiful and tall, and well versed in glorious handiworks,
and spoke aloud to him and addressed him in winged words, saying: 290
'It would be a sharp one, and a stealthy one, who would ever get
past you in any contriving; even if it were a god against you.
You wretch, so devious, never weary of tricks, then you would not
even in your own country give over your ways of deceiving
and your thievish tales. They are near to you in your very nature.
But come, let us talk no more of this, for you and I both know
sharp practice, since you are far the best of all mortal
men for counsel and stories, and I among all the divinities
am famous for wit and sharpness; and yet you never recognized   300
Pallas Athene, daughter of Zeus, the one who is always
standing beside you and guarding you in every endeavor.
And it was I who made you loved by all the Phaiakians.
And now again I am here, to help you in your devising
of schemes, and to hide the possessions which the haughty Phaiakians
bestowed—it was by my thought and counsel—on you, as you started
for home, and tell you all the troubles you are destined to suffer
in your well-wrought house; but you must, of necessity, endure
all, and tell no one out of all the men and womenthat you have come
back from your wanderings, but you must endure
much grief in silence, standing and facing men in their violence.'   310

Primary Source 4.8   Herodotus, *The Histories* 1.74

(Source: de Sélincourt, A. (trans.) revised by J. Marincola (2003) *Herodotus: The Histories*, London, Penguin, pp. 33–4)

One battle was fought at night. But then, after five years of indecisive warfare, a battle took place in which the armies had already engaged when day was suddenly turned into night. This change from daylight to darkness had been foretold to the Ionians by Thales of Miletus, who fixed the date for it in the year in which it did, in fact, take place. Both Lydians and Medes broke off the engagement when they saw this darkening of the day: they were more anxious than they had been to conclude peace ...

Primary Source 4.9   Aristotle, *On the Heavens*

(Source: Waterfield, R. (trans.) (2000) *The First Philosophers*, Oxford, Oxford University Press, p. 13)

Others say that the earth rests on water. This is the oldest account that has been passed down to us today, and they say it was the view of Thales of Miletus, that the earth stays where it is as a result of floating like a piece of wood or something similar (for none of these things is so constituted as to keep its position on air, but they do so on water)—as though the same argument did not apply to the water supporting the earth just as much as to the earth itself. After all, water is just as incapable of staying suspended in mid-air, and is also so constituted as to keep its position only when it is on something.

Primary Source 4.10   Seneca, *Questions about Nature*

(Source: Waterfield, R. (trans.) (2000) *The First Philosophers*, Oxford, Oxford University Press, p. 13)

Thales says that the world is held up by water and rides on it like a ship, and that what we call an earthquake happens when the earth rocks because of the movement of the water.

Primary Source 4.11   Theophrastus, *Commentary on Aristotle's 'Physics'*

(Source: Waterfield, R. (trans.) (2000) *The First Philosophers*, Oxford, Oxford University Press, p. 14)

Anaximander said that the first principle and element of existing things was the boundless; it was he who originally introduced this name for the first principle. He says that it is not water or any of the other so-called elements, but something different from them, something boundless by nature, which is the source of all the heavens and the worlds in them. And he says that the original sources of existing things are also what existing things die back into 'according to necessity'; for they give justice and reparation to one another for their injustice in accordance with the ordinance of Time', as he puts it, in these somewhat poetic terms. It is clear that, having noticed how the four elements change into one another, he decided not to make any of them the underlying thing, but something else beside them; and so he has creation take place not as a result of any of the elements undergoing qualitative change, but as a result of the opposites being separated off by means of motion, which is eternal.

Primary Source 4.12   Aristotle, *Physics*

(Source: Waterfield, R. (trans.) (2000) *The First Philosophers*, Oxford, Oxford University Press, pp. 15–16)

Moreover, they take the infinite not to be subject to generation or destruction, on the grounds that it is a kind of principle, because anything generated must have a last part that is generated, and there is also a point at which the destruction of anything ends. That is why, as I say, the infinite is taken not to *have* an origin, but to *be* the origin of everything else—to contain everything and steer everything, as has been said by those thinkers who do not recognize any other causes (such as love or intelligence) apart from the infinite. They also call it the divine, on the grounds that it is immortal and imperishable; on this Anaximander and the majority of the natural scientists are in agreement.

Primary Source 4.13   Herodotus, *Histories* 4.36.2

(Source: Waterfield, R. (trans.) (2000) *The First Philosophers*, Oxford, Oxford University Press, p. 14)

I am amazed when I see that not one of all the people who have drawn maps of the world has set it out sensibly. They show Ocean as a river flowing around the outside if the earth, which is as circular as if it had been drawn with a pair of compasses, and they make Asia and Europe the same size.

Primary Source 4.14   Agathemerus, *Geography* 1.1–2

(Source: Waterfield, R. (trans.) (2000) *The First Philosophers*, Oxford, Oxford University Press, p. 14)

Anaximander of Miletus, who studied under Thales, was the first who dared to draw the inhabited world on a tablet; subsequently Hecataeus of Miletus, a well-travelled man, improved the accuracy of this drawing and made it a thing of wonder. ... The ancients made the inhabited world round, with Greece in the centre and Delphi in the centre of Greece, since the navel of the earth is to be found there.

Primary Source 4.15   Hippolytus, *Refutation of All Heresies* 1: 6.4–7

(Source: Waterfield, R. (trans.) (2000) *The First Philosophers*, Oxford, Oxford University Press, pp. 16–17)

He says that the stars are created as a circle of fire, which is separated off from the fire in the universe and surrounded by vapour. There are breathing-holes—pipe-like channels, as it were—where the stars appear; and so eclipses occur when the breathing-holes are blocked up. The moon appears to wax or wane at different times as a result of the blocking or opening of the channels. The circle of the sun is twenty-seven times the size of the earth, while the circle of the moon is eighteen times the size of the earth. The sun is the highest, and the circle of the fixed stars are the lowest ... Winds occur when the finest vapours of the mist are separated off, gathered together, and set in motion. Rainfall is the result of the vapour which is sent up from the earth under the influence of the sun. Lightning occurs when wind breaks out and splits the clouds.

Primary Source 4.16   Aëtius, *Opinions* 3.3.1

(Source: Waterfield, R. (trans.) (2000) *The First Philosophers*, Oxford, Oxford University Press, p. 17)

Anaximander says that all these things [*the phenomena of thunderstorms*] are caused by wind: when wind has been enclosed within a dense cloud and compressed, and then breaks out as a result of its fineness and lightness, the rupture causes the noise, and the sundering, in contrast with the blackness of the cloud, causes the flash.

Primary Source 4.17   Aëtius, *Opinions* 5.19.4

(Source: Waterfield, R. (trans.) (2000) *The First Philosophers*, Oxford, Oxford University Press, p. 17)

Anaximander says that the first living creatures were born in a moist medium, surrounded by thorny barks, and that as they grew older they began to be fitted for a drier medium, until the bark broke off and they survived in a different form.

Primary Source 4.18   Censorinus, *On Birthdays* 4.7.1–5

(Source: Waterfield, R. (trans.) (2000) *The First Philosophers*, Oxford, Oxford University Press, p. 17)

Anaximander of Miletus imagined there arose from heated water and earth either fish or fish-like creatures, inside which human beings grew and were retained as fetuses up until puberty; then at last the creatures broke open, and men and women emerged who were already capable of feeding themselves.

Primary Source 4.19   Aristotle, *On Celestial Phenomena*

(Source: Waterfield, R. (trans.) (2000) *The First Philosophers*, Oxford, Oxford University Press, p. 16)

They say that at first the whole region around the earth was wet, and that part of it began to dry up under the influence of the sun; this evaporating water causes winds and the turnings of the sun and moon, while the rest is the sea. And so they believe that the sea is still in the process of drying up and becoming less, and that eventually, some time in the future, it will all be dry.

Primary Source 4.20   Aristotle, *On the Heavens*

(Source: Waterfield, R. (trans.) (2000) *The First Philosophers*, Oxford, Oxford University Press, p. 16)

There are some (including, among the thinkers of long ago, Anaximander) who say that the earth stays where it is because of equality. For something which is established in the centre and has equality in relation to the extremes has no more reason to move up than it does down or to the sides; it is impossible for it to move in opposite directions at the same time, and so it is bound to stay where it is.

Primary Source 4.21   Plutarch, *Miscellanies* 2.5–11

(Source: Waterfield, R. (trans.) (2000) *The First Philosophers*, Oxford, Oxford University Press, p. 16)

Anaximander says that the earth is cylindrical in shape, and three times as wide as it is deep. He says that, at the point when this universe was created, the part of the eternal which is productive of hot and cold was separated off, and that a kind of sphere of flame emerged from this and grew all around the vapour that surrounds the earth, like bark on a tree. The sun and the moon and the stars came into being, he says, when this fiery sphere broke off and became enclosed in certain circles.

origin myths

Xenophanes
c.570 – 490 BCE

Primary Source 4.22   Clement, *Miscellanies* 5.109.2

(Source: Waterfield, R. (trans.) (2000) *The First Philosophers*, Oxford, Oxford University Press, p. 27)

> But mortals think that the gods are born,
> Wear their own clothes, have voices and bodies.

Primary Source 4.23   Clement, *Miscellanies* 7.22.1

(Source: Waterfield, R. (trans.) (2000) *The First Philosophers*, Oxford: Oxford University Press, p. 27)

> Ethiopians say that their gods are flat-nosed and black,
> And Thracians that theirs have blue eyes and red hair.

Primary Source 4.24   Clement, *Miscellanies*

(Source: Waterfield, R. (trans.) (2000) *The First Philosophers*, Oxford, Oxford University Press, p. 27)

> If cows and horses or lions had hands,
> Or could draw with their hands and make things as men can,
> Horses would have drawn horse-like gods, cows cow-like gods,
> And each species would have made the gods' bodies just like their own.

Primary Source 4.25   Sextus Empiricus, *Against the Professors* 9.193.3–5

(Source: Waterfield, R. (trans.) (2000) *The First Philosophers*, Oxford, Oxford University Press, p. 27)

> Homer and Hesiod have attributed to the gods
> Everything that men find shameful and reprehensible—
> Stealing, adultery, and deceiving one another.

Primary Source 4.26   Herodotus, *The Histories* 3.38

(Source: de Sélincourt, A. (trans.) revised by J. Marincola (2003) *Herodotus, The Histories*, London, Penguin, p. 187)

For if anyone, no matter who, were given the opportunity of choosing from amongst all the nations in the world the beliefs which he thought best, he would inevitably, after careful consideration of their relative merits, choose those of his own country. Everyone without exception believes his own native customs, and the religion he was brought up in, to be the best; and that being so, it is unlikely that anyone but a madman would mock at such things. There is abundant evidence that this is the universal feeling about the ancient customs of one's country. One might recall, in particular, an account told of Darius. When he was king of Persia, he summoned the Greeks who happened to be present at his court, and asked them what they would take to eat the dead bodies of their fathers. They replied that they would not do it for any money in the world. Later, in the presence of the Greeks, and through an interpreter, so that they could understand what was said, he asked some Indians, of the tribe called Callatiae, who do in fact eat their parents' dead bodies, what they would take to burn them. They uttered a cry of horror and forbade him to mention such a dreadful thing. One can see by this what custom can do, and Pindar, in my opinion, was right when he called it 'king of all'.

Primary Source 4.27   Clement, *Miscellanies* 5.109.1

(Source: Waterfield, R. (trans.) (2000) *The First Philosophers*, Oxford, Oxford University Press, p. 26)

> One god, greatest among gods and men,
> In no way similar to mortal men in body or in thought.

Primary Source 4.28   Sextus Empiricus, *Against the Professors* 9.144.4

(Source: Waterfield, R. (trans.) (2000) *The First Philosophers*, Oxford, Oxford University Press, p. 26)

Complete he sees, complete he thinks, complete he hears.

Primary Source 4.29   Simplicius, *Commentary on Aristotle's 'Physics'*

(Source: Waterfield, R. (trans.) (2000) *The First Philosophers*, Oxford, Oxford University Press, p. 27)

> He remains for ever in the same place, entirely motionless,
> Nor is it proper for him to move from one place to another.
> But effortlessly he shakes all things by thinking with his mind.

Primary Source 4.30   Diogenes Laertius, *Lives of the Eminent Philosophers* 9.51

(Source: Waterfield, R. (trans.) (2000) *The First Philosophers*, Oxford, Oxford University Press, p. 211)

Protagoras was the first to claim that there are two contradictory arguments about everything, and he used them to develop the consequences of contradictory premises, being the first to use this argumentative technique. He began one of his books as follows: 'Man is the measure of all things—of things that are, that they are, and of things that are not, that they are not'.

Primary Source 4.31   Diogenes Laertius, *Lives of the Eminent Philosophers* 9.52

(Source: Waterfield, R. (trans.) (2000) *The First Philosophers*, Oxford, Oxford University Press, p. 211)

[Protagoras speaks] Where the gods are concerned, I am not in a position to ascertain that they exist, or that they do not exist. There are many impediments to such knowledge, including the obscurity of the matter and the shortness of human life.

Primary Source 4.32   Sextus Empiricus, *Against the Professors* 9.54

(Source: Waterfield, R. (trans.) (2000) *The First Philosophers*, Oxford, Oxford University Press, p. 305)

CRITIAS:

> There was a time when human life was chaotic,
> As subject to brute strength as the life of beasts,
> When not only did the good go unrewarded,
> But neither was there any punishment for the bad.
> And then, or so it seems to me, men introduced   5
> The restraint of law, so that justice would be the tyrant
> Of the human race, the master of abuse
> And punisher of any transgression.
> Next, since the laws made it impossible
> For people to commit obvious crimes of force,   10
> They began to act in secret; this was the point, I think,
> At which some shrewd and clever man first
> Invented fear of the gods for mortal men, so that
> The wicked might have something to fear, even if
> Their deeds or words or thoughts were secret.   15
> So that is why he introduced the divine ...
> He claimed that the home of the gods is the place
> Whose merest mention would fill men with utter terror ...
> There were flashes of lightening, terrifying thunderclaps,
> And the brilliance of the stars in the heavens ...   20
> Also from the sky heavenly bodies come in a gleaming mass,
> And moist rain proceeds from there into the earth ...
> This, I think, is how in the first place someone persuaded
> Mortal men to worship the race of gods.

Primary Source 4.33   Aristophanes, *Clouds* 364–72

(Source: Sommerstein, A. (trans.) (2002) *Aristophanes: Clouds*, London, Penguin, p. 89)

STREPSIADES: Holy earth, what a sound they make! How divine and majestic and wondrous!

SOCRATES: Yes, you know, these are the only gods; all the rest is codswallop.

STREPSIADES: But look, in the name of Earth, don't you consider Olympian Zeus a god?

SOCRATES: What do you mean, Zeus? Will you stop talking nonsense? Zeus doesn't even exist.

STREPSIADES: What do you mean? Who makes the rain, then? That's the first thing I want to know.

SOCRATES: These clouds do, of course; and I'll prove it to you by strong evidence. Tell me, where have you ever yet seen it raining without clouds? And yet we might have expected Zeus to make rain by himself from a clear sky while the clouds were away from home.

Primary Source 4.34   Plato, *Defence of Socrates*

(Source: Gallop, D. (trans.) (1997) *Plato: Defence of Socrates, Euthyphro, and Crito,* Oxford, Oxford University Press, pp. 29, 31, 38–9)

19b-c6

Let us examine, from the beginning, the charge that has given rise to the slander against me—which was just what Meletus relied upon when he drew up this indictment. Very well then, what were my slanderers actually saying when they slandered me? Let me read out their deposition, as if they were my legal accusers:

'Socrates is guilty of being a busybody, in that he inquires into what is beneath the earth and in the sky, turns the weaker argument into the stronger, and teaches others to do the same.'

The charges would run something like that. Indeed, you can see them for yourselves, enacted in Aristophanes' comedy: in that play, a character called 'Socrates' swings around, claims to be walking on air, and talks a lot of other nonsense on subjects of which I have no understanding, great or small.

26b8-e5

Then, Meletus, in the name of those very gods we are now discussing, please clarify the matter further for me, and for the jury here. You see, I cannot make out what you mean. Is it that I am teaching people to acknowledge that some gods exist—in which case it follows that I do acknowledge their existence myself as well, and am not a complete atheist, hence am not guilty on that count—and yet those gods are not the ones acknowledged by the city, but different ones? Is that your charge against me—namely, that they are different? Or are you saying that I acknowledge no gods at all myself, and teach the same to others?

—I am saying the latter: you acknowledge no gods at all.

—What ever makes you say that, Meletus, you strange fellow? Do I not even acknowledge, then, with the rest of mankind, that the sun and the moon are gods?

—By God, he does not, members of the jury, since he claims that the sun is made of rock, and the moon of earth!

My dear Meletus, do you imagine that it is Anaxagoras you are accusing? Do you have such contempt for the jury, and imagine them so illiterate as not to know that books by Anaxagoras of Clazomenae are crammed with such assertions? What's more, are the young learning those things from me when they can acquire them at the bookstalls, now and then, for a drachma at most, and so ridicule Socrates if he claims those ideas for his own, especially when they are so bizarre? In God's name, do you really think me as crazy as that? Do I acknowledge the existence of no god at all?

—By God no, none whatever.

20d7-21a8

You see, fellow Athenians, I have gained this reputation on account of nothing but a certain sort of wisdom. And what sort of wisdom is that? It is a human kind of wisdom, perhaps, since it might just be true that I have wisdom of that sort. Maybe the people I just mentioned possess wisdom of a superhuman kind;

otherwise I cannot explain it. For my part, I certainly do not possess that knowledge; and whoever says I do is lying and speaking with a view to slandering me—

Now please do not protest, fellow Athenians, even if I should sound to you rather boastful. I am not myself the source of the story I am about to tell you, but I shall refer you to a trustworthy authority. As evidence of my wisdom, if such it actually be, and of its nature, I shall call to witness before you the god at Delphi.

You remember Chaerephon, of course. He was a friend of mine from youth, and also a comrade in your party, who shared your recent exile and restoration. You recall too what sort of man Chaerephon was, how impetuous he was in any undertaking. Well, on one occasion he actually went to the Delphic oracle, and had the audacity to put the following question to it—as I said, please do not make a disturbance, gentlemen—he went and asked if there was anyone wiser than myself; to which the Pythia responded that there was no one.

Primary Source 4.35   Xenophon, *Memoirs of Socrates* 1.1

(Source: Tredennick, H. and Waterfield, R. (trans.) (1990) *Xenophon: Conversations of Socrates*, London, Penguin, pp. 68–9)

With regard to the first charge, that he did not recognize the gods recognized by the State, on what evidence can they possibly have relied? Everyone could see that he sacrificed regularly at home and also at the public altars of the State; and he made no secret of using divination; in fact it was common gossip that Socrates claimed that the divine communicated to him. This, I imagine, was the chief reason for accusing him of introducing new deities. Yet he was no more heretical than any other people who believe in divination and rely on portents and omens and chance meetings and sacrifices. They do not suppose that the birds they see or the people they meet know what is the right course for those who are consulting the diviner; they believe that these things are simply means used by the gods to communicate, and Socrates took the same view. But whereas most people say that it is the omen or the encounter that dissuades or encourages them, Socrates asserted what he actually believed: he said that the divine does the communicating. He often warned his associates to do this or not to do that, at the prompting of the divine, and those who took his advice benefited from it, while those who did not were sorry for it afterwards. Surely anyone would agree that Socrates did not want to seem either a fool or an impostor to his companions; and he would have been thought both if he had been manifestly mistaken in making what he claimed to be divine revelations about the future. It seems obvious, then, that he would not have predicted the future if he had not been sure that his statements would come true; and who could base this trust on anything other than a god? And if he trusted in gods, he surely must have believed in gods.

Primary Source 4.36 Plato, *Euthyphro* 5e3–6c8

(Source: Gallop, D. (trans.) (1997) *Plato: Defence of Socrates, Euthyphro, and Crito,* Oxford, Oxford University Press, p. 8)

EUTHYPHRO:	See how strong my evidence is, Socrates, that this is	5e3
	the law—evidence I've already given others that my conduct was	5
	correct: one must not tolerate an impious man, no matter who he may	
	happen to be. The very people who recognize Zeus as best and most	6a
	righteous of the gods admit that he put his father in bonds for wrong-	
	fully gobbling up his children; and that that father in turn castrated *his*	
	father for similar misdeeds. And yet they are angry with me, because	
	I'm prosecuting *my* father as a wrongdoer. Thus, they contradict	5
	themselves in what they say about the gods and about me.	
SOCRATES:	Could this be the reason why I'm facing indictment,	
	Euthyphro? Is it because when people tell such stories of the gods,	
	I somehow find them hard to accept? That, I suppose, is why some will	
	say that I've gone astray. But now, if these stories convince you—with	10
	your great knowledge of such matters—then it seems that the rest of us	b
	must accept them as well. What can we possibly say, when by our own admission	
	we know nothing of these matters? But tell me, in the name of friendship, do you	
	really believe that those things happened as described?	
EUTHYPHRO:	Yes, and even more remarkable things, Socrates, of which	5
	most people are ignorant.	
SOCRATES:	And do you believe that the gods actually make war upon	
	one another? That they have terrible feuds and fights, and much more of the	
	sort related by our poets, and depicted by our able painters, to adorn our	c
	temples—especially the robe which is covered with such adornments, and	
	gets carried up to the Acropolis at the great Panathenaean festival? Are we to say	
	that those stories are true, Euthyphro?	
EUTHYPHRO:	Not only those, Socrates, but as I was just saying, I'll	5
	explain to you many further points about religion, if you'd like, which I'm	
	sure you'll be astonished to hear.	

Primary Source 4.37 Plato, *Euthyphro* 6e4–8a9

(Source: Gallop, D. (trans.) (1997) *Plato: Defence of Socrates, Euthyphro, and Crito,* Oxford, Oxford University Press, pp. 9–11)

SOCRATES:	Then teach me about that character, about what it might	6e4
	be, so that by fixing my eye upon it and using it as a model, I may call	5
	holy any action of yours or another's, which conforms to it, and may deny to be	
	holy whatever does not.	
EUTHYPHRO:	All right, if that's what you want, Socrates, that's what I'll tell you.	
SOCRATES:	Yes, that *is* what I want.	10
EUTHYPHRO:	In that case, what is agreeable to the gods is holy, and what	
	is not agreeable to them is unholy.	7a
SOCRATES:	Splendid, Euthyphro!—You've given just the sort of answer	
	I was looking for. Mind you, I don't yet know whether it's correct, but	
	obviously you will go on to show that what you say is true.	5
EUTHYPHRO:	I certainly will.	

SOCRATES: All right then, let's consider what it is we're saying. A thing
             or a person loved-by-the-gods is holy, whereas something or someone
             hated-by-the-gods is unholy; and the holy isn't the same as the unholy, but
             is the direct opposite of it. Isn't that what we're saying?   10

EUTHYPHRO: Exactly.

SOCRATES: And does it seem well put?   b

EUTHYPHRO: I think so, Socrates.

SOCRATES: And again, Euthyphro, the gods quarrel and have their differences, and there is
             mutual hostility amongst them. Hasn't that been
             said as well?

EUTHYPHRO: Yes, it has.   5

SOCRATES: Well, on what matters do their differences produce hostility and anger, my good
             friend? Let's look at it this way. If we differed, you and I, about which of two things
             was more numerous, would our difference
             on these questions make us angry and hostile towards one another? Or   10
             would we resort to counting in such disputes, and soon be rid of them?   c

EUTHYPHRO: We certainly would.

SOCRATES: Again, if we differed about which was larger and smaller,
             we'd soon put an end to our differences by resorting to measurement,   5
             wouldn't we?

EUTHYPHRO: That's right.

SOCRATES: And we would decide a dispute about which was heavier and lighter, presumably,
             by resorting to weighing.

EUTHYPHRO: Of course.

SOCRATES: Then what sorts of questions would make us angry and   10
             hostile towards one another, if we differed about them and were unable to reach a
             decision? Perhaps you can't say offhand. But consider my
             suggestion, that they are questions of what is just and unjust, honourable   d
             and dishonourable, good and bad. Aren't those the matters on which our
             disagreement and our inability to reach a satisfactory decision occasionally make
             enemies of us, of you and me, and of people in general?   5

EUTHYPHRO: Those are the differences, Socrates, and that's what they're about.

SOCRATES: And what about the gods, Euthyphro? If they really do differ, mustn't they differ
             about those same things?   10

EUTHYPHRO: They certainly must.

SOCRATES: Then, by your account, noble Euthyphro, different gods   e
             also regard different things as just, or as honourable and dishonourable,
             good and bad; because unless they differed on those matters, they wouldn't quarrel,
             would they?

EUTHYPHRO: Correct.   5

SOCRATES: And again, the things each of them regard as honourable,
             good, or just, are also the things they love, while it's the opposites of those things
             that they hate.

EUTHYPHRO: Indeed.

SOCRATES: And yet it's the same things, according to you, that some
             gods   10

consider just, and others unjust, about which their disputes lead them to quarrel and make war upon one another. Isn't that right? 8a

EUTHYPHRO: It is.

SOCRATES: Then the same things, it appears, are both hated and loved by the gods, and thus the same things would be both hated-by-the-gods and loved-by-the-gods.

EUTHYPHRO: It does appear so.

SOCRATES: So by this argument, Euthyphro, the same things would be both holy and unholy.

EUTHYPHRO: It looks that way.

Primary Source 4.38 Hippocrates, *The Sacred Disease* I–II

(Source: Jones, W.H.S. (trans) (1959) *Hippocrates, Vol. II* (Loeb edn), London/Cambridge MA, William Heinemann/Harvard University Press, pp. 139–41)

I. I am about to discuss the disease called "sacred." It is not, in my opinion, any more divine or more sacred than other diseases, but has a natural cause, and its supposed divine origin is due to men's inexperience, and to their wonder at its peculiar character. Now while men continue to believe in its divine origin because they are at a loss to understand it, they really disprove its divinity by the facile method of healing which they adopt, consisting as it does of purifications and incantations. But if it is to be considered divine just because it is wonderful, there will be not one sacred disease but many, for I will show that other diseases are no less wonderful and portentous, and yet nobody considers them sacred. For instance, quotidian fevers, tertians and quartans seem to me to be no less sacred and god-sent than this disease, but nobody wonders at them. Then again one can see men who are mad and delirious from no obvious cause, and committing many strange acts; while in their sleep, to my knowledge, many groan and shriek, others choke, others dart up and rush out of doors, being delirious until they wake, when they become as healthy and rational as they were before, though pale and weak; and this happens not once but many times. Many other instances, of various kinds, could be given, but time does not permit us to speak of each separately.

II. My own view is that those who first attributed a sacred character to this malady were like the magicians, purifiers, charlatans and quacks of our own day, men who claim great piety and superior knowledge. Being at a loss, and having no treatment which would help, they concealed and sheltered themselves behind superstition, and called this illness sacred, in order that their utter ignorance might not be manifest. They added a plausible story, and established a method of treatment that secured their own position.

Primary Source 4.39 Hippocrates, *The Sacred Disease* V–VI

(Source: Jones, W.H.S. (trans) (1959) *Hippocrates, Vol. II* (Loeb edn), London/Cambridge MA, William Heinemann/Harvard University Press, pp. 151–5)

V. But this disease is in my opinion no more divine than any other; it has the same nature as other diseases, and the cause that gives rise to individual diseases. It is also curable, no less than other illnesses, unless by long lapse of time it be so ingrained as to be more powerful than the remedies that are applied. Its origin, like that of other diseases, lies in heredity. For if a phlegmatic parent has a phlegmatic child, a bilious parent a bilious child, a consumptive parent a consumptive child, and a splenetic parent a splenetic child, there is nothing to prevent some of the children suffering from this disease when one or the other of the parents suffered from it; for the seed comes from every part of the body, healthy seed from the healthy parts, diseased seed from the diseased parts.

Another strong proof that this disease is no more divine than any other is that it affects the naturally phlegmatic, but does not attack the bilious. Yet, if it were more divine than others, this disease ought to have attacked all equally, without making any difference between bilious and phlegmatic.

VI.   The fact is that the cause of this affection, as of the more serious diseases generally, is the brain. The manner and the cause I will now set forth clearly. The brain of man, like that of all animals, is double, being parted down its centre by a thin membrane. For this reason pain is not always felt in the same part of the head, but sometimes on one side, sometimes on the other, and occasionally all over. Veins lead up to it from all the body, many of which are thin, while two are stout, one coming from the liver, the other from the spleen. The vein from the liver has the following character. One part of it stretches downwards on the right side, close by the kidney and the loin, to the inner part of the thigh, reaching down to the foot; it is called the hollow vein. The other part of it stretches upwards through the right diaphragm and lung. It branches away to the heart and the right arm. The rest leads upwards through the collarbone to the right of the neck, to the very skin, so as to be visible. Right by the ear it hides itself, and here it branches, the thickest, largest and most capcious part ending in the brain, another in the right ear, another in the right eye, and the last in the nostril.

Such is the character of the veins from the liver. From the spleen too extends a vein downwards and upwards to the left; it is similar to the one from the liver, but thinner and weaker.

Primary Source 4.40   Homer, *The Iliad* 15.187–92

(Source: Lattimore, R. (trans.) (1951) *The Iliad of Homer*, Chicago and London, The University of Chicago Press, p. 314)

> Since we are three brothers born by Rheia to Kronos,
> Zeus, and I, and the third is Hades, lord of the dead men.
> All was divided among us three ways, each given his domain.
> I when the lots were shaken drew the grey sea to live in   190
> forever; Hades drew the lot of the mists and the darkness,
> and Zeus was allotted the wide sky, in the cloud and the bright air.

Primary Source 4.41   Pindar, *Fragment*

(Source: Garland, R. (1985) *The Greek Way of Death*, London, Gerald Duckworth & Co. Ltd., p. 61)

Prosperous is he who having seen these things passes beneath the earth. He knows the end of life and its god-given beginning (or 'principle', *archē*).

Primary Source 4.42   Pindar, *Olympians* 2.56–77

(Source: Kirk, G.S., Raven, J.E. and Schofield, M. (eds) (1984) *The Presocratic Philosophers* (2nd edn), Cambridge, Cambridge University Press, p. 237)

Those of the dead that are lawless in mind pay the penalty straightaway here [*sc.* on earth] – but the sins committed in this realm of Zeus are judged below the earth by one who pronounces sentence with hateful necessity. The good, upon whom the sun shines for evermore, for equal nights and equal days, receive a life of lightened toil, not vexing the soil with the strength of their hand, no, not the water of the sea, thanks to the ways of that place; but in the presence of the honoured gods, all who rejoiced in keeping their oaths share a life that knows no tears, while the others endure labour that none can look upon. And those who, while dwelling in either world, have thrice been courageous in keeping their souls pure from all deeds of wrong, they traverse the highway of Zeus to the tower of Kronos, where the ocean-breezes blow around the Island of the Blest; and flowers of gold are blazing, some on the shore from radiant trees, while others the water fosters; and with chaplets they entwine their hands, and with crowns, according to the righteous councils of Rhadamanthys – for he sits ready with advice beside the great Father, the lord of Rhea with her throne exalted over all.

Primary Source 4.43   Empedocles, fr. 115 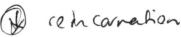 reincarnation

(Source: Kirk, G.S., Raven, J.E. and Schofield, M. (eds) (1984) *The Presocratic Philosophers* (2nd edn), Cambridge, Cambridge University Press, p. 315)

There is an oracle of Necessity, ancient decree of the gods, eternal, sealed with broad oaths: when anyone sins and pollutes his own limbs with bloodshed, who by his error makes false the oath he swore – spirits whose portion is long life – for thrice ten thousand years he wanders apart from the blessed, being born throughout that time in all manner of forms of mortal things, exchanging one hard path of life for another. The force of the air [*lit.* aither] pursues him into the sea, the sea spews him out onto the floor of the earth, the earth casts him into the rays of the blazing sun, and the sun into the eddies of the air; one takes him from the other, but all abhor him. Of these I too am now one, an exile from the gods and a wanderer, having put my trust in raving Strife.

Primary Source 4.44   Xenophanes, fr. 7

(Source: Raven, J.E. Kirk, G.S. & Schofield, M. (ed. and trans.) (1984) *The Presocratic Philosophers*, Second Edition, Cambridge: Cambridge University Press p. 219)

On the subject of reincarnation Xenophanes bears witness in an elegy which begins: 'Now I will turn to another tale and show the way.' What he says about Pythagoras runs thus: 'Once they say that he was passing by when a puppy was being whipped, and he took pity and said: "Stop, do not beat it; for it is the soul of a friend that I recognized when I heard it giving tongue."'

Primary Source 4.45   Aristophanes, *The Frogs* 136–64 and 178–208

(Source: Lattimore, R. (trans.) *The Frogs*, in Arrowsmith, W. (ed.) (1971) *Aristophanes: Four Comedies*, Ann Arbor, MI, University of Michigan Press, pp. 16–21)

HERAKLES   It's a long voyage.
          The first thing that you'll come to is a great swampy lake.
          It's bottomless.

DIONYSOS   Well then, how do I get across?

HERAKLES   There's an ancient mariner with a little tiny boat.
          He'll take you across. And you'll give him two bits for it.

DIONYSOS   Oh, gee.
           Those two bits. You can't ever get away from them.
           How did they ever get here?

HERAKLES   Theseus brought them along from
           Athens.
           After that, you'll see snakes, and armies of wild animals,
           monsters.

DIONYSOS   Stop trying to scare me out of this.
           You'll never stop me.

HERAKLES   Next comes a great sea of mud
           and shitten springs eternal, and people stuck therein,
           whoever did an injury to his guest or host,
           debauched some child and picked its pockets in the process,
           or beat his mother up, or broke his father's jaw,
           or swore an oath and broke it,
           or copied out a tragic speech of Morsimos.

DIONYSOS   Don't stop. I've got another one to add to those.
           Whoever learned the war-dance by Kinesias.

HERAKLES   Next a sweet sound of flutes will come upon your ears,
           and you'll see a lovely light like the sunlight here above,
           myrtles, and solemn troops and sweet societies
           of men and women, and an endless clapping of hands.

DIONYSOS   And who are they?

HERAKLES   The blessed, the Initiates.

XANTHIAS   And I'm the donkey carrying mystic properties,
           but I don't mean to keep them from the rest of time.

HERAKLES   Ask them. They'll tell you everything else you need,
           for they live closest to the road you have to go.
           Their habitation is by Pluto's doors.
           So, good luck, little brother.

Herakles disappears, shutting the door.

DIONYSOS   Oh, the same to you;
           Keep healthy. You there, Xanthias, pick the bundles up.

XANTHIAS   You mean, before I've put them down?

DIONYSOS   Get a move on.

XANTHIAS   Oh please, please don't make me do it. Why don't you hire
           one of these stiffs they're carrying out? There'll be one soon.

DIONYSOS   What if I can't get one?

XANTHIAS   Then I'll do it.

DIONYSOS   Fair enough.
           Look, here comes a corpse now being carried out.

Corpse is brought in on a stretcher.

           Hey! Hey, you there, the dead one. I'm talking to you.
           Want to carry some luggage to Hades?

Corpse sits up.

CORPSE   How much?

DIONYSOS   *Showing his hand.*
                                    That much.

CORPSE   Give me two bucks?

DIONYSOS   My god no, that's too much.

Corpse lies down again.

CORPSE   Keep carrying me, you guys.

DIONYSOS   Hey, what's the matter, wait, we've got to work this out.

CORPSE   Two bucks. Put up or shut up.

DIONYSOS   Make it one and a half.

CORPSE   I'd sooner come to life again.

Corpse is carried off.

XANTHIAS   Stuck up bastard, isn't he? The hell with him!
            I'll take the baggage.

DIONYSOS   You are nature's nobleman.
            Let's go catch a boat.

Off stage.

CHARON   Woo-oop! Coming alongside!

XANTHIAS   What's going on here?

DIONYSOS   What indeed. Oh, here, it's the lake right
            where he said it would be, and now here comes the boat.

Charon, in a little boat (on wheels) is pushed in.

XANTHIAS   So help me Poseidon, so it is, and Charon too.

DIONYSOS   O carry me Charon o sweet chariot carry me home.

CHARON   Who wants a cruise? Relaxation from business worries?
            The Meadows of Forgetting, or Horsefeatherland?
            To go to the Dogs? To go to the Birds? To go to Hell?

DIONYSOS   Me.

CHARON   Get aboard and shake a leg.

DIONYSOS   Where d'you think we're bound?
            Strictly for the Birds?

CHARON   We sure are, with you aboard.
            Get on, get on.

DIONYSOS   Here, boy!

CHARON   No, I won't take a slave.
            Only a veteran of our hide-saving sea battle.

XANTHIAS   I would have made it but I was sick. I had the pinkeye.

CHARON   Then you can just take a little walk around the lake.

XANTHIAS   Where shall I wait for you?

CHARON   By the Stone of Parching Thirst,
            at the pull-off.

DIONYSOS   Got it?

XANTHIAS   Oh, I've got it. Wish I were dead.
            What kind of bad-luck-sign did I run into this morning?

Xanthias trudges off, carrying the bundles. Dionysos climbs awkwardly, into the boat.

CHARON   You, sit to your oar.

Dionysos sits on his oar.

                                                Anyone else going? Hurry it up.

A few Extras (the ones who carried the corpse), get into the boat, each taking an oar.

                    Hey, *you* there. What d'you think you're doing?

DIONYSOS   *I* am sitting
                    to my oar. Exactly what you told me to do.

Rearranging him.

CHARON   Well, sit *here,* fatso. Sit like this. Got it?

DIONYSOS   Okay.

CHARON   Now get your hands away and bring them back.

DIONYSOS   Okay.

CHARON   Stop being such an ass, will you? Bring your weight forward.
                    Get your back into it.

DIONYSOS   What do you want? I never rowed before.
                    I'm no Old Navy Man. I didn't make the First Crew.
                    How'm I supposed to row?

CHARON   Easily. Just begin to do it,
                    and you'll get a pretty song to give you the time.

DIONYSOS   Who's singing?

CHARON   It's a swan song, but the swans are lovely frogs.

DIONYSOS   Go ahead.
                    Give me the stroke.

CHARON   OO-pah, oo-pah.

Primary Source 4.46   Aristophanes, *The Frogs* 322–52

(Source: Lattimore, R. (trans.) *The Frogs*, in Arrowsmith, W. (ed.) (1971) *Aristophanes: Four Comedies*, Ann Arbor, MI, University of Michigan Press, pp. 30–1)

CHORUS

In white, as Initiates

                    Iacchos! Well beloved in these pastures o indwelling
                    Iacchos o Iacchos
                    come to me come with dance steps down the meadow
                    to your worshipping companions
                    with the fruited, the lifebursting,
                    the enmyrtled and enwreathed garland on your brows, bold-footed
                    stamp out the sprightly measure
                    of the dancing that's your pleasure,
                    of the dancing full of graces, full of light and sweet and sacred
                    for your dedicated chosen ones.

XANTHIAS	Demeter's daughter, Persephone, holy lady and queen, ineffable fragrance wafts upon me. Roasting pigs!
DIONYSOS	If I promise you a handful of tripes, will you shut up?
CHORUS	Let flames fly as the torch tosses in hand's hold Iacchos o Iacchos star of fire in the high rites of the night time. And the field shines in the torch light, and the old men's knees are limber, and they shake off aches and miseries and the years of their antiquity drop from them in the magical measure. Oh, torch-in-hand-shining. Iacchos go before us to the marsh flowers and the meadow and the blest revel of dances.

Parabasis. The Chorus advances down stage and the leader addresses the audience directly.

Primary Source 4.47   Thucydides, *Launching of the Sicilian Expedition* 6.27

(Source: Warner, R. (trans.) (1972) *Thucydides: History of the Peloponnesian War*, Harmondsworth, Penguin, p. 426)

While these preparations were going on it was found that in one night nearly all the stone Hermae in the city of Athens had had their faces disfigured by being cut about. These are a national institution, the well-known square-cut figures, of which there are great numbers both in the porches of private houses and in the temples. No one knew who had done this, but large rewards were offered by the state in order to find out who the criminals were, and there was also a decree passed guaranteeing immunity to anyone, citizen, alien, or slave, who knew of any other sacrilegious act that had taken place and would come forward with information about it. The whole affair, indeed, was taken very seriously, as it was regarded as an omen for the expedition, and at the same time as evidence of a revolutionary conspiracy to overthrow the democracy.

Primary Source 4.48   Plato, *Apology* 40 c5– 41 c8

(Source: Gallop, D. (trans.) (1997) *Plato: Defence of Socrates*, Oxford, Oxford University Press, pp. 57–8)

And let us also reflect upon how good a reason there is to hope   40c5
that death is a good thing. It is, you see, one or other of two things:
either to be dead is to be non-existent, as it were, and a dead person
has no awareness whatever of anything at all; <u>or else, as we are told,
the soul undergoes some sort of transformation , or exchanging of this
present world for another.</u> Now if there is, in fact, no awareness in
death, but it is like sleep—the kind in which the sleeper does not even   10
dream at all—then death would be a marvellous gain. Why, imagine   d
that someone had to pick the night in which he slept so soundly that
he did not even dream, and to compare all the other nights and days of
his life with that one; suppose he had to say, upon consideration, how   5
many days or nights in his life he had spent better and more agreeably
than that night; in that case, I think he would find them easy to count   e
compared with his other days and nights—even if he were the Great
King of Persia, let alone an ordinary person. Well, if death is like that,

then for my part I call it a gain; because on that assumption the whole of time would seem no longer than a single night.

death in Hades

On the other hand, if death is like taking a trip from here to another place, and if it is true, as we are told, that all of the dead do   5
indeed exist in that other place, why then, gentlemen of the jury, what could be a greater blessing than that? If upon arriving in Hades, and   41a
being rid of these people who profess to be 'jurors', one is going to find those who are truly judges, and who are also said to sit in judg-ment there—Minos, Rhadamanthys, Aeacus, Triptolemus, and all other demigods who were righteous in their own lives—would that be a disappointing journey?   5

Or again, what would any of you not give to share the company of Orpheus and Musaeus, of Hesiod and Homer? I say 'you; since I personally would be willing to die many times over, if those tales are true. Why? Because my own sojourn there would be wonderful, if   b
I could meet Palamedes, or Ajax, son of Telamon, or anyone else of old who met their death through an unjust verdict. Whenever I met them, I could compare my own experiences with theirs—which would   5
be not unamusing, I fancy—and best of all, I could spend time ques-tioning and probing people there, just as I do here, to find out who among them is truly wise, and who thinks he is without being so.

What would one not give, gentlemen of the jury, to be able to question the leader of the great expedition against Troy, or Odysseus,   c
or Sisyphus, or countless other men and women one could mention? Would it not be unspeakable good fortune to converse with them there, to mingle with them and question them? At least that isn't a   5
reason, presumably, for people in that world to put you to death—because amongst other ways in which people there are more fortunate than those in our world, they have become immune from death for the rest of time, if what we are told is actually true.

Primary Source 4.49   Plato, *Republic* 2.377b5–3.389d5

(Source: Reeve, C.D.C. (trans.) *Plato: Republic*, Indianapolis, Hackett, pp. 57–70; footnotes edited)

SOCRATES:	Shall we carelessly allow our children to hear any old 377b5 stories made up by just anyone, then, and to take beliefs into their souls that are, for the most part, the opposite of the ones we think they should hold when they are grown up?
ADEIMANTUS:	We certainly won't allow that at all.
SOCRATES:	So our first task, it seems, is to supervise the storytellers: if they make up a good story, we must accept it; if not, we must reject it. We will persuade nurses and mothers to tell the acceptable ones to their children, and to spend far more time shaping their souls with these stories than they do shaping their bodies by handling them. Many of the stories they tell c now, however, must be thrown out. 5
ADEIMANTUS:	Which sorts?
SOCRATES:	In the more significant stories, we will see the less significant ones as well. For surely the more significant ones and the less significant ones both follow the same pattern and have the same effects. Don't you think so? d

ADEIMANTUS: Indeed, I do. But I do not understand at all what more significant ones you mean.

SOCRATES: The ones Homer, Hesiod, and other poets tell us. After all,   5
               they surely composed false stories, which they told and are still telling to people.

ADEIMANTUS: Which stories do you mean? And what is the fault you find in them?

SOCRATES: The first and most important fault that one ought to find, especially if the falsehood
               has no good features.

ADEIMANTUS: Yes, but what *is* it?   10

SOCRATES: Using a story to create a bad image of what the gods and   e
               heroes are like, just as a painter might paint a picture that is not at all like the
               things he is trying to paint.

ADEIMANTUS: Yes, you are right to find fault with that. But what cases in particular, what sorts of
               cases, do you mean?   5

SOCRATES: First, the biggest falsehood about the most important things has no good
               features—I mean Hesiod telling us about how Uranus behaved, how Cronus
               punished him for it, and how he was in turn punished by his own son.[1] But even if
               these stories were true, they should be passed   378a
               over in silence, I would think, and not told so casually to the foolish and the
               young. And if, for some reason, they must be told, only a very few people should
               hear them—people who are pledged to secrecy and have had to sacrifice not just a
               pig, but something so large and scarce   5
               that the number of people who hear them is kept as small as possible.

ADEIMANTUS: Yes, those stories are certainly troubling.

SOCRATES: And they should not be told in our city, Adeimantus. No   b
               young person should hear it said that if he were to commit the worst crimes, he
               would be doing nothing amazing, or that if he were to inflict every sort of
               punishment on an unjust father, he would only be doing the same as the first and
               greatest of the gods.   5

ADEIMANTUS: No, by Zeus, I do not think myself that these stories are fit to be told.

SOCRATES: Indeed, we must not allow *any* stories about gods warring, fighting, or plotting
               against one another if we want the guardians of our city to think that it is shameful
               to be easily provoked into mutual hatred. After all, those stories are not true either.
               Still less   c
               should battles between gods and giants, or the many other multifarious hostilities
               of gods and heroes toward their families and friends, occur in the stories the
               guardians hear or in the embroidered pictures they see. On the contrary, if we are
               somehow going to persuade our people that no   5
               citizen has ever hated another, and that it is impious to do so, then *those* are the
               things their male and female elders should tell them from childhood on. And the
               poets they listen to as they grow older should be compelled   d
               to tell them the same sort of thing. Stories about Hera being chained by her son, on
               the other hand, or about Hephaestus being hurled from heaven by his father when
               he tried to save his mother from a beating, or   5
               about the battle of the gods in Homer, should not be admitted into our city, either
               as allegories or non-allegories. For the young cannot distinguish what is allegorical
               from what is not. And the beliefs they absorb at that age are difficult to erase and

---

[1]   Uranus prevented his wife, Gaia, from giving birth to his children by blocking them up inside her.
Gaia gave a sickle to one of these children, Cronus, which he used to castrate his father when the
latter next had intercourse with her. Cronus ate the children he had by his wife, Rhea, until, by
deceiving him with a stone, she was able to save Zeus from suffering this fate. Zeus then overthrew
his father. See Hesiod, *Theogony* 154–210, 453–506.

tend to become unalterable. For these reasons, then,   e
we should probably take the utmost care to ensure that the first stories they hear
about virtue are the best ones for them to hear.

ADEIMANTUS: Yes, that makes sense. But if, at this point too, someone were once
again to ask us what stories these are, how should we reply?   5

SOCRATES: You and I are not poets at present, Adeimantus, but we are
founding a city. And it is appropriate for the founders to know the   379a
patterns on which the poets must base their stories, and from which they must not
deviate. But they should not themselves make up any poems.

ADEIMANTUS: That's right. But what precisely are the patterns that   5
stories about the gods must follow?

SOCRATES: Something like this: whether in epic, lyric, or tragedy, a god must always be
represented as he is.

ADEIMANTUS: Yes, he must.   10

SOCRATES: Now, gods, of course, are really good, aren't they, and must be described
as such?   b

ADEIMANTUS: Certainly.

SOCRATES: And surely nothing good is harmful, is it?

ADEIMANTUS: I suppose not.

SOCRATES: Well, can what is not harmful do any harm?   5

ADEIMANTUS: No, never.

SOCRATES: And can what does no harm do anything bad?

ADEIMANTUS: No, it can't do that either.

SOCRATES: But what does nothing bad could not be the cause of anything bad, could it?

ADEIMANTUS: No, it could not.   10

SOCRATES: What about what is good? Is it beneficial?

ADEIMANTUS: Yes.

SOCRATES: So, it is the cause of doing well?

ADEIMANTUS: Yes.

SOCRATES: What is good is not the cause of all things, then. Instead, it is the
cause of things that are good, while of bad ones it is not the   15
cause.

ADEIMANTUS: Exactly.

SOCRATES: So, since gods are good, they are not—as the masses claim—the cause of
everything. Instead, they are a cause of only a few things that happen to human
beings, while of most they are not the cause. For good things are fewer than bad
ones in our lives. Of the good things, they alone are the cause, but we must find
some other cause for the bad
ones, not the gods.   5

ADEIMANTUS: That's absolutely true in my view.

SOCRATES: Then we won't accept from Homer—or from anyone else—the foolish mistake he
makes about the gods when he says: "There   d
are two urns at the threshold of Zeus, one filled with good fates, the other with bad
ones," and the person to whom Zeus gives a mixture of these   5
"sometimes meets with a bad fate, sometimes with a good one." But the one who

receives his fate entirely from the second urn, "evil famine drives over the divine earth." Nor will we tolerate the saying that "Zeus is the dispenser of both good and bad to mortals." As for the breaking of   e
the oaths and the truce by Pandarus, if anyone tells us that it was brought about by Athena and Zeus, or that Themis and Zeus were responsible for strife and contention among the gods, we won't praise him. Nor will we allow the young to hear the words of Aeschylus: "A god makes mortals   5
guilty, when he wants to destroy a house utterly."[2] And if anyone composes a poem, such as the one those lines are from, about the suffering of Niobe, or about the house of Pelops, or the tale of Troy, or anything else   5
of that sort, he should be required to say that these things are not the works of a god. Or, if they are the works of a god, then the poet must look for roughly the sort of account of them we are now seeking: he must say that the actions of the gods are good and just, and that the people they punish are benefited by them. We won't allow him to say that those who   b
are punished are made wretched, and that it was a god who made them so; but we will allow him to say that bad people are wretched because they are in need of punishment, and that in paying the penalty they are benefited by that god. But as for saying that a god, who is himself good, is the   5
cause of evils, we will fight that in every way. We won't allow anyone to say it in his own city, if it is to be well governed, or anyone to hear it either—whether young or old, whether with meter or without meter. For   c
these stories are impious, disadvantageous to us, and not in concord with one another.

ADEIMANTUS: I like your law, and I will vote with you for it.

SOCRATES: This, then, will be one of the laws or patterns relating to gods that speakers and poets will have to follow: that gods are not the cause of all things, but only of good ones.

ADEIMANTUS: And an entirely satisfactory one it is.   10

SOCRATES: Now, what about this second law? Do you think that gods are sorcerers who deliberately take different forms at different times,   d sometimes by changing on their own and altering their own form into a large number of shapes, sometimes by deceiving us into thinking they have done so? Or are they simple beings, and least of all likely to   5 abandon their own form?

ADEIMANTUS: I can't say offhand.

SOCRATES: Well, if something abandons its own form, mustn't it either cause the change itself or be changed by something else?   e

ADEIMANTUS: It must.

SOCRATES: Now, the best things are least liable to alteration or change, aren't they? For example, a body is altered by food, drink, and labors, and all plants by sun, winds, and other similar affections—but the healthiest   5 and strongest is least altered, isn't that so?

ADEIMANTUS: Of course.

SOCRATES: And wouldn't a soul that is most courageous and most knowledgeable be least disturbed or altered by any outside influence?

---

[2]   The first three quotations are from *Iliad* 24.527–32. The sources for the fourth, and for the quotation from Aeschylus, are unknown. The story of Athena urging Pandarus to break the truce is told at *Iliad* 4.73–126.

ADEIMANTUS: Yes.   5

SOCRATES: And the same account surely also applies even to manufactured items, such as implements, houses, and clothes: those that are good and well made are least altered by time or any other influences.

ADEIMANTUS: That's right.   10

SOCRATES: So whatever is in good condition—whether due to nature or craft or both—is least subject to change by something else.   b

ADEIMANTUS: It seems so.

SOCRATES: But gods, of course, as well as the things belonging to them, are best in every way.

ADEIMANTUS: They certainly are.   5

SOCRATES: So, on this view, gods would be least likely to have many forms.

ADEIMANTUS: Least likely, indeed.

SOCRATES: Then would they change or alter themselves?

ADEIMANTUS: Clearly so, if indeed they are altered at all.

SOCRATES: Do they change themselves into something better and more beautiful, or into something worse and uglier, than themselves?   10

ADEIMANTUS: It would have to be into something worse, if indeed they are altered at all. For surely we won't say that gods are deficient in   c
either beauty or virtue.

SOCRATES: You are absolutely right. And do you think, Adeimantus, that anyone, whether god or human, would deliberately make himself worse in
any way?   5

ADEIMANTUS: No, that is impossible.

SOCRATES: It is also impossible, then, for a god to want to alter himself. On the contrary, since each god is, it seems, as beautiful and as good as possible, he must always unqualifiedly retain his own form.

ADEIMANTUS: In my view, at least, that is absolutely necessary.

SOCRATES: None of our poets, then, my very good man, is to say that   d
"The gods, like strangers from foreign lands, assume many disguises when they visit our cities."[3] Nor must they tell lies about Proteus and Thetis, or present Hera, in their tragedies or other poems, disguised as a priestess collecting alms for "the life-giving sons of the Argive river Inachus,"[4] or tell us any of the many other such lies. Nor should mothers, influenced   e
by these stories, which terrify children, tell bad tales about gods who go wandering around at night in the guises of many strange and multifarious beings, lest they blaspheme the gods and, at the same time, make their   5
children too cowardly.

ADEIMANTUS: Indeed, they should not.

SOCRATES: But, though the gods themselves are the sorts of things that cannot change, do they make us think that they appear in multifarious guises, deceiving us and using sorcery on us?   10

ADEIMANTUS: Perhaps they do.

---

[3] *Odyssey* 17. 485–6.

[4] Inachus was the father of Io, who was persecuted by Hera because Zeus was in love with her. The source for the part of the story Plato quotes is unknown.

SOCRATES:	What? Would a god be willing to lie by presenting in word or deed what is only an illusion?	382a
ADEIMANTUS:	I don't know.	
SOCRATES:	Don't you know that all gods and humans hate a *true* lie, if one may call it that?	5
ADEIMANTUS:	What do you mean?	
SOCRATES:	I mean that no one intentionally wants to lie about the most important things to what is most important in himself. On the contrary, he fears to hold a lie there more than anything.	
ADEIMANTUS:	I still don't understand.	10
SOCRATES:	That's because you think I am saying something deep. I simply mean that to lie and to have lied to the soul about the things that are, and to be ignorant, and to have and hold a lie there, is what everyone would least of all accept; indeed, they especially hate it there.	b 5
ADEIMANTUS:	They certainly do.	
SOCRATES:	But surely, as I was saying just now, it would be most correct to say that it is truly speaking a lie—the ignorance in the soul of the one to whom the lie was told. For a lie in words is a sort of imitation of this affection in the soul, an image of it that comes into being after it, and not an altogether pure lie. Isn't that so?	10
ADEIMANTUS:	Yes, it is.	
SOCRATES:	A real lie, then, is hated not only by the gods, but also by human beings.	
ADEIMANTUS:	I think it is.	
SOCRATES:	What about a lie in words? Aren't there times when it is useful, and so does not merit hatred? What about when we are dealing with enemies, or with so-called friends who, because of insanity or ignorance, are attempting to do something bad? Isn't it a useful drug for preventing them? And consider the case of those stories we were talking about just now—those we tell because we do not know the truth about those ancient events: by making the lies that they contain as much like the truth as possible, don't we make them useful?	10 d
ADEIMANTUS:	We most certainly do.	
SOCRATES:	In which of these ways, then, could a lie be useful to a god? Would he lie by making likeness of the truth about ancient events because of his ignorance of them?	5
ADEIMANTUS:	It would be ridiculous to think that.	
SOCRATES:	Then there is nothing of the lying poet in a god?	
ADEIMANTUS:	Not in my view.	10
SOCRATES:	Would he lie, then, through fear of his enemies?	
ADEIMANTUS:	Hardly.	e
SOCRATES:	Because of the foolishness or insanity of his family or friends then?	
ADEIMANTUS:	No one who is foolish or mad is a friend of the gods.	
SOCRATES:	So a god has no reason to lie?	
ADEIMANTUS:	None.	5
SOCRATES:	So both what is daimonic and what is divine are entirely free of lies.	
ADEIMANTUS:	Absolutely.	

SOCRATES: A god, then, is altogether simple, true in both word and deed. He does not change himself or deceive others by means of images, by words, or by sending signs, whether they are awake or dreaming.   10

ADEIMANTUS: That is my view—at any rate, now that I have heard what you have to say.   383a

SOCRATES: You agree, then, that this is the second pattern people must follow when speaking or composing poems about the gods: the gods are not sorcerers who change themselves, nor do they mislead us by telling lies in word or deed.   5

ADEIMANTUS: I agree.

SOCRATES: Even though we praise many things in Homer, then, we won't approve of Zeus' sending the dream to Agamemnon, nor of Aeschylus when he makes Thetis say that Apollo sang, in prophecy at   b
her wedding:

About the good luck my children would have,
Free of disease throughout their long lives,
And of all the blessings the friendship of the gods would bring me.
I hoped that Phoebus' divine mouth would be free of lies,
Endowed as it is with the craft of prophecy.
But the very god who sang, the one at the feast,
The one who said all that, he himself it is
Who killed my son.[5]

Whenever anyone says such things about a god, we will be angry with him, refuse him a chorus,[6] and not allow teachers to use what he says for the   c
education of the young—not if our guardians are going to be as god-fearing and godlike as human beings can be.   5

ADEIMANTUS: I agree completely about these patterns, and I would use them as laws.

Book 3
SOCRATES' NARRATION CONTINUES:

SOCRATES: Where the gods are concerned, then, it seems that those   386a
are the sorts of stories the future guardians should and should not hear from childhood on, if they are to honor the gods and their parents, and not treat lightly their friendship with one another.

ADEIMANTUS: I am sure we are right about that.   5

SOCRATES: What about if they are to be courageous? Shouldn't they be told stories that will make them least likely to fear death? Or do you think that anyone ever becomes courageous if he has that fear in his   b
heart?

ADEIMANTUS: No, by Zeus, I do not.

SOCRATES: What about if someone believes that Hades exists and is full of terrible things? Can anyone with that fear be unafraid of death   5
and prefer it to defeat in battle and slavery?

ADEIMANTUS: Not at all.

SOCRATES: Then we must also supervise those who try to tell such stories, it seems, and ask them not to disparage the life in Hades in this undiscriminating way, but to speak

[5]   At *Iliad* 2.1–34, Zeus sends a dream to Agamemnon to promise success if he attacks Troy immediately. The promise is false. The source for the quotation from Aeschylus is unknown.

[6]   I.e., deny him the funding necessary to hire a chorus of actors and produce his play.

well of it, since what they now tell us is neither true nor beneficial to future
warriors.   c

ADEIMANTUS: Yes, we must.

SOCRATES: We will start with the following lines, then, and expunge everything like them: "I
would rather labor on earth in another man's service, a man who is landless, with
little to live on, than be king over all the dead";[7] and this: "He feared that his home
should be revealed to mortals and immortals as dreadful, dank, and hated even by
the gods;"[8] and: d
"Alas, there survives in the Halls of Hades a soul, a mere phantasm, with its wits
completely gone";[9] and this: "He alone can think others to be flitting shadows";[10]
and: "The soul, leaving his limbs, made its way to Hades, lamenting its fate,
leaving manhood and youth behind",[11] and   387a
this: "His soul went below the earth like smoke, screeching
as it went",[12] and:

As when bats in an awful cave
Fly around screeching if one of them falls
From the cluster on the ceiling, all clinging to one another,
so their souls went screeching.[13]

We will beg Homer and the rest of the poets not to be angry if we delete   b
these and all similar passages—not because they are not poetic and pleasing to the
masses when they hear them, but because the more poetic they are, the more they
should be kept away from the ears of children and men who are to be free and to
fear slavery more than death.

ADEIMANTUS: Absolutely.

SOCRATES: Then, in addition, we must also get rid of the terrible and frightening names that
occur in such passages: Cocytus, Styx,[14] "those below," "the sapless ones," and all
the other names of the same pattern that supposedly make everyone who hears
them shudder. Perhaps they are useful for other purposes, but our fear is that all
that shuddering will make our guardians more emotional and soft than they ought
to be.   5

ADEIMANTUS: And our fear is justified.

SOCRATES: Should we remove them, then?

ADEIMANTUS: Yes.

SOCRATES: And follow the opposite pattern in speech and poetry?

ADEIMANTUS: Clearly.   10

SOCRATES: Shall we also remove the lamentations and pitiful speeches
of famous men?   d

ADEIMANTUS: If what we did before was necessary, so is that.

---

[7] *Odyssey* 11.489–91. Odysseus is being addressed by Achilles in Hades.

[8] *Iliad* 20.64–5. Hades is afraid that the earth will split open and reveal what his home is like.

[9] *Iliad* 23.103–4. Achilles speaks these lines as the soul of the dead Patroclus leaves for Hades.

[10] *Odyssey* 10.493–5. Circe speaking to Odysseus about the prophet Tiresias.

[11] *Iliad* 16.856–7. The words refer to Patroclus, who has just been mortally wounded by Hector.

[12] *Iliad* 23.100. The soul referred to is that of Patroclus.

[13] *Odyssey* 14.6–9. The souls are those of Penelope's suitors, whom Odysseus has killed.

[14] "Cocytus" means river of wailing or lamenting, "Styx", river of hatred.

| SOCRATES: | Consider, though, whether we will be right to remove them or not. What we claim is that a good man won't think that death is a terrible thing for another good one to suffer—even if the latter happens to be his friend. | 5 |

ADEIMANTUS: Yes, we do claim that.

SOCRATES: So, he won't mourn for him as if he had suffered a terrible fate.

ADEIMANTUS: Certainly not.   10

SOCRATES: But we also claim this: a good person is most self-sufficient when it comes to living well, and is distinguished from other people by having the least need of anyone or anything else.   e

ADEIMANTUS: True.

SOCRATES: So it is less terrible for him than for anyone else to be deprived of a son, brother, possessions, or the like.

ADEIMANTUS: Yes, much less.   5

SOCRATES: So, he will lament it the least and bear it the most calmly when some such misfortune overtakes him.

ADEIMANTUS: Of course.

SOCRATES: We would be right, then, to remove the lamentations of famous men. We would leave them to women (provided they are not   10
excellent women) and cowardly men, so that those we say we are   388a
training to guard our land will be ashamed to do such things.

ADEIMANTUS: That's right.

SOCRATES: In addition, then, we will have to ask Homer and the other poets not to represent
Achilles, who was the son of a goddess,   5
as:

Lying now on his side, now on his back, now again
On his belly; then standing up to wander distracted
This way and that on the shore of the unharvested sea;[15]

or to make him pick up ashes with both hands and pour them   b
over his head, weeping and lamenting to the extent and in the manner Homer
describes;[16] or to represent Priam, a close descen-   5
dant of the gods, as "begging and rolling around in dung, as he calls upon each of
his men by name."[17] And yet more insistently than that, we will ask them at least
not to make the gods lament and say: "Woe is me, unfortunate that I am, wretched
mother of   c
a great son."[18] But, if they do make the gods do such things, at least they must not
dare to represent the greatest of the gods in so unlikely a fashion as to make him
say: "Alas, with my own eyes I see a man who is most dear to me being chased
around the city, and my heart laments";[19] or "Woe is me, that Sarpedon, who is
most dear to me, should be fated to be killed by Patroclus, the son of   d
Menoetius."[20] You see, my dear Adeimantus, if our young people listen seriously
to these stories without ridiculing them as not worth hearing, none of them is going
to consider such things to be unworthy of a mere human being like himself, or

---

[15] *Iliad* 24.3–12.

[16] *Iliad* 18.23–4.

[17] *Iliad* 22.414–5.

[18] *Iliad* 18.54. Thetis, the mother of Achilles, is mourning his fate among the Nereids.

[19] *Iliad* 22.168–9. Zeus is watching Hector being pursued by Achilles.

[20] *Iliad* 16.433–4.

rebuke himself if it occurred to him to do or say any of them. On the contrary, with-   5

out shame or perseverance, he would chant many dirges and laments at the slightest sufferings.

ADEIMANTUS: That's absolutely true.   e

SOCRATES: But that must not happen, as our argument has shown—and we must remain persuaded by it until someone shows us a better one.

ADEIMANTUS: No, it must not.

SOCRATES: Moreover, they must not be lovers of laughter either. For   5
whenever anyone gives in to violent laughter, a violent reaction pretty much always follows.

ADEIMANTUS: I agree.

SOCRATES: So, if someone represents worthwhile people as overcome by laughter, we must not accept it, and we will accept it even less if they represent the gods in that way.

ADEIMANTUS: Much less.   389a

SOCRATES: Then we must not accept the following sorts of sayings about the gods from Homer: "And unquenchable laughter arose among the blessed gods as they saw Hephaestus limping through the hall."[21]   5
According to your argument, they must be rejected.

ADEIMANTUS: Yes, if you want to attribute it to me, but they must be rejected in any case.   b

SOCRATES: Moreover, we have to be concerned about the truth as well. For if what we said just now is correct and a lie is really useless to the gods, but useful to human beings as a form of drug, it is clear that it must be assigned to doctors, whereas private individuals must have nothing to do with it.   5

ADEIMANTUS: It is clear.

SOCRATES: It is appropriate for the rulers, then, if anyone, to lie because of enemies or citizens for the good of the city. But no one else may have anything to do with it. On the contrary, we will say that for a private individual to lie to such rulers is as bad a mistake as for a sick person not to tell his doctor or an athlete his trainer the truth about his physical   c
condition, or for someone not to tell the captain the things that are true about the ship and the sailors, or about how he himself or one of his fellow sailors is faring—indeed, it is a worse mistake.   5

ADEIMANTUS: That's absolutely true.

SOCRATES: So, if anyone else is caught telling lies in the city—"any   d
of the craftsmen, whether a prophet , a doctor who heals the sick, or a carpenter who works in wood"[22]—he will be punished for introducing a practice that is as subversive and destructive of a city as of a ship.   5

---

[21]   *Iliad* 1.599–600.

[22]   *Odyssey* 17.384.

Primary Source 4.50   Plato, *Gorgias* 523a–527e

(Source: Emlyn-Jones, C. (ed. and trans.) (2004) *Plato: Gorgias*, Harmondsworth, Penguin, pp. 131–6, 149–50; footnotes edited)

SOCRATES: Give ear then, as they say, to a very fine story, which   523
will, I suppose, seem just a legendary tale to you but is fact to me; what
I am going to tell you as the truth.[1]

Homer relates that, when they succeeded their father, Zeus and Poseidon and Pluto
divided his empire between them.[2] Now, there was in the time of Kronos a law
concerning mankind which has remained in force among the gods from that time to
this. The law ordains that, when his time comes to die, a man who has lived a
righteous and holy life   b
shall depart to the Isles of the Blessed and there live in complete happiness, free from
evils, but that the man whose life has been wicked and godless shall be imprisoned in
the place of retribution and judgement, which is called Tartarus.

In the time of Kronos and in the early days of the reign of Zeus humans were tried
while still alive by living judges on the very day on which they were fated to die.
This led to wrong verdicts, so Pluto and the overseers of the Isles of the Blessed came
to Zeus and complained that people were arriving at both destinations contrary to
what they deserved. Then Zeus said: 'I will put an end to this. At present verdicts are
wrongly   c
given. The cause of this is that men are being tried in their clothes, for they are still
alive when this happens.[3] Many whose souls are wicked are dressed in the trappings
of physical beauty and high birth and riches, and when their trial takes place they are
supported by a crowd of witnesses who come to testify to the righteousness of their
lives.

'This causes confusion to the judges, who are also hampered by   d
being clothed themselves, and their soul is hidden behind eyes and ears and the rest
of the body, and all of this, as well as their own clothes and those of the accused form
a barrier in front of them. Our first task, then,' said Zeus, 'is to take from mortals the
foreknowledge of the hour of their death which at present they enjoy. Prometheus has
been given orders[4] to   e
bring this to an end. Next, they must all be tried naked after they have died, and, so
that the verdict will be just, the judge too must be naked and dead himself, viewing
with bare soul the bare soul of every man as soon as he is dead, when he has no
friends and relations to aid him and has left behind   524
on earth all his former glory. I realized this before you did, and I have appointed my
own sons[5] as judges, two from Asia, Minos and Rhadamanthus, and one from
Europe, Aeacus. These, when they are dead, shall sit in judgement in the meadow at

---

[1] *Legendary ... truth*: 'Legendary tale' translates *muthos*; 'fact' translates *logos*, which has a basic
meaning of 'word' or 'story', but also implies a *rational* account'.

[2] *divided ... between them*: In Homer (*Iliad* 15.187 ff.), Zeus takes the Heavens, Poseidon the sea
and Pluto the Underworld. Socrates presents a bowdlerized version of the succession story;
'succeeded' replaces the violent overthrow of Kronos related in Hesiod's *Theogony* 453 ff. Plato
elsewhere objects to this story on moral grounds, e.g. *Republic* 377e ff.

[3] *I will put ... happens*: The short sentences of Zeus' pronouncements reflect the simple narrative
style of the Greek at this point.

[4] *take ... foreknowledge ... orders*: Prometheus ('Foresight') can also take away foreknowledge;
possibly here there is an echo of Aeschylus, *Prometheus Bound* 248 ff., where Prometheus explains
that he stopped mortals from foreseeing their fate by giving them 'blind hopefulness', or the story
may go back to an ancient folk-tale source.

[5] *my own sons*: All three were traditionally judges in Hades. Minos and Rhadamanthus were from
Crete (which was reckoned as part of Asia) and Aeacus was born on the island named after his
mother Aegina (near Athens).

the parting of the ways from which the two roads lead, the one to the Isles of the Blessed and the other to Tartarus. Rhadamanthus shall try the men of Asia and Aeacus the men of Europe, but to Minos I will give the supreme function of delivering judgement when his colleagues are in doubt. This will ensure that the judgement about the ultimate destiny of mortals is decided as justly as possible.'

This, Callicles, is what I have heard and believe to be true, and   b
from this account I draw the following conclusions. Death, it seems to me, is nothing but the complete separation of two separate entities, body and soul, and, when this separation takes place, each of them is left in much the same state as when the person was alive. The body retains its natural characteristics with the consequences of its treatment and experience all still visible. For instance, if a man's body during life has grown large by nature or nurture or both, his corpse will be large in death; if fat, his c
corpse will be fat, and so on. Again, if the deceased was in the habit of wearing his hair long, his corpse will be long-haired; if he was a convict, whose body was marked during life with the scars of blows inflicted by whips or in other ways, the same marks will be visible on his body after death; if his limbs were broken or deformed in life, you will see the same when he is dead. In a word, all or almost all the physical characteristics   d
which a person has acquired during life remain visible for a time even after death. The same, I believe, Callicles, is true of the soul; once it is stripped of the body all its qualities may be seen, not only its natural endowments but the modifications brought about by the various habits which its owner has formed.

So when the dead reach the judgement-seat, in the case of Asiatics the judgement seat of Rhadamanthus, Rhadamanthus summons them   e
before him and inspects each person's soul, without knowing to whom it belongs. Often, when it is the king of Persia or some other monarch or potentate that he has to deal with, he finds that there is no soundness in the soul whatever; it is a mass of weals and scars imprinted on it by   525
various acts of perjury and wrongdoing which have been stamped on his soul; it is twisted and warped by lies and vanity and has grown crooked because truth has had no part in its development. Power, luxury, pride and debauchery have left it so full of disproportion and ugliness that when he has inspected it Rhadamanthus dispatches it in ignominy straight to prison, where on its arrival it will undergo the appropriate treatment.

The object of all punishment which is rightly inflicted should be   b
either to improve and benefit its subjects or else to make them an example to others, who will be deterred by the sight of their sufferings and reform their own conduct. Those who are helped by undergoing punishment, whether by gods or men, are those whose faults are curable; yet both here and in Hades this benefit comes only at the cost of pain and anguish; there is no other
way in which men can be cured of wrongdoing. Those who   c
have committed the worst crimes and are consequently incurable become examples to others. Being incurable they are no longer capable of receiving benefit themselves, but they do good to others, who see them suffering an eternity of the most severe and painful and terrible torment on account of their sins. They are literally hung up as object-lessons there in the prison-house
of Hades, in order that every newly arrived wrongdoer may contemplate them and take the warning to heart.[6]

---

[6] *object-lessons ... heart*: This only makes sense if the curable souls return again to the upper world. This is the theory of the transmigration of souls, which Plato expounds in detail later in *Republic*, but which does not feature explicitly in *Gorgias*, although the doctrine here seems to presuppose it.

If what Polus says about him is true, I maintain that Archelaus will   d
be one of these, together with any other tyrant of like character. Indeed, I think that
the majority of these warning examples are drawn from among tyrants and kings and
potentates and politicians, whose power gives them the opportunity of committing the
greatest and worst impieties. In support of
this view I can quote Homer, in whose Hades those whose punishment   e
is everlasting, Tantalus and Sisyphus and Tityus, are kings and potentates, whereas
Thersites – and any other common criminal – has never been represented as suffering
the extremity of punishment assigned to the incurable. The reason is, I think, that he
did not have sufficient power for wrongdoing, and to that extent was more fortunate
than those who did.[7]

However, Callicles, even if the extremely wicked are found among men in power,
there is nothing to prevent good men arising in this class,   526
and those who do so are greatly to be admired. For it is difficult, Callicles, and very
praiseworthy, to live a life rightly when there is ample opportunity to do wrong. But
such men are rare. There have been, both here and in other countries, and no doubt
there will be in the future, fine, good men who have shone in the righteous conduct of
affairs committed to their charge; one of
the most illustrious, Aristides[8] the son of   b
Lysimachus, won a reputation which extended over the whole of Greece; but the
majority of men in power, my friend, go to the bad.

As I was saying, then, when Rhadamanthus gets such a person before him, he is quite
ignorant of his identity or parentage; his knowledge is confined to the man's guilt,
and having considered this and made a mark to indicate whether he regards him as
curable or incurable, he dispatches him to Tartarus, where he undergoes the
appropriate treatment. But   e
sometimes the eye of the judge lights on a soul which has lived in purity and truth; it
may or may not be the soul of a private person, but most often, Callicles, if I am not
mistaken, it is the soul of a lover of wisdom who has kept to his own calling during
his life and has not meddled in city affairs.[9] Then Rhadamanthus is struck with
admiration and sends him off to the Isles of the Blessed. Aeacus discharges the same
judicial function, holding, like Rhadamanthus, a staff of office in his hand; Minos,
who sits as president of the court, enjoys the unique distinction of a golden sceptre –
you may remember that Odysseus in Homer says that he saw him   d
'wielding a sceptre of gold and pronouncing judgement among the dead'.[10]

Personally, Callicles, I put faith in this story, and make it my aim to present my soul
to its judge in the soundest possible state. That is why, dismissing from consideration
the honours which stimulate most people's ambition, and pursuing the truth, I shall
try to be as good as possible, both in life and when my time comes to die, in death.
To this way of life and to   e
this struggle, in which the prize, I assure you, outweighs all the prizes of this world, I
challenge all others to the best of my ability. In your case, Callicles, it is a counter-
challenge, coupled with a warning that when the time comes for you to stand the trial
of which I have just spoken, you will be quite unable to defend yourself; you will

---

[7] *Homer ... who did*: For the punishment of Tantalus, Sisyphus and Tityus, see *Odyssey*
11.576–600. Thersites was a subordinate in the Greek army at Troy who abused the leaders of the
expedition and got punished by Odysseus for his insubordination (*Iliad* 2.211 ff.).

[8] *Aristides*: Known as 'the Just', he took a prominent part in the battles of the Persian Wars and the
political aftermath.

[9] *not meddled ... affairs*: Socrates here recommends the *apragmosune* ('detachment from political
affairs') of the private citizen over *polupragmosune* ('involvement in political affairs') – an important
tension in fifth-century politics.

[10] *Minos ... 'wielding ... dead'*: Homer, *Odyssey* 11.569.

stand at the judgement-seat   527

of the son of Aegina, when he summons you before him, as gaping and dizzy as I will be here,[11] and possibly someone will slap you in the face with impunity and subject you to every kind of insult.

Perhaps you may despise what I have told you as no more than an old wives' tale. There would be every reason why you should if our search had disclosed to us any better or truer account of the matter; but as things are you see that the three of you, yourself and Polus and Gorgias, the   b

wisest men in Greece, are unable to show that there is any better way of life than this one now, which also turns out to benefit us in the world to come. All the other theories put forward in our long conversation have been refuted and this conclusion alone stands firm: that one should avoid doing wrong with more care than being wronged, and that the supreme object of a man's efforts, in public and in private life, must be the reality rather than the appearance of goodness. Moreover, if a person goes wrong in any way he must be punished, and the next best thing to being good is to become good by submitting to punishment and paying the penalty for one's faults. Every form of pandering, whether to oneself or to others, whether to large groups or to small, is   c

to be shunned; oratory is to be employed always in the service of right, and the same holds true of every other activity.

Be guided by me then and join me in the pursuit of what, as our argument shows, will secure your happiness both in life and after death. Let people despise you for a fool and insult you if they wish; yes, by Zeus, even if they inflict the ultimate indignity of a blow in the face, take it cheerfully: if you are really a good man devoted to the practice   d

of virtue they can do you no harm.

And then, when we have adequately exercised ourselves in this way in partnership with one another, finally we can, if we think fit, set our hand to politics or to giving our opinion about any other subject that attracts us: our opinions will be better worth having then than they are now. It would be shameful for men in our present condition, who are so uneducated that we never think the same for two moments together, even on subjects of the greatest importance, to give ourselves the airs   e

of persons of importance. Let us then allow ourselves to be led by the argument now made clear to us, which teaches that the best way of life is to practise righteousness and all virtue, whether living or dying; let us follow that way and urge others to follow it, instead of the way which you in mistaken confidence are urging upon me, for that way is worthless, Callicles.

[11] *gaping and dizzy ... here*: Not Socrates' demeanour at his actual trial, according to Plato's *Apology*! But note that there is a non-Platonic tradition that Socrates offered no defence at his trial.

Secondary Sources

Block 3   Ovid and the reception of myth

Secondary Source 3.1   Andrew Feldherr, 'Metamorphosis in the *Metamorphoses*'

(Source: Hardie, P. (ed.) (2002) *The Cambridge Companion to Ovid*, Cambridge, Cambridge University Press, pp. 163–79 and selected references)

> As Gregor Samsa awoke one morning from uneasy dreams, he found himself transformed in his bed into a monstrous insect.

The first sentence in Kafka's *Metamorphosis*, a work whose moral seriousness has sometimes seemed to place it at the opposite pole from Ovid's epic in the literature of transformation, is as baffling for the reader as the event it describes is for Gregor Samsa. As he has become a monstrous insect so we are immediately confronted with the question of how to make sense of and interpret this monstrous and bizarre subject. The first words, with their resemblance to the classic fairy tale beginning 'once upon a time', seem to offer one possibility: we can normalize this supernatural event by assuming the story belongs to a genre that doesn't ask us to take it seriously, and even rejoice in the distance that separates us from a fictional world where such things are possible. So for Samsa there is the fleeting possibility that he is still dreaming. But if the time when this event takes place is re-assuringly indeterminate, other elements of this story bring it much closer to home. Gregor Samsa is too specific to be the name of a fairy tale prince, and the transformation takes place in his own bed – it could indeed be ours. Throughout the story, the particularity with which Gregor's condition is described suggests a kaleidoscopic variety of strategies for making sense of it. Perhaps one of the most tempting is to neutralize its strangeness by treating it as a figure of speech, so that its significance becomes symbolic rather than literal. Gregor Samsa is merely like an insect – because of the alienating effects of bourgeois culture? because he is going through some psychological transformation? What we decide the image means matters less than the initial decision that it means something other than that one Gregor Samsa really did turn into an insect. After this move, the possibility of identifying with Samsa, seeing his condition as one that we somehow share, becomes much easier.

The opening lines of Ovid's poem make it even more explicit that the comprehension of metamorphosis provides a crucial analogue for the reader's experience of the poem:

> In noua fert animus mutatas dicere formas
> corpora: di coeptis (nam uos mutastis et illa)
> adspirate meis primaque ab origine mundi
> ad mea perpetuum deducite tempora carmen.

(1.1–4)

> My spirit impels me to speak of bodies changed into new forms:
> gods, inspire my beginnings – for you have changed even those –
> and draw my song without breaks from the first beginning of the
> world to my own times.

The text itself, like the bodies it announces as its subject matter, has been transformed. Indeed the syntax of the opening sentence changes shape before the eyes of the reader, who might initially have taken the first line as a self-sufficient whole meaning 'my mind prompts a new venture, to speak of changed forms' but must reconstrue it upon *corpora* (bodies) at the beginning of the second verse.[1] The kind of changes the poem exhibits on a larger scale include shifts in tone, subject matter, and even generic affiliation, among the 250 or so narratives of metamorphosis it contains. Thus in the first book we move suddenly from Apollo's destruction of the monstrous dragon Python to the story of Daphne, in which the same god figures not as a heroic bringer of order but as a lover, reminiscent of the protagonists of contemporary elegy. Yet this tale itself ends with a panegyric to Augustus and a glimpse ahead to the time when the laurel tree into which the resisting Daphne is transformed will adorn the emperor's triumphs.

Paradoxically, recognition of this metamorphic aspect of the text's construction has sometimes gone together with an undervaluation of the thematic centrality of transformation itself, which becomes a narrative leitmotif valuable solely because its omnipresence allowed the poem to travel freely among the varied stories of Greek myth. Indeed those occasions when the poet can be seen bending over backwards to slip a reference to metamorphosis into a story where it seems to have little place draw attention to his own invention and away from the story he is telling. Correspondingly, according to this view, the fairy-tale elements of metamorphosis distance the reader from the story by neutralizing the tragic and distressing. Thus in a story like that of Myrrha (10.298–502), who succumbs to sexual passion for her father, consummates it under cover of darkness, and is driven into exile when discovered, her final transformation into a myrrh tree acts as a kind of narrative *deus ex machina*. As opposed to the nightmarish overtones of Gregor Samsa's metamorphosis, Myrrha's leaves the real conflicts and consequences of the human situation far behind.[2] Yet using Kafka's tale as a positive model reminds us that the choice of metamorphosis as a subject transforms a narrative in far more complex ways than simply providing for frequent changes of subject. Each individual metamorphosis opens up possibilities for contrasting responses: humour, terror, allegorization, even boredom. Of course these responses are largely conditioned by the text itself – if a story begins 'once upon a time', for example, we have a pretty strong clue about how to read it. On the other hand, the changing implications of metamorphosis among the many kinds of literary discourse in which it occurs make it a narrative element that invites contrasting readings and opens out interpretative possibilities. Ovid himself participates in this process by introducing multiple points of view on transformation itself as well as raising questions about the generic status of his work. Thus metamorphosis continually compels readers to refigure their relationship to the text, their understanding of the narratives it contains, and ultimately how it functions as a literary representation.

The tradition of using the metamorphosis theme to emphasize the *Metamorphoses*' essential lack of seriousness begins with Ovid himself, who in a later work tells us that his tales of transformation were 'not to be believed' (*Trist.* 2.64), a claim that highlights the first assumption a contemporary reader might bring to any such story. The rhetorical training that played such a crucial role in informing ancient responses to literature divided narratives into three classes according to their relationship to reality: histories (*historiae*) told what actually happened; *argumenta*, exemplified by the plots of new comedy, presented plausible stories, things that might have happened, and finally 'tales'

---

[1]   For the fullest treatment of these lines' shifting meaning, see now Wheeler (1999) 8–20.

[2]   For the classic statements of this position, see Fränkel (1945) esp. 97–100 and Galinsky (1975) 62–9.

(*fabulae*) describe events that are not only 'untrue, but separated even from the appearance of truth' because they are unnatural or impossible.[3] Illustrations of this last category often include tales of transformation.[4] Yet for all Ovid's overt acceptance of the 'fairy tale' status of his narrative, other aspects of his poem suggest that in raising such traditional distinctions between fiction and reality he also challenges them. Thus while the second word of his poem, *nova*, which in Latin can mean not only 'new' but also 'strange' or 'unattested', perhaps hints at the miraculous nature of the stories to follow, the progress 'into the new' also points forward to the overall chronological schema of his work. This organizational pattern itself connects the 'fabulous' to the real world of the poet, the 'my times' that mark the poem's conclusion: rather than being limited to an undifferentiated mythical past, the miraculous transformations will be integrated into a framework that can also be described historically. Indeed throughout the poem, mortals will be punished precisely for failing to recognize that their capacity for metamorphosis allows the Olympian gods of legend to appear as unremarkably realistic figures. When, for example, the character Pirithus explicitly rejects a story as a fiction because it describes the gods changing shape,[5] he is admonished to be more careful with the story of Baucis and Philemon, which describes the punishment of those who failed to offer hospitality to gods disguised as mortals and the rewards of those who did.

In defining the place of his poem in the poetic tradition, Ovid challenges readers' expectations in another way by suggesting his allegiance to two kinds of poetry often opposed and again his choice of metamorphosis as a topic accentuates this ambiguity. The verb *deducere* (1.4), used in the proem to describe how the gods 'draw out his song', was frequently used programmatically by Augustan poets to summon up the taste for short, elaborately refined poems codified above all by the Alexandrian Greek Callimachus (see also Harrison in this volume, p. 87). Yet in the same sentence Ovid describes his poem as *perpetuum*, continuous or unbroken, a translation of the Greek word used by Callimachus of the kind of chronologically arranged, loosely composed narratives that he defined his work against. While it is certainly possible to reconcile these characteristics, and as a Callimachean scholar has recently pointed out, no reader could bring against Ovid's poem the charges of monotony and sloppy construction that lay behind the rejection of 'continuous' poems, the reader continually experiences a tension between the epic architecture of the poem and the artful episodes of which it is made up.[6]

---

[3]   For examples of this classification see Sext. *Math.* 1.263. *Rhet. ad Her.* 1.13, Cic. *Inv.* 1.27, and Quint. *Inst.* 2.3.4 (quoted in the text); see Graf in this volume, p. 109.

[4]   Thus Sextus (1.264) includes the tales 'of the companions of Diomedes changed into sea birds, of Odysseus changed to a horse, and of Hecuba to a dog', in this class, and Martianus Capella (550) presents the transformation of Daphne as a paradigmatic *fabula*. Ovid himself explicitly alludes to the generic distinction in an earlier poem (*Amores* 3.12) where he protests that poets should not be treated as if they were witnesses in a courtroom (19–20). He then proves his point that the 'licence of poets' is not constrained by the criterion of credibility that applies to the genre of history (*historica fide*, 42) by cataloguing the miraculous mythological stories to be found in their works. In most of these tales, the unbelievable element is precisely metamorphosis. Yet the context of the poet's plea not to be believed undercuts its ostensible message: Ovid has portrayed his (fictional) mistress in such terms that now everyone is in love with her and he himself is jealous. He therefore demands that his readers understand his praise for her as false. For the poem's manipulation of the rhetorical categories of believable and unbelievable stories see McKeown (1979).

[5]   '*ficta refers nimiumque putas, Acheloe, potentes | esse deos' dixit 'si dant adimuntque figuras.*' ('you retail fictions, Achelous,' he said, 'and you think the gods too powerful if they give and take away shapes.') (8.614–15) – lines that refer back to the *Metamorphoses*' programmatic description of its subject matter.

[6]   Cameron (1995) 359–61.

The claims to alternative generic allegiances in these lines open up very different possibilities for understanding the poet's choice of metamorphosis as a subject. If we are to read the poem as a series of discrete, refined narratives such a topic would seem entirely appropriate.[7] Although their works are almost completely lost, Ovid's most important predecessors for building tales of metamorphosis into larger poetic units seem to have worked very much in the tradition of Callimachean brevity. In the second century BCE, for example, Nicander of Colophon, whose only surviving works are a pair of didactic poems about snakebites and antidotes, produced the *Heteroioumena* (*Transformations*), in which he collected what seem to have been particularly obscure metamorphoses associated with the monuments and rites of far-flung cities and usually featuring local rustic divinities rather than the Olympian gods. While we are not in a position to tell what kind of larger structures Nicander used to organize his material, it is fairly clear that the poem was on a significantly smaller scale than Ovid's: five books, probably, as opposed to fifteen. Nothing can be said for certain about the scope, or even the date, of another source and antecedent of the *Metamorphoses*, the *Ornithogonia* (*Bird Origins*) of Boios, but his apparent aim of demonstrating that every species of bird was at one time a man again indicates a much more restricted canvas than Ovid's universal history.

By contrast to its suitability for these catalogue poems, the fabulous aspect of metamorphosis tales made them very difficult to reconcile with the aesthetic principles of serous epic, where supernatural solutions to human problems are pointedly avoided. In the Homeric poems, for example, stories of metamorphosis occur either in Odysseus' account of his wanderings, a narrative space reserved for all sorts of miraculous figures, or their very strangeness marks them out as communications from the gods, like the serpent and the bird's nest turned to stone mentioned in *Iliad* 2.301–29. And even these examples do not form a part of the poet's own narrative; they are described and interpreted by characters within the poem.[8]

In the works of Ovid's immediate epic predecessor, Virgil, the phenomenon of metamorphosis assumes a more prominent but deeply ambiguous role, one that in many respects looks ahead to its complex function in the *Metamorphoses*.[9] On the one hand Virgil seems to give an ideological dimension to Homer's reticence about transformation stories. Beyond raising questions about the plausibility of the narrative, metamorphosis suggests a world of unstable ephemerality that can only be at odds with the poem's motion towards the foundation of Rome as the centre of a stable cosmos, and indeed comes to be associated with the dehumanizing violence and immorality of Rome's civil wars. The bleeding bush that manifests the presence of Polydorus, a Trojan prince murdered by an avaricious and impious Thracian king, at the beginning of book 3, and the howling of the bestialized inhabitants of Circe's realm (*Aen.* 7.10–24) signpost regions where neither Aeneas' mission nor Virgil's narrative should go.[10] Virgil swerves just shy of metamorphosis in another sense when one of the poem's final similes figures Aenas and Turnus, in the climactic duel that decides the fate of Italy, as battling bulls (*Aen.* 12.715–22). Animal rage

---

[7]   For a general discussion of the treatment of metamorphosis in earlier literature, and detailed accounts of Nicander and Boios see Forbes-Irving (1990) 7–37. See also Hardie (1999a) for a discussion of metamorphosis as a way of commenting on the representational strategies of earlier epics.

[8]   On the avoidance of the miraculous in Homer see Griffin (1977).

[9]   For a fuller treatment of metamorphosis in the *Aeneid* see Hardie (1992).

[10]   For the re-emergence of these Circean dangers later in *Aen.* 7 see Putnam (1995) 100–20.

and undifferentiated violence are hardly the stuff from which the reader expects the tapestry of Roman history to be woven. But since this is just a figure of speech, it can always be read as but a partial, imprecise image of the combatants, or even as a foil to them. Metamorphosis within Virgil's poem is not, however, merely the favoured *modus operandi* of the forces of darkness and dissolution. Of the contrary, the victory of Aeneas, and by implication the emergence of Roman order from the chaotic final books of the poem, is in a sense a tale of metamorphosis, requiring the hero's transformation from the last remnant of a city doomed to fall to the founder of a civilization fated to endure. And in one important instance, his account of how the goddess Cybele saves the Trojan ships from destruction by turning them into nymphs (*Aen.* 9.77–122), Virgil highlights his inclusion of a miraculous transformation to make clear the special status of his epic. The passage has jolted Virgil's readers since antiquity, and even within the poem characters struggle to make sense of it.[11] The poet himself seems to hold the story at arm's length, presenting it as a legend, yet the transformation as an event is anchored in the plot of his epic.[12] But rather than regard Virgil's treatment of the episode as either half-hearted or misjudged, we can rather take it as a self-conscious deployment of the vexed status of metamorphosis within epic, alerting readers all too ready to dismiss the tale as fantasy that Aeneas' divinely guided foundation of Rome requires a different poetics than do the exploits of Homer's mortal heroes. As Ovid will later, Virgil here makes metamorphosis an occasion to reorient his readers' expectations of the poem.

If metamorphosis generally marks the limit of what is consistent with the moral seriousness of heroic epic, this is the line on which *Metamorphoses* dances. The poem's metre, size, and its incorporation of the Trojan and Roman subject matter of epic invite the reader to view the work in its entirety as a rival to those earlier works. Yet within that tradition, especially in the *Aeneid*, metamorphosis denoted a world of instability distinctly at odds with the clear and stable endings to which those works aspire – even if they notoriously fail to attain them. Should we read metamorphosis through epic eyes, with an even greater awareness of its essential unbelievability and trivializing effect? Can the epic form even save the work from itself by transfiguring its fabulous subject matter into a grand history of the Augustan world, just as Virgil allows metamorphosis a new role in his poem? Or is the work fundamentally an anti-epic, lending the gravity of the Homeric and Virgilian form to an antithetical vision of man's place in the cosmos? Or, a final alternative, should we simply avoid the question by allowing the poem to decompose itself into a Hellenistic assemblage of separate tales? Since Ovid often positions metamorphoses at the end of episodes, the transformations within the narrative tend to occur precisely where the structure of the work as a whole is most up for grabs. In deciding whether each metamorphosis marks an ending, or merely a transition, readers are continually confronted with the question of what kind of work they are reading.

To get a sense of what is at stake ideologically in the differing responses to metamorphosis offered by the poem, let us take a look at the poem's very first

---

[11]   Thus the ancient body of Virgilian commentary known as 'Servius Danielis' mentions two slightly different objections to the passage: one implies that the poet should never make up anything so remote from truth (3.46), and the other, though allowing poetic fictions, insists that they should have some precedent in earlier authors (9.81).

[12]   The verb *fertur* ('it is said', 9.82) provides the most obvious sign of this authorial distancing – although even that can be treated as a learned reference to an earlier poetic authority. According to Servius Danielis, 'some have objected to this "fertur" because it denies authority to the tale; others have praised it as a sign that the poet was unwilling to lend authority to an unbelievable event.' (*Ad Aen.* 9.81).

account of the transformation of a human being into an animal, the tale of Lycaon (1.209–43), an episode whose prominent position invites us to treat it as a paradigm for what is to come. This story follows after the poem's account of the formation of the cosmos, a process which involves not the creation of new substances out of nothing but rather a sorting into an ordered hierarchy of elements already present in the confused mass of primordial chaos. At first this story will seem to further the suggestion that metamorphosis itself serves as a tool for imposing a familiar, stable order on things, as opposed to representing the irruption of the unaccountable as it does in Kafka. Jupiter has heard of the impious behaviour of human beings, and in hopes of finding the story is false, he disguises himself as a mortal and descends from Olympus to investigate. When he enters Lycaon's realm, he gives signs of his divinity and begins to receive the worship of the people. The king, however, refuses to acknowledge Jupiter as divine and plots to prove him mortal by killing him in his sleep. He also kills a hostage and attempts to serve his cooked limbs to the god. In punishment, the god destroys the palace and Lycaon is driven into exile, at which point 'he wails and tries in vain to speak. His countenance takes upon itself all his madness; he turns his innate love of slaughter against sheep and even now rejoices in blood. His clothes turn into hair; his arms into legs. He becomes a wolf and preserves the traces of his old form. There is the same grayness, the same violent countenance. His eyes still gleam, and the appearance of bestiality remains.' (1.233–9).

Jupiter's account suggests that Lycaon has been quite literally put in his place. He had violated human norms by murdering a hostage and even attempted to usurp Jupiter's prerogative here by imposing his own test on the god. He subsequently undergoes a transformation that seems at once to punish his attempt to take on the god's role in the story and to express his own innate bestiality. (Notice that Jupiter never claims responsibility for the transformation, which appears to happen spontaneously, as if nature were simply taking its course.) Just as the creation of the world involved the separation of the lighter elements from water and earth, so here this wild beast who had somehow been grouped among men has finally been returned to his rightful category. The change that has taken place is merely one of form. And Lycaon's new shape not only more clearly reveals his essence, it also manifests and enforces the cosmic hierarchies he has violated. The wolf itself becomes a reminder of the consequences of behaving as either a beast or a god. There is also a more narrowly political significance to the metamorphosis. Before recounting this story Jupiter had been compared to the emperor Augustus, and the assembly of gods he addresses takes on the form of the Roman senate. The little epiphany of order that results from this metamorphosis, in which the natural world as we know it becomes a sign of the proper distribution of authority among gods and men, also serves as a reminder of the specifically Roman order that now, as Augustan artistic imagery so often implied, had embraced the cosmos itself.[13] The very name Lycaon derives from the Greek word for wolf (*lykos*), again suggesting that metamorphosis is above all a clarification of who he really is,[14] and that because of metamorphosis even verbal signs now more clearly represent the world. But of course in Ovid's text, Lycaon hasn't become a *lykos* but a *lupus*: metamorphosis as cosmic clarification depends upon the translation of Greek into Latin.

[13] For a good introduction to this pattern of imagery in the visual arts see Zanker (1988) 183–92 and Nicolet (1991) 29–56, and for an example of its development in literature see Hardie's (1986) 336–76 reading of the Virgilian shield of Aeneas.

[14] Solodow (1988) 174 defines 'clarification' as the central function of metamorphosis.

if it is nature, is it the god who is kinder.

is transformation a punishment.

or a transformation to a situation of rightful place ā the move from order to chaos? Lycaon acts like a wolf, displays wolf-like characteristics.

Such readings as this have produced a sense that the real emphasis in Ovid's poem of changes should be on stability. Far from suggesting a world of flux and shifting appearance, metamorphosis, which is always to be located in the past, results in a firm natural and political order in the present. The human beings who undergo metamorphosis, an emphatically final process that leaves no possibility of a return to their prior shape,[15] do not lose the enduring aspects of their being, rather they take on a form that reveals them – an idea that closely resembles influential stoic accounts of identity.[16] And indeed by narrating stories of this type, Ovid seems to be contributing to the semantic clarification and revelation that Jupiter sets in motion, by offering a world whose natural elements, like wolves, become transparent to human qualities and divine actions. But the very neatness of this interpretation results precisely from the tale's univocality and from the erasure of alternative points of view. Indeed this is the one story in the poem narrated by Jupiter himself, the ultimate representation of authority in the epic universe. Yet the metamorphosis that seems to provide such unanswerable closure in fact allows competing readings back into the text precisely because it makes the shutting down of alternative points of view so explicit. The first thing that happens to Lycaon is that he loses his power to speak – precisely the eloquence that allows Jupiter to tell his version of events. The last body parts mentioned are Lycaon's shining eyes, eyes that are depicted only as seen, not as seeing. Points of view opposed to Jupiter's would have been ready to hand for an informed reader of the text. For, as nearly as we can tell, no other account of Lycaon is so relentless in its condemnation of the king. Greek versions, in fact, present a highly ambivalent figure whose outrageous treatment of the gods is balanced by his role as a civilizing hero, an institutor of religious practices, whose name would be preserved not just by the wolf, but by the cult of Zeus Lykaios which he founded.[17] Even with Ovid's Jovian account, the boundaries between gods, humans, and animals seem dangerously permeable. Jupiter sets the plot in motion by his own shape-shifting, the assumption of human form – a disguise that anticipates the paradox of the final metamorphosis by simultaneously masking and revealing his divine nature. It might even be argued that Lycaon's outrage results less from his attempt to deprive the gods of the honour due them than from his scrupulous belief in the reality of appearances and his efforts to use those appearances to distinguish different orders of being. His very plot to kill Jupiter shows that he has taken his disguise seriously: far from attempting to dishonour the god, he assumes that the figure before him is a mortal impostor. And if Lycaon's error is really a failure to recognize that gods can disguise themselves as men, his experience is very relevant to Ovid's own readers who are making their first acquaintance with anthropomorphized gods in the work.[18] If they were to attempt to apply the same criterion of truth to their reading, then the entire epic machinery that underlies the moralizing/politicizing interpretation of the story would be called into question. To expose the gods as

---

[15]   Though even to the 'rule' that metamorphosis for humans is irreversible, there are occasional exceptions like Mnestra, the daughter of Erysichthon (8.843–78). When her father sells her into slavery as a way of supporting his insatiable hunger, the god Neptune gives her the power to change shape as a way of escaping from her buyers.

[16]   Dörrie (1959) connects the perpetuation of such an essence after metamorphosis with the view represented by the philosopher Posidonius (fr. 96) that each individual possesses a distinctive quality independent of his material existence.

[17]   For earlier accounts of the Lycaon story see Forbes-Irving (1990) 90–5 and 216–18; see also Barkan's (1986) 24–7 integration of the legend of Lycaon the sacrificer with Ovid's story.

[18]   For another adversarial reading of Jupiter's account of Lycaon see Anderson (1989); for the balance between contrasting readings in the story see Wheeler (1999) 171–81.

mere projections of human authority is to short-circuit their political use to glorify any individual human potentate – a central issue in Augustan iconography.[19]

Another tale from the first book reveals even more clearly how interpretation of the poem's thematic emphases hinges on the reading of a metamorphosis. When the nymph Daphne realizes that she will never win the foot-race against Apollo and will forfeit her virginity, she prays to be transformed and so to lose the external form (*figura*) that has caused her downfall by arousing the god's desire.

> Scarcely had she ended her prayer when a heavy sluggishness took possession of her limbs; her soft breast clothes itself in thin bark. Her hair grows into leaves, her arms into branches. Her foot once so swift cleaves to sluggish roots. A bough holds her face; only her beauty remains.
>
> (1.548–52)

Here the relationship between the new shape and the old becomes much more complicated. Far from fixing her in a state that permanently expresses her essential qualities, Daphne's metamorphosis strips her of the swiftness by which she has been characterized in the narrative; Ovid figures the transformation itself as a process of occlusion and possession. To try to read this metamorphosis according to the Lycaon paradigm by stressing the persistence of her beauty raises new problems, for it was her external attractiveness that warred against her desire to remain a virgin (*uotoque tuo tud forma repugnat*, 1.489). Indeed if anything has been preserved of Daphne it is the tragic discrepancy between her inner will and outer appearance. To read her metamorphosis as a clarification, then, implies that her essence lay in what she seemed to others to be rather than recognizing her as subject in her own right.

Such a reading is put forward by the divine interpreter within the poem, none other than Apollo himself, the god who pursued her on account of her form:

> Though you cannot be my wife, you will be my tree. My locks will always possess you, laurel, so will my lyre and my quiver. You will accompany the Latin chiefs when the joyful voice sings "Triumph" and the Capitoline witnesses long (triumphal) processions ... And as my youthful head is perpetually unshorn, so you will always retain the honour of leaves.
>
> (1.557–65)

Apollo's response to Daphne's metamorphosis in a sense completes the processes of the transformation by converting her form into a symbol, yet a symbol that recalls not so much who Daphne was as who Apollo is. It is his hair that her leaves are now made to recall, not her own once disordered tresses. Apollo's strategy also bears on the question of the poem's genre; by placing Daphne's transformation in an extensive historical context, recalling the broad temporal sweep proclaimed in the poet's prologue, and converting her into an instrument of praise, Apollo epicizes her story.[20] In doing so he fits it into the continuum prepared for by the poet himself, who introduced the story as an explanation for how the laurel tree came to be the sign of victory in the games that celebrated Apollo's conquest of the Python. Thus the tale that might have been thought to show how the god lost an archery contest with Cupid, and was

---

[19]   For a discussion of how Ovid's hyper-anthropomorphized gods undercut imperial religious innovations see Feeney (1991) 205–24.

[20]   For an introduction to the sophisticated pattern of generic play in this story see Nicoll (1980).

forced to shed his typical attributes by assuming the role of a lover, becomes instead a celebration of his once and future triumphs. For Daphne, though, does her metamorphosis mark the beginning of her epic significance, or is it in fact the end of the story? Again her changed form holds the key. The final lines at first appear to close the gap between Daphne's perspective and Apollo's by suggesting that Daphne herself consented to the role Apollo offered her by nodding her bough 'as if it were a head'. But perhaps the bough is just a bough. In other words, perhaps Daphne's will has been masked completely by her own form, and the attempt to claim her participation in this future as though she were still there marks merely the final stage in her possession.

The readings offered so far suggest that the event of metamorphosis in Ovid mobilizes two coherent interpretations of the poem, and that the choice between them depends on the point of view adopted on the transformation itself. First, to focus on the new shape, which is often a form familiar from the actual experience of the reader, in several senses normalizes metamorphosis, subordinating a manifestly unbelievable process to an undeniably real product. The world is, reassuringly, not a place where metamorphosis happens every day, and the very stories Ovid tells about wolves and laurel trees gives them a new significance as the manifest products of cosmic and political order and as *exempla* that perpetuate that order by recalling the consequences of violating it. In depicting metamorphosis from this perspective not only is Ovid in several senses doing the Lord's work, but he is also making his poem function like Virgilian epic, granting legendary events a privileged function for explaining the here and now, and conversely exalting the here and now by linking it to the grand sagas of past myth.[21] The reader's distance from the narrative, his recognition that this story by its nature must be fiction, becomes anything but a disadvantage. Lycaon's tale, for example, readily lends itself to allegorization, an interpretative strategy that allows the dubious motives of Jupiter as character to fade from view. The alternative, to continue to recognize the human subjects of metamorphosis, dissolves the epic structure of the poem by making metamorphosis seem ultimately both inexplicable and very much the end of the story. Each transformation appears less a stage in the history of the cosmos than the shutting down of an individual consciousness, locked in opposition to the ordering forces of the universe. Here, far from retaining a comfortable position in the world after metamorphosis, the reader is drawn back into the unstable past, entering into the fiction rather than marking it off as such.

The pair of internal *Metamorphosis* that Ovid places at the beginning of his sixth book, in which the goddess Minerva and her human rival Arachne assemble stories and transformation for the two tapestries they weave in competition with each other, enshrine these polar alternatives for interpreting the process, for again the ideological differences between the two 'texts' result not just from the discursive use each artist makes of metamorphosis but from the perspective they present on the process itself (6.1–145).[22] Minerva depicts four tales of metamorphosis, designed explicitly to warn Arachne of the dangers of rivalling the gods, symmetrically at the corners of a tapestry whose centrepiece shows her own triumph in a contest with Neptune for possession of Athens. In each case only the names of the victims and the final form they have assumed are indicated. By contrast the gods themselves are depicted in forms that, like the disguise Jupiter assumes in the Lycaon tale, are presented as at once anthropomorphized and authentic; 'His own appearance marks each god:

[21]   On aetiology in Ovid see Myers (1994) and Graf (1988) 62.

[22]   Leach (1974), Vincent (1994), and Feeney (1991) 190–4 offer particularly stimulating readings of this much discussed episode.

Jupiter's is the image of a king' (6.73–4). In answer to Athena's use of metamorphosis as a warning against human presumption, Arachne presents a catalogue of the animal forms the gods have used to deceive the victims of their lust. Here, rather than manifesting an essentially immutable hierarchy of powers, metamorphosis destabilizes such structures by revealing how the gods themselves can quite literally turn into beasts. Far from offering an absolute guide to behaviour, the visual forms that result from the god's metamorphoses highlight the shifting and uncertain nature of appearances; only the spatial settings of the crimes and the human faces of the victims preserve constant and reliable markers of identity.[23] A heavy emphasis in the account of Arachne's portrayal of these scenes falls on the verb *reddidit* (6.122) which here means 'render', but whose primary force is 'give back', as though her artistic depiction were returning countenance that these women had lost. While obviously this is not the case here – the victims she depicts never underwent metamorphosis – this nuance shows how Arachne's choice to portray rapes where the god changes form pointedly reverses the programmatic rape narrative of book 1, where the object of the god's passion does indeed lose her form. There the reader's 'recognition' of the victim under her new shape was a possibility that, if realized, radically reoriented his/her response to the tale. In Arachne's more one-sided presentation it is impossible not to see the rape victim as a human subject. Indeed Arachne's realistic descriptive technique – or rather Ovid's technique for presenting her depiction as narrative – works to draw the viewers into this world of deceptive fictions precisely by granting them access to the victim's point of view: thus in describing how the god Jupiter took on the form of a bull to abduct Europa, he comments that 'you would think it was a real bull', as if 'you' were Europa.

The tapestry's demonstration of the dependency between the work's competing ideological strands and the antithetical strategies of representation it employs takes us back to the point where we began, the analogy between making sense of the process of metamorphosis and interpreting the text that represents it. Here I want to go further by suggesting that changed appearances are even more closely connected to artistic representations of change. If metamorphosis produces an apprehensible trace of distant or incredible events in the real world of the readers, so too does a statue, a painting, or the book-roll before them. Thus metamorphosis becomes a way of dramatizing the act of representation itself and the alternative political valences the process of transformation acquires within the work apply also to what Ovid's own text is doing. As Solodow and others have shown, much of the poet's vocabulary for the product of metamorphosis, such as the word *imago*, overlaps with terms for artistic depictions.[24] And in cases of petrification, the frozen forms, like those produced by the head of Medusa (5.177–209), are essentially indistinguishable from statues. Another way of suggesting the same point is by alluding to the visual iconography of the figures described; so the second book ends with a description of Europa riding on the bull's back, her clothes billowing behind her in the breeze, precisely the aspect in which she was most commonly shown in actual paintings.[25] The connection between representation and the ordering, clarifying aspects of metamorphosis can apply to literary as well as visual representations. This becomes particularly clear when we examine the relationship between metamorphosis and metaphor. Niobe's transformation into a stone begins when she 'stiffens with evils', a common Latin metaphor.

[23] *omnibus his faciemque suam, faciemque locorum | reddidit*, 6.121–2.

[24] Solodow (1988) 203–6; see also Anderson (1963).

[25] Kenney (1986) 390.

Thus not only does her final form again appear motivated by some essential quality of her experience – as Lycaon's innate bestiality makes him a wolf – it also offers a means for the figurative to become something more than figurative, for a trope to become reality.[26]

But as with the process of transformation itself, there is another side to the story. If metamorphosis figures the production of images it also resembles the subsequent transformation these images themselves undergo when they evoke the very figures they represent: just as the laurel tree can be read as Daphne, so an image or indeed a story of Daphne can be perceived as what it really is – a statue, painting or a text – or as the nymph it depicts. For statues and images do not only appear within the poem as the final products of metamorphosis, they also undergo metamorphosis by coming to life. Throughout the work, art and nature are notoriously unstable categories: elements of the natural world seem to aspire to the perfection and order of art, but the ultimate manifestation of artistic excellence is the illusion of reality.[27] So too the static, plastic images Ovid evokes ultimately contrast with the flow of the narrative in which they are embedded.[28] It thus seems better to speak of an oscillation between two processes: the distant and other becomes 'real' through translation into an artistic product, which in turn becomes 'real' in the opposite sense, in the sense that its illusion works, that it ceases to be a representation and gives the viewer/reader access to what it represents.[29]

The deployment of artefacts in the story of Phaethon illustrates just such an oscillation (1.747–2.366). Phaethon approaching the palace of the sun encounters a set of images that represent nothing less than the ordered cosmos whose construction we witnessed in the first book.[30] These images are embossed on the very door of the palace, and when Phaethon passes through it he moves into a world of animated artistic figures, beginning with his father himself, who with his radiate crown is not so much the sun as it really is as a symbol of the sun endowed with autonomous existence, very like the Tritons who represent the sea on the doors. So too on his wild ride through the cosmos, Phaethon will encounter the constellations not as clusters of stars but as the animals that represent them. The allotted boundaries between things are only restored when Phaethon is killed by Jupiter's thunderbolt, buried, and quite literally replaced by an inscribed tombstone. Thus the story achieves its ending, and the world returns to its regular form, when the one whose adventures animated the static image of the cosmos is himself transformed into a text. Yet this is not quite the end of the sequence of metamorphoses, for if the tombstone will not exactly come back to life, so

[26] For the relation between metaphor and metamorphosis see especially Pianezzola (1979), Barkan (1986) 20–5, and Hardie (1999a). The extension of this thesis, most fully developed by Schmidt (1991) is that Ovid's text invests reality with a set of metaphorical meanings, translating the world as it is into a storehouse of images which can be read as tropes for human qualities and experiences.

[27] See the examples collected by Solodow (1988) 210–14, in particular the description of the setting for Actaeon's encounter with Diana: 3.157–64. The conundrum of the priority of art over nature receives special attention already in the initial description of the ordering of chaos, where as Wheeler (1995) has shown, the terms in which the actions of the creator god are described are themselves modelled on Homer's account of the crafting of the shield of Achilles.

[28] Cf. Hardie (1999a) for a complementary treatment of the effects of metaphor and allegory.

[29] Indeed one wonders whether the tapestries of Arachne and Minerva would have been quite so clear if they had depicted whole narratives rather than just scenes from narratives. Then Minerva might have had to show her criminals as human subjects, and conversely Arachne's work might have depicted the various civilizing heroes whose birth resulted from the gods' deceptions. For a fuller discussion of the relationship between metamorphosis and literary and artistic representation see Sharrock (1996).

[30] On this image see Brown (1987).

powerfully does it evoke the absent figure it represents that Phaethon's mother actually treats it as a substitute for her lost son, covering it with tears and clasping it to her breast. So too the funerary rituals that his sisters undertake at his tomb prompt their own metamorphosis into poplar trees.

In an earlier chapter in this volume Thomas Habinek pointed out the paradoxical status of Ovid as at once a member of the Roman élite and as a subject, indeed a prominent victim, of the imperial order. This discussion of the poet's treatment of metamorphosis has pointed toward a corresponding set of ambiguities in the way the poet positions his audience in relation to the hierarchies depicted within the poem, and in how he portrays his own representation of that cosmos alternatively as a form of participation in the creation of the structured world we know, and as an exposure of the flux, change, and victimization that underlies it. My own experience as a reader of the work convinces me that an interpretation that privileges one tendency at the expense of the other remains fundamentally incomplete. The challenge of comprehending metamorphosis means that each instance compels the reader to make a choice between different interpretations of the poem that bring into play all its discursive levels – the literary, the political, the theological. Some readers may make the same set of choices every time and achieve a remarkably consistent reading of the work, others will have more difficulty negotiating its transformations. Yet if such a proliferation of competing points of view seems but a new route to an impasse of equivocation all too familiar to students of Latin poetry, where every positive thesis the work advances about the world necessarily implies its own antithesis, Ovid's emphasis on metamorphosis suggests an antidote by refocusing our attention on the processes of representation and reading. Rather than search for the poem's political dimension in the propagation of a particular ideological stance, we might rather observe that the very task of interpreting Ovid's involves the vivid experience of contrasting perspectives on many different manifestations of authority. As the author can 'play god' by measuring his creation against the cosmos, so the reader can assume the role of Apollo, or of Daphne. By marking out the poem as a set of fictions metamorphosis may indeed facilitate such by reminding the reader of the distance that separates Ovid's text from the real centres of seriousness and significance in the Augustan world. Yet the same phenomenon also points out the poem's capacity to redraw the line between reality and mere representation and so between Ovid's cosmos and Augustus's. The fundamental ambiguity of metamorphosis thus at once reflects, and helps bring about, the transformation of Ovid's text into a dynamic locus for defining and codifying political and social roles.

FURTHER READING

Wheeler's (1999) application of reader-response criticism to the *Metamorphoses* offers a fuller development of many of the issues and approaches discussed here. Two more general book-length studies of the *Metamorphoses* presenting highly contrasting view of metamorphosis are Galinsky (1975) and Solodow (1988). Tissol (1997) and Ahl (1985), a still controversial book, explore in different ways the manifestations of metamorphosis in Ovid's language and style. Though they focus less directly on the metamorphosis theme, both Otis (1970) and Due (1974) offer stimulating book-length readings of the poem. The essential modern works on Ovid's manipulation of genre in the poem are Knox (1986b) and Hinds (1987). Barkan's (1986) dazzling history of metamorphosis in medieval and Renaissance culture commences with an extensive treatment of Ovid's poem. Feeney (1991) similarly includes an important chapter on Ovid, addressing both the poem's status as fiction and its relation to Augustan politics. For more on reception of the poem as a fiction, see the article by Konstan (1991), and, on ancient attitudes to fiction more generally, the collection edited by Gill and Wiseman (1993). On the relationship between metamorphosis and the body, see both the older article of Curran (1978) and Segal (1998). Forbes-Irving (1990) treats the religious and mythical aspects of metamorphosis in Greek culture and catalogues earlier versions of many of Ovid's tales. Antoninus Liberalis' *Metamorphoses*, a compendium of Hellenistic metamorphosis narratives that provides our evidence for the works of Nicander and Boios, is available in English translation by Celoria (1992). For those with the relevant languages, Rosati's (1983) treatment of illusion and representation, Schmidt's (1991) account of metamorphosis, and Galand-Hallyn (1994), on metamorphosis and poetic creation, are especially recommended.

References

Ahl, F. (1985) *Metaformations: Soundplay and Wordplay in Ovid and Other Classical Poets*. Ithaca

Anderson, W. S. (1963) 'Multiple change in the *Metamorphoses*', *Transactions of the American Philological Association* 94: 1–27

Anderson, W. S. (1989) 'Lycaon: Ovid's deceptive paradigm in *Metamorphoses* 1', *Illinois Classical Studies* 14: 91–101

Barkan, L. (1986) *The Gods Made Flesh. Metamorphosis and the Pursuit of Paganism*. New Haven and London

Brown, R. (1987) 'The Palace of the Sun in Ovid's *Metamorphoses*', in M. Whitby, P. Hardie, M. Whitby, eds., *Homo Viator: Classical Essays for John Bramble*, 211–20. Bristol

Cameron, A. (1995) *Callimachus and His Critics*. Princeton

Celoria, F. (1992) *The Metamorphoses of Antoninus Liberalis: A Translation with Commentary*. London

Curran, L. C. (1978) 'Rape and rape victims in the *Metamorphoses*', *Arethusa* 11: 213–41

Dörrie, H. (1959) 'Wandlung und Dauer: Ovids Metamorphosen und Poseidonios' Lehre von der Substanz', *Altsprachliche Unterricht* 4.2: 95–116

Due, O. S. (1974) *Changing Forms: Studies in the Metamorphoses of Ovid*. Copenhagen

Feeney, D. C. (1991) *The Gods in Epic: Poets and Critics of the Classical Tradition*. Oxford

Forbes-Irving, P. M. C. (1990) *Metamorphosis in Greek Myths*. Oxford

Fränkel, H. (1945) *Ovid, a Poet between Two Worlds*. Berkeley and Los Angeles

Galand-Hallyn, P. (1994) *Le reflet des fleurs: Description et métalanguage poétique d'Homère à la Renaissance*. Geneva

Galinsky, K. (1975) *Ovid's Metamorphoses: An Introduction to the Basic Aspects*. Oxford and Berkeley

Gill, C. and Wiseman, T. P., eds. (1993) *Lies and Fiction in the Ancient World*. Exeter

Graf, F. (1988) 'Ovide, les Métamorphoses, et la véracité du mythe', in C. Calame, ed., *Métamorphoses du mythe en Grèce antique*, 57–70. Geneva

Griffin, J. (1977) 'The Epic Cycle and the uniqueness of Homer', *Journal of Hellenic Studies* 97: 39–53

Hardie, P. R. (1986) *Virgil's Aeneid: Cosmos and Imperium*. Oxford

Hardie, P. R. (1992) 'Augustan poets and the mutability of Rome', in Powell, A., ed., *Roman Poetry and Propaganda in the Age of Augustus*, 59–82. London

Hardie, P. R. (1999a) 'Metamorphosis, metaphor, and allegory in Latin epic', in M. Beissinger, J. Tylus, S. Wofford, eds., *Epic Traditions in the Contemporary World: The Poetics of Community*, 89–107. Berkeley

Harrison, S. J., ed. (2001) *Texts, Ideas and the Classics*. Oxford

Hinds, S. E. (1987) *The Metamorphosis of Persephone. Ovid and the Self-conscious Muse.* Cambridge

Kenney, E. J. (1986) Introduction and notes to Melville, A. D., trans., *Ovid. Metamorphoses*. Oxford

Knox, P. E. (1986b) *Ovid's Metamorphoses and the Traditions of Augustan Poetry.* Cambridge

Konstan, D. (1991) 'The death of Argus, or what stories do: audience response in ancient fiction and theory', *Helios* 18: 15–30

Leach, E. W. (1974) 'Ekphrasis and the theme of artistic failure in Ovid's *Metamorphoses*', *Ramus* 3: 102–42

McKeown, J. C. (1979) 'Ovid *Amores* 3.12', *Papers of the Liverpool Latin Seminar* 2: 163–177

Myers, S. (1994) *Ovid's Causes. Cosmogony and Aetiology in the Metamorphoses.* Ann Arbor

Nicolet, C. (1991) *Space, Geography, and Politics in the Early Roman Empire.* Ann Arbor

Nicoll, W. S. M. (1980) 'Cupid, Apollo, and Daphne (Ovid *Met.* 1.452ff.)', *Classical Quarterly* 30: 174–82

Otis, B. (1970) *Ovid as an Epic Poet*, 2nd edn. Cambridge

Pianezzola, E. (1979) 'La metamorfosi ovidiana come metafora narrativa', *Quaderni del circolo filologico-linguistico padavano* 10: 77–91

Putnam, M. C. J. (1995) *Virgil's Aeneid: Interpretation and Influence.* Chapel Hill

Rosati, G. (1983) *Narciso e Pigmalione. Illusione e Spettacolo nelle Metamorfosi di Ovidio.* Florence

Schmidt, E. A. (1991) *Ovids poetische Menschenwelt: Die Metamorphosen als Metapher und Symphonie.* Heidelberg

Segal, C. P. (1998) 'Ovid's metamorphic bodies: art, gender, and violence in the *Metamorphoses*', *Arion* 5.3: 9–41

Sharrock, A. (1996) 'Representing metamorphosis', in Elsner, J., ed., *Art and Text in Roman Culture*, 103–30. Cambridge

Solodow, J. B. (1988) *The World of Ovid's Metamorphoses.* Chapel Hill

Tissol, G. (1997) *The Face of Nature. Wit, Narrative, and Cosmic Origins in Ovid's Metamorphoses.* Princeton

Vincent, M. (1994) 'Between Ovid and Barthes: ekphrasis, orality, textuality in Ovid's "Arachne"', *Arethusa* 27: 361–86

Wheeler, S. M. (1995) '*Imago mundi*: another view of the creation in Ovid's *Metamorphoses*', *American Journal of Philology* 116: 95–121

Wheeler, S. M. (1999) *A Discourse of Wonders: Audience and Performance in Ovid's Metamorphoses.* Philadelphia

Zanker, P. (1988) *The Power of Images in the Age of Augustus*, trans. A. Shapiro. Ann Arbor

Secondary Source 3.2   Eric Csapo, 'Totalizing structure'

(Source: Csapo, E. (2005) *Theories of Mythology*, Malden, MA and Oxford, Blackwell Publishing Ltd, pp. 247–54 and selected references)

Vernant's Pandora: The grammar of actions

The French classicist Jean-Pierre Vernant (1914–) is responsible for several of the most successful structuralist interpretations of myth. Unlike Lévi-Strauss, whose chief interest is in the relatively stable traditional societies of native North and South America, Vernant is a student of the voluble *historical* culture of archaic and classical Greece. Highly sensitive to the different nature of his material, Vernant pays closer attention to the temporal and historical elements in narrative. As a result, he shares with Greimas the same reserve about Lévi-Strauss's manner of conceptualizing the relationship between the syntagmatic and paradigmatic axes of mythic narrative. He recommends a three-stage approach to the analysis of myth which combines syntagmatic, paradigmatic, and ideological analysis (1974: 244–6). In the *first* stage he recommends one stick close to the text in question and focus upon the narrative's temporal sequence and causal relations. The goal is not to examine the articulation of the plot but the logic or "grammar" governing the permutation of its actions. At a *second* stage of the analysis one may depart from the specific text to examine other versions of the same myth or even different myths with comparable contents. Here the aim is to locate the homologies and oppositions deployed by the myth (whether they involve places, times, objects, agents, actions, or the contrast between initial and final situations). In doing so one should pay close attention to the links between the framework established by the grammar of the tale and its concrete semantic contents. The *third* stage is a cultural or ideological analysis aimed at placing the myth within its social context. What are the categories of thought, what the systems of opposition and classification which allowed this particular myth to be produced in this particular form? How did the society which generated the myth carve up its reality and encode it in its language and cultural artifacts?

The procedure is beautifully illustrated by Vernant's analysis of the myth of Pandora in Hesiod. (The following account follows Vernant 1974: 177–94 in outline, but I have modified considerably the exposition of "the grammar of actions" in order to sharpen and foreground their logical structure and to make some points about the relation between syntagmatic and paradigmatic analysis.) Hesiod tells the tale in two different works, the *Theogony* and *Works and Days*. The versions are closely related and make implicit reference to one another. Hesiod, *Theogony* 535–616:

> At the time when the gods and mortal men were coming to a settlement at Mekone, [Prometheus] eagerly divided a large ox into portions and placed it before Zeus, attempting to trick him. For men he laid out flesh and entrails rich with fat which he had placed in the oxhide and hidden inside the ox's stomach. For Zeus he laid out the ox's white bone which had been carefully arranged for a stratagem of deception and hidden in white fat. The father of gods and men then addressed him saying "Son of Iapetus, most distinguished among all the lords, my dear fellow, how unfairly you have divided the portions." In this way Zeus, whose schemes never fail, reproached him. Prometheus, of subtle cunning, answered with a slight smile and a mind busy with the art of deception: "Zeus, most glorious and greatest of the immortal gods, take whichever of these suits your fancy." This he said with treacherous intent. Zeus, whose schemes never fail, fully

detected and was not unaware of the deceit. And he contemplated evil for mortal men in his heart, which the future brought to pass. He nevertheless took up the white fat with both hands, but his mind seethed with rage, and anger filled his heart, when he saw the white oxbones set for a stratagem of deception. And ever since then the race of men on earth make white bones burn on the smoking altars for the immortal gods. Greatly vexed cloud-gathering Zeus addressed him: "Son of Iapetus, clever beyond all others, my dear fellow, your mind is still full of the art of deception." In this way Zeus, whose schemes never fail, spoke in anger.

From that moment he kept brooding on this deceit, and he did not give the power of undying fire to the ash trees for mortal men, who inhabit the earth. But the good son of Iapetus tricked him by stealing the gleam of far-beaming, undying fire in a hollow fennel stalk. And it stung high-thundering Zeus to the depths of his spirit and enraged his very heart, when he saw the far-beaming gleam of fire amongst men. At once he devised an evil for men in exchange for fire. The famous supple-limbed god [Hephaestus] fashioned from earth the likeness of a chaste maiden after the design of Kronos's son. The gray-eyed goddess Athena dressed and adorned her with a white garment and with her hands drew a colorful veil down around her head, a wonder to look at. And Pallas Athena wrapped lovely garlands of herbs blooming with flowers. And when he had fashioned this beautiful evil in exchange for good, he led her, beautified with the finery of the gray-eyed daughter [Athena] of the mighty sire, out into the presence of the other gods and of men. Wonder took hold of the immortal gods and mortal men when they gazed on this deep deceit. From her came the female sex. They [women] live with their husband as a great affliction for mortals, unadapted to wretched poverty, but only to abundance. As the bees in their roofed hives feed the drones who conspire in evil deeds, and the former bustle about every day all day until the setting of the sun and build the white honeycomb, while the latter wait inside the covered cells to gather another's labor to their bellies, just so high-thundering Zeus made women, conspirators in pernicious deeds, to be an evil for mortal men.

And he provided another evil in exchange for good. He who avoids the destructive acts of women and does not wish to marry, will come to a grievous old age bereft of support. While he lives he is not short of means, but when he dies distant relations will divide up his livelihood. But for him whose lot it is to marry, if he has a good wife endowed with good sense, good will match evil continually all his life; whereas the man who gets the troublesome kind lives with unrelenting sorrow in his breast, mind and heart, and the evil is incurable.

In *Works and Days*, after explaining to his brother Perses the virtue of honest hard work, Hesiod explains how the need for hard work originated (42–105):

For the gods have hidden from men their livelihood. Otherwise you would easily work enough in even a single day to provide for yourself and be at your ease for an entire year. You would quickly place the steering oar above the smoke [to preserve it while unused] and the labours of oxen and steadfast mules would cease. But Zeus hid [men's livelihood] when angry at heart because Prometheus, of subtle cunning, deceived him. As a result he schemed grim troubles for men. He hid fire. From cunning Zeus the good son of Iapetus [Prometheus] stole it for men in a hollow fennel stalk unseen by Zeus who delights in lightning. In anger cloud-gathering Zeus addressed him: "Son of Iapetus, clever beyond all others, you are pleased that you have stolen fire and beguiled my wits, but this will prove a great calamity for you yourself and for men in the future. I will give them an evil in exchange for good, such that they will all delight in their hearts as they embrace their evil." This is the father of gods and men said and he laughed out loud. He commanded famous Hephaestus at once to mix earth with water, to put in it a human voice and strength, and to liken in appearance the beautiful, lovely form of the maiden to an immortal goddess. Then he commanded Athena to teach her crafts, to weave the embroidered loom, and Aphrodite to pour golden charm around her head and painful longing, and debilitating erotic fixation. He bid Hermes, the messenger who killed Argus, to put into her the mind of a bitch and a thievish disposition.

This he commanded, and they obeyed Lord Zeus, son of Kronos. Immediately the famous supple-limbed god molded from earth the likeness of a chaste maiden after the design of Kronos's son. The gray-eyed goddess Athena dressed and adorned her. The Graces and Lady Persuasion placed golden necklaces about her neck, and the lovely-haired Seasons crowned her with spring flowers. The messenger who killed Argus put lies, wheedling words and a thievish disposition in her breast at the bidding of deep-resounding Zeus. The herald of the gods also put voice into her and called the woman Pandora, since all [*pan*] who inhabit Olympus gave her as a gift [*doron*], a calamity for grain-eating men. Then when he completed this deep inescapable deceit, the father sent the famous killer of Argus, leading the gift, to Epimetheus. And Epimetheus did not call to mind that Prometheus warned him never to receive a gift from Olympian Zeus, but to send it back, lest it prove to be some evil for men. Only after he received it, when he had the evil, did he realize.

Formerly the races of men lived on the earth without evil, hard work, and grievous ailments, which brought men death. For mortals age quickly amidst hardships. But they escaped after women removed the great lid from the jar with her hands: she contrived grim troubles for humankind. Hope alone remained there inside in her secure home under the lips of the jar and did not fly out, because she [woman] put back the lid of the jar by the design of cloud-gathering, aegis-bearing Zeus. But countless troubles wander among humans: the earth is full of evil and full the sea. Illnesses visit humans uninvited by day and by night silently carrying evil for mortals, since cunning Zeus deprived them of voice. And so there is no way whatsoever to escape the will of Zeus.

Vernant's first level of analysis is based on the precise wording of the original texts. Hesiod's account presents us with a series of actions which represent a battle of wits fought out by the two protagonists, Prometheus, the champion of men, backed by his brother, Epimetheus, and Zeus, king of the gods, backed by the other Olympians. The actions can be summarized as follows:

I *Syntagmatic structure: Narrative sequence*

   A Hesiod's *Theogony* 535–616:

      1 Prometheus *tricks* Zeus *into accepting* the inedible parts of the sacrifice.

2 Zeus *pretends to accept* "but he was not unaware of the deceit."

3 Zeus *withholds* ("did not give") the celestial fire from men.

4 Prometheus *steals* fire and gives it to men.

B Hesiod's *Works and Days* 42–105:

1 The gods *hide* from men their means of livelihood.

2 Zeus *hides* fire from men.

3 Prometheus *hides* fire in a fennel stalk.

4 Prometheus *steals* fire from the gods.

5 Zeus *tricks* Epimetheus *into accepting* Pandora.

6 Epimetheus *accepts*.

Each action has not only a linear or sequential relationship with all the others but also a conceptual relationship. All are permutations of acts of giving and taking. The battle of wits is conducted as an exchange of gifts between Zeus and the gods on the one hand and Prometheus, Epimetheus, and humankind on the other. But this is no straightforward exchange. Throughout, the narratives insist on one quality Zeus and Prometheus have in common, their cunning intelligence (Greek *metis*), an "art" or "craft" of trickery and deception. By it their manner of gift-giving is distinguishable from ordinary gift-giving. Ordinary gift-giving is open and acknowledged and would have little purpose without the recognition and appreciation which this openness allows. But the exchange between Zeus and Prometheus is a perverse form of gift-giving in which both the intent and the true nature of the objects of exchange are concealed. Each action of the myth's syntagmatic structure expresses in the mode of cunning intelligence – let us call it "the mode of concealment" – one of the four possibilities of gift exchange. In normal gift exchange one can either give or not give, take or not take. To each of these actions there correspond special forms of giving and not giving, taking and not taking, in the mode of concealment. We can tabulate the following *Grammar of Actions*.

A Giving

	giving	*not giving*
openness	offer	withhold
concealment	trick into accepting	hide

B Taking

	taking	*not taking*
openness	accept	refuse
concealment	steal	pretend to accept

By insisting upon a grammar of actions Vernant makes a significant break with Lévi-Strauss's paradigmatic method. For Lévi-Strauss the syntagmatic axis of the myth was something clearly separable from the paradigmatic, while the latter alone seemed systematic and meaningful: syntagmatic stood to paradigmatic much the same way as Saussure's "material" signifiers to his "conceptual" signified. But Jakobson was able to show that a phoneme, though the smallest element of the signifier and the smallest element of the syntagmatic chain, was so far from being neatly separable from the paradigmatic order that it was itself already an expression of a complex paradigmatic order. In the same way Vernant invites us to see that the smallest units of the narrative syntax are already manifestations of a system of paradigmatic relations. The actions of the grammar belong to both orders simultaneously.

If we were to express Vernant's grammar of actions in terms of Greimas's elementary structures of signification and redraw our charts as "semiotic squares," we would find that each mode, that of openness and that of concealment, expresses the Greimasian algorithm *A:B :: -A:-B*.

Semantic square in the mode of openness

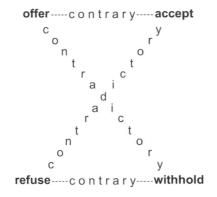

Thus, in the mode of open gift-giving, *to offer* is opposed to *to accept*, but the contradictory of *to offer* is *to not offer*, i.e., *to withhold*. Similarly, the contradictory of *to accept* is *to refuse* (i.e., *to not accept*): one either accepts or does not.

There are in fact two distinct logical domains accessed by the myth's grammar of actions. The one we have just looked at (which joins pairs diagonally across the square) is a sort of absolute logic of contradiction: one either offers or does not offer – one either does a thing or one does not. But this is somewhat different from the logic which links the horizontal pairs. Here we oppose two distinct actions like offering and accepting. These terms are not opposed by a logic of positive and negative, do or don't, but by the groundrules of a particular cultural institution, namely, that of gift exchange. It is not necessarily true that one either offers or accepts. One could share, for example, or ride a bicycle or eat cake, actions which have nothing to do with exchange relations. But the actions in the Hesiodic tale are special forms of non-participation in a gift-exchange relationship. They do not ignore the rules of the game but invert them.

In the mode of concealment, the internal logic of the square is only intelligible with relation to the mode of openness which it perverts. This perversion is a form of negated gift exchange, a negative logic which stands to the mode of openness as the algebraic equation *-A: -B :: —A:-B* stands to the Greimasian *A:B :: -A:-B*. A concealed form of *offering* is *to trick someone into accepting*; a concealed form of *accepting* is *to steal*; *to with-hold* something in covert fashion is *to hide* it; and *to refuse* something deviously is *to pretend to accept* while not really accepting as such. Therefore, a strictly symmetrical logic binds the mode of concealment.

When we look at the syntagmatic structure of the myth of Prometheus, we see that it shows a duel of wits between men and gods conducted by means of gift-giving. If we take both tales together as one, we might see that the actions are true to the qualities of the actors. Prometheus and Zeus are both characterized by their cunning intelligence and they act in the mode of concealment: Prometheus *tricks into accepting*, *hides*, and *steals*; Zeus *pretends to accept*, *hides*, and *tricks into accepting*. The other gods obey Zeus's commands and

Semantic square in the mode of concealment

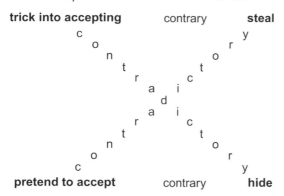

trick into accepting   contrary   **steal**

pretend to accept   contrary   **hide**

participate in his schemes. But Epimetheus fails to obey Prometheus. Moreover, he fails to play the game of gift-giving-and-taking by the rules of cunning intelligence. He simply *accepts* the gift of Pandora, naively acting in the mode of openness. The tale tells how humanity fell from a trouble-free existence to a life of toil. Its main function is to delineate what is divine and what is human. On the basis of this analysis we could say that cunning intelligence is divine, but humanity partakes of both modes of intelligence, the cunning of Prometheus (foresight) and the guileless naivety of Epimetheus (aftersight). Humanity falls from grace when it loses a battle of wits, because of inferior cunning and foresight.

If we compare the two versions, however, we notice that each narrative has the same structure. In each a battle of wits is lost, because one of the protagonists lapses into the mode of openness. We notice that in *Works and Days* Hesiod states that Zeus hid fire as he hid grain, but in the *Theogony* (563), Zeus "did not give" fire, i.e., he withheld it, acting in the mode of openness. If we follow the language of the *Theogony*, the story will break down into two symmetrical confrontations. In one, Zeus attempts to withhold something which Prometheus steals. In the other, Prometheus warns Epimetheus to refuse Zeus's gifts but Zeus outwits him. An attempt to withhold, outwitted by Prometheus, is balanced by an attempt to refuse, outwitted by Zeus. Each version represents a battle of wits which is lost when one of the combatants slips from the mode of concealment into the mode of openness. Each confrontation ends in man's receipt of a divine "gift": fire and woman. The shifting of the treatment of fire by Zeus (whether "withholding" or "hiding") from one narration to the other preserves the syntagmatic parallelism between one story and the other.

Superficially the story signifies, as Hesiod puts it, that man cannot compete with the gods; though he partakes of the divine intelligence represented by Prometheus, he also partakes of the qualities of Epimetheus. At a deeper level it indicates that there is something devious about the way gods deal with men, their generosity is perversely mixed with hidden malice, their gifts a deceptive mixture of evil and good. From a purely theoretical perspective, the beauty of the analysis lies in the demonstration that the paradigmatic structure, just as much as the syntagmatic structure, can be expressed as a function of time, as a shift from an initial state or thematic situation in the mode of concealment (here truly a *contenu inversé*) to a final state or resolution of the conflict in the mode of openness.

Reference

Vernant, J-P. 1974. *Myth & société en Grèce ancienne*. Paris. Trans. J. Lloyd, *Myth and Society in Ancient Greece*, Brighton, 1980.

Secondary Source 3.3   Carolyn Higbie, 'Hellenistic mythographers'

(Source: Woodard, R.D. (ed.) (2007) *The Cambridge Companion to Greek Mythology*, New York, Cambridge University Press, pp. 237–50)

From sometime in the fourth century BC on, Greeks developed an interest in collecting, documenting, and interpreting the important literary works of their past. The central texts to which they devoted much of their energies were the Homeric epics, the *Iliad* and *Odyssey*, but these were not the only ones. They also acquired the works of the lyric poets, tragedians, comedians, orators, historians, and philosophers. The centers for these projects became the great libraries of antiquity, most notably in Alexandria and Pergamum, but there were others, including some that focused on philosophical texts.[1] Scholars who worked in these libraries faced a monumental task of organizing the texts, before they could begin real study of them. As part of their initial work, they had to create a catalog of the collection, which may be the reason for one of two lists that Callimachus, an Alexandrian scholar and librarian of the third century BC, was said to have composed, in addition to his learned poetry: *Tables of Illustrious Persons in Every Branch of Learning Together with a List of their Works*.[2] This seems to have been some sort of catalog to the holdings of the Alexandria Library, though the fragments are so brief and so few that it is difficult to be certain.

Once these preliminaries were complete, though additions to the libraries, particularly that in Alexandria, continued for centuries, scholars could turn their attention to studying the works themselves. The texts reflected an often double transmission, since many had probably survived through both oral transmission and then as written documents that had been copied and recopied in different cities, by different scribes with varying abilities, and for many purposes. Generations of oral transmission of poems meant they had been reworked and adapted each time they were performed, depending on the abilities of the performer, the setting of the performance, and the response of the audience. Mistakes that inevitably accompany the copying and recopying of written texts, especially those that contain unusual dialect forms and archaisms or difficult metrical patterns, meant that the Alexandrian scholars would have been confronted by texts that not only were difficult to read but also were filled with a bewildering array of versions of the most popular authors and works. These might also contain versions of myths peculiar to a location, which might either contradict another or might simply be otherwise unknown. In the Homeric *Odyssey*, for example, a central theme is Penelope's twenty years of faithfulness to her husband and her clever trick with the burial shroud for Laertes, which enables her to put off the suitors. The second-century-AD traveler Pausanias, however, reports that the Mantineans in the Peloponnese preserve a very different account of life on Ithaca during Odysseus' absence: Penelope was unfaithful to Odysseus with many suitors. When Odysseus returned home and discovered this, he threw Penelope out of the house, and she returned to the home of her father in Sparta and then died in Mantinea (Paus. 8.12.6–7). Another tradition, also perhaps from Arcadia, said that Penelope had had an

[1]   See, for example, Strabo 13.1.54 (= C608), Plutarch, *Life of Sulla* 26.1–2, and Athenaeus 5.214d–e for different versions of the fate of Aristotle's books.

[2]   This title is not that given to the work by Callimachus, but a descriptive title given to it by a later author. We do not know what Callimachus called his catalog, which also had the much shorter title *Pinakes*. On Callimachus as a bibliographer, see Rudolf Blum, trans. by Hans H. Wellisch, *Kallimachos: The Alexandrian Library and the Origins of Bibliography* (Madison, WI: University of Wisconsin Press, 1991) 124–60, esp. 150–60.

affair with either Hermes or Apollo or all the suitors and had given birth to Pan (Herodotus 2.145.4; Apollodorus, *Epitome* 2.7.38; Duris of Samos *Die Fragmente der griechischen Historiker* 76 F 21; Pindar fr. 100).

Mythography and Paradoxography

Some Hellenistic scholars devoted themselves to attempting to restore what they believed to be the original version of a work. Their focus on the text then led them to produce commentaries and essays. Others saw in texts mines of material to be extracted for any number of uses. From this double opportunity – the need for texts to be explicated and the wealth of material contained within them – developed at least two genres, mythography[3] and paradoxography, which flourished for some four centuries, from the mid-third century BC into the second century AD. Students of literature scanned texts and extracted from them material grouped around a theme or focus, such as stories of the weird or unusual (paradoxography) and stories about the gods and heroes (mythography).

In addition to his list of the library holdings, in fact, Callimachus was also credited with a second catalog, *A Collection of Wonders from the Entire Earth Arranged by Locality.*[4] This seems to be an early, if not the first, example of paradoxography. Unfortunately, Callimachus' work does not survive complete, but the third-century BC writer Antigonus of Carystus includes forty-four selections from Callimachus in his own *Historiae mirabiles* 129–73 (= fr. 407 Pfeiffer).

The fate of Callimachus' collection of oddities was not unique. Many other paradoxographies and mythographies survive only in fragments, as excerpts in the work of later authors. More than twenty Greek paradoxographers, of whom only seven survive, compiled collections of the bizarre from the time of Callimachus until the third century AD.[5] Of the many mythographies written during the same period, very few survive even in fragmentary or abridged form. We know the mythographical work *Diegesis* of Conon, for example, only from a summary made by Photius in the ninth century AD, supplemented by a few lines from a papyrus fragment (FGrH 26).[6] Such collections, in straightforward and generally plain prose, without any attempt to achieve literary effects and usually lacking documented sources, seem to have been regarded not so much as the work of a single author to be preserved in its original form but rather as material available to subsequent generations of readers for their own purposes. These later writers might be thought of more as compilers rather than authors, more interested in presenting the stories briefly and clearly than in achieving some sort of literary effect (there are no speeches, similes, or metaphors, for example) or elucidating the presentation of the myth in an earlier text of a poem or play. In compiling their own collections, they seem not to have returned to the early literary sources used by their predecessors

[3] See Albert Henrichs, "Three Approaches to Greek Mythography," in Jan Bremmer, ed., *Interpretations of Greek Mythology* (London: Croom Helm, 1987): 242–77, for an invaluable introduction to the topic. His definition of mythography is worth quoting (243): "Once a myth became fixed in the literary tradition, it would either survive indefinitely along with the poem, play or other work of literature in which it was recorded, or it would eventually perish together with that record, unless some interested scholar saved it for posterity by including it in a collection of various myths. Such collectors of myths, who wrote down the mythical stories in plain prose, are called mythographers, and their collective product is mythography, a handmaiden of mythology."

[4] See Blum, *Kallimachos*, 134.

[5] See Alexander Giannini, *Paradoxographorum Graecorum Reliquiae* (Milan: Instituto Editoriale Italiano, 1965).

[6] Henrichs, "Three Approaches to Greek Mythography," 244–7, has a very useful introduction to Conon.

in the field, but simply to have drawn on the collections of their predecessors. The original and complete versions of these texts thus disappeared, since the digests satisfied readers' needs. It is difficult, therefore, always to attribute to any one author a particular collection or to be confident about the purpose he had in collecting, especially if the author is early in the history of writing in these genres, unless there is a specific statement about sources, goals, and authorship.

A story from Phlegon of Tralles' *De mirabilium libellus* (*Book of Marvels*), compiled in the second century AD, illustrates the kind of lurid tales and the prosaic style typical of paradoxography, as well as its links with mythography (chapter):[7]

> In Messene not many years ago, as Apollonius says, it happened
> that a big jar [*pithos*] was broken up by the force of a storm when
> a lot of water came pouring down. From it there fell out a triple
> head of human form. It had two rows of teeth. When they tried to
> find out whose head it was, an inscription revealed it: for "Idas"
> had been inscribed. The Messenians prepared another jar [*pithos*]
> at public expense and put the head in it. They attended to the
> hero more carefully, since they understood that this was the one
> about whom Homer says [*Il.* 9.558–60]:
>
> And of Idas, who of men on earth at that time
> Was the strongest. He drew his bow against lord
>   Phoebus
> Apollo for the sake of his lovely-ankled bride.

In this anecdote, there are many clichés or elements of folktale – the storm that reveals an ancient artifact, a monstrous relic, an inscription, the identification of a Homeric hero's remains, and the creation of a hero shrine. Whereas the Messenians draw on their own sense of the past, supported by their knowledge of the Homeric poems, to gain status in their world through mythology,[8] Phlegon of Tralles, loosely citing Apollonius, an earlier paradoxographer, as a source, tells the story as an example of the oddities in the world. Other tales in his collection concern the discovery of immense bones and coffins, the birth of deformed babies and animals to women, the birth of children to men, and the existence of living centaurs. He offers no comment on any aspect of the stories that are in his collection, nothing about their believability, the evidence for them, or any context into which they might fit.

When we read of Idas in the most famous book of mythography to survive from the ancient world, that identified as the work of Apollodorus, we first meet him in the narrative of important families in Calydon, preparatory to the story of the Calydonian boar hunt (1.7.8–9):

> Evenus fathered a daughter, Marpessa, whom Apollo sought, but
> Idas, the son of Aphareus, took her away in a winged chariot
> from Poseidon. When Evenus pursued him in a chariot, he came
> to the Lycormas river, but he could not overtake him, and so he

[7]   See William Hansen, ed., *Anthology of Ancient Greek Popular Literature* (Bloomington, IN: Indiana University Press, 1998): 249–58. For a complete translation of Phlegon of Tralles' work, see William Hansen, *Phlegon of Tralles' Book of Marvels* (Exeter: University of Exeter Press, 1996).

[8]   See Carolyn Higbie, *The Lindian Chronicle and the Greek Creation of Their Past* (Oxford: Oxford University Press, 2003); also "Ancient Greek Archaeology?", forthcoming in the Acta of the 16th International Congress of Classical Archaeology.

killed his horses and threw himself into the river. And the river is called Evenus after him. Idas came to Messene and when Apollo came across him, he took away the girl. When they fought over marriage to the girl, Zeus separated them and allowed the girl to choose which one she wished to live with. Since she was afraid that Apollo would abandon her when she grew old, she chose Idas as her husband.

In Apollodorus' narrative, the story of Idas is introduced by a long string of genealogical links (not translated here) and includes an etymologizing explanation for the name of a river before the tale of how Idas finally won his bride is told. Unlike Phlegon of Tralles, who seeks to highlight the grotesque element in stories, Apollodorus concentrates on genealogies, etymologies, and the deeds of heroes. The authors share a similar tone and style and compile their materials from already published works, but they have different interests.

The Roots of Mythography and Paradoxography: Mythology and Chronography

Mythography and paradoxography both developed in the late fourth century BC, although the roots of each can be traced further back in Greek thought. The immediate impetus for the development of mythography lies in the awareness of their literary past and the desire to preserve it that Greeks felt by the end of the fourth century BC, but other genres, mythology and chronography, together with genealogy and local history, also lay behind mythography. In some respects, mythology itself can be seen as a counterpart to chronography in early Greece, especially in the hexameter catalogs that recorded the names, families, and deeds of the gods and heroes. Organized roughly by generations of families, such poems were a chronological guide of sorts to the Greek mythological past and enabled Greeks of historical times to link their families with gods and heroes. Catalog poetry also provided both material and a structuring principle to later prose works.[9] No version could be claimed as Panhellenic and definitive, but the poems did impose a structure on the stories. Two excerpts from the Hesiodic *Catalog of Women* illustrate the kind of information that such poems offered and how they might survive into later times (frr. 1, 53):

> That Deucalion was the son of Prometheus and Pronoea
> Hesiod says in the first *Catalogue*, and also that Hellen was
> the son of Deucalion and Pyrrha.

About the Myrmidons Hesiod says thus:

> She became pregnant and bore Aeacus, delighting in
>   horses.
> But when he came to the boundary of lovely youth,
> he was distressed at being alone. The father of both
>   men and gods made whatever ants there were
>   on the beautiful island
> into men and deep-girdled women.
> These were the first to yoke rolling ships
> and the first to use sails, the wings of a sea-crossing ship.

These two fragments from the catalog, the first a paraphrase and the second a direct quotation, survive only because they became part of the scholia – marginal

---

[9]   See M.L. West, *The Hesiodic Catalogue of Women: Its Nature, Structure, and Origins* (Oxford: Oxford University Press, 1985); Henrichs, "Three Approaches to Greek Mythography," 248–9.

notes – to other poems: the genealogy of Deucalion and his son Hellen appears in a scholion to Apollonius of Rhodes' *Argonautica* 3.1086 and the origins of the Myrmidons are in a scholion to Pindar's *Nemean* 3.21. Scholia such as these are an important source of obscure mythological stories for modern readers, since the texts from which they were taken do not often survive.

Myths certainly appeared in prose texts before the Hellenistic world, but they lack, so far as one can tell from the fragmentary remains, the flavor of a compilation, of time spent in libraries gathering stories from different sources. Instead they often are part of a work that covers a wider chronological range than the era of gods and heroes, and that is not simply a catalog of mythological stories.[10] Mythological figures play an often major role in narrative of early prose writers such as Hecataeus (FGrH 1), Acusilaus (FGrH 2), Pherecydes (FGrH 3), Hellanicus (FGrH 4 and 323a), and Herodotus. Later authors remark that Hellanicus and Acusilaus disagree about genealogies and that Acusilaus often corrects Hesiod, or they claim that Acusilaus merely reworked Hesiod in prose and then published the work as his (FGrH 2 T 5–6).

Mythological figures turn up in these early prose works often because of the importance that the past played for Greeks in debates over contemporary matters. The political allegiance of the island of Salamis, for example, depended in part on where Trojan War figures, such as Ajax, were said to have been born, lived, or died. In his history of the Persian Wars, Herodotus crosses the divide between mythological and human time:[11] he opens his account with a look at the kidnapping of women such as Io, Europa, and Helen and ends with the second invasion of Greece by Persians in 480–479 BC, perhaps about the time that he was born. Even as he spans these two kinds of time, he recognizes that they are in some way different, as he shows in his comment about "the human generation" in his discussion of Polycrates (3.122.2). Pherecydes was said in his ten books of *Histories* or *Genealogies* to have traced the family of Thucydides the historian back through Miltiades to Philaeus, son of Ajax, and thus to Zeus (FGrH 3 F 2).[12]

The second genre that influences mythography is chronography. By the end of the fifth century BC, some Greek thinkers developed a view of the past as a time different from their own, one that could be studied through documents. Hellanicus of Lesbos produced lists of priestesses at the Argive Heraion (FGrH 4 F74–84) and of victors at the musical competitions of the Carnea (F85–86), Hippias of Elis gathered names of Olympic victors in the *stadion* (FGrH 6 F 2), and someone compiled a list of the archons in Athens and inscribed it on stone at the end of the fifth century BC.[13] Aristotle, an innovator in the study of

---

[10]   As Robert L. Fowler states, "'mythography' is not a fifth-century genre" (*Early Greek Mythography*, vol. 1 [Oxford: Oxford University Press, 2000]: xxvii). Fowler includes 29 authors in his edition of Greek mythographers up to the early fourth century BC; see his discussion of his choices in the Introduction to his text, xxvii–xxxviii. He excludes any text that records events after the Ionian migration and the return of the Heraclidae (xxx).

[11]   See Fowler, *Early Greek Mythography*, xxx–xxxi.

[12]   See Carolyn Higbie, "The Bones of a Hero, the Ashes of a Politician: Athens, Salamis, and the Usable Past," *Classical Antiquity* 16 (1997): 279–308; Rosalind Thomas, *Oral Tradition and Written Record in Classical Athens* (Cambridge, UK: Cambridge University Press, 1989): 161–95.

[13]   Russell Meiggs and David Lewis, eds., *A Selection of Greek Historical Inscriptions to the End of the Fifth Century BC* (Oxford: Oxford University Press, 1969): no. 6. For a translation, see Charles W. Fornara, ed. and trans., *Archaic Times to the End of the Peloponnesian War* (Cambridge, UK: Cambridge University Press, 1977): no. 23.

literary texts, was also innovative in his use of inscriptions to answer historical questions: he seems to have read through inscriptions at Delphi in order to compile a list of victors at the Pythian games, for example, and he, together with his adherents, gathered information from inscriptions in his project on the constitutions of Greek city states. Craterus of Macedon, perhaps part of Aristotle's circle, even assembled and placed in chronological order public inscriptions from fifth-century BC Athens, though no historian following him seems to have made much use of his sourcebook.[14]

The *Bibliotheca* of Apollodorus

The most famous and influential, in modern times, of these mythological compendia is the *Bibliotheca* – "Library."[15] Although the *Bibliotheca* has been attributed to the famous second-century BC researcher Apollodorus of Athens, who did write on mythology, it is probably not his work, and no other author has been identified. Nevertheless, the author is still referred to as Apollodorus. Photius, who read and excerpted Conon's *Diegesis*, also knew of this work and said of it (*Bibliotheca* 186):[16]

> It encompassed the antiquities of the Greeks, whatsoever time had brought them to believe about both gods and heroes, as well as the naming of rivers and lands and peoples and cities as to their origins, and whatever else runs back into the past. It comes down to the Trojan War and it runs through both the battles with one another of certain men and their deeds, and their wanderings from Troy, especially of Odysseus with whom the account of the far past [*archaeologia*] stops. Most of the book is a summary account and not unhelpful to those seeking to understand the distant past.

Photius neatly summarizes both the chronological range of Apollodorus' work and its subject matter. The *Bibliotheca*, having devoted perhaps one-half of its narrative to the Trojan War, ends with Odysseus, whose final journey and death are the last story in the work. It agrees with other texts in seeing a division at this point in the Greek past. Along the way, the *Bibliotheca* offers explanations, often based either on folk etymology or on an event in a hero's life, for names of rivers, towns, and regions.

Apollodorus organizes his text by family and generations, as he makes clear in the opening to book 2, for example, (2.1.1): "Since we have worked our way through the family of Deucalion, we next speak of that of Inachus." This chronographical element can be traced to works such as Hesiod's *Theogony* or *Catalog of Women*, the works of Hecataeus and Acusilaus of Argos entitled *Genealogies*, and the attempts to place a chronological structure on the past. One consequence of this approach is the appearance of many long lists of names in the text – names of daughters and sons, names of heroes on expeditions (in the Trojan horse, for example), names of rivers, and names of hunting dogs.

Hesiod

[14]   See Carolyn Higbie, "Craterus and the Use of Inscriptions in Ancient Scholarship," *TAPA* 129 (1999): 43–83.

[15]   See Aubrey Diller, "The Text History of the Bibliotheca of Pseudo-Apollodorus," *TAPA* 66 (1935): 296–313; M.H.A.L.H. Van der Valk, "On Apollodori Bibliotheca," *REG* 71 (1958): 100–168; Marc Huys, "125 Years of Scholarship on Apollodoros the Mythographer: a Bibliographical Survey," *L'Antiquité Classique* 66 (1997): 319–51.

[16]   See René Henry, *Photius, Bibliothèque*, 3 vols. (Paris: Budé, 1962).

Unlike other mythographers, so far as we can tell, Apollodorus devotes a certain amount of space to citing sources. The references are brief and generally unspecific, as these sentences from his discussion of the family of Io reveal (2.1.3):

> Iasus was the son of Argos and Ismene, daughter of Asopus, and he [Iasus] was said to be the father of Io. But Castor, who wrote the *Chronologies*, and many of the tragedians say that Io was the daughter of Inachus. But Hesiod and Acusilaus say that she was the daughter of Peiren. ... Pherecydes says [Argos] was the son of Arestor, but Asclepiades says of Inachus, and Cercops a son of Argos and Ismene, the daughter of Asopus. But Acusilaus says that he was born of the earth.

This section of the text may contain rather more references than is usual in the *Bibliotheca*, but is otherwise very typical of the work. Apollodorus cites a wide range of sources, including hexameter poets (Hesiod, Homer, Eumelus, Panyassis, and Apollonius of Rhodes), lyric poets (Pindar and Simonides), tragedians (Euripides), and prose authors (Acusilaus of Argos and Pherecydes, in particular.) He also cites authors such as Asclepiades of the late fourth century BC who gathered mythological stories from the tragedians (FGrH12). Most often, such references are to provide additional or conflicting versions of a story, frequently, as here, about the identification of a figure's parents; Apollodorus does not argue for one version or another, but simply includes the different sources. His aim in citation may be completeness in source material, just as he is complete in his chronological range of stories.

The *Bibliotheca* is difficult to date, though many scholars place it roughly in the first century AD. The author gives no explanation for its composition in a preface or anywhere else; modern writers refer to it as a "handbook," which reflects modern attitudes toward it, but may not accurately convey its role when it was compiled. Finally, the work has not survived whole: we have a full text for most of the first three books that breaks off in the story of Theseus, but we have only epitomes – summaries – of the other seven books.[17] Nevertheless, because of its existence in a more complete form than any other mythography and because of the wide scope of the stories included, it is the best known and most used of such collections today.

Other Mythographic Works

Unlike the all-inclusive Apollodorus, other mythographers gathered together stories focused on a theme. Eratosthenes retold myths about stars in a work known as *Catasterisms*. Eratosthenes' collection survives not in its original form, but only because it was helpful in understanding Aratus' astronomical poem, *Phaenomena*, and so it appears in the scholia to that work and in an epitome of star myths, as well as a couple of Latin texts. A manuscript, probably of the ninth century AD, preserves a wide range of texts, including the only surviving version of two mythographers: Parthenius of Nicaea of the first century BC, who collected myths of love, and Antoninus Liberalis, probably of the second century AD, who collected myths culminating in metamorphosis.

---

[17]   Epitomes became an important part of literary life from the time of the Hellenistic world. There were even epitomes of epitomes, as in the case of the *Historia animalium,* epitomized by Aristophanes of Byzantium, which in its turn was epitomized by Sopater.

Parthenius

The Greek literary man Parthenius of Nicaea, who was brought to Rome after being taken captive during the Third Mithridatic War, composed a mythographic work known as the *Erotica Pathemata*. It is important not only as an example of mythography but of Greek prose from the middle of the first century BC.[18] As Parthenius says in his dedicatory epistle to Cornelius Gallus, the *Erotica Pathemata* were thirty-six tales of love taken from Greek works, perhaps to be used by the Roman as a source for his poetry:

> Because, Cornelius Gallus, I thought that the collection of sufferings in love suited you very much, I have selected them and sent them to you in as abbreviated form as possible. For those among the present collection that occur in certain poets where they are not narrated in their own right, you will find out for the most part from what follows.[19] The ones which are most agreeable can be put by you into hexameters and elegiacs. Do not look down on them because there is not present that elegance which you seek. For I have collected them in the style of a little notebook, and they will serve you in a similar manner, perhaps.

Parthenius emphasizes the fact that he has collected these tales from different authors and that he presents them to Gallus as source material, which the latter might versify.[20] The prose, Parthenius asserts, is straightforward and lacks any elegance or style, but this is of no consequence, since he expects that the stories will be reworked. The stories themselves often involve incest, homosexuality, and disasters associated with ill-fated love. Some are not set in the mythological world, but in the generations some time after, but those that take place in historical times seem as distant as those from the mythological era.

Parthenius' proposal to Gallus reflects two different, but parallel traditions. In first-century-BC Rome, prominent Romans might present a client, especially one with a reputation for literary or historical work, with notes from him to work up into a text that would enhance their joint reputations. Among others, Cicero sent notes on his year as consul to the historian Lucceius, in hopes of seeing them transformed into a history glorifying his deeds of 63 BC (Cicero, *Ad familiares* 5.12.10). The second tradition goes back to the work done in the Library at Alexandria and perhaps even to Peripatetic monographs, in which notes were abstracted either from lectures or books and then organized by topic. Such notes could then be put to use in any of several different genres, including mythography, paradoxography, ethnography, and even poetry. We might speculate both about the sources of Callimachus' poetry, for example, and the purposes to which he intended to put his *Collection of Wonders*.[21]

One, rather brief, tale from the *Erotica Pathemata* may serve as an example of the collection. Parthenius reports what happens to Odysseus after he returns to Ithaca and kills the suitors (III):[22]

> Odysseus did wrong not only to Aeolus [see tale II], but even after his wanderings, when he killed the suitors, he came to Epirus because of

[18]   See J.L. Lightfoot, *Parthenius of Nicaea* (Oxford: Oxford University Press, 1999).

[19]   I have taken the translation of this difficult and corrupt sentence from Lightfoot, *Parthenius*; see her discussion in the commentary ad loc.

[20]   See Lightfoot, *Parthenius*, 74, 217–24, on the significance of this dedication and epistolary preface.

[21]   See Lightfoot, *Parthenius*, 217–20.

[22]   See Lightfoot's discussion of this story in her commentary ad loc.

some oracles. There he seduced the daughter of Tyrimmas, Evippe; he had been very hospitable to him and had been his host with every kindness. The child born to Odysseus from this girl was Euryalus. His mother, when he came of age, sent him to Ithaca, having given him some tokens hidden in a wax tablet. As it happened, Odysseus was not there then and Penelope discovered all these things, since she had already known of Odysseus' love affair with Evippe. She persuaded Odysseus, when he came back, before he knew anything of these goings on, to kill Euryalus because he was plotting against him. And Odysseus, because he lacked strength of character and he was not otherwise reasonable, killed his son himself. And not much time after he did this, wounded by the prickle of a stingray, he died at the hands of his own offspring.

Like Phlegon of Tralles' story of Idas, Parthenius' tale is full of folktale motifs. The tokens in a wax tablet remind us of the sandals and sword that served as tokens to identify the young Theseus, while Penelope's actions recall those of Medea, who attempted to kill her stepson Theseus when he turned up in Athens, or Phaedra, whose false accusations against her stepson Hippolytus caused Theseus to bring about his death. Parthenius draws no moral, but presumably any poet who used this narrative could.

The sources for Parthenius' stories are not often identified by the author. Only in three instances does he briefly name them: in his story of Byblis, Parthenius states, "Nicaenetus says ..." (XI); in that of Antheus, he prefaces some verses that he quotes with the name of Alexander the Aetolian (XIV); similarly, in the story of Corythus, he prefaces a quotation of verses with the name of Nicander (XXXIV). An oddity of the single manuscript that preserves the *Erotica Pathemata* is the presence of marginal notes, in the same hand as that of the main text, that name authors and works that also tell the story.[23] Thus, for the tale of Odysseus quoted above, the marginal note remarks, "Sophocles tells the story [*historeî*] in his *Euryalus*." Where these attributions can be checked, they seem to be accurate, but this does not necessarily mean that Parthenius drew either on that text or a summary of it; an earlier author can tell the same story as a later one without being the source for it. Notably, the three names mentioned by Parthenius in XI, XIV, and XXXIV do not appear in the marginal notes for those stories.

Antoninus Liberalis

Antoninus Liberalis' collection of forty-one stories all culminate in metamorphosis, which is visited by the gods on a human either as a punishment for outrageous behavior or as a release from some sort of disaster. Some of his tales explain the establishment of a cult, and his language can be repetitive. Typical is this story about the war between the pygmies and cranes with its concluding remark that provides the link to a story familiar to his readers (XVI):[24]

Among the people known as pygmies there was a girl named Oenoe, who was not without beauty, but who was unpleasant in character and arrogant. She had no thought for either Artemis or Hera. After she was

---

[23]   These notes also survive for the mythography of Antoninus Liberalis. See Lightfoot, *Parthenius*, 246–56 and 303–5.
[24]   See Manolis Papathomopoulos, *Antoninus Liberalis, Les Métamorphoses* (Paris: Budé, 1968).

married to Nicodamas, a reasonable and upright citizen, she gave birth to a son, Mopsus. And to her all the pygmies because of their good nature took very many presents for the birth of her son. But Hera, who was angered at Oenoe, because she did not honor her, made her into a crane, lengthened her neck, and created a lofty-flying bird. And she brought on a war between Oenoe and the pygmies. Oenoe, on account of her love for her son Mopsus, kept on flying around their houses and did not cease. The pygmies armed themselves and pursued her. And from then until now there has been war between the pygmies and the cranes.

Antoninus Liberalis seems to have drawn on two sources almost exclusively. From Boios' *Ornithogonia* (FGrH 328 F 214), he took tales involving birds, and from Nicander's *Metamorphoses* came stories not only about birds, but also animals, trees, and stones.[25] Like Parthenius, Antoninus Liberalis' sources – or authors who told the same tales – were also identified in marginal notes.

Conon

About other collections it is impossible to say what their purpose or focus was. Conon's *Diegesis* is a good example of such a miscellany.[26] Alive during the reign of Augustus, Conon assembled some fifty stories that lack any thematic link or any other discernable organizational principle, at least as far as can be determined from the later summary of it by Photius. The dedication of the work to King Archilaus of Cappadocia offers no hint of its structure or purpose (FGrH 26 T1). There are myths that explain the foundation of cities and establishment of cults, stories of love, and stories that explain proverbs or place names, and even three examples of paradoxography.[27] Perhaps of most interest are the three stories preserved in no other source: the foundation of Olynthus, the establishment at Ephesus of the cult of Apollo Gypaieus, and how the oracle of Apollo at Didyma was transferred from Branchus to the Evangelidae. Conon gives the myth behind Olynthus (FGrH 26 F 1 [IV]):

> The fourth book of the *Diegesis* reports on the affairs concerning the city of Olynthus and Strymon, king of the Thracians, from whom the ancient Eioneus River took its name. And that there were three sons of his, Brangas and Rhesus and Olynthus. And Rhesus, who fought at Troy for Priam was killed at the hands of Diomedes. Olynthus, who fought with a lion unintentionally, died on a hunt. And Brangas, his brother, after he lamented greatly his misfortune, buried Olynthus on the spot where he died. When he came into Sithonia, he founded a prosperous and great city, which he called Olynthus after the boy.

The details of the story are not unique and could be paralleled from many other such tales, but no other source gives this foundation myth for Olynthus. Unfortunately for modern scholars interested in such matters, Conon seems not to have identified his sources. Completely absent from Conon's text is any story in which a god is a major character.

---

[25]   On Nicander, see A.S.F. Gow and A.F. Scholfield, *Nicander: The Poems and Poetical Fragments* (Cambridge, UK: Cambridge University Press, 1953): 205–8. On Boios, Nicander, and Antoninus Liberalis, see P.M.C. Forbes Irving, *Metamorphosis in Greek Myths* (Oxford: Oxford University Press, 1990): 20–36.

[26]   See Henrichs, "Three Approaches to Greek Mythography," 244–7.

[27]   See Henrichs, "Three Approaches to Greek Mythography," 268–9.

Homeric Myth and Scholarship

The Homeric poems received the greatest attention from scholars over the centuries, attention that was directed both to explicating the language and meter of the epics and to elucidating some of the more obscure figures. It is difficult to say in exactly what form these studies were originally published, whether texts of the poems were accompanied by commentaries or whether texts were prepared separately from commentaries and essays on various subjects. Nothing has come down to us in its original form, and we are often dependent either on compilations and abridgements of works or on hostile remarks about someone's scholarship as we try to reconstruct this scholarship. Nor is it always certain for whom these treatises were written: although some texts were clearly directed to other scholars and some to students just learning to read the poems,[28] many surviving fragments of Homeric scholarship are not obviously designed for a particular audience. Part of the problem may be yet again the endless working and reworking of previous material, recasting, for example, comments that were originally designed for scholars so that they might be useful to students. Nonetheless, mythographers clearly found much to interest them in the Homeric poems; their work is preserved for us today in the scholia, particularly the so-called D scholia, the scholia minora, and in independent texts such as the Mythographus Homericus.[29]

The Mythographus Homericus is an example of Hellenistic scholarship on the mythological stories in the Homeric epics. Although it existed for the first five centuries of our era as a text in its own right, it has not been published as such in our time.[30] Study of it is complicated by the wide variety of forms in which fragments have survived: the manuscript tradition must be supplemented with fragments in papyri and on ostraca. But the basic structure and purpose of the collection are clear: to elucidate the Homeric epics by giving brief versions of myths wherever relevant. The stories are introduced by a word or phrase from the poem, followed by the comment or mythological tale, and the entry concludes most often with a subscription in which an authority is cited. Within the *Iliadic* D scholia, in which the Mythographus Homericus has become embedded, there are approximately 200 of these *historiae*, as they are known; there are many fewer for the *Odyssey*.

Preserved in the D scholia and probably from the Mythographus Homericus is, for example, a different version of the story told in the *Iliad* about the rebellion of the gods against Zeus.[31] In the *Iliad*, Hera, Poseidon, and Athena are identified as the gods who sought to overthrow Zeus (1.399–400). In a long narrative of this rebellion, a D scholion names the ring-leaders: "Poseidon and Hera and Apollo and Athena plotted to bind him and then subdue him." The scholion describes punishment taken by Zeus against only three of the gods; Athena seems to escape their fate. At the end of the entry comes this statement about the source of the story: "Didymus tells the story [*historeî*]." This scholion

---

[28]   On the sort of help that a student beginning to read Homer was given in the Hellenistic and Roman worlds, see Teresa Morgan, *Literate Education in the Hellenistic and Roman Worlds* (Cambridge, UK: Cambridge University Press, 1998): 166; also Raffaella Cribiore, *Gymnastics of the Mind: Greek Education in Hellenistic and Roman Egypt* (Princeton: Princeton University Press, 2001): 140–42, 204–5.

[29]   See Cribiore, *Gymnastics of the Mind*, 207–8, for a brief introduction. More information is to be found in Franco Montanari, "The Mythographus Homericus," in eds. J.G.J. Abbenes, S.R. Slings, and I. Sluiter, *Greek Literary Theory after Aristotle* (Amsterdam: VU University Press, 1995): 135–72.

[30]   See Henrichs, "Three Approaches to Greek Mythography," 243 and fn. 5.

[31]   See Montanari, "The Mythographus Homericus," 158–61.

does not discuss the significance of the participation of the various gods, as other scholia on the lines do, and seems to conflate versions without regard for the differences. But it does cite a learned source for the variant, the Homeric commentator Didymus of the first century BC, and it uses the verb *historeî*, which we have already seen in the marginal notes to the mythographies of Parthenius and Antoninus Liberalis.

Modern scholars have identified a number of writers of the Hellenistic era as mythographers, writers who collected stories of gods and heroes from a variety of sources and presented them in unadorned prose narratives. Almost none of these mythographers survives intact; for most, we have either fragments cited in later authors, often in scholia, or only a name with or without a book title. This means that we must depend on reconstruction and analogy in our studies of these authors, but they form an interesting and neglected part of the Hellenistic literary culture.

Mythographies seem to have been compiled for a wide range of purposes. They could serve a scholarly function, providing readers of archaic and classical poetry with explanation of myths and rituals, and offering explanations for place names. In this regard, they were the scholarly counterpart of essays on grammar and language in the early poets. Some of the material from these mythographies seems to have been abstracted and reworked for students just beginning to read poets like Homer. Such students needed more basic help than scholars, so were given stories of the gods as well as explanations of verb forms and glossaries for obscure and difficult words. Mythographies might also have provided reading material which was interesting, but not taxing to the reader. In this guise, it could be seen as a parallel to paradoxography, in which oddities from the natural world were compiled for reading pleasure.

The rich and complex Hellenistic world fostered the rise of literary scholarship and the development of new genres. Readers became aware of new texts and authors, as well as different versions of works already well known. They drew from these texts, once they were accessible, material that could be organized and juxtaposed in new ways. Thus, compilers of paradoxographies showed their readers bizarre phenomena and compilers of mythographies enabled readers either to explore the whole of the mythological past or to read stories focused on a theme.

Modern readers of mythographies are able to discover the variety and obscurity of Greek myth. These collections can illuminate otherwise mysterious references in poets and preserve local traditions which might vary greatly from a Panhellenic version. These texts enable us to have a greater understanding of the Hellenistic literary world, which we can get in no other way.

Further Reading

To learn more about Hellenistic mythography, the best place to begin is Albert Henrichs, "Three Approaches to Greek Mythography," in Jan Bremmer, ed., *Interpretations of Greek Mythology* (London: Croom Helm, 1987) 242–77. For accessible translations of some of the most important texts, see Michael Simpson, trans., *Gods and Heroes of the Greeks: The Library of Apollodorus* (Amherst, MA: University of Massachusetts, Press, 1976); William Hansen, ed. and trans., *Anthology of Ancient Greek Popular Literature* (Bloomington, IN: Indiana University Press, 1998); William Hansen, *Phlegon of Tralles' Book of Marvels* (Exeter: University of Exeter Press, 1996).

Secondary Source 3.4   Philip Hardie, 'In pursuit of Daphne'

(Source: Hardie, P. (2002) *Ovid's Poetics of Illusion*, Cambridge,
Cambridge University Press, pp. 46–51)

The story of the god of poetry's pursuit of the beautiful nymph tells of a desire that is terminally thwarted of its bodily goal, as the girl is changed into a tree, but a desire that is always kept alive in memory, and more specifically in writing. It is also a story about the god of knowledge's frustrated pursuit of sexual knowledge, as the male gaze proves unable to penetrate the secrets of the female body. But Daphne's body is transformed into another object, the laurel-tree, that is a multiply determined bearer of meaning. The metamorphosis of Daphne is an excellent example of what Peter Brooks calls the 'semioticization of the body'[1] as her body is turned into a site of signification – the place for the inscription of stories – and itself a signifier'.[2]

Apollo ought to be the ultimate knowing subject, but the god of oracular certainty, through whom is laid bare (*patet*) what will be, what has been, and what is (*Met.* 1.517–18), spectacularly falls short not merely of foreknowledge of his own failure (491 *suaque illum oracular fallunt* 'his own oracles fail him'), but also of the knowledge he seeks of the object of desire. At her first sighting by the god scantily clad Daphne is subjected to a fetishistic scopophilia,[3] that fragments her person into a blazon of body parts (hair, eyes, mouth, fingers, hands, arms, legs), and phantasises about what remains hidden to view (502 *siqua latent, meliora putat* 'whatever is hidden he thinks even better').[4] Similarly in *Amores* 1.5 the reader's gaze on the body of the naked Corinna had travelled downwards over her body parts, only to come to a halt at the text's refusal to display her inmost secrets. In the case of Daphne metamorphosis ensures that these secrets will always remain hidden, both from Apollo and from the reader, under the bark that grows round her soft body. As a consequence of the pressure of Apollo's desire, Daphne now exists for her lover only in substitutions for and displacements of herself. The symbolism of her arboreal form as a phallic fetish is perhaps too obvious to point out. For the reader Daphne is for ever on display, but for ever concealed, within the text. She has indeed been converted into a *tenuis liber* (549), 'thin bark' / 'slender book', thus suffering Corinna's fate of becoming that impossible, but most seductive, object of desire, a text, a potent screen for the projection of male fantasy.

Apollo also fails because he is incapable of bringing his own subjectivity into a satisfactory relationship with the object of desire. Here Lacan's notion of the Desire of the Other as the constitutive moment in the formation of the subject may be brought into play. Lacan equivocates on the objective and subjective genitives in the phrase 'Desire of the Other': the divided subject's desire for the other is also the wish to be recognised unconditionally by the other, to be the desire of the other.[5] This is an impossible request, since the person to whom it is addressed is likewise a divided subject, and therefore unable to answer it unconditionally. Apollo demands recognition from Daphne, asking her to ask

---

[1]   Brooks (1993) 25.

[2]   Brooks (1993) 5–6.

[3]   The phrase used in the classic discussion of the male gaze in Hollywood cinema by Mulvey (1975) 14.

[4]   On the fetishistic blazon made out of Daphne's body by Apollo and its importance for the Petrarchan tradition see Enterline (2000) 99.

[5]   Lacan (1977) 288 9; Bowie (1991) 135–6.

who *he* is (1.512 *cui placeas, inquire tamen* 'yet ask who it is who fancies you'), but she will not pause long enough to give him an answer (526 *cumque ipso uerba inperfecta reliquit* 'she left him and his unfinished words'). At the end of the story Apollo forges a relationship of a kind with the tree into which Daphne has changed, but one that operates in the order of the Imaginary, through mirror-images and identifications, in an attempt to elide the otherness of the object of desire. Apollo reasserts his prophetic power as he verbally appropriates the laurel (558 '*arbor eris certe*'[6] *dixit 'mea'* '"at any rate you will be my tree", he said'), and effects a metaphorical identification between himself and the tree 564–5 '*utque meum intonsis caput est iuuenale capillis,* | *tu quoque perpetuos semper gere frondis honores*' '"just as the hair on my youthful head is unshorn, so may you always wear the everlasting glory of your leaves"' (Apollo's comparison of the foliage with his hair is eased by the frequent metaphorical use of *coma* 'hair' to refer to the leaves of a tree). The renewed power of Apollo's knowledge of the future is guaranteed by the reader's

proof of the perpetuity of desire and memory as much as of the power of Apollonian prophecy.

Apollo's *self*-knowledge, on the other hand, is questionable. A kind of recognition of the god by Daphne/the laurel does come at the very end of the story, 566–7 *factis modo laurea ramis* | *adnuit utque caput uisa est agitasse cacumen* 'the laurel nodded with its new-made branches and seemed to shake its tip as if it were a head'. One way of making sense of what has happened to Daphne is to regard Apollo's words to the laurel as the consecration of a kind of cult statue, an idol, as the repeated hymnic apostrophes (*te...te...*etc.) at 559–65 conjure up the presence of divinity within her blockish image, just as Corinna is transformed into a kind of goddess under the gaze of her lover. The laurel's nod will then suggest stories about miraculously animated statues.[7] But another model hints that the nod should be construed neither as the sign of the presence of a divinity within a cult statue, nor as the sign of recognition by a desiring Other, but only as the token of the presence of Apollo himself. The shaking laurel is the Callimachean sign of the epiphany of the god (*Hymn to Apollo* 1–7): 'See how the laurel branch of Apollo has shaken! ... The god is no longer far off.'[8] Paradoxically it is through the perpetuation of the narcissism that has characterised all of his words and actions hitherto that Apollo betrays his own lack of insight into his own subjectivity. The 'hymn' to the laurel at 557–65 turns out to be as much a hymn to himself as had been the

---

[6]   For the certitude of the Delphic oracle cf. Lucr. 1.738–9 *multo certa ratione magis quam* | *Pythia quae inpodi a Phoebi lauroque profatur*' with 'reasoning far more certain than that uttered in prophecy by the Pythian priestess from Apollo's tripod and laurel' (Lucretius polemicises against the conventional acceptance of Pythian certitude). The laurel is Apollo's oracular tree.

[7]   E.g. Livy 5.22.5 (Roman soldiers carry off the statue of Juno from Veii) *cum quidam ... 'Visne Roman ire Iuno?' dixisset, adnuisse ceteri deam conclamauerunt.* 'After one of them said "Do you want to go to Rome, Juno?", the others shouted that the goddess had nodded yes.'

[8]   Cf. also the shaking laurel at Callim. *Iamb.* 4, fr. 194–10, with Kerkhecker (1999) 86 n. 18. In her contest with the olive tree the laurel shows herself as obsessed with her own status and self-praise. 'The laurel knows only herself', Kerkhecker (1999) 99: another hint that the Ovidian Daphne turns into a mirror image of Apollo? For further possible Ovidian allusion to the fourth *Iambus* at *Met.* 1.557–65 see Kerkhecker (1999) 91 n. 37.

hymnically formulated praise of his own powers in his futile wooing of Daphne at 515 –18.[9] He cannot escape from self-knowledge into a relationship with another, in an ironical and blinkered obedience to the Delphic maxim 'know thyself' that will be closely paralleled by the disastrous self-knowledge of the Ovidian Narcissus.

Apollo can touch Daphne only through the physical contact between his own person and the leaves of the laurel. For this to happen, the laurel's 'hair' cannot remain unshorn like Apollo's (564): the branches have to be plucked to be worn. The plucking of plants or picking of fruit is a common image for defloration and marriage; but for Apollo metaphor cannot translate into the actuality of a fulfilled sexual desire. The laurel's *perpetui frondis honores* 'everlasting glory of leaves' are a perpetual icon of perpetual virginity, an answer to her initial prayer to her father at 486–7 '*da mihi perpetua ... uirginitate frui*' 'grant that I may enjoy everlasting virginity'. Thus the laurel becomes an inscribed body, declaring the unalterable truth about Daphne, that she will always be a virgin. The inmost secrets of her body will never be revealed, will always lie hidden (*latere*), even from the god through whom all is revealed (*patere*).

My claim that Apollo's power of prophecy, at least, is vindicated at the end of the story needs qualification, for the failure of the one 'hymn', and the success of the other, result from an equivocation on the unexpressed term *uates*, both 'prophet' and 'poet'. At 1.517–18 Apollo had boasted of his power to control time through prophecy, 'through me is revealed what shall be, what has been, and what is'. The control over time of a prophet-*uates* is of course power only over knowledge of events, not the power to shape those events; but as poet-*uates* Apollo will have power over the future praise, *laus*, of the *laurus* itself[10] and also over the *laudes*, such as those of Augustus, of which the laurel will be the signifier. The conversion of Apollo-prophet into Apollo-poet is an essential part of the comprehensive textualisation of the mythical events narrated in the story. Daphne, as we have seen, is transformed into a book. Daphne can never by physically conjoined with Apollo, she cannot be his *con-iunx* 'wife' (557), but, like 'Corinna' and 'Ovid', the names of 'Daphne' and 'Apollo' will for ever be joined in their story. Within the text Apollo asserts that she will always be with him as an appendage of his attributes, the first in the list of those attributes being the one most closely attached to Apollo's person, his hair, *coma* (559), another way of saying that the laurel will attach *ad mea tempora*, both 'to my times' and 'to my temples', a favourite Ovidian pun.[11] The word *tempora* occurs at 451, immediately preceding the story of Daphne, where we had been told that at that time (451–2) *nondum laurus erat, longoque decentia crine | tempora cingebat de qualibet arbore Phoebus* 'as yet there was no laurel and Apollo used to garland his fair long-haired temples from any tree'. The perpetuity of the memorialisation is doubly marked by the two occurrences of *semper*, at 558 'my hair, my lyre, my quiver, will always have you', and 565 'you too bear always the everlasting glory of your leaves'. The 'everlasting glory' of the laurel is another way of saying the immortality granted by poetry, in this case *this* poetry, immortalising Daphne, a part of Ovid's own *perpetuum carmen* (1.4), which is an 'everlasting' as well as a 'continuous song'.[12]

---

[9]   On Apollo's 'hymn to himself' see Feeney (1998) 72.

[10]   The standard ancient etymology: Maltby (1991) 331.

[11]   Hinds (1999) 56 n. 13.

[12]   For this sense of *perpetuum* e.g. Lucr. 3.12–13 *aurea dicta, | aurea, perpetua semper dignissima uita* 'golden words, golden, always most worthy of everlasting life'.

Apollo's gift of evergreen perpetuity to the laurel foreshadows Ovid's own claim for his own textual perpetuity at 15.878–9 *perque omnia saecula fama ... uiuam* 'through all ages I shall live in fame'. Even before he sees Daphne Apollo has a deep concern for the continuing fame of his 'work': after killing the Python he institutes the Pythian Games (445) *neue operis famam posset delere uetustas* 'so that length of years might not wipe out the fame of his work'. From the verb *delere* comes the adjective applied to the 'indelible name' to which Ovid looks forward at the end of the poem (15.876), *nomen indelebile*.

For the reader the laurel in the landscape is a memorial of the erotic narrative that is the *aition* of the laurel, a 'book' to be read, in the larger Book of the Immortal Poet. The limit to the reader's knowledge of Daphne will be the recognition that Daphne/laurel is a proleptic memorial for the achievement of the poet himself, her evergreen leaves an icon of the perpetual freshness and life of the text, and the attribute not only of Apollo's but also of the poet's *tempora*.

Reading the book offers us some kind of possession of the poet's evergreen laurels and of the objects of desire in the text: for us of course all the desirable bodies in the *Metamorphoses* have a purely textual existence. Our pursuit of Daphne will always leave us in possession of a book, a *tenuis liber* (and the same is true of the reader's pursuit of Corinna). But my reading has revealed that the reader's frustration of satisfied desire is parallel to that of the characters in the poem. Others have pointed to ways in which characters within the text of the *Metamorphoses* function as figures for the reader outside the text. My argument tends to work in the opposite direction, allegorising the reader's experience into the experience of actors in the text, with the result that desiring actors end up as readers or spectators, but not possessors, of their objects of desire. In this respect, too, the Apollo and Daphne narrative functions as commentary on the relationship between lover-poet and reader in the *Amores*, where, as we saw, the climactic encounter between Corinna and Ovid in 1.5 leaves the poet in possession of an object that is hardly less textual, less written, than that which the reader holds in his hands.

References

Bowie, M. (1991) *Lacan*, London

Brooks, P. (1993) *Body Work. Objects of Desire in Modern Narrative*, Cambridge, Mass. and London

Enterline, L. (2000) *The Rhetoric of the Body from Ovid to Shakespeare*, Cambridge

Feeney, D. C. (1986) '"Stat magni nominis umbra." Lucan on the greatness of Pompeius Magnus', *CQ* 36: 239–43

Hinds, S. E. (1999) 'After exile: time and teleology from *Metamorphoses* to *Ibis*', in Hardie, Barchiesi, Hinds (1999) 48–67

Lacan, J. (1977) *Ecrits. A Selection* (transl. A. Sheridan), London and New York

Maltby, R. (1991) *A Lexicon of Ancient Latin Etymologies*, Leeds

Mulvey, L. (1975) 'Visual pleasure and narrative cinema', *Screen* 16.3: 6–18

Secondary Source 3.5   Diana Winstanley, 'Phaethon: seizing the reins of power'

(Source: Gabriel, Y. (ed.) (2004) *Myths, Stories, and Organizations: Premodern Narratives for Our Times*, Oxford, Oxford University Press, pp. 176–91[1])

> On what wings dare he aspire?
> What the hand dare seize the fire?
>
> (William Blake, 'The Tyger' from 'Songs of Experience'[2], 1789/1967: 42)

Reading Ovidly—Introducing Phaethon

THE story of Phaethon is both a personal, as well as an epic tale; in this chapter, I shall first present the version of Phaethon as told in Ovid's *Metamorphoses* (written c. 5 BCE), and then explore its relevance to our times. On the face of it, the story of Phaethon is about a young man goaded by his peers into trying to take hold of the reins of power. In an attempt to show everyone, not least himself, that he is the true son of the Sun God, he seeks to ride the brilliant chariot of his father across its daily, trail-blazing arc over the earth. Unable to control the wild horses that pull the chariot, he ends up ablaze and crashes down on the earth below, causing much damage, and finally dying in his father's great shadow. The value of a good story is above all its capacity for retake, and before Ovid, Euripides had already used the story of Phaethon in a tragic play, of which some fragments still remain (see Diggle 1970). Like many of Ovid's tales (Hughes 1997), the story of Phaethon lends itself to reflection on a variety of current concerns (Hofman and Lasdun 1994); in this chapter, I offer a few contemporary retakes from the spheres of organization and of private life, demonstrating the versatility of the myth and highlighting its capacity to resonate with a contemporary audience.

Ovid is one of our greatest authors, a storyteller who writes of the ancient gods in ways which offer a deep insight into the human condition; his unique and sophisticated narrative skills have earned him the title of a 'modern' poet. In this chapter, I go further, arguing that he is also a postmodern poet—his greatest work, *Metamorphoses*, is about the fluidity of form and content, where not only people and landscapes are transformed, but the work itself shifts in ways that makes it impervious to fixed interpretations: Ovid is a protean poet par excellence.

The Story of Phaethon

The story of Phaethon is part of a fantastical panorama populated by heroes and Gods, monsters, and nymphs, who encounter continual change and transformation as they stride and soar through the pages of Ovid's *Metamorphoses*. The very name Phaethon means 'the shining or beaming one', evoking the nature of his divine father, and at the same time tragically prefiguring his fiery fate. Ovid tells us that Phaethon is a young boy whose mother is Clymene, a sea nymph, and whose father is Phoebus,[3] the

---

[1]   Thanks are due to Dr Paula James, Senior Lecturer, Open University, Department of Classical Studies, who gave guidance on Ovid's narrative and poetic interpretation of the myth, as well as on current Ovidian scholarship.

[2]   The Tyger appears in William Blake's 'Songs of Experience', the antithesis of his 'Songs of Innocence', where his feelings over the suffering of mankind and the corruption of innocence are aired.

[3]   The Sun god, Helios; originally, however, the Sun god was distinct from Phoebus and Apollo.

Sun God. The linking of 'son' and 'sun' is certainly an interesting modern homophone.[4] Clymene marries Merops, a mortal king who adopts Phaethon as his son. This makes Phaethon a mortal prince, and a mix of godly fire and water; in Ovid's version, he is also portrayed as a typically mixed-up teenager.

The story opens with two boys, Phaethon and Epaphus, playmates rivalling each other over the status of their parents. As far as we know, these two boys had not been linked before by any of the earlier tellers or illustrators of these myths, and their appearance, therefore, in this story is one of Ovid's first metamorphoses. Growing into manhood, and taking up an adult role in the world, is inexorably fraught with dangers; Phaethon and Epaphus, however, have even more reasons than most to be anxious, because their divine parentage adds genetic chaos into the already heady cocktail of adolescent hormones: it makes their pubescent rites of passage even more difficult. Phaethon boasts that his father is the Sun God, Phoebus; Epaphus dismisses this claim as puffed up pride, and accuses Phaethon of creating an 'image of a false father' (*Tumidus genitoris imagine falsi*, 1.754). Phaethon goes 'crying' back to his mother for reassurance. She seeks to reassure him, but to no avail. He then enters the heavenly realm, and sets off for the nearby palace of the Sun God to ask for proof. This will give Phaethon the closure he needs regarding his own identity, as well as tremendous status in the eyes of others. Being an amazing weaver of tales, Ovid transforms in this way the ever-present sun into the always-absent father.

At the meeting of Phaethon and Phoebus, Phaethon stands in wonder at the magnificence of his father's palace; he is dazzled by the halo of sunbeams that crowns his father's head, and overawed by his chariot, inlaid with gold and jewels. Phoebus embraces his son warmly and proudly, and foolishly gives a promise of anything the boy might like, in order to help prove his identity. Once given, however, such promises cannot be broken. This proves to be the fateful gift, as the foolish Phaethon asks to be allowed, just for a day, to take his father's place on the chariot that hauls the Sun through the sky. As any father would, Phoebus begs his son to reconsider, but his pleas are in vain. Can we blame Phaethon for making such a demand on his father? By riding the chariot of the Sun he will be recognized by the world as his father's son; as the charioteer, he will be able to look down on all his classmates and cast off his own nagging anxieties. He will have the strength and power of a master of the universe.

Phaethon is only a teenager, and passing into the adult world is far harder than he can ever imagine. He attempts a truly heroic rite of passage—and fails to make the grade. He fails, because even as a temporary loan, he attempts to get his inheritance by wheedling out of an over-indulgent father a dangerous promise. He also fails because the offspring of immortal fathers cannot receive an inheritance from their parents who never die. Phaethon is thus one of Ovid's examples of the young and of those with delusions of grandeur, who attempt recklessly and fatally to short-circuit apprenticeship and the acquisition of skill—Icarus and Semele[5] being two others who, in seeking god-like stature, fall to earth or are burnt to ashes.

serve an apprenticeship.

[4]   The pun implied in the English translation through homophones would also have rung strong for Ovid's own readers: the son's name, Phaethon, was also a regular epithet of the Sun, his father, as for example, in Vergil's *Aeneid* (5.105), where dawn is ushered by 'Phaethontis equi'—by the steeds of Phaethon, that is, Helios himself (from the Greek Phaos—Phôs, meaning 'Light'). The Sun-Phaethon, therefore, would also be here Phaethon-the-Son.

[5]   Semele was a human mistress of Jove (Jupiter), who asks him to make love to her the way he does to his divine wife Juno; this act leads to her dying consumed by flames.

The Sun God next advises Phaethon how to steer his chariot, telling him of the wheel tracks in the sky that can provide a marker; clearly, the lad is not listening, and once he is careering through the sky, tackling the constellations, he takes leave of his senses. Not long into the fiery ride, Phaethon becomes all too witless to bring his workforce to order. The fact that he has no godly weight has already disturbed the horses' psychological equilibrium, as well as the actual physical balance of the chariot: the unfamiliar driver lacks any authority, and the horses, unnerved by the mortal novice at the reins, career and gallop out of control across the universe, setting the earth ablaze and wreaking havoc in the heavens. Here Phaethon can be juxtaposed with Arachne; where Phaethon claims a role through kinship with a God, and loses it through lack of skill, Arachne claims a role through skill and mastery (at weaving), and loses it through challenging a God, and through refusing to acknowledge the debt to the one who is not just a goddess of weaving, but weaving itself.

Once Phaethon has dropped the reins, the horses run both free and fearful of their freedom. Phaethon himself is plunged into the darkness, blinded by the conflagration around him; what should have been a moment of exhilaration and intoxication becomes instead the start of his total annihilation. Phaethon's hands have dropped not just the horses' reins, but those of the narrative as well. From this moment on, Phaethon is caught up in the whirlwind of cosmic chaos, and the focal point of the story is no longer himself, but rather all that surrounds him.

Numberless myths of causation erupt around the planetary and earthly havoc that ensues. Ovid suggests this conflagration is the reason why Africans are black, as their blood was driven by the heat to the surface of their bodies; it is also the reason why Libya is a desert, and the myth suggests that the terrified Nile hid its head, so that even today its source remains unknown (see Wise 1976: 51). As the fate of the universe hangs in balance, Mother Earth calls upon Jupiter for assistance: he launches the lightning shaft that will destroy Phaethon, and send the Sun chariot reeling from the skies. Phaethon's final plummet back to earth gives him a moment of glory as a brief trailblazer, compared by Ovid to a comet. His embers plunge to the earth, and, around the stone marking his demise, his mother grieves, while his sisters, weeping in their sorrow, turn to trees; the amber itself that is formed by their tears will be used, in the distant future, as Roman wedding jewellery. Although Phaethon may have proved his divine ancestry, he remains mortal—and his human fallibility means he can never become a God like his father.

Phaethon Retakes: Rereading Ovidian Myths Today

A Personal Retake of Absence and Identification

There was something in the Phaethon story that resonated strongly with the author; my father was a politician, a Liberal MP and then life peer, as well as a TV presenter, TV doctor, and weekly columnist in the *Manchester Evening News*. Every day before the six o'clock news and the Magic Roundabout, on his programme 'This is Your Right', his presence would beam through the television sets of friends and classmates, as well as my own. In Manchester, where I grew up, he was known by everyone, but not by me, although, like Phaethon, I basked in his reflected glory, enjoying and bragging about the connection. He made speeches that were recorded in Hansard; conducted hustings in draughty halls and entertained as an after dinner speaker, night after night; I can still remember my awe as he crowned a local beauty queen: both appeared dazzling from my position on the ground, and this reminded me of

Phaethon's amazement at Phoebus's beaming crown. One of my few mementos of my father since his death is a video of the announcement of the voting in the first general election that he won as MP for Cheadle and Hazel Grove, in 1966. The video shows clearly the few minutes that were the happiest of his life. It is not often that a video captures such a moment, but his aura and delight beams through the footage, as he leans, amongst the excited clapping and cheers, to hug my mother. Like Phaethon, my experience of my father was of that of a beaming presence, omnipresent to everyone, but not present to me. In discussing this story with the editor, he reminded me of Leonardo de Vinci's comment that the sun can never see a shadow. If you are the sun, you are inevitably always in the sunshine, and maybe you cannot see what lurks in the shadows. Likewise, if you are the child of the sun, it can be hard to see yourself as a separate human being.

All children want to feel 'special', but this is much harder if the parent is revered on the public stage, and absent from home. What must it be like for other children of famous, 'god-like' parents—for Prince William, for example, walking in the shadow of a famous mother, Princess Diana, whose early and tragic death only elevated her further to almost immortal status; or for the sons of Tony Blair (and children of other prime ministers), as he is seen daily in handshakes with foreign dignitaries or grappling across the dispatch box of the Commons—is he still there to help with homework and play football? Growing up in the shadow of another can create a complex net of emotions, which can tangle up one's sense of identity and role.

Like many powerful magnates, Phoebus never seriously believed anyone other than himself could bring in the sun—not even Jupiter, the king of the gods. He is all-powerful and unique. If only Phaethon had followed in the footsteps of his mortal stepfather, Merops, he would have inherited a kingdom and been groomed in the arts of leadership. This is a key dilemma of adolescence—whether to follow fantastical dreams and whims, or take a more solid established path to adulthood. As a young adult, I tried to follow in my father's footsteps, studying politics at university and becoming chair of the students' union; I was well along the path to becoming an MP in his wake, then, when the ride began to feel bumpy, I suffered from debilitating asthma, tired from breathing air into this image of myself. Unlike Phaethon, I voluntarily threw myself off the chariot: my descent was bruising, but only slightly so.

The desire to emulate famous, god-like fathers, and prove oneself through imitation, can paradoxically lead not to confirmation of identity and kinship, but to a doomed existence where one is a poor replica, a shadow of oneself. So, then, Phaethon's is the sad story of a child who yearns for his father, and seeks identification with him, but fails to construct a viable identity of his own (De Levita 1965: 76–95). Newbold (2001: 175) suggests that father identification is an essential part of our identity formation; but the absence of the father renders it impossible for Phaethon to shed his infantile ego-ideal and develop a more mature identity of his own, as separate from that of the ideal of the father. It is not easy for an ordinary mortal to create a mature identity through identification with a father who is a Sun God, who is omnipresent and absent at the same time; Phaethon failed in his attempt to become like his ego-ideal, while I abandoned mine when I found it to be unattainable.

One meaning of identity, discussed at length by de Levita (1965), is the social identity bestowed upon us by others, and this is the catalyst for Phaethon's journey. Our peers are our mirrors, acknowledging the sense of self that we project to them. When the image we have of ourselves, and wish others to have of us, becomes violently severed from the way others actually see us, there can be deep inner turmoil and crisis, particularly in those teenage years when our sense of self is so fragile that it cannot ward off the battering of peers. Fragmented and disjointed identities are the source and manifestation of many psychiatric disorders, such as, for example, borderline personality disorder. It is really no wonder that Phaethon splits in two, the fearless warrior on a mission to prove himself, and the fearful boy, anxious and afraid. Phaethon provides an almost archetypical example of someone who is in search of identity, with delusions of grandeur and aspirations to emulate a god-like state. He is part of an impressive and diverse company of mortals who appear in Ovid's text, and whose transformations, whether defence mechanisms, punishments, rewards, or spontaneous manifestations of an inner essence, can be detected in modern life as a feature of the human condition under social stress and personal crisis. *Fiducia Formae*—having faith in one's form of beauty, and being unassailable in terms of identity and shape—is shaken to the core by Ovid in every possible way. Changing identity, whether it is an assumed change, such as Phaethon's taking on his father's mantle, or a forced change, such as when Phaethon is destroyed by his grandiosity and his sisters are turned into trees, is an unsettling idea, developed in a myriad of ways by Ovid.

[handwritten margin note: this is what Ovid is writing about.]

The story of Phaethon can be seen as that of an identity crisis played out at the physical and the psychological, the earthly and the god-like levels, using the device of uncertain parentage to light the fuse which sets the explosions in train. In facing their identity crises, Epaphus and Phaethon fit well into patterns of adolescent narcissism, manifested in 'self-absorption, delight in boasting and insult, sensitivity to shame and mockery, self-inflation, delusions of grandeur' (Newbold 2001: 175). As Newbold suggests, 'Most fantasies of power betray an underlying narcissism as they replace feelings of helplessness and separation with those of mastery and control' (p. 175). Phaethon's identity crisis exhibits itself in narcissism, and seeks resolution through merging with a father figure in order to assume mastery and control, and to gain the admiration of others. The greater the power of the father, the more helpless the child, and the stronger the fantasy of omnipotence becomes.

Rites of Passage and Contemporary Family Life

In contemplating my personal retake of the Phaethon story, I realised that they were other aspects of family life that it also reflected: beyond the identity crises of adolescence, and its delusions of grandeur, the story also comments more broadly on the social rites of passage into adulthood. In contemporary life, with the help of the media, we often find ourselves as voyeurs of the tragic and comic aspects of growing up. This theme is played out exhaustively in dramas, soap operas, and films (such as American Beauty, or The Graduate), where audiences are fascinated by the personal tragedies that can mark the transition through adolescence and middle age. Viewed from this angle, Phaethon's story highlights the confusion, bravado, and recklessness of male adolescence, and the rituals in which it seeks solace. Using the humorous style of an American high school heist, McHugh (1986) frames the story as a teenage son borrowing his father's Ferrari in order to take his girlfriend to a prom.

Here is an extract from the tale:

> "Phaethon, my son." Called the noble god in surprise.
> "Why do you come here to this lofty garage?
> What do you seek? ...
> Answered this: "Dad, I've got a problem,
> And I really need your help. You see.

There's this girl. I like her a lot. We're
Going to the Prom together, if the Fates
Be with me." ...
"Well Dad,
It's like this, I told her my father was a god.
She said that modern technology disproved
The existence of all gods. She said she learned that fact
In her Computer Math class. Now I'm beginning
To believe it myself, and I'm the son of a God!
Isn't there some way that I could prove our existence?"
(*after some sighing and stalling*)
... The Sun God said "... If your girlfriend
Wants proof, she shall have it; ... Go on ask me anything."
Phaethon got right to the point. "I need some wheels, Dad"
He said, looking fondly at the Sun God's Ferrari
Now gleaming from its recent waxing.
"I can't take my girl to the Prom unless I have a car.
Taking her in a god's Ferrari would be really cool." ...

Phaethon, the hot-headed boy struggling to be accepted by his peers, wants to be seen as 'cool', a James Dean of the skies. However, rather than assert his identity, as in the ancient heroic tradition, through a series of deeds that build his strength and character and win him the respect of others, he attempts, like many a rash adolescent, to do it with a single act of emulation and self-destruction—he crashes his dad's 'car'.

Branding the Image

It is telling then that the car industry has seen the marketing potential of branding a vehicle that can be associated with a spectacular teenage crash. Pelzer (2002) discusses the choice of Volkswagen to call their new car the 'Phaeton',[6] and asks why 'they chose the name of the first car crash victim in history'. Apparently, the Volkswagen speaker claimed the car had survived without damage despite the driver's demise. The branding of Phaeton, and the act of integrating the driver's name into the vehicle, begs comparison with the chariot of the sun, and can be seen as a symbol of mankind's aspiration to god-like status. The death of the driver does not so much suggest the failure of the vehicle, as it does its super-human power, which would take more than adolescent power to control. Cars and other fast machines have notoriously been extensions of the adult male ego, masculinity, power, and sexual prowess. Donald Campbell and his illustrious father Malcolm were between them 'the joint architects of 11 speed records on water as well 10 on land'. Tremayne (2003) tells the story of this fated son's emulation of the father. Donald grew up in his father's shadow, a hero of land speed records, a strict disciplinarian who sent his son to prep school at eight years, where the boy is said to have sold his father's autograph and 'basked in the reflected glory of having the fastest man on earth as a parent'. Donald grew up yearning to be like him, but also feeling that nothing he could do would ever be quite good enough. In watching an early film, his widow commented 'There was this little boy, so proud of his father, and his father didn't even notice...', yet he worshipped him. Like Phaethon, no proof of his own capability was enough, and he took over

---

[6]   One might argue that already in the past 'Phaeton' was the name of a well-known, light, and sporty type of open four-wheeled carriage for two horses—yet the contradiction inherent in the mythological allusion remains ... 'Phaeton' (an alternative Latin form of the name and a long-established French spelling) is also considered easier to pronounce than 'Phaethon'.

Sir Malcolm's speedboat *Bluebird* after his father's death. It was in a later version Bluebird K7 that he attempted to break the 300 mph barrier in 1966 on Coniston Water. At a speed estimated at 328 mph, '*Bluebird* climbed inexorably into the sky before flipping back into the murky waters of the lake', (Tremayne 2003). Ironically, less than ten years later, I swam across Coniston Water above the wreck of Bluebird, in an attempt to impress my father who chugged alongside in his boat, on one of his few breaks from work ...

Public Retakes—Space Travel, Consumption, and Spectacle

It is not just the car industry that sees the commercial opportunity of a spectacle; this contemporary 'retake' is conducted through the eyes of the ever-present media, where stories have many facets, exploited in the search for understanding, 'truth', and an audience. It is not just our personal, private, and family lives that come under scrutiny; the *camera oscura* also takes on the public realm and dissects it for private consumption.

Phaethon's conflagration in space evokes the treatment of a modern day spectacle by the mass media: there is fascination, dread, and awe at witnessing spectacles like airplanes being driven into buildings on 11 September 2001. In Glyn Maxwell's version of Phaethon (in Hofmann and Lasdun, 1994: 65–78), the story is told in a journalist fashion, as a series of interview fragments with the drama's different characters brought together in the manner of an investigative documentary. Clymene, Phaethon, the horses, a spokesperson of the sun, a scientist, and the people of Africa, each have an entirely different take, and the reader is left to sift through the evidence and make sense of the fragments of the tale. This postmodern narrative tradition is one which echoes the playful contradictions and metamorphoses of Ovid, and shifts both perspective and storyteller for the sake of dramatic effect and voyeuristic entertainment.

Here are some extracts from Maxwell (1994: 65–78):

> Film of Epaphus
>
> Epaphus, his friend,
> Now drunk, shakes him and leers. Was this the time
> He told him his father wasn't his father really
> And Phaeton, stunned,
>
> Backed into space?
> No this time he grins ...
> Eous (one of the horses)
>
> How did I know it was him?
>   When we were torn through clouds and the East wind
> I felt no weight on my back, heard no command,
> And felt no pull, no hand,
> No pilot. No escape now. Kingdom come.
>
> Three images, that's all.
>   One was his face, the boy, his face when he lost
> The reins and then his footing—that was the last
> We saw of him—he must
>   Presumably have gone in a fireball—

A Scientist

Would he have suffered? Would he have suffered pain?
Would he have suffered? Lady let me explain.
He bore the worst
Of Heaven, curved
With Poison, Scorpio! ...

Clymene, his mother

Death was instantaneous,
Death is always instantaneous.
Loss was instantaneous.
Loss is always.

The strong visual image of Phaethon exploding in the skies readily evokes the Challenger shuttle disaster, and the more recent Columbia crash. Space flight has parallels with the Phaethon myth: human beings trying to extend beyond this world and into the heavens, in the pursuit of omnipotence and god-like aspirations. It is eerie how similar to Maxwell's (1994) perspectives on Phaethon have been reports of the Columbia space shuttle disaster in 2003, encompassing testimonies of NASA scientists and safety experts, and the tributes of politicians and relatives. Here are four quotations from the *Observer*, on the day after the disaster (1 February 2003):

The Correspondent:

The space shuttle Columbia erupted in flames yesterday as it re-entered the Earth's atmosphere at 12,000 miles per hour, killing all seven crew members and plunging America into mourning and despair.

President Bush:

These men and women assumed a great risk in the service of all humanity. These astronauts knew the dangers and faced them willingly knowing they had a high and noble purpose in life.

James Milford—a Barber and Resident of Nacogdoches:

It's all over Nacogdoches. There are several little pieces, some parts of machinery ... there's been lots of pieces about three feet wide.

Ron Dittemore, Head of the Shuttle Programme:

'We cannot discount that there might be a connection' (referring to an earlier incident which resulted in loosening of a heat resistant tile). An hour before the disaster, transmission of data from hydraulic sensors sited on the left wing, stopped abruptly. 'It was as if someone had cut a wire'.

Our interest, capitalized on and nurtured by the media, can become voyeuristic and intrusive. An entire industry has developed around journalists and pundits, whose role is to interpret occurrences across the world or in space through the voices of whoever has an angle or story to give. The Challenger space shuttle disaster in 1986 spawned a host of investigations (the main one being Rogers Commission 1986), books (e.g. see McDonnell 1987), book chapters (such as Feynman 1993), case studies (e.g. Morgan 1989), articles, videos, films, and documentaries (such as the BBC *Panorama* broadcast 'The Dream that Fell out of the Sky', 28 April 1986, and even as recently as 2000, the BBC2 programme 'Challenger'), broadcast on 23 January of that year. The common threads that seem to preoccupy accounts of space spectacles derive from a fascination, in contemporary times, to find out what happened, who or what was to blame, what pain has been caused, and how people have reacted to it, at the political or personal level. As well as seeking detail, there is a drive to seek meaning and make sense of it all.

In seeking the meaning of such events, Phaethon's story can be instructive. It is well-established that the Challenger's mission was not meant as a scientific breakthrough, but rather as the symbolic illustration of America's political and technological dominance over the skies, and a celebration of its multicultural make-up: this was a flight intended to impress the world with American superiority. The symbol conjured by the flight was that of 'prevailing over death through competence' (Schwartz 1988: 10). Yet, and while crowds watched the flight on the frosty morning of 28 January, 1986, seventy-three seconds after take-off the shuttle exploded—killing the five men and two women astronauts. Like Phaethon, the astronauts were blind to the incompetences that lay behind the mission; like Phoebus, however, there were also those who knew of the catalogue of shortcomings that lay behind the plan, yet felt powerless to stop this compulsion to fly. We may question how Phoebus could knowingly send his son on such an ill-fated mission, but the experience of the Challenger suggests that opposition can be futile in the face of an exigency to satisfy the demands of a stubborn superego.

The Challenger accident was subsequently found to be the result of the poor design of the O-rings, the rocket's safety seals on the field joints which circled the circumference of the spacecraft. These had been known to erode at low temperatures. Robert Boisjoly, an engineer, had declared in a letter earlier, to Robert Lund, Vice President of Engineering at Morton Thiokol, that 'it is my honest and very real fear that if we do not take immediate action to dedicate a team to solve the problem, with the field joint having the number one priority, then we stand in jeopardy of losing a flight along with all the launch pad facilities'. Later, Robert Lund was to recommend that no launch take place at temperatures of less than 53°C, and on that chilly morning the temperature was around 28°C. This information was available, the part had even been on the criticality list, and yet they still proceeded to fly.

The political and managerial will to proceed proved irresistible. One senior engineer at NASA exclaimed that under Lund's recommendation, 'we would be unable to launch until April!' There was a sense of urgency—the President, and NASA, needed, like Phaethon, to prove themselves immediately. The shuttle had cost the nation millions of dollars, $5 billion had been spent on a space shuttle programme which went back to the 1970s and to Richard Nixon's desire to woo the sunbelt's aerospace industries, a key heartland for the Republican vote, at a time when Vietnam and Watergate were eroding confidence in the American administration. Subsequently, President Reagan's 1982 policy consisted of two priorities—maintaining US leadership in space and expanding private-sector involvement and investment. At the time of the launch, President Reagan was relying on his talking directly with Christa McAuliffe, the teacher launched into space to give lessons from the skies, to boost his popularity. This, then, was part of the American Dream, turned into a narcissistic fantasy to match Phaethon's adolescent delusions of grandeur. The president and the space industry were both in need of reassurance.

Robert Boisjoly continued strenuously to voice his concerns. In his account to the Presidential Commission of Inquiry, he said: 'Mr Mason said we had to make a management decision. He turned to Bob Lund and asked him to take off his engineering hat and put on this management hat. From this point on, management formulated the points to base their decision on.'

From this point on, the flight was doomed; like Phaethon, they were not willing to let lack of technical competence, or the fear of failure, stand in their way. In the face of obsessive compulsion, technical incompetence as well as risks and fears can be overlooked. The experience of Challenger suggests that the fantasy of omnipotence in the skies, of power and mastery in times of national identity crisis and insecurity, can lead to almost anything.

Of course there are key differences. NASA (the National Aeronautics and Space Administration) and all its subcontracting organizations are not the same as one boy. Real stories of space flight involve millions of hours of arduous labour, whereas a myth can dream up a palace, gods, and unbelievable flights and drama in seconds, without having to go through the arduous process of creation. However, marketing, advertising, and the media can blur the edges between reality and fiction, where the launch of space shuttles becomes a Disneyland-in-space (Schwartz 1988), and where even the branding of a new car becomes a heroic adventure. Myths such as Phaethon can offer a commentary on our times, but they can also be used to lure us with their glitter to consume, lock, stock, and barrel, the story, the image, and the product.

On its own, a technological disaster does not make as powerful a story as one which incorporates human suffering and the individual at its centre. Each story unfolds into another. In his television broadcast to the nation on 28 January 1986, Reagan alluded to someone else's aspirations in the skies, when he concluded his tribute to the Challenger crew with the words: 'We will never forget them this morning as they prepared for their journey and waved goodbye and slipped the surly bonds of earth to touch the face of God.' President Bush more recently made similar allusions in tribute to the Columbia crew. In researching Phaethon, this quotation drove me to seek out its origin. I was fascinated to discover another story which also seemed to capture some of Phaethon's spirit. Reagan was quoting 'High Flight', a sonnet written by John Gillespie Magee, a pilot with the Royal Canadian Air Force in the Second World War. Magee was killed at the age of nineteen, on 11 December 1941, during a training flight from the airfield near Scopwick, having come to Britain to fly in a Spitfire squadron (Rees 1992). In a letter to his parents, Magee says 'I am enclosing a verse I wrote the other day. It started at 30,000 feet and was finished soon after I landed'. The full text of the poem is:

> Oh! I have slipped the surly bonds of Earth
> And danced the skies on laughter-silvered wings;
> Sunward I've climbed and joined the tumbling mirth of sun-split clouds,
> And done a hundred things you have not dreamed of
> Wheeled and soared and swung
> High in the sunlit silence. Hov'ring there,
> I've chased the shouting wind along, and flung
> My eager craft through footless falls of air ...
> Up, up the long, delirious, burning blue
> I've topped the wind-swept heights with easy grace
> Where never lark, nor ever eagle flew—
> And, while with silent lifting mind I've trod

The high, untrespassed sanctity of space,
Put out my hand and touched the face of God.

('High Flight' was published in 1943 in a volume called 'More Poems
from the Forces', here transcribed by Rees from the original manuscript
in the Library of Congress, and quoted by Rees 1992.)

Magee, like Phaethon, fell to and was buried on earth. Parts of his poem are engraved on his gravestone amid the military graves at Scopwick in Lincolnshire; he has been acclaimed as an early poet of the Second World War. In the same way that Nigel Rees talks of being drawn to visit Magee's grave, where even the petrol pump attendant at the service station was immediately able to size up his interest and direct him to the burial ground, so I, too, felt compelled to visit the Challenger Grave at the Arlington Cemetery in Washington during a visit to the USA, where NASA and the White House can be viewed at a distance. The images of the explosion which filled the TV coverage, and the pictures taken whilst silently contemplating the grave, are still present with me today; like Phaethon's sisters, I felt rooted to the spot.

Concluding Comments

This journey through stories of Phaethon began with Ovid. Ovid's myths are about being playful with the banality of human existence, and his interests are human and contemporary:

Ovid takes mythology as a free space in which to play, in which to mock and extend, embrace, reject, invent and foreclose as he sees fit. He transposes it to the most familiar terms by removing that which is distant, divine, or supernatural and making the stories purely human and contemporary instead; his mythological world is very matter of fact. He turns mythology away from its concentration on the general and the generic, toward the illumination of unique moments in the life of the individual.

(Solodow 1998: 75).

Ovid is prescient; the multi-dimensionality of stories, and the confusion between truth and fiction, fact and interpretation, is a current concern, but it is forestalled by Ovid, who enables the plasticity of his stories to celebrate metamorphosis and change. He baffles our senses as we soar from one level to the other, left reeling like Phaethon, like a fragment caught up in the chaos of the universe. His multi-dimensional approach to Phaethon, in his constant changing of register from distant to close, from the human to the supernatural, from exaggeration to understatement, underscores the plurality of ways in which a myth can be absorbed and interpreted. Ovid is an irreverent storyteller, something that keeps him apart from some of his more serious contemporaries such as Virgil, possibly a reason too for his exile from Rome by Augustus; he also knows how to tell a good story.

Ovid gives us just one author's perspective of Phaethon. The story of Phaethon had already been stolen by Ovid from others. Euripides had also written about this ancient myth and other authors had chosen different focal points—Heliades for example had concentrated on the story of Phaethon's sisters. Every writer taking up an ancient myth has their own tale to tell, their own angle of retake or deceit. It is not just authors and authorial intention, however, that breathe life into myths—the reader also has his or her own retake and motive. Barthes (1995: 127–9) has argued that: 'To give a text an Author is to impose a limit on that text, to furnish it with a final signified, to close the writing.'

Myths exist outside and beyond the author. But this does not mean that we have to go as far as Barthes, and kill the author, moving away from seeing 'him or her' as someone who nourishes a story or myth 'in the same relation of antecedence to his work as a father is to his child'. The handing down of a myth or a story from father to son, from mother to daughter, is an important part of its life; each telling and each reinterpretation creates the space for many more authors and readers.

We become attached to some myths, so that we may treat them as our personal property to mould to our will. But we cannot stop others from doing the same—no more than Ovid could stop Volkswagen from appropriating his Phaethon, or Euripides could stop Ovid, in turn, from doing the same. Nor can the families of the Challenger or Columbia victims prevent the stories of their children proliferating in the newspapers and media.

The power of a myth is to make thieves of us all; we may appropriate it in order to use it as our own lens. Myths, such as Phaethon's, can represent a number of different things to us, personal or social, entertainment or spectacle, product or branding, thrill or tragedy. Myths, more than any other type of story expand beyond the boundaries of their authors: they are gifts from one generation to the next, and belong to us all.

References

Barthes, R. (1995). 'The Death of the Author', in S. Burke (ed.), *From Plato to the Post Modern*. Edinburgh: Edinburgh University Press. (Originally his preface to Brillat-Savarin's *The Physiology of Taste*, 1971).

Blake, W. (1789/1967). *Songs of Innocence and of Experience: Showing the Two Contrary States of the Human Soul*, a reproduction of the original. Oxford: Oxford University Press.

Diggle, J. (ed.) (1970). *Euripides Phaethon*. Cambridge: Cambridge University Press.

Feynman, R. (1993). *What Do You Care What Other People Think*. London: HarperCollins, Part 2.

Hofmann, M. and Lasdun, J. (1994). *After Ovid: New Metamorphoses*. London: Faber and Faber.

Hughes, T. (1997). *Tales from Ovid*. London: Faber and Faber.

Levita, D.J. de (1965). *The Concept of Identity*. New York: Basic Books. [Section 111 'Intermezzo—Phaethon'; 76–83.]

McDonnell (1987). *Challenger: A Major Malfunction*. New York: Simon and Schuster.

McHugh, P. (1986). 'Phaethon Goes Back to the Future', winner of Classical Association of New England Essay Contest, 1995, published in *New England Classical Newsletter*.

Maxwell, G. (1994). 'Phaethon and the Chariot of the Sun—fragments of an Investigative documentary', in M. Hofmann and J. Lasdun (eds.), *After Ovid: New Metamorphoses*. London: Faber and Faber.

Morgan, G. (1989). 'The Challenger Disaster: A Case of Discouraged Feedback', in G. Morgan *Creative Organisation Theory*. London: Sage, 1–4.

Newbold, R.F. (2001). 'Narcissism and Leadership in Nonnus'. *Dionysiaca' Helios*, 28(2): 173–90.

Ovid (1987). *Metamorphoses*. (tr A.D. Melville) Oxford: Oxford University Press (with introduction and notes by E.J. Kenney).

Pelzer, P. (2002). 'Art for Management's Sake? A Doubt' unpublished paper.

Rees, N. (1992). 'High Flier' in *The* "quote ... unquote". *Newsletter*, 1(2).

Rogers Commission (William P. Rogers, Chair) (1986). Report to the President by the Presidential Commission on the Space Shuttle Challenger Accident, Printing Office, Washington, DC.

Schwartz, H. (1988). 'The Symbol of the Space Shuttle and the Degeneration of the American Dream'. *Journal of Organizational Change Management*, 1(2): 5–20.

Solodow, J.B. (1988). *The World of Ovid's Metamorphoses*. Chapel Hill: University of North Carolina Press.

Tremayne, D. (2003). *Donald Campbell: The man behind the mask*, Transworld; and quotes drawn from article of the same title by D. Tremayne, in *Classic and Sportscar Magazine*, 1997.

Wise, V. (1976–77) 'Flight Myths in Ovid's Metamorphosis: An interpretation of Phaethon and Daedalus'. *RAMUS*, 5–6: 44–57.

Secondary Source 3.6   Andrew Zissos and Ingo Gildenhard, 'Problems of time in *Metamorphoses 2*'

(Source: Hardie, P., Barchiesi, A. and Hinds, S (eds) (1999) *Ovidian Transformations: Essays on The Metamorphoses and its Reception*, Cambridge, Cambridge Philological Society, pp. 31–47)

1. Time flies

In book 2 of the *Metamorphoses*, as numerous scholars have observed, Ovid's chronology of mythological time seems to go awry.[1] Inconsistencies in sequence and causality arise with surprising frequency, as linear time is repeatedly made to collapse – to fragment, skip forward, or fall back on itself. Unstable and shifting temporal structures result in radical departures from a straightforward chronological sequence. Attempts have been made to explain these temporal rifts by appeals to Ovid's impressionist mode of composition,[2] but there are strong indications that the poet's erratic chronology is a deliberate and self-conscious effect.[3] In particular, Ovid devotes a good deal of space at the beginning of book 2 to forging a strong symbolic link between the mechanics of time and the movement of the sun. Thus the subsequent coincidence of temporal disruption and ostentatiously random solar motion in the Phaethon episode suggest a purposeful deviation from a 'natural' temporal sequence – and one with a precise philosophical underpinning.[4]

The connection between time and solar flight was no doubt a commonplace for many of Ovid's contemporary readers. Among earlier writers, Plato had posited a providential connection between time and the movement through the sky of heavenly bodies, suggesting that the latter 'were created by [God] in order to

[1] Diggle (1970) 196; Coleman (1971) 463: Galinsky (1975) 93–4; Mack (1988) 110–11: cf. Anderson (1997) 251.

[2] E.g. Galinsky (1975) 93–4.

[3] Deviations from 'natural' temporal sequence are fairly common in modern fiction, and critics have begun to explore more systematically the differences (or potential differences) between the temporal structures of fiction and those of 'reality.' As Ronen (1994) 202 has observed 'Fictional worlds allow, in principle at least, radical deviations form the regularities of time in the actual world. That is, fictional worlds can include time paradoxes where time is presented as reversible or bilateral ... Such cases reveal that fictional time forms part of a separate, although analogous, world system.'

[4] In a forthcoming study of Seneca's *Thyestes*, to which the present analysis is much indebted, Alessandro Schiesaro suggests that the reversal of the sun's course is a motif in Senecan tragedy that sometimes evokes the notion of temporal regression in the context of morally depraved acts. Cf. Sen. *Med.* 28–31: *... spectat hoc nostri sator | Sol generis, et spectatur, et curru insidens | per solita puri spatia decurrit poli? | non redit in ortus et remetitur diem?*

distinguish and preserve the numbers of time' (*Tim.* 38c).[5] For Greeks and
Romans alike, time was virtually indistinguishable from periodic celestial
motion: the only reliable means of marking its passage was by the cyclic
recurrence of heavenly bodies in flight.[6] Hence the importance of the sun, whose
course determined two of the three 'natural' divisions of time, solar year and day.[7]
As the swiftest and most mobile of the heavenly bodies, the sun inevitably came
to be thought of as creating and controlling time through its very movement.[8] In
his nostalgic compendium of scientific lore, Macrobius would make this equation
explicit, stating that time was simply the product of the *cursus soli* (*Sat.* 2.10.9).

2. The palace of the Sun

The poetic universe which unfolds in the opening books of the *Metamorphoses*
constitutes a creative fusion of philosophical speculation and a rampantly
anthropomorphic theology. In such a complex and eclectic narrative domain, the
interdependence of solar motion and chronology would need to be strongly
signalled at the outset in order to be appreciated by the reader. In this case,
the signalling takes place in the ecphrasis of the palace of Sol at the opening of
book 2, where the association of the sun with time is symbolically established.
After dwelling on the external artwork, Ovid proceeds to offer a detailed
description of the scene inside the palace, where Sol sits surrounded by allegorical
figures which 'symbolize his close association with the orderly passage of time':[9]

> purpurea velatus veste sedebat
> in solio Phoebus claris lucente smaragdis.
> a dextra laevaque Dies et Mensis et Annus
> Saeculaque et positae spatiis aequalibus Horae ... (2.23–6)

> Clad in a purple gown, Phoebus sat on a throne glittering with
> emeralds. To the left and right [stood] Day and Month and Year,
> along with the Centuries and the Hours, arrayed at equal intervals ...

The sun's status as supreme temporal regulator has evidently carried over into
the mythological domain, where Sol is portrayed as a divine 'patriarch of time'.
The interplay between physics and mythology is thus mediated by the figure of
the sun-god, through which Ovid has elevated a social convention (time) to the
level of a character with its own narrative identity. In this respect, the initial
image of the patriarch is noteworthy for its overtones of power, control,
and order: the cosmos, it would appear, is in good hands. Personifications of
the 'natural' temporal divisions (day, month, year) are appropriately located in
Sol's palace, and the poet lists them together on the same line. Included with
them, but grouped together on the following line, are the 'artificial' divisions
of *Horae* and *Saecula*. By grouping natural and artificial units on separate lines
the poet offers an implicit typology of chronological registers.

[5]   On the interrelation of time and the heavens cf. *Tim.* 38b: 'Time and the Heavens came into being at the same instant in order that, having been created together, if there ever were to be a dissolution of them, they might be dissolved together.'

[6]   Dicks (1970) 123.

[7]   The months are controlled by the moon, often considered to be the sister of Sol, as here by Ovid (cf. 2.208–9). Anderson (1997) 251 suggests that the sibling relationship arises primarily through syncretism of Apollo–Sol and Diana–Luna.

[8]   For the belief that the sun was the swiftest of the heavenly bodies see Sen. *QNat.* 1.3.10. The sun's status as supreme temporal indicator was no doubt reinforced by the calendar reform of Julius Caesar in 46 BCE.

[9]   Anderson (1997) 229: cf. Brown (1987) 213.

The physical deployment of the *Horae*, often depicted as divine attendants to Sol, is striking.[10] Ovid takes special care in describing these figures, which are most obviously subject to the movement of the sun: indeed, their arrangement is reminiscent of a sundial. In Roman times, the days (and the nights) were divided into twelve equal hours, whose length varied according to season. Thus, the hours themselves were not fixed temporal units; it was their proportionate division of the daylight period, that is, the relative spacing of the individual hours over the course of the day that was important. This spacing was of course rendered concretely: the hours were marked at equal intervals on sundials, and it seems to be this device that lies behind the deployment of the hours in equal intervals about the sun-god. Thus the phrase *spatiis aequalibus* (2.26), with its pun on the spatial and temporal meaning of *spatium*, perfectly encapsulates the reprocessing of temporal orderliness in physical terms. As a result, the dependence of the operation of time upon the sun is insinuated in a particularly effective manner.

Likewise, the presence of allegorical figures of the seasons suggests Sol's status as the divine patriarch presiding over the annual cycle of time. As Robert Brown has observed, the symmetrical textual arrangement of the four seasons, with each being assigned exactly one verse, again reflects a principle of properly ordered time:[11]

> Verque nouum stabat cinctum florente corona
> stabat nuda Aestas et spicea serta gerebat,
> stabat et Autumnus calcatis sordidus uuis
> et glacialis Hiems canos hirsute capillos. (2.27–30)

> Youthful Spring stood wrapped in a crown of flowers; naked Summer stood wearing a wreath of corn; there too stood Autumn, stained from the trampling of grapes; and frosty Winter, with shaggy grey hair.

Taken as a whole, the ecphrasis offers both a visual and textual instantiation of temporal regularity, thereby underscoring the sun's status as universal guarantor of consistent chronology.[12] By its unvarying annual movement the sun determines the seasons of the year, and the poet offers an equality of verse length to match the uniform duration of the seasons themselves.[13] Both by textual organization and by physical arrangement, Ovid creates a picture of well-ordered time. But, as Brown notes of other aspects of the description of the palace of the Sun, this harmonious scene serves to throw into relief the subsequent chronological ruptures.[14] At the opening of book 2, Ovid presents a picture of universal order so as to provide a backdrop against which the chaotic disorder caused by Phaethon may be more fully appreciated. In a similar fashion, the image of well-ordered temporality, focused around Sol as 'time guardian,' establishes a standard of normalcy against which the subsequent chronological distortions are more readily perceived.[15]

[10]   The *Horae* had become more strongly associated with hours than seasons by the Roman period (e.g. Virg. *Aen.* 3.512; Val. Fl. 4.92; Stat. *Theb* 3.410). For the *Horae* as divine attendants of the Sun god cf. Val. Fl. 4.92.

[11]   Brown (1987) 214.

[12]   Denis Feeney suggests that even this picture may be partially destabilized by cross-reference to the *Fasti*, which will install Janus as Chaos at 2.25–30.

[13]   Moreover, from the third century BCE onwards, sundials which marked the date and season were common: see Gibbs (1976), 7–8.

[14]   Cf. Brown (1987) 214.

[15]   Cf. Ronen (1994), 200, who observes that the analogy between actual and fictional temporality is 'one of the strongest conventions assumed by readers of fiction'.

3. The chariot ride

Through this ever-renewed journey across the sky, Sol brings the day into existence and takes it out of existence. As noted earlier, the endless and precise repetition of solar motion was thought to constitute the essential determinant of nature's law of ordered time. Ovid affirms this notion of precise repetition with the intriguing description of the sun's path marked in the sky (*manifesta... uestigia*, 2.133).[16] But here scientific notions collide with the anthropomorphic theology of the *Metamorphoses*. Erratic solar motion is introduced into the narrative when Phaethon, ignoring his father's pleas, insists on attempting to ride Sol's chariot. The young boy thus assumes responsibility for conveying the light of the sun across the sky, and thereby marking and controlling the passage of one day (cf. *diem*, 2.48). Once the journey is under way, it does not take long for Phaethon's adventure to go drastically wrong. The youth is not up to the task; he proves unable to control the chariot as he rides through the sky, and his journey takes on a chaotic aspect. The chariot veers off its habitual course (*tritumque relinquunt ... spatium*, 2.167–8), now approaching too close to earth, now too close to heaven.[17] Not only is the chariot ride itself chaotic, so are its effects; the Phaethon tale becomes an adventure narrative with cosmic repercussions. The poet provides both a description of vast celestial displacements and a lengthy account of the heat-induced transformations of the earth's surface caused by Phaethon's excessively close passage (2.201–71).

Finally, as the fate of the universe hangs in the balance, Tellus calls upon Jupiter for assistance – or at least a speedy resolution of the situation. The goddess laments in *chaos antiquum confundimur* (2.299). This harks back to the opening of the poem, to the description of the original *Chaos* (1.7) which existed before the universe came into being, and suggests the possibility of chronological regression.[18] In Tellus' complaint that the erratic solar course is causing a reversion to the original state of chaos there is an explicit temporal dimension (*antiquum*) to the cosmic destruction. Here there is a strong hint that time is among the disintegrating cosmic hierarchies caused by the erratic course of Sol's chariot through the heavens.[19]

[16]   It might further be noted that Sol's admonition to Phaethon to maintain a precise distance between Earth and Heaven (2.134–7) offers a close echo, unmentioned by Bömer (1969) ad loc., of Xenophon's description at *Mem*. 4.3.8 of the sun on its voyage around the earth, careful never to approach too close to the planet for fear of scorching the inhabitants, but likewise careful not to veer too far away for fear of freezing them. Once again, a reference to Socratic thought looks likely. Cf. Plato's discussion of the myth at *Tim*. 22c–23b, in which the interlocutor attempts a scientific explanation for Phaethon's 'inability to drive the horses in the path of his father'.

[17]   The language used to describe the route invests Phaethon's chariot ride with a metapoetic force. In the phrase *tritumque ... spatium* there is a suggestive echo of the 'well-known highways' of Callimachus. Likewise, Sol's aforementioned advice against deviations in the chariot's course: *hac sit iter, manifesta rotae uestigia cernes* (2.133) is couched in poetological language. These 'wheeltracks' (*uestigia*) in the sky are a remarkable touch, which, as Kenney (1986) 386 notes, commentators have strangely passed over in silence. The item *uestigia* had taken on in earlier Roman poets a well-established poetological signification. The image of the poet 'making tracks' had been popularized by Callimachus in the prologue to the *Aetia*, where the word ἴχνια (1.26) became a poetological trope. Hor. *Epist*. 1.19 employs the Latin equivalent *uestigia* for a claim of poetic innovation (cf. Lucr. 3.3–4; Virg. *Georg*. 3.291–2). The word *uestigium*, then, has a clear poetological pedigree. Ovid exploits such language to inform his deviations from accepted narrative decorum with a level of self-consciousness: it is precisely when the chariot leaves the 'well-worn highway' (*tritumque relinquunt ... spatium*. 2.167–8) that temporal paradox arises.

[18]   Cf. Stephen Hinds' similar comments in this volume, 61, on the same phrase at *Ibis* 83–4.

[19]   The suggestion of temporal regression voiced here by Tellus undermines the proleptic references to subsequent episodes in the description of the disastrous chariot ride (*nondum Oeagrius Haemon*, 2.219; *arsurusque iterum Xanthus*, 2.245). The progressive 'temporal vector' of Ovid's epic is ruptured by Tellus' declaration that Phaethon's voyage is having a regressive chronological impact. Cf. Denis Feeney's interesting remarks on 2.364–6 and 2.538–9, in this volume, 27.

The reversal of time and the threatened reversion to original chaos suggest once again a philosophical correlation of time and the heavens. At *Tim.* 37d–e, Plato observes that 'days and nights and months and years did not exist before the heavens came into being' (πρὶν οὐρανὸν γενέσθαι). Time was a vital constituent of the universe that evolved from initial chaos: according to numerous ancient thinkers, it did not exist prior to universal creation. Thus Macrobius:

> cum chaos esset, tempora non fuisse, siquidem tempus est certa dimensio quae ex caeli conuersione colligitur. (Macrobius, *Saturnalia* 1.8.7)

> While Chaos lasted, time did not exist, since time has fixed measurements and those are determined by the revolution of the heavens.

The sun normally moves with precision on a fixed and regular course through the sky. But in the *Metamorphoses* passage the solar chariot moves through unfamiliar regions (2.202–3) and according to no cosmic law: *sine lege ruunt* (2.204). The phrase points to the loss of uniform periodic motion by which the heavenly body made possible the measurement, and even the existence, of time. This anomalous state is reinforced by the picture of the Moon seeing the solar chariot below her own:

> inferiusque suis fraternos currere Luna
> admiratur equos ... (2.208–9)

> The Moon is astonished to see her brother's horses running below her own ...

Here the two celestial bodies whose movements regulate all three 'natural' divisions of time (solar year, lunar month, and day) are shown to be wholly out of kilter. The sibling relationship that Ovid asserts between Sol and Luna helps to reinforce their paired status as temporal regulators, and thus to suggest the anomaly of their lack of respective alignment.

The result of Phaethon's haphazard course is a violation of the temporal mechanics of the cosmos, as laid out in such treatises as Plato's *Timaeus*. Given the philosophical underpinning outlined above, it is perhaps unsurprising that Phaethon's eccentric journey through the sky on Sol's chariot should result in numerous paradoxical effects, including temporal distortion. There is a radical destabilization of precisely those temporal norms that were instantiated in the palace ecphrasis at the beginning of book 2. This is seen in a number of chronological ruptures: the Triones are mentioned prior to their creation, while the waters forbidden to them (*uetito ... aequore*, 2.172) are mentioned in advance of the prohibition (2.527–31).[20] Ovid amusingly suggests that this constellation, which never sets in the ocean, tries to do so because of the intense heat. Likewise, the mountain Atlas is mentioned in the speech of Tellus (*Atlans en ipse laborat | uixque suis umeris candentem sustinet axem*, 2.296) in advance of its creation, which occurs more than two books later (4.631–2).[21]

---

[20]   Anderson (1997) 248 suggests that by calling the constellation *Triones* (Oxen) Ovid avoids direct anticipation of the story of Callisto. Ovid, however, does refer to the new constellation as *Triones* in the Callisto episode, which somewhat weakens the claim; moreover, Anderson's observation does not resolve the problem of the anticipated prohibition.

[21]   A further temporal anomaly arises from the fact that Phaethon finally falls into the Po river, which is still apparently flowing with water (cf. *abluit* 2.324), only moments after his disastrous chariot ride had dried it out (2.257–8). That the river is identified first by its conventional Latin name (*Padumque*, 2.258) and subsequently by its more legendary Greek name (*Eridanus*, 2.324) does little to obscure this gratuitous inconsistency, given that Ovid describes the desiccation of all western rivers.

4. Aftermath

The conclusion of the Phaethon episode serves to further elaborate the collapse of temporal norms. Ovid incorporates a series of endings, involving successive waves of distraught loved ones – grieving nymphs, grieving father, grieving mother, grieving sisters, grieving uncle, and then, rather bizarrely, grieving father once again. This is a veritable catalogue of endings, for most of which exemplars can be found in earlier poets.[22] In the curious repetition of closural gestures, and the encyclopedic approach to variants, the poet creates a very confusing chronological picture. At first glance, this might appear to be a developed instance of the kind of chronological blurring that Coleman in particular has addressed.[23] There is, however, a problematization of closure in this sequence, which results in a more radical effect than blurred chronology.[24] Though each 'ending' is more or less self-contained and satisfactory in itself, taken in combination they tend to contradict each other and thus disrupt the narrative time line. A brief examination of the closural sequence will demonstrate the temporal anomalies that arise. Following the death and burial of Phaethon, Ovid provides an account of paternal grief and its apparently short-lived cosmic implications:

> nam pater obductos luctu miserabilis aegro
> condiderat uultus: et si modo credimus, unum
> isse diem sine sole ferunt ... (2.329–32)

> For the wretched father hid his face in a veil of misery; and they say
> (if only we believe) that one day went by without the sun ...

The orderly routine of the heavens has been overturned; Phaethon's disaster has resulted in temporary annulment of the alternation of day and night. The loss of distinction between day and night is symptomatic of the disruption of natural order caused by the disastrous chariot ride. The breakdown of temporal mechanics is nicely evinced by the phrase *unum isse diem sine sole ferunt*, which constructs a beguiling contradiction. Since a day is defined by the movement of the sun across the sky, the measurement of this unit of time in the absence of solar motion is paradoxical in the extreme.[25] This sly reference to the sun's role as guarantor of temporal regularity problematizes linear chronology just as the episode appears to be drawing to a conclusion. The force of *unum* seems to place a limit to the term of active paternal grief: *one* day went by without the sun – but how?

Next follow the accounts of additional grieving relatives. First in the sequence is the mother Clymene, whose traversal of the whole world (*totum percensuit orbem*, 2.335) clearly implies the passage of a certain amount of time. Her grief

---

[22]   E.g. Euripides, *Phaethon*. Virg. *Aen.* 10.185–93 (for Cycnus), and possibly Aeschylus' (very fragmentary) *Heliades*, which obviously emphasized Phaethon's sisters, who formed the chorus and grieved for him after his death.

[23]   Coleman (1971) 463 offers a helpful discussion on the 'blurring of chronology needed to incorporate temporally parallel sequences of stories belonging to different geographical locations into a linear narrative line'; he is nonetheless mistaken in the assertion that, with the single exception of the Syrinx episode, there is an uninterrupted and linear chronological progression from the cosmogony to the end of the Callisto episode, overlooking the convoluted closure of the Phaethon episode.

[24]   An issue touched on by Bass (1977) 402, who notes that 'the question of the [Phaethon] episode's endpoint does not admit of a single, simple answer.'

[25]   The phrase *isse diem* underscores the paradoxical effect by making the day 'move' instead of the sun. Likewise Ovid's parenthetical *si modo credimus* prepares the reader for an impossibility.

is matched by Phaethon's sisters, the Heliades, whose term of grief is measured at no less than four months (*luna quater iunctis inplerat cornibus orbem*, 2.344). In the wake of their miraculous transformation into poplar trees, Phaethon's uncle Cycnus pines away until he becomes a swan (2.367–80).

At this point several months have clearly passed since Phaethon's death caused Sol to eclipse for a day. But rather remarkably, the grief narratives now come full circle with an incongruous reprise of the reaction of Sol (2.381–400). The *interea*, used to introduce this new sequence, seems to imply a recursive temporal structure, suggesting that an overlapping time sequence is being described. Nevertheless, it is unclear how far back *interea* is supposed to reach.[26] It is a little hard to imagine, given the passing of several months in the intervening grief sequences, that Ovid is returning to that initial day which passed without the light of the sun.

In his grief and anger, the bereaved Sol now goes on strike, refusing to provide the universe with its customary daylight (2.385–8). Ovid now describes the sun in continuous eclipse at 2.381–5. This is particularly problematic, because it reopens an issue that had seemed to be settled in the earlier account of Sol's grief (*unum | isse diem sine sole ferunt*, 2.330–1). If in the first scene the withdrawal of the sun had somehow been fixed at one day, now it appears to be rather more open-ended.

In the end, Jupiter's embassy to the striking sun-god combines pleas and (unspecified) threats in effective combination (2.394–7). Thus threatened, Sol immediately caves in, gathers together his frightened horses and resumes fulfilment of his cosmic duty. Ovid concludes with a description of the sun-god's smouldering anger and resentment which now find a convenient outlet:

> conligit amentes et adhuc terrore pauentes
> Phoebus equos stimuloque dolens et uerbere saeuit
> (saeuit enim) natumque obiectat et inputat illis. (2.398–400)

> Phoebus gathers his horses, still frenzied and fearful, and applies the goad and savage whip, blaming them in his rage for the death of his son.   *spite?*

The temporality of this scene is distinctly problematic. As Diggle notes, 'the description of Phoebus gaining control of his dazed horses (2.398–400) suggests the immediate sequel to the thunderbolt.' That is, the narrative seems to locate itself at the moment of Phaethon's death, obviously prior to the lamentation sequences that followed the burial. Moreover, the horses were last seen at 2.315, as they scattered in panic from the shattered chariot. But, to quote Diggle once again, 'there is no question here of repairing a wrecked chariot; that Phoebus at once applies the goad suggests that the horses are still in full career through the heavens rather than wandering aimlessly among the poplars on the banks of the Eridanus.'[27] It is worth recalling that Sol's chariot was last seen at 2.316–18, where it had been 'smashed to pieces, its splendid parts lying scattered far and wide'[28] to grasp the importance of Diggle's observations. In effect, in the bizarre conclusion of the Phaethon episode time is presented as reversible or, perhaps better, radically fragmented. Narrative 'reality' seems

---

[26]   For the use of *interea* as a conveniently vague temporal connective in epic narrative see Hardie (1994) 104.

[27]   Diggle (1970) 196.

[28]   Brown (1987) 215.

to be torn between competing variants, creating an obvious disruption of continuity and linear progress. Chronological order has succumbed to a kind of metaliterary multiplicity, and 'natural' temporal sequence has been abandoned.

5. Callisto: relative regression

Ovid's Callisto tale unfolds in the immediate aftermath of Phaethon's disaster, starting with Jupiter's inspection of the terrestrial damage resulting from the cataclysmic chariot ride. Indeed, Jupiter is described effecting a fresh act of universal re-creation, restoring order to the scorched universe, especially in Arcadia:

> ... Arcadiae taumen est inpensior illi
> cura suae, fontes et nondum audentia labi
> flumina restituit, dat terrae gramina, frondes
> arboribus laesasque iubet reuirescere siluas. (2.405–8)

> ... but Arcadia is his greater concern: he restores its fountains, and the rivers that still fear to flow; he gives grass to the ground, leaves to the trees, and he orders the damaged forests to grow green again.

The effect is to evoke a kind of palingenesis on the cosmic level, which is reinforced by reminiscences of the Callimachean *Hymn to Zeus*. The points of contact with the Hymn are three: first, the common location of Arcadia for both narratives. More specifically, the phrase *Arcadiae...suae* (2.405–6) signals the notorious claim of the Callimachean Hymn that Zeus was born in Arcadia (Callim. *Iou.* 6–9). Secondly, the absence of springs and rivers flowing in Arcadia (*fontes et nondum audentia labi | flumina*, 2.406–7) – a result of Phaethon's disaster in the *Metamorphoses* passage – invokes the primordial waterlessness of Arcadia in the Hymn (Callim. *Iou.* 18–20: ἔτι δ' ἄβροχος ἦεν ἅπασα Ἀρκαδίη μέλλεν δὲ μάλ εὔυδρος καλέεσθαι | αὖτις ...).[29] Thirdly, both narratives mention the triad of Callisto, Arcas and Lycaon.[30] These Callimachean reminiscences serve to evoke an act of universal creation, and this again hints at a movement backwards in universal time.

The close connection of the Callisto episode with the preceding Phaethon tale is reinforced through a further assault on the conventions of temporality. The Callisto tale continues and indeed escalates the rupture in chronological sequence by highlighting a breakdown in the chain of causation in Ovid's global narrative. This emphasis derives from a singular feature of the Callisto narrative – namely, that the heroine is never directly identified. The poet, apparently playing to the reader's erudition, persistently uses the device of antonomasia to refer to Callisto. In the earlier stages of the narrative she is referred to as *uirgine Nonacrina* (2.409), and *Parrhasis* (2.460). The adjective *Nonacrinus* (i.e. Arcadian) is an Ovidian coinage found in no other Latin authors;[31] the substantive *Parrhasis* is likewise first found in Ovid.[32] This is a deliberate effect: the heroine's identity is set up as a puzzle for the reader, who is provided with increasingly explicit clues as the narrative unfolds.

[29] Note furthermore the verbal parallel between *nondum* and ἔτι.

[30] Interestingly, Callisto is not explicitly named by Callimachus and this antonomastic ploy is picked up and further elaborated by Ovid, as discussed below.

[31] Bömer (1969) ad loc.

[32] Moore-Blunt (1977) ad loc. The coinage may constitute a further nod to the Callimachean *Hymn to Zeus*, which opens in that particular area of Arcadia (Callim. *Iou.* 10: ἐν δέ ... Παρρασίη). Cf. above, n. 30.

When Callisto's identity is made clear, the disclosure is made through mention of her son Arcas (2.468) and her father Lycaon (2.496).

As it happens, the identity of Callisto's father was a matter of considerable debate in ancient literature.[33] Ovid was certainly under no obligation to follow the tradition that Callisto was Lycaon's daughter, and her paternity is not directly relevant to the plot of the *Metamorphoses* tale. The choice is evidently a deliberate one, and the manner of Callisto's indirect identification by the poet only serves to increase attention on the question of paternity. Indeed, Callisto's father is progressively and rather craftily brought into focus. In an initial cryptic reference, the poet notes that his metamorphosed heroine is afraid of wolves even though her father is among them (*pertimuitque lupos, quamuis pater esset in illis*, 2.495). This recalls the narrative of book 1, where Lycaon's outrageous hospitality to Jupiter results in a punitive lupine transformation. In the following line, the poet explicitly identifies the heroine's father, Lycaon:[34]

> Ecce, <u>Lycaoniae</u> proles ignara <u>parentis</u>.
> Arcas adest ter quinque fere natalibus actis ... (2.496–7)

> And now Arcas had reached his fifteenth year, knowing nothing of his mother born of Lycaon ...

At this point, a chronological difficulty arises, one that Ovid clearly has been leading up to. No careful reader of the *Metamorphoses* could fail to recollect that Lycaon had attempted to kill Jupiter, while the latter was his guest.[35] Indeed, it was primarily because of Lycaon's wickedness that Jupiter decided to eradicate the entire human race. Since all mortal beings of Lycaon's era except Pyrrha and Deucalion were supposed to have perished in the flood (1.253–312), his presence and that of his progeny at this stage in the narrative is distinctly problematic. The usage of the patronymic *Lycaoniae* underscores the anachronism. The spectre of the narrative past, a past that should be beyond recall, is here creeping into the narrative present.

By emphatically identifying Callisto through her father, Ovid underscores the chronological contradiction in his narrative.[36] The disruption of continuity and linear progress is thus strongly marked. Indeed, the narrator draws attention to the tampering with temporal modality through the bitter outburst of Juno which follows. During her meeting with Tethys and Oceanus, Jupiter's jealous spouse ironically suggests that he should marry Callisto and take Lycaon as his father-in-law:

> cur non et pulsa ducit Iunone meoque
> conlocat in thalamo socerumque Lycaona sumit? (2.525–6)

> Why not, pushing me aside, marry her and set her in my bedchamber, taking Lycaon as father-in-law?

---

[33] For the different identifications of Callisto's father (Ceteus, Nycteus, Lycaon) see Sale (1965) 21.

[34] Anderson (1997) 291 opines that the marked separation of the Lycaon and Callisto episodes suggest that the relationship between them is 'gratuitous information'.

[35] As Due (1974) 181 points out, the murderous attempt on his guest Jupiter appears to be an Ovidian innovation. He further notes (ibid.) that Ovid makes Lycaon's earlier outrage worse: in Apollodorus he kills a boy from the neighbourhood: in the *Metamorphoses* he slaughters a foreign hostage. These innovations clearly make Lycaon all the more offensive to Jupiter in his capacity as protector of guests.

[36] Which distinguishes the Ovidian treatment from the more muted approach at Apollod. 3.98.

Juno's suggestion that a familial bond be established between Jupiter and Lycaon is clearly meant ironically to recall the antipathy of the pair as described in book 1.[37] But it also appears to imply that Lycaon is still alive, thereby further underscoring the departure from chronological consistency.[38] Ovid's genealogical connection of Callisto and Lycaon thus introduces a gratuitous breach in the narrative chain of causation.[39] Far from 'glossing over' the chronological contradiction, the Callisto episode is carefully structured to make it emphatic, so that time essentially falls back upon itself in this episode.

In fact there are further temporal rifts in the narrative. As mentioned earlier, the catasterism of Callisto and her son (2.505–7) creates a constellation that had already been mentioned in the Phaethon tale (2.171); here the two episodes work in tandem to problematize causality and chronological sequence. Likewise, Ovid's ingenious mythological explanation for the fact that the Great Bear constellation does not set (2.528–30) openly contradicts the earlier Phaethon passage in which the prohibition was clearly already in effect. As the Callisto tale is an aetiological myth intended to explain the origin of this prohibition, Ovid's causal and chronological inversions are particularly rich in paradoxical effect.[40]

6. Ocyrhoe: thinking ahead

The Phaethon and Callisto tales offer extended and purposeful deviations from the principal of temporal linearity. Taken together, the episodes open up new possibilities in the poetic universe of the *Metamorphoses*. It is perhaps worth concluding with an examination of a more overtly self-conscious treatment of chronological rupture, though one that is informed by these initial poetic explorations.

Later in book 2, following the death of Coronis, the prophetess Ocyrhoe strides into the narrative in a state of vatic possession, and immediately begins to foretell the dramatic life of Apollo's child Aesculapius:

> ergo ubi uaticinos concepit mente furores
> incaluitque deo, quem clausum pectore habebat,
> adspicit infantem 'toto' que 'salutifer orbi
> cresce puer' dixit, 'tibi se mortalia saepe
> corpora debebunt; animas tibi reddere ademptas
> fas erit, idque semel dis indignantibus ausus
> posse dare hoc iterum flamma prohibebere auita
> eque deo corpus fies exsangue deusque,
> qui modo corpus eras, et bis tua fata nouabis. (2.640–8)

> And so when her mind had been overcome with vatic frenzy and she
> grew warm with the god, whom she held enclosed within her breast,

---

[37] Anderson (1997) 296 calls it 'a particularly catty remark'.

[38] O'Bryhim (1990) 79 suggests that the explanation for Ovid's departure from his chronological scheme is that 'he wanted to emphasize Callisto's pollution and exile'.

[39] A fragment of Hesiod (181 C) records that Lycaon had committed his great offence against Jupiter precisely because of the rape of his daughter by the supreme god. According to this fragment Lycaon, feigning ignorance of his daughter's rape by Jupiter, invited the gods to a feast and served a meal of human flesh. This version is also reported by pseudo-Eratosthenes *Catast.* fr. I. Cf. Lactantius Placidus on *Theb.* 7.414: *Lycaon pater Helicae ursae fuisse dicitur, qui dolore stupratae a Ioue filiae deos humanorum cranium cibis uiolauit.* Thus in these narratives which make Lycaon the father, there is a causal relationship between the rape of Callisto and Lycaon's offence against Jupiter. But Ovid has reversed the order of his two events, telling of the ultimate fate of Lycaon long before any mention of his daughter. He thereby destroys any meaningful causal relationship between the two events, and removes any necessity for the genealogical connection.

[40] For Otis (1966) 119 the tale ends with a 'comically motivated *aition*'.

she looked upon the infant and said: 'Grow quickly, child, healer of
the whole world! Often will mortal bodies owe their lives to you; for it
will be allowed for you restore to life departed souls. But having dared
to give back life once against the gods' will, your grandfather's
thunder-bolt will prevent you from doing so a second time. And from
a god you will become a bloodless corpse; but then from a corpse you
will become a god again, thereby twice renewing your fates.

Like most epic prophets, Ocyrhoe is interested in the future rather than the
present; authentic prophecy generally involves a gesture towards the τέλος
of the poem. In this case, the narrative elements predicted by Ocyrhoe are found
in the final book of the *Metamorphoses*. Aesculapius' prophesied role as global
healer, anticipated in the phrase *salutifer orbi*, finds its fulfilment at the end
of the poem in the phrase *salutifer urbi* (15.744), as Alison Keith has noted.[41]
The resurrection of a departed soul without divine sanction, foretold by
idque semel dis indignantibus ausus (2.644–5), is realized in the tale of
Hippolytus/Virbius:

> 'uidi quoque luce carentia regna
> et lacerum foui Phlegethontide corpus in unda,
> nec nisi Apollineae ualido medicamine prolis
> reddita uita foret; quam postquam fortibus herbis
> atque ope Paeonia Dite indignante recepi ...' (15.531–5)

> 'I even saw the lightless realm and bathed my mangled body in the
> waters of Phlegethon. Nor would I be here now if the son of Apollo
> had not by powerful cures given me back my life; and after I had
> received back my life against Dis' will through strong herbs and
> Paean's help ...'

There are two verbal echoes here that point back to Ocyrhoe's prophecy.[42] First,
as Keith observes,[43] the phrase *reddita uita* recalls *animas...reddere* (2.644).
Likewise, the phrase *Dite indignante* used by Hippolytus/Virbius elegantly
picks up *dis indignantibus* (2.645). In the second case, both phrases are ablative
absolutes, and there is an appropriate increase in specificity as to the divine
reaction in the progression from prophecy (book 2) to reported fact (book 15).[44]

At first glance, Ocyrhoe's prophecy involves a conventional form of
anticipation, and indeed one that is perfectly acceptable within the conventions
of a linear narrative. There is, however, a subtle chronological disruption in this
passage as well. Ocyrhoe's prophecy goes beyond merely gesturing towards
later narrative; it appropriates the temporality of the Hippolytus/Virbius tale of
book 15. Ovid achieves this effect by a cunning and under-appreciated
chronological slippage in the transition to the following segment. This transition

---

[41]   Keith (1992b) 72.

[42]   For cross-references between the Hippolytus tales in the *Metamorphoses* and the *Fasti* see Keith
(1992b) 69–72.

[43]   Keith (1992b) 72, who notes further that *anima* is used as the equivalent of *uita* by many Latin
poets.

[44]   A further parallel may arise through the *lusus etymologici* in the Hippolytus/Virbius episode of
book 15. On that scene, Kenney (1986) 464 notes that the context suggests punning etymologies:
Hippo-lytus 'loosed (undone) by horses'; Vir-bi(u)s 'twice a hero (or hero-alive)'. The name
Hippolytus may thus equate to Ocyrhoe through the horse motif (*in equum cognataque corpora
uertor,* 2.663), the name of Virbius through the prophecy of a doubled life (*bis tua fata nouabis,*
2.648).

describes the unhappy reaction of her father Chiron after Ocyrhoe's punitive transformation into a horse (2.665–75):

> flebat opemque tuam frustra Philyreius heros,
> Delphice, poscebat, nam nec rescindere magni
> iussa Iouis poteras, nec, si rescindere posses,
> tunc aderas: Elin Messeniaque arua colebas,
> illud erat tempus, quo te pastoria pellis
> texit onusque fuit baculum siluestre sinistrae,
> alterius dispar septenis fistula cannis;
> dumque amor est curae, dum te tua fistula mulcet ... (2.676–83)

The semi-divine son of Philyra wept, and in vain sought your aid, god of Delphi. For you could not revoke the decrees of great Jupiter – and even if you could, you were not then at hand, but were dwelling in Elis and the fields of Messina. For that was the time when you were covered by a shepherd's cloak and you carried in your left hand a staff and in your right a pipe of uneven reeds. And while your thoughts were turned to love, and your pipe played soft soothing tunes ...

The reference her, as Bömer blandly observes, is to the period of Apollo's servitude to Admetus in Thessaly.[45] But this is problematic: Jupiter had forced this servitude upon Apollo as the final act in a series of retaliations that started with Jupiter killing Aesculapius by thunderbolt for daring to bring Hippolytus/ Virbius back to life. The phrase *bis tua fata nouabis* refers to two 'deaths' of Aesculapius: first in his mother's womb and again when Jupiter slays him for bringing Hippolytus back to life – in both cases he is saved by Apollo. This brings up the end of the poem (15.531–5), where the second event occurs. The servitude to Admetus, however, must be based on the second death – and yet it is, both in narrative and in temporal terms, located in book 2.

The problem here is that there has been a slippage from the narrative moment of the prophecy into the projected time of that prophecy. The narrative that follows the prophecy requires the event that was just predicted to be already fulfilled. Ocyrhoe has just foretold Aesculapius' resurrection of a dead man, yet by the end of the prophecy, as Chiron grieves and calls on Apollo for aid, the narrative has already jumped well beyond the time of that act: for Apollo is being punished for his retaliation to Jupiter's punishment of that original deed. Somehow, Ocyrhoe's prophecy has not just foretold future events, but has actually redirected the future into the narrative present: the phrase *illud erat tempus* (2.680) seems rather archly to hint at the temporal breach. In the ingenious slippage from the grief of Chiron to the paternal loss of Apollo the poet effects not just a gesture towards the later narrative, but an appropriation of it.

The Ocyrhoe tale offers one more example of fluctuating chronology. That the temporal slippage of this episode is a deliberate and self-conscious effect is suggested by the poetologically charged language used to describe the prophetess. Indeed, her very name constitutes something of a literary-critical witticism which helps to identify a metaliterary function.

Ocyrhoe's status as prophet provides for the possibility of that now familiar linguistic confusion between the categories of prophecy and poetry.[46] The language of the passage helps to create this duality: the adjective *uaticinos* (2.640)

[45]   Bömer (1969) on 2.679.
[46]   See in particular O'Higgins (1988).

is reinforced by the fact that Ocyrhoe 'sings' (*canebat*, 2.639) just as the poet does.[47] In short, Ocyrhoe is a studied instance of the self-consciously constructed Augustan poet/prophet figure. Further evidence for Ocyrhoe's metapoetic status may be adduced from the emphasis on the prophetess' rather unusual name. As soon as Ocyrhoe appears in the narrative, the poet digresses in learned Alexandrian fashion to provide an actiological explanation for her name:[48]

> ecce uenit rutilis umeros protecta capillis
> filia centauri, quam quondam nympha Chariclo
> fluminis in rapidi ripis enixa uocauit
> Ocyroen ... (2.635–8)

> Then the centaur's daughter arrived, her shoulders covered with auburn hair, whom the nymph Chariclo bore on the banks of a swift stream and named Ocyrhoe ...

This name is, in fact, an Ovidian innovation.[49] The usual Greek names for Chiron's daughter are Hippe (Ἵππη, 'Mare') or Melanippe (Μελανίππη, 'Black Mare').[50] Moreover, as Keith rightly points out, the poet makes a fleeting reference to the better attested names at the end of the episode: *in equam cognataque corpora uertor ... nomen quoque monstra dedere* (2.663, 675).[51] What, then, is the significance of Ovid's innovation?

Ocyrhoe is a Greek compound whose constituents are the adjective ὠκύς and the noun ῥοή; she is named after the 'swift stream' on whose banks she was born. Now in the context of Greek literature the image of flowing water conjures up two strong metaphoric associations: poetry and time. From the archaic period onwards, this image is regularly used as a poetological trope.[52] In the Hellenistic period, the celebrated *sphragis* to Callimachus' *Hymn to Apollo* made the stream image a virtual synonym for poetic composition.[53] Considered against this literary background, Ovid's innovation in naming his prophetess suggests a metapoetic implication, establishing Ocyrhoe as a poet figure, and thus as an emblem of the poetic process itself. A second well-established usage of the river image was as a metaphor for the flow of time, a trope which Ovid himself frequently deploys.[54] In this compound symbolism there is an indication that the issue of temporal modality is being raised self-consciously by the poet.

---

[47]   As Moore-Blulnt (1977) 134 notes, the compound *uaticinus* occurs only here in classical poetry. From Augustan poetry on the word *uates* and its cognates are regularly used to signify either prophet or poet.

[48]   For further demonstrations of etymological erudition in the passage see Keith (1992b) 85–92.

[49]   Moore-Blunt (1977) 133.

[50]   Keith (1992b) 66.

[51]   Keith (1992b) 66.

[52]   E.g. ῥέεν αὐδή (*Il.* 1.249); χέει ...φωνήν (*Od.* 19.521); ῥέεν αὐδή (*Th.* 39), ἔπε' ... ῥεῖ (*Th.* 84). For an example from the fifth century, the treatment of Aristophanes, *Knights* 526–8 in Asper (1997) 113, is particularly valuable. The implicit *tertium comparationis* which gives the metaphor its vigour is continuity of movement: like a river, song and speech 'stream along'. By the time of Pindar at the latest, the flowing water image had become a standard figure of speech, used by poets to describe their own work. Pindar uses the very word ῥοή in this sense of a 'stream of song or poetry' (e.g. *Nem.* 7.12).

[53]   The literary-critical metaphor μέγας ῥόος at Callim. *Ap.* 108–9 is a striking precedent for Ocyrhoe.

[54]   E.g. *Met.* 15.179–80, *Am.* 1.8.49–50, etc.: see McKeown (1989) 227–8.

Combining the double significance of the word ῥοή with the other element in the Greek compound, the adjective ὠκυς ('swift'), a more precise sense begins to emerge. In the context of a poetic endeavour the image of a 'swift stream' suggest the tendency of a narrative to develop rapidly, or, put another way, the impulse towards chronological anticipation. As has been shown, this is precisely the narrative tendency that the figure of Ocyrhoe embodies: her prophecy produces a forward-looking temporal rift.

In other words, the metapoetic implications of Ocyrhoe's name – that is, the impulse to speedy plot development – alludes to the temporal rift that her prophecy generates. In the aftermath of her prophecy it becomes clear that some of what Ocyrhoe predicted must already by assumed by the narrative. Like all prophetic figures in epic she gestures towards later narrative events; but unlike other prophets, Ocyrhoe briefly effects a kind of narrative 'fast-forward', thereby instantiating in the text the metapoetic implication of her name. In other words, Ocyrhoe symbolizes the poetic urge for a speedy plot-development and temporal distortion, which she herself brings about.

The sequential ordering of time is more important to epic than to other genres. Epic is teleological in its narrative unfolding, and Ovid's proemic promise of a poem moving inexorably from universal creation *ad mea tempora* is an implicit declaration of a masterplot that will organize and construct meaning through time. The figure of Ocyrhoe embodies the teleological drive of Ovid's poem, both in name and narrative function. But that drive is momentarily undercut, nullified by the temporal rift with which the episode concludes.

7. Temporality and the *Metamorphoses*

In the course of book 2 of the *Metamorphoses*, then, Ovid repeatedly deviates from a 'natural' temporal structure. These deviations appear to constitute a sustained and self-conscious exploration of the possibilities of temporal modalities inherent in fictional worlds. After forging a powerful symbolic link between solar movement and time, the poet thematizes the breakdown of temporal norms, thereby abandoning perhaps the most familiar of narrative conventions. The time warp affected by the chaotic chariot ride of Phaethon has both thematic implications in determining the behaviour of the universe in its wake and also broader narratological ramifications as the issue of the representation of time and temporality is explored.

At least one important question remains to be asked: why book 2? To answer this, it will be useful to return briefly to the ecphrasis with which the book opens. The description of the palace of the Sun marks a new beginning in Ovid's epic, reprocessing the cosmogony of the first book in ecphrastic terms.[55] The reworking of the initial cosmogony is heavily flagged at 2.5–7, and the extended reminiscences have been well catalogued by Brown.[56] Ecphrasis spatializes time, making it stand still, or reordering linear time in a spatial pattern. This static quality is perhaps hinted at by the threefold *stabat* of the seasons (2.27–30, cited above), which of course should never stand still.[57] Ovid seems to be making a general point here about the potential of ecphrasis to

[55] Brown (1987) 215–9, esp. 219: 'Vulcan's [artistic rendering of the] universe recalls Ovid's account of creation in the corresponding part of book 1, and therefore contains a self-reference.' Brown further notes important parallels between the creative activity of Vulcan and the Demiurge of the first book.

[56] Brown (1987). Stephen Wheeler (1995a) has argued that the cosmogony in book 1 is itself ecphrastic, a narrativization of the cosmic Shield of Achilles.

[57] Cf. the account of the passage of the seasons at 15.199–213.

disrupt time. On a more fundamental level, book 1 already contains a number of 'beginnings'. The re-creation of the world after the flood (*redditus orbis erat.* 1.348) anticipates the palingenesis following Phaethon's disastrous adventure (2.401–8), and there is a notorious plurality of myths of human origins.[58] This is an epic that has problems with beginnings as well as endings: to that extent the problems of time in book 2 are a continuation of book 1.[59]

References

Anderson, W.S. (1977) *P. Ovidii Nasonis Metamorphoses*

Asper, M. (1997) *Onomata allotria. Zur Genese, Struktur und Funktion poetologische r Metaphern bei Kallimachos*

Bass, R.C. (1977) 'Some aspects of the structure of the Phaethon episode in Ovid's *Metamorphoses*', *CQ* 27: 402–8

Bömer, F. (1969) *P. Ovidius Naso, Metamorphosen: Kommentar*, Buch I–III

Brown, R. (1987) 'The palace of the sun in Ovid's *Metamorphoses*', in Whitby, Hardie, Whitby (1987): 211–20

Coleman, R. (1971) 'Structure and intention in the *Metamorphoses*', CQ 21: 461–77

Dicks, D.R. (1970) *Early Greek astronomy*

Diggle, J. (1970) *Euripides: Phaethon*

Due, O.S. (1974) *Changing forms: studies in the Metamorphoses of Ovid*

Feeney, D.C. (1991) *The gods in epic: poets and critics of the classical tradition*

Feeney, D.C. (1992) '*Si licet et fas est*: Ovid's *Fasti* and the problem of free speech under the Principate', in Powell (1992a): 1–25

Galinsky, G.K. (1975) *Ovid's Metamorphoses: an introduction to the basic aspects*

Gibbs, S.L. (1976) *Greek and Roman sundials*

Hardie, P. (1994) *Virgil. Aeneid Book IX*

Keith, A.M. (1992b) *The play of fictions: studies in Ovid's Metamorphoses Book 2*

Kenney, E.J. (1986) Introduction and notes to Melville (1986)

Mack, S. (1988) *Ovid*

McKeown, J.C. (1989) *Ovid: Amores. Volume II. A commentary on book one*

Melville, A.D. (trans.) (1986) *Ovid, Metamorphoses*

Moore-Blunt, J.J. (1977) *Ovid: Metamorphoses 2*

O'Bryhim, S. (1990) 'Ovid's version of Callisto's punishment', *Hermes* 118: 75–80

O'Higgins, D. (1988) 'Lucan as vates', *ClAnt* 7: 208–26

Otis, B. (1966, 1970 ed. 2) *Ovid as an epic poet*

Ronen, R. (1994) *Possible worlds in literary theory*

Sale, W. (1965) 'Callisto and the virginity of Artemis', *RhM*: 108: 11–35

Wheeler, S.M. (1995a) '*Imago mundi*: another view of the creation in Ovid's *Metamorphoses*', *AJP* 116: 95–121

Whitby, M., Hardie, P. and Whitby, M. (eds.) (1987) *Homo uiator: classical essays for John Bramble*

[58] Bömer (1969) 70; Feeney (1991) 194.

[59] We would like to thank the editorial team for their valuable suggestions and contributions at all stages of the rewriting process.

Secondary Source 3.7   Stephen M. Wheeler, 'Transforming time'

(Source: Wheeler, S.M. (1999) *A Discourse of Wonders: Audience and Performance in Ovid's* Metamorphoses, Philadelphia, PA, University of Pennsylvania Press, pp. 125–35, endnotes omitted)

Earlier I suggested that there are two levels of continuity: that of the story-world and that of the discourse. The history of the world justifies a linear reading of the poem, but the order of the discourse continually undermines the audience's attempt to build a consistent temporal framework. One cause of historical discontinuity within the *Metamorphoses* is the frequent incidence of chronological contradictions or anachronisms. Some scholars assume that such inconsistencies are intrinsic to an unsystematic mythological tradition and are an insignificant byproduct of Ovid's synthesis of incompatible sources. As critics are increasingly recognizing, however, chronological inconsistencies may be a deliberate poetic device by which the *poeta doctus* demonstrates his knowledge of different mythological traditions and raises questions about narrative reliability and the construction of the past. Similarly, anachronisms within the *Metamorphoses* may be significant if the audience attempts to build a consistent chronology. By scrambling the order of events and providing evidence for alternative chronologies, the poet challenges and reshapes the audience's understanding of time.

What evidence is there that Ovid may have projected an audience with the expectations of a systematic chronology of Greco-Roman myth? Galinsky asserts that "any effort to establish a systematic chronology ... would be futile for the simple reason that such a chronology did not exist in classical times" (1975: 85). This statement does not gibe well with the proliferation of universal chronicles in the first century B.C. We know, for example, that Castor of Rhodes assembled a six-book *Chronological Epitome* (*FGrH* 250), which was the first systematic chronology to cover the mythical period of Greek prehistory, from the period of the Assyrian king Ninus (2123 B.C.) to Pompey's settlement of the East (61 B.C.). Catullus may have been familiar with this chronological work (Weber 1983: 270–71), and Varro used it in *De Gentre Populi Romani*, a historical work that placed Rome's remote past in a Greek context. Varro divided the past into three periods: the obscure; the mythical; and the historical (Varro, *De Gente Populi Romani*, fr. 3 Peter; cf. Wiseman 1979: 158–59). The mythical period ran from the flood to the first Olympiad and was reckoned by Censorinus to be roughly sixteen hundred years (*De Die Nat.* 21.1).

Another important chronological compendium from the same time in Rome was the three-book *Chronica* of Cornelius Nepos. According to Catullus, this was the first universal history attempted in Latin (1.5–6, "ausus es unus Italorum / omne aevum tribus explicare cartis / doctis"). Evidently this work included the reign of Saturn and so must have covered the mythological period before the Trojan war (cf. Wiseman 1979: 158). A little later, Diodorus Siculus took the trouble to work out a systematic mythological chronology in his *Library of History*. In his preface to the fourth book, he acknowledges the difficulty of the chronological contradictions of Greek myth (4.1.2), but makes an effort to present what he calls an "archaeology" of heroic deeds (4.1.4). His point of departure is the rape of Europa, Cadmus, the foundation of Thebes, and the birth of Dionysus — the material with which Ovid begins the third book of the *Metamorphoses*. Whether or not Ovid was familiar with the work of Diodorus, much less the work of Castor or Nepos, is impossible to demonstrate. Yet Roman audiences would surely have been familiar with the Greco-Roman impulse to write universal histories and systematize mythological chronology. Hence Ovid's own framework for a universal history could reasonably arouse the expectation of a systematic chronology.

Ovid's audience can also be assumed to be aware of the problem of historical anachronisms. For example, in *Metamorphoses* 15, the poet-narrator follows the tradition that Numa Pompilius, the second king of Rome, was a student of Pythagoras in Croton. The narratorial audience, however, must know that the story was a chronological impossibility. Cicero (*Rep.* 2.28–29; *Tusc.* 4.2) and Livy (1.18.2–5) point out that Pythagoras did not come to Italy until the fourth year of the reign of Tarquinius Superbus (c. 530 B.C.), 140 years after Numa's death. The Ovidian narrator, however, exploits the audience's awareness of the anachronism to launch one of the greatest non-events in his poem.

Numa travels to Croton where he learns from an old man the foundation story of the city (15.9–59). Ovid then makes an abrupt transition in which he makes no further mention of Numa but introduces Pythagoras as an exiled resident of Croton (15.60–74). The gap in Ovid's transition to Pythagoras compels the narratorial audience to assume that Numa has something to do with Pythagoras, even though the narrator studiously avoids making the connection. Pythagoras then lectures to a general audience — again, without specific reference to Numa (15.75–478). All the while, the narratorial audience may assume that Numa is among these auditors. Finally, at the end of the speech, Ovid returns to Numa, who was last mentioned 470 lines earlier when he arrived in Croton:

> Talibus atque aliis instructo pectore dictis
> in patriam remeasse *ferunt*. ultroque petitum
> accepisse Numam populi Latialis habenas

(Met. 15.479–81)

> [After he had been indoctrinated by such arguments and others like it, *they say* that he returned to his homeland and that upon petition Numa voluntarily accepted the reins of power over the people of Latium.]

This transition from the speech of Pythagoras to Numa is deceptively indirect. In lines 479–80, the audience must assume that it was Numa who had heard the speech of Pythagoras before returning to his homeland, for Ovid does not name Numa until line 481. More important, the narrator distances himself from the "truth" of what he says by attributing it to tradition ("ferunt"). If poet and audience know that the meeting between Numa and Pythagoras is an anachronism, then the "ferunt" acknowledges the fictionality of Numa's meeting with Pythagoras. It reminds the audience that it has been listening to a story, not an event that actually occurred.

Anachronisms within the *Metamorphoses* also constitute a significant form of communication between poet and audience. They deauthorize any single version of mythological history by opening up alternative possibilities and force the audience to reevaluate its understanding of the poem's narrative. To illustrate how chronological problems involve the audience in the *Metamorphoses*, let us consider a few exemplary cases.

Callisto

One does not need to read long in the *Metamorphoses* to discover that the poet plays with the audience's sense of time. When Phaethon loses control of the solar chariot and veers off course in Book 2, the first sign of global warming is recorded near the north pole: "tum primum radiis gelidi caluere Triones / et vetito frustra temptarunt aequore tingi" (2.171–72, "then for the first time the rays of the sun made the cold *Triones* hot, and they vainly tried to bathe in the forbidden sea"). The *Triones* ("Plow-oxen") or *Septentriones* ("Seven plow-oxen") is an old Roman designation for the group of stars that the Greeks identified as the Great Bear (Ursa Maior) or Wain – the constellation that never sets below the horizon. Of course, it is a witty paradox that the arctic constellation should try to cool off in the sea; however, the full significance of the joke can only be understood with reference to the famous Homeric ecphrasis of Achilles's shield. Homer concludes his description of the heavens on the shield by saying that the constellation of the Bear does not "partake of the baths of Ocean" (*Il.* 18.489, οἴη δ᾽ ἄμμορός ἐστι λοετρῶν Ὠκεανοῖο [= *Od.* 5.275]). In alluding to this passage, Ovid not only presents his audience with a humorous example of *oppositio in imitando* (cf. Giangrande 1967: 85); he programmatically illustrates the "counter-classical" disintegration of the Homeric *imago mundi* (cf. W.R. Johnson 1970: 126).

So far so good. Yet, at the same time, Ovid deliberately sets up a chronological inconsistency with the very next episode. After Jupiter restores the world to order after Phaethon's conflagration, he rapes Callisto (2.401–40) and sets in motion her transformations into a bear (2.466–95) and the constellation of the Bear (2.496–505). Juno then petitions Oceanus and Tethys to ban the new constellation from their waters: "'gurgite caeruleo Septem prohibete triones, / ... ne puro tingatur in aequore paelex'" (2.528–30, "'keep the *Septentriones* from the blue deep ... so that my husband's mistress may not bathe in the pure sea'"). Here Juno explicitly identifies the *Septentriones* with Callisto and echoes the earlier passage in the Phaethon episode (cf. 2.172, "vetito ... aequore tingi"). The story of Callisto thus explains why the constellation of the Bear is forbidden from bathing in the sea and patently prefigures the earlier mention of the *Septentriones* in the Phaethon episode.

The Callisto story poses other chronological problems that complicate the audience's expectations of linear narrative. Callisto is the daughter of Lycaon, the Arcadian tyrant, whose transformation into a wolf was narrated by Jupiter in order to justify the destruction of the human race by flood (1.163–243). Callisto therefore belongs to a time before the flood, some thousand lines earlier in the poem. It is possible, of course, that Callisto is a survivor of the flood, but Ovid states categorically that all humans and animals were destroyed except for Deucalion and Pyrrha (cf. 1.325–26). Furthermore, the new generation of Epaphus and Phaethon suggests that the era of Lycaon is past. Consequently, when Ovid introduces Callisto after the tale of Phaethon, the audience is faced with a temporal inconsistency.

Instead of glossing over this problem, the poet-narrator takes trouble to flaunt it. After Callisto's transformation into a bear, he remarks that she feared wolves, even though her father was among them (2.495, "pertimuit-que lupos, quamvis pater esset in illis"). Here the audience is asked to remember Lycaon's transformation and to view Callisto's fate as a sequel to her father's. When

[handwritten margin note: Ovid does much explaining of why the world is the way it is. Stars, sun, constellations, night, day, hours, months ... birds, animals, stones, trees, rocks etc etc]

Jupiter transforms Callisto into a constellation, Juno laments the insult to her power and envisions a new scenario for Jupiter:

> "vindicet antiquam faciem vultusque ferinos
> detrahat, Argolica quod in ante Phoronide fecit!
> cur non et pulsa ducit Iunone meoque
> conlocat in thalamo socerumque Lycaona sumit?"

(Met. 2.523–26)

> ["Let him champion her old appearance and take away her beastly features, as he did before in the case of the Argive Io! Why does he not drive off Juno too, marry the mistress, install her in my bedroom, and take Lycaon as a father-in-law?"]

First, Juno recalls the end of the Io tale (1.734–46), when Jupiter liberated Io from Juno through a false promise of marital fidelity. Next, she suggests that Jupiter remarry and take Lycaon as *socer*. This brilliant stroke of sarcasm depends on the audience's memory of Jupiter's representation of Lycaon as his arch enemy. Juno's references to earlier events in the poem lead to a reconstruction of the audience's experience of time. The episodes of flood and fire fade into the background as the earlier episodes of Lycaon and Io move to the foreground. The chronological inconsistencies in the Callisto episode could lead to the bland conclusion that temporal order does not matter in the *Metamorphoses* (cf. E.A. Schmidt 1991: 21). Yet, in the process of reading the poem, what emerges is a series of challenges to the audience's attempts to build a consistent chronology. The audience gradually learns that the narrative's chronological order is constantly changing: events are shuffled and reordered to create rhetorically effective views of past and present.

The Raven

The next instance of play with chronology follows the Callisto episode (2.531–41), as the poet-narrator introduces the series of tales involving the raven, crow, Apollo, and Coronis (2.542–632). The transition begins with Juno taking leave of Ocean and Tethys:

> Di maris adnuerant: habili Saturnia curru
> ingreditur liquidum pavonibus aethera pictis,
> tam nuper pictis caeso pavonibus Argo,
> quam tu nuper eras, cum candidus ante fuisses,
> corve loquax, subito nigrantes versus in alas.

(Met. 2.531–35)

> [The gods of the sea had assented: Juno entered the clear sky with her chariot drawn by painted peacocks, peacocks painted as recently by the bloodshed of Argus as you had been suddenly transformed into black plumage, talkative raven, though you had been previously white.]

The poet-narrator shifts attention from Juno to her peacocks and then remembers the time when their feathers were decorated with the eyes of Argus (1.722–23). The poet thus establishes a chronological relationship and point of continuity between the Io and Callisto tales. Then, without warning, he addresses a "you" which turns out to be the raven that was once white but is now black. The apostrophe is a typical device by which the poet brings a new character to the audience's attention, but this character has no immediate relation to the narrative context at the end of the Callisto tale. The occasion for addressing the raven is that his plumage changed at the same time as the peacock's, an event that occurred six hundred lines earlier in the poem. In order to tell this story, the poet must stage a flashback to the time of Argus's death.

Temporal regression does not end with the transition between Callisto and the raven. Ovid must backtrack further in time to narrate how the raven witnessed the adultery of Coronis and how he intended to inform Apollo of the crime (2.542–47). On his way to Apollo, the raven meets the crow who attempts to warn him from his purpose by telling the cautionary tale of her own fall from divine grace — another occasion for a flashback. The crow had informed Minerva about the disobedience of the daughters of Cecrops and instead of a reward she lost her position of divine favor to the owl (2.549–65). Not content with her treatment by Minerva, the crow tells yet an earlier story about how Minerva was responsible for transforming her into a bird when she was threatened with rape by Neptune (2.566–88). The narrative pattern of this story recalls the attempted rapes of Daphne and Syrinx in book 1, and so suggests that the poem's narrative continuum has not progressed but is circling backward. Finally, the crow complains of the owl's elevation in honor by alluding to the "famous" story of Nyctimene's incest with her father (2.589–95). After this series of flashbacks, the raven finally accomplishes his business of repeating the crow's mistake — with disastrous results for Apollo and Coronis (2.598–630). Instead of receiving the reward he seeks, he is banished from the ranks of white birds (2.631–32).

In the hundred lines that follow the Callisto episode, Ovid turns time on its head in order to pursue a miniature "Ornithigonia." The unsystematic treatment of time is not a product of careless composition or a sign of facile temperament, as critics once used to maintain. In Ovid's hands, the formal narrative technique of the flashback becomes an object lesson in how time can be broken up into segments and reordered for rhetorical purposes. The raven's error, for example, seems all the more egregious because he does not pay attention to the crow's cautionary tales. However, the raven may have some right to be skeptical. The crow ostensibly warns him against bearing bad news, but undermines her own argument by suggesting that she was unjustly punished by Minerva. Instead of telling her own history from the beginning – *ab ovo*, so to speak – she reorders events to accentuate her victimization and the injustice of the incestuous owl's position of honor. When the poet-narrator makes the order of the narrative discourse run counter to the temporal order of the story-world, he invites the audience to ask what purpose the restructuring of time serves.

Atlas

We have already seen that the Ovidian narrator deliberately commits a chronological error in the Phaethon episode that can only be detected later in the Callisto episode. A different sort of problem arises when he introduces Atlas in the Phaethon episode. When the conflagration reaches its worst point, Tellus makes an appeal to Jupiter to prevent the world from returning to chaos (2.279–300). She points out that the ordinarily stalwart Atlas is struggling to bear the heavens on his shoulders: "Atlas en ipse laborat / vixque suis umeris candentem sustinet axem" (2.296–97). Commentators often assert that Tellus is referring to Mount Atlas and remark that this is an anachronism because Atlas will not be turned into a mountain until the Perseus episode in Book 4. This reading from hindsight is misleading. From the narratorial audience's perspective, the knowledge that Atlas will be transformed into a mountain is not available. Furthermore, Ovid has already enumerated the mountains that are on fire in an epic catalog, and Atlas is not among them (2.216–26). Finally, Tellus's language does not indicate that Atlas is a mountain. The idea of Atlas struggling ("laborat") because the world-axis is burning his shoulders ("vixque suis umeris ... sustinet") evokes an anthropomorphic figure (cf. Anderson 1997: ad loc.). This Atlas is the Titanic son of Iapetus and Clymene, who famously strains under the weight of heaven as punishment for his part in the gigantomachy (cf. Hes. *Theog.* 517–20, 746–48; Hug. *Fab.* 150). From Tellus's brief description, the audience might envision the Hellenistic and Roman type of Atlas bearing the celestial sphere on his shoulders. In the ideological environment of Augustan iconography and myth, the figure of Atlas could be said to guarantee "the continued stability of the universe against a return to the primeval confusion of the divisions of the universe" (P.R. Hardie 1986: 374). Accordingly, when the giant threatens to drop his burden, Tellus sounds the alarm with etymologizing urgency: "si freta, si terrae pereunt, si regia caeli, / in chaos antiquum confundimur" (2.298–99, "If the seas, lands, and palace of heaven perish, we are confounded with primeval chaos"). The shift from a mythological picture of Atlas to the imagery of cosmic dissolution implies that Atlas may also be regarded as the personification of the world-axis (cf. P.R. Hardie 1983: 223). There is nothing in this passage, however, to suggest that Atlas is a mountain.

When Ovid reintroduces Atlas in the Perseus episode (4.621–662), the narratorial audience may recognize that its narrator not only departs from the traditional mythological view of the giant, but also that he contradicts the early account of Atlas given by Tellus. Atlas is now king of Hesperia and does not bear the weight of heaven on his shoulders. Furthermore he is on the lookout for a son of Jupiter who is fated to steal his golden apples. Grimal (1958: 247) argues that this is a different, euhemerized Atlas who is a later, human descendant of Iapetus. Consequently, there is no contradiction with the earlier representation of Atlas in the Phaethon episode. However, the new Atlas retains the rare and distinctive Hesiodic patronymic *Iapetionides* (4.632 "son of Iapetus"), which suggests that he may be equated with the Titan himself. When Perseus petrifies Atlas with Medusa's gaze, the gods contribute to the metamorphoses by increasing the size of his mountainous form so that he supports heaven (4.657–62). The narratorial audience is thus presented with a new version of the Atlas myth that contradicts the traditional anthropomorphic image of Atlas represented by Tellus, but which provides a metamorphic explanation for why Atlas supports heaven.

After introducing this new variant of the Atlas myth, Ovid promptly allows it to be contradicted. A little over one hundred lines later, Perseus tells the court of Cepheus the story of how he obtained Medusa's head. He sets the scene with a geographical description of Medusa's home which is fortified by the mountainous mass of icy Atlas (4.772–73, "gelido sub Atlante iacentem / esse locum solidae tutum munimine molis"). This is blatant anachronism. Ovid's narratorial audience would remember a different order of events: that Perseus decapitated Medusa and then transformed Atlas with her stony stare. This contradiction casts doubt upon Perseus's reliability as a storyteller. Conversely, one might view this contradiction as a sign of the primary narrator's own unreliability. Be this as it may, the narratorial audience knows more than the internal audience. The latter does not know that there is another version of the story wherein Perseus transformed Atlas into a mountain. When Perseus tells his adventures after the beheading of Medusa, the narrator summarizes in a way that casts further doubt upon Perseus's story: "addidit et longi non falsa pericula cursus" (4.787, "and he added the perils of his long journey that were not false"). The "non falsa pericula" should include the transformation of the giant Atlas, but there is no indication that Perseus tells this story to his Ethiopian audience.

The contradictory treatment of Atlas suggests the arbitrariness of the events themselves. Stories are shaped to effect a particular response on a given occasion. Ovid expects these discrepancies to be noticed; they are not to be dismissed as the product of a miscellany of unrelated stories. Nor is the narrator simply displaying his *doctrina* by juxtaposing different mythological traditions about Atlas; rather, he expects his audience to remember and to notice the different constructions of "reality" depending upon who is the narrator. At the level of communication between narrator and narratorial audience, this conflict leads to ambiguity and doubt about what is believable and what is not, which version is authoritative and which is not.

The encounter between Perseus and Atlas produces yet another inconsistency that has to do with Hercules. Atlas has received an oracle from Themis saying that a son of Jupiter will steal his golden apples (4.644–45). The mythologically adept audience should recognize that this is a reference to a forthcoming Herculean labor. When Perseus seeks hospitality from King Atlas, he announces that he is a son of Jupiter and so is mistaken for Hercules. This case of mistaken identity proves unflattering to Perseus because he does not quite live up to the heroism of his illustrious half-brother. When Atlas tries to send the wrong son of Jupiter away, a scuffle ensues in which Perseus resorts to his magic weapon. The narrator excuses Perseus's action on the grounds that he is "inferior in strength" (4.653, "viribus inferior") and forestalls the audience's disapproval with a rhetorical question: "quis enim par esset Atlantis / viribus?" (4.653–54, "For who could be the equal of Atlas in strength?"). Hercules, the audience might answer; according to tradition, he proves equal to Atlas in strength when he holds up the sky. However, Ovid outwits the audience with a contradictory version of the Atlas myth in which Perseus transforms the Titan into the mountain that supports heaven.

Later in the *Metamorphoses*, Atlas is referred to as the anthropomorphic mythological figure of Book 2. Hercules claims to have borne heaven on his shoulders (9.198, "hac caelum cervice tuli"), and so alludes to the time when he persuaded Atlas to fetch him the golden apples of the Hesperides. When the deified Hercules enters heaven, the narrator jokes that Atlas felt the weight: "sensit Atlas pondus" (9.273). This a replay of the image of the labouring Atlas in the Phaethon episode with the difference that the Titan must now bear the additional weight of his enemy Hercules. Ovid returns to Atlas one last time in the speech of Pythagoras. In a moment reminiscent of Lucretius's praise of Epicurus, Pythagoras says that it pleases him to travel through the stars, to leave the earth behind on a cloud, and to stand on the mighty shoulders of Atlas (15.149, "validisque umeris insistere Atlantis"). Is the philosopher speaking literally or figuratively when he mentions Atlas? Is this Atlas the mythological giant or the personification of the world-axis? Or is Atlas the euhemerized astronomer, mathematician, and philosopher, and hence a predecessor of Pythagoras himself (cf. Diod. Sic. 3.60.1–3)? The literal image of Pythagoras standing on the shoulders of Atlas recalls Hercules's own earlier ascent to heaven, but it also has a comic specificity that undercuts the philosopher's pretensions.

Each time Ovid mentions Atlas, his purpose is to deform and reform the audience's conception of the giant as the figure who sustains heaven. But this is not simply play for play's sake. Atlas is an ideologically loaded figure. In the Augustan context, he is neither the reminder of Zeus's victory over the Titans, nor the slow-witted figure duped by Hercules. Vergil, for example, reforms the mythological Atlas and closely associates him with Aeneas in the *Aeneid*. As P.R. Hardie argues, Aeneas shoulders the burden of his cosmic shield just as Atlas does the heavens (1986: 372–75; cf. Galinsky 1972: 111). Atlas also stands for the emperor in imperial panegyric. Ovid himself describes the emperor in Atlantean terms in the *Fasti*: "omine suscipiat, quo pater, orbis onus" (*F.* 1.616, "May he take upon himself the burden of the world with the same omens as his father"). In light of these associations, Ovid's changing representations of Atlas continue the renegotiation of the Titan's meaning. On the one hand, the poet exploits the potential for comedy in the image of the giant straining to support heaven; on the other, he introduces a new type of Atlas whose metamorphosis explains a prominent geographical feature of North Africa.

References

Anderson, W. S., ed. 1997. *Ovid's Metamorphoses Books 1–5*. Norman, Okla.

Galinsky, G. K. 1972. "Hercules Ovidianus." *WS* N.F. 6:93–116.

Galinsky, G. K. 1975. *Ovid's Metamorphoses: An Introduction to the Basic Aspects*. Berkeley and Los Angeles.

Grimal, P. 1958. "La chronologie légendaire dans les Métamorphoses." In *Ovidiana: Recherche sur Ovide, publiées à l'occasion du bimillénnaire de la naissance du poète*, ed. N. I. Herescu, 245–257. Paris.

Hardie, P. R. 1983. "Atlas and *axis*." *CQ* 33:220–28.

Hardie, P. R. 1986. *Virgil's Aeneid: Cosmos and Imperium*. Oxford.

Johnson, W. R. 1970. "The Problem of the Counter-Classical Sensibility and Its Critics." *CSCA* 3:123–52.

Schmidt, E. A. 1991. *Ovids Poetische Menschenwelt: Die Metamorphosen als Metapher und Symphonie*. Sitzungsberichte der Heidelberger Akademie der Wissenschaften. Philosophische-historische Klasse. 1991, 2. Heidelberg.

Weber, C. 1983. "Two Chronological Contradictions in Catullus 64." *TAPA* 113: 263–71.

Wiseman, T. P. 1979. *Clio's Cosmetics: Three Studies in Greco-Roman Literature*. Leicester and Totowa, N.J.

Secondary Source 3.8   Stephen M. Wheeler, 'Introduction: The Fate of the Audience'

(Source: Wheeler, S.M. (1999) *A Discourse of Wonders: Audience and Performance in Ovid's* Metamorphoses, Philadelphia, University of Pennsylvania Press, pp. 1–7, endnotes omitted)

> αἵδε δὲ νύκτες ἀθέσφατοι· ἔστι μὲν εὕδειν,
> ἔστι δὲ τερπομένοισιν ἀκούειν· οὐδέ τί σε χρή,
> πρὶν ὥρη, καταλέχθαι· ἀνίη καὶ πολὺς ὕπνος.

[These nights are endless: there is time to sleep and time to enjoy hearing stories. No need for you to go to bed before it's time: a lot of sleep is a bad thing too.]

— Homer, *Odyssey* 15.392–94

In the first book of the *Metamorphoses*, Ovid playfully reflects on the danger of the audience falling asleep during the performance of his poem. Mercury begins to tell Argus, the hundred-eyed watchman of Io, a story that explains the recent invention of the panpipe. Before the tale is scarcely under way, however, Argus loses interest and dozes. The price that the sentinel pays for sleeping on duty is nothing less than his head. That Argus forfeits his life for not listening to a story is of undoubted metanarrative significance. Even if it is a cruel prank, the fate of Argus tells us that continuing participation in the narrative transaction is, figuratively speaking, a matter of life and death. Ovid's method of drawing the audience's attention to its role in narrative discourse has parallels in the performance of oral poetry. Investigators of modern oral epic report the case of a Romanian singer who accused his backup musician of falling asleep in order to make the audience aware that its own attention was being taken to task (Martin 1989: 5). While it is unlikely that Ovid is criticizing his own audience's heedfulness through the somnolence of Argus, the death of a dull listener cannot but serve as a warning. Ovid's self-conscious treatment of the boredom of one listener raises the question of the audience's responsibility to Ovid's immense narrative which clearly challenges the staying power of any mortal. To read the *Metamorphoses* from beginning to end without pause would require an ideal insomnia.

How then are we to read and interpret this poem that presents countless transformation tales from the creation of the world to the poet's own day? Are we to treat it as a loosely integrated collection of autonomous stories that can be read at random? Or should we be carried along by the poem's narrative flow from one moment to the next? Of course, Ovid highlights the continuous aspect of his discourse at the beginning of his poem by referring to it as a *carmen perpetuum*. Yet many critics have downplayed the significance of the poem's continuity, assuming that the individual episode is the poet's main unit of composition. Gordon Williams, for example, credits Ovid with the introduction the 'cult of the episode' into Latin epic. As Williams explains: "This is a new kind of poetry: a reader can take it up at any point, and, provided he is careful to identify the beginning of an episode, he can read without needing to know what has preceded — in fact, straight progress through the work is probably the worst way to treat it; its essential lack of unity breeds tedium" (1978: 247). Clearly Williams does not believe that reading through the poem is an imperative. He is not alone. Otto Steen Due (1974: 164) also prefers to treat the poem as an anthology. Although he accepts that the *Metamorphoses* is suitable for continuous reading, he "can hardly imagine any narrative work which it is easier or more pleasant to use as a 'bed-side book.'"

Be this as it may, many of the poem's stories simply cannot stand on their own. Our opening example of Mercury's tale about Syrinx illustrates this point well on a number of levels. First, it is inseparable from the Io tale in which it is embedded. Second, if one were to read the Io tale in excerpted form, the metanarrative significance of the Syrinx would be lost. The audience would not be able to tell that Syrinx was a doublet of Daphne and hence an ironic twist on the danger of tedious repetition (*similitudo*). The very fact that Ovid constructs a self-referential joke about the repetition of a narrative pattern suggests that the audience needs to know what has preceded, contrary to what Williams claims. Many readers, especially those who are sympathetic to Ovid's skill at transforming one story into another, are liable to disagree with the view that the poem is supposed to be read as a florilegium of Greek myth. Still the tendency of most current criticism on the *Metamorphoses* is to read and interpret each episode in isolation, focusing on the poet's use of sources, literary models, and generic conventions. The problem with a *pars pro toto* approach to the interpretation of the poem is that it fails to address aspects of the poem's diachronic development.

The purpose of this book is to establish a new basis upon which to read the *Metamorphoses* as a *carmen perpetuum*. In the past, critics have addressed the issue of the poem's continuity by focusing on structural and thematic unity, attempting to describe the relation of the parts of the poem to the whole. The search for a unifying scheme, however, has proven difficult because the poem's structure is indeterminate. Structural studies founder on the assumption that the

Metamorphoses can be described as an autonomous visualizable object that represents the author's intended design. In this respect, the remarks of the reader-response critic Wolfgang Iser are a helpful corrective (1978: 27): "Literary texts initiate 'performances' of meaning rather than actually formulating meanings themselves. Their aesthetic quality lies in this 'performing' structure, which clearly cannot be identical to the final product, because without the participation of the individual reader there can be no performance." Iser locates literary meaning in the reader's cognitive processing of the text. In other words, the text is a set of instructions by which the reader assembles an aesthetic literary experience. In the act of reading, however, the reader's participation in the construction of the literary experience involves more than what is explicitly stated in the text. Here Iser's concept of the "wandering viewpoint" (Iser 1978: 118) is useful for understanding what happens in the act of reading. The wandering viewpoint is the place where "memory and expectation converge, and the resultant dialectic movement brings about a continual modification of memory and an increasing complexity of expectation." This reciprocal spotlighting of what precedes and what follows in a text compels the reader to synthesize interrelated but not necessarily similar perspectives into new configurations of meaning. This synthesizing activity, which Iser terms "consistency building" is the means by which the audience becomes involved in the text and participates in the production of its meaning. If consistency building is a natural human cognitive activity, then it is likely that some readers are going to find different versions of consistency in the *Metamorphoses*. Others may argue on the contrary that the poem defeats the process of consistency building.

For these reasons, I suggest that we discard the questionable assumption that Ovid's poem represents a fixed structure that the reader is supposed to imagine. I propose a new approach to the problem of continuity in the *Metamorphoses*! My thesis is that Ovid presents his poem as a fictive viva-voce performance. This is obviously a different kind of performance from the kind described by Iser above, but Iser's principle that texts initiate performances remains valid. In order for Ovid's fiction of performance to be realized the reader must produce it. Furthermore, in producing the text, the reader is invited to play the part of the audience which hears the poem for the first time and whose experience of it is filtered through the "wandering point of view." This is not to deny the textuality of the *Metamorphoses*, its division into books, or the freedom of the reader to dip in and out of the poem. Indeed, as we will see, the tension between the poet's fiction of performance and the implicit textuality of his work both complicates and enriches the experience of the *Metamorphoses*. What makes the poem continuous, however, is the underlying fictional framework of the poet reciting his work before an audience from beginning to end. Nowhere in the poem does the poet refer to the act of narrative communication as one that is mediated by writing, which implies the poet's absence. On the contrary, poet and audience are both present and participating in the poem's discourse. I will argue, further, that the relationship between poet and audience is the basis upon which the *Metamorphoses* can be reckoned a poetic and conceptual unity which is aware of but ultimately resistant to the forces that threaten to undermine that unity.

The main contribution of this book is to flesh out the role of the audience in Ovid's *Metamorphoses*, and so to provide a firmer basis upon which the audience's response to the poem's continuity may be described and interpreted. I begin with a 'first reading' of the proem of the *Metamorphoses* that demonstrates how Ovid engages the reader in the process of formulating the meaning of the text and specifically its conceptual transformations. The method of reading employed follows the example of the early reader-response criticism of Stanley Fish. However, this preliminary sounding in a Fishian mode raises questions about the occasion of Ovid's narrative and who its recipient is. In order to address these issues, I develop a model of narrative communication which is based upon the rhetorical and narratological criticism of Wayne Booth, Gérard Genette, Seymour Chatman, and Gerald Prince. Through this model I investigate the form of the 'narrating instance' in the *Metamorphoses* and the poem's different levels of audience. In the final part of the book I turn to the identification and interpretation of signs of the audience's participation in the narrative of the poem.

The impetus for my inquiry into the audience of Ovid's *Metamorphoses* arises from a growing interest in the role of the reader in literary criticism. In recent years, there has also been a growing number of contributions to this topic in the study of the *Metamorphoses*. A brief survey of the relevant secondary literature may help give an idea of where my own work fits. To start with, Michael von Albrecht pays considerable attention to the psychology of the reader in his monograph on Ovidian parenthesis and its poetic function (1964). He observes that Ovid uses parenthesis to make an aside to his audience that anticipates or manipulates its response. In a later essay 'Ovide et ses lecteurs' (1981a), von Albrecht examines other evidence for the way that Ovid takes the reader into his confidence. In particular he notes how generalizing second person address and literary allusion effect a closeness between poet and reader. The key idea that links both of von Albrecht's studies is the 'dialogue' between poet and reader.

Ernst Jürgen Bernbeck's treatment of the narrative style of the *Metamorphoses* (1967) also takes into account the role of the reader. He challenges the claim that the *Metamorphoses* exemplifies the norms of epic style, as it was formulated by Richard Heinze in *Ovids elegische Erzählung* (1919, reprint 1960). Bernbeck demonstrates, on the contrary, that Ovid disrupts the reader's expectations of epic continuity as defined by Heinze himself in *Virgils epische Technik* (1915, reprint 1972). In an exemplary reading of the Ino episode (1967: 1–39), Bernbeck points out how the poet omits the traditional transitional devices that ensure dramatic continuity between scenes and speeches; instead the poet makes allusive or playful logical connections that reflect the arbitrariness of his own train of thought. As a result, Ovid's narrative does not unfold naturally and realistically, but jumps unexpectedly and abruptly from one scene or speech to the next without sufficient connection, thus causing surprise and suspense in the reader. Consequently, the reader does not view the mythological action directly but is continually challenged by the poet's mental gymnastics with epic conventions. Although Bernbeck may overstate the discontinuity of the *Metamorphoses* by implicating it too much in a normative conception of epic, his basic point remains valid. The reader is responsible for filling in the gaps of the narrative created by the poet's abrupt transitions, ellipses, and allusive references.

The first direct study of the reader in the *Metamorphoses* is to be found in Due's book *Changing Forms* (1974: 9–89). He addresses the question of how the *Metamorphoses* would have been understood by the majority of readers in Imperial Rome. Using the tools of classical philology and the evidence of language, literature, and material culture, Due reconstructs a 'model' Roman reader of the Augustan Age through whose eyes he attempts to read the poem. As far as Ovidian criticism was concerned, Due's book was ahead of its time. It held the unorthodox premise that authorial intention does not matter and that "the only meaning of a poem is the way in which it is actually understood" (1974: 9). Although Due acknowledges that a reader's impressions of a poem are subjective, they can be validated and made objective when they are shared with others. It is this kind of community of interpretation that Due wishes to describe, but he recognizes that this too changes with time. He concludes by saying that "we have to give up the theory that there is one and only one correct understanding of a poem" (10–11). Whereas von Albrecht and Bernbeck focus on the text as a medium that communicates the poet's intention to the reader, Due severs the tie between the two, placing control of meaning in the hands of readers — a meaning which is subject to change from era to era. Given these circumstances, one may question the credibility of Due's attempt to recuperate a normative Augustan age response to the *Metamorphoses*, especially because he does not adduce much evidence for ancient readings of the poem.

In recent years, a significant development in Ovidian criticism has been the recognition that the act of storytelling is a central theme of the *Metamorphoses* and that the interaction between internal narrators and audiences is a model for the poet's interaction with the reader. An early example of such criticism is found in Gianpiero Rosati (1981) who examines the embedded narratives in *Metamorphoses 5* as a mirror for communication between the poet and the reader. Also of interest are the narratologically oriented essays by Betty Rose Nagle (1983, 1988a, 1988b, 1988c, 1989) which deal with various narrative transactions between speakers and addressees in the story-world of the *Metamorphoses*. The books of A. M. Keith (1992) and K. Sara Myers (1994a) likewise take a narratological approach to the poetic significance of internal storytelling in the poem, making special reference to Ovid's Callimachean models, the *Hecale* and *Aetia*.

On another front, it has been increasingly recognized that Ovid accommodates different and indeed opposing responses to his narrative. In his study of the differential responses to Mercury's tale of Syrinx and Pan, David Konstan (1991) identifies two kinds of reader, one that identifies with desire of Pan and the other that is philosophically detached like Argus. D. C. Feeney (1991: 229–32) similarly sees the poem as dramatizing two positions which are identified with belief and disbelief. Stephen Hinds (1988: 23–29) and Alessandro Barchiesi (1994: 245–78 = 1997b 181–208) politicize this polarity: Ovid enables both a naive reading of Augustan panegyric and a subversive one.

Most recently, Garth Tissol's book, *The Face of Nature* (1997), revives interest in the affective qualities of Ovid's style and observes that the reader's experience of stylistic change, punning wordplay, narrative disruption, and literary allusion is thematically significant — and indeed transformative. Tissol argues further that the process of reading the work is an embodiment of the theme of flux which dominates Ovid's world view. R. A. Smith's book on Ovidian allusion to Vergil (1997) also contributes to the question of how to read the *Metamorphoses*. Unfortunately, it appeared just as I was finishing this work and so could not be included in my discussion.

What is left to be said on the topic of audience and response in the *Metamorphoses*? There has been little systematic study of the poet-narrator's own audience: that is, how it is structured and how it affects our interpretation of the poem. Von Albrecht's rhetorical approach to the poet's communication with his reader is an important first step, but more remains to be said about who the reader is. Bernbeck's model of the reader is essentially a description of the literary expectations appropriate to Vergilian epic as they are described by Heinze. Yet is it safe to say that Ovid's audience is perforce an epic audience? As for recent narratological studies of the poem, they have focused exclusively on internal audiences, and have provided limited description or interpretation of the role of the poet's own audience or reader. Once it is clarified who the primary recipient of Ovid's narrative is, more can be said about the relationship between external and internal audiences. These are just some of the issues that remain to be addressed in considering the role of the reader or audience in the performance of Ovid's *carmen perpetuum*.

References

Barchiesi, A. 1994. *Il poeta e il principe*. Rome and Bari.

Bernbeck, E. J. 1967. *Beobachtungen zur Darstellungsart in Ovids Metamorphosen*. Zetemata 43. Munich.

Due, O. S. 1974. *Changing Forms: Studies in the Metamorphoses of Ovid*. Copenhagen.

Feeney, D. C. 1991. *The Gods in Epic: Poets and Critics of the Classical Tradition*. Oxford.

Heinze, R. [1915] 1972. *Vergils Epische Technik*. 3d ed. Leipzig. Reprint. 5th ed. Stuttgart.

Hinds, S. E. 1988. "Generalising about Ovid." In *The Imperial Muse: Ramus Essays on Roman Literature of the Empire* (= *Ramus* 16 [1987]), ed. A. J. Boyle, 4–31. Victoria.

Iser, W. 1978. *The Act of Reading*. Baltimore.

Keith, A. 1992. *The Play of Fictions: Studies in Ovid's Metamorphoses Book 2*. Ann Arbor.

Konstan, D. 1991. "The Death of Argus, or What Stories Do: Audience Response in Ancient Fiction and Theory." *Helios* 18:15–30.

Martin, R. 1989. *The Language of Heroes*. Ithaca.

Myers, K. S. 1994a. *Ovid's Causes: Cosmogony and Aetiology in the Metamorphoses*. Ann Arbor.

Nagle, B. R. 1983. "Byblis and Myrrha: Two Incest Narratives in the *Metamorphoses*." *CJ* 78:301–15.

Nagle, B. R. 1988a. "A Trio of Love-Triangles in Ovid's *Metamorphoses*." *Arethusa* 21:75–98.

Nagle, B.R. 1988b. "Erotic Pursuit and Narrative Seduction in Ovid's *Metamorphoses*." *Ramus* 17:32–51.

Nagle, B. R. 1988c. "Ovid's 'Reticent' Heroes." *Helios* 15:23–39.

Nagle, B. R. 1989. "Ovid's *Metamorphoses*: A Narratological Catalogue." *SyllClass* 1:97–125.

Rosati, G. 1981. "Il racconto dentro il racconto: funzioni metanarrative nelle 'Metamorfosi' di Ovidio." Atti del convegno internazionale: "Letterature classiche e narratologia." *Materiali e contributi per la storia della narrativa greco-latina* 3:297–309.

Smith, R. A. 1997. *Poetic Allusion and Poetic Embrace in Ovid and Virgil*. Ann Arbor.

Tissol, G. 1997. *The Face of Nature: Wit, Narrative, and Cosmic Origins in Ovid's Metamorphoses*. Princeton.

von Albrecht, M. 1964. *Die Parenthese in Ovids Metamorphosen und ihre dichterische Funktion*. Spudasmata 7. Hildesheim.

von Albrecht, M. 1981a. "Ovide et ses lecteurs." *REL* 59:207–15.

Williams, G. W. 1978. *Change and Decline*. Berkeley and Los Angeles.

Secondary Source 3.9   Thomas A. Schmitz, 'Reader-Response Criticism'

(Source: Schmitz, T.A. (2007) *Modern Literary Theory and Ancient Texts: An Introduction*, Malden, MA and Oxford, Blackwell Publishing, pp. 86–97)

The theoretical positions we have seen so far were, by and large, approaches that developed out of Saussure's linguistic structuralism or engaged in a discussion with it. This chapter will leave this straightforward line of development behind, at least temporarily. In Germany, structuralist ideas and the reactions to these developments that are often referred to by the somewhat vague term of 'poststructuralism' have never played as important a role as in the intellectual debate in France or the USA. There are a number of social, political, academic, and intellectual reasons for this difference about which one could speculate at length (there is a fascinating account in Robert C. Holub's book [188]). One of them is rather simple: around the time when structuralism became so important in other countries, a different strand of literary criticism became dominant in Germany and monopolized the public's attention, the so-called "theory of reception." Its origin can be dated with a great deal of precision: in 1967, Hans Robert Jauss (1921–97), who worked in the field of French literature, delivered his inaugural lecture at the University of Constance; it was entitled "Literary History as a Challenge to Literary Theory" (English translation in [203.3–45]). In the same year, Wolfgang Iser (1926–2007) accepted a position in the English department at Constance, and Harald Weinrich (b. 1927) published his article "Towards a Literary History of the Reader" (in German; reprinted in [373.21–36]). Hence, for a number of years, Constance became the center of this approach to literary studies which is often referred to as the "Constance school."

Occasionally, reception theory made polemical arguments against other positions and was attacked in its own turn, yet these debates were always relatively tame, compared to the embittered war of words that was provoked by some varieties of poststructuralism such as deconstruction [...]. One reason why reception theory was less controversial and contentious among more traditional philologists in Germany and elsewhere may be that it can be considered some sort of bland, "low-fat" theory: it is less rooted in philosophical speculations, and its language is less rich in specialized technological vocabulary than the idiom of poststructuralism. Moreover, it could lay claim to a series of illustrious forebears. Its main argument, to put the audience (in most cases, this means the reader [...]) into the focus of interpretative attention, can be traced back to antiquity. When Aristotle, in chapter 6 of his *Poetics* (1449 b 27), sees the main aim of tragedy in providing a purification from excessive emotions by means of "fear and pity", or when Horace, in his *ars poetica* 333, defines that poets attempt to "enlighten or delight," this is a clear signal that for them, the audience is the most important part of literary communication, where author and text have to follow its lead. If we are willing to accept sweeping generalizations, we can say that this was the dominant view of literature until well into the eighteenth century. It was only Romanticism which emphasized the "genius" and individual creativity in literature and all artistic activity and thus foregrounded the producers of literature to the detriment of its receivers. And it was precisely during Romanticism's heyday, in the nineteenth century, that philology and literary criticism emerged as academic disciplines and developed their methodology. Hence, the Romantic view of literature prevailed in these fields and was hardly ever challenged. Reception studies criticized this bias and postulated that the reader be restored in her or his rights. A literary work, its adepts argued, cannot be said to exist in the same manner as a material object such as a table; much rather, it can be compared to a musical score which will only be transformed into music when it is performed. Analogously, a literary text has only a virtual existence until a reader picks it up and concretizes it in her or his reading.

Empirical Reception Studies

The idea that literary texts do not become "real" until they are actualized in the experience of a reader's mind and that accordingly, the reader should be at the center of literary studies can be pursued in two quite distinct directions. The first current can be described as a pragmatical approach: it asks in which ways literary texts have been concretized by different readers, in different periods, in different social classes, or in different national contexts. Scholars following its lead have, for example, explored the ways in which texts were read in certain periods and areas: Who read novels? How was such reading seen and judged by society? How were texts understood and interpreted? Classical students have been engaged in this kind of research for a long time; for example, Birger Munk-Olsen has examined who read classical texts during the Middle Ages and how these texts were studied [272]. There are numerous studies of the history of transmission and reception of single authors (such as Monique Mund-Dopchie's book on Aeschylus [271]). However, concerning classical antiquity itself, we are in a much more difficult situation than students of modern literature: we do not have contemporary evidence such as diaries, private letters, or published reviews at our disposal for studying the attitudes and criteria of readers in antiquity (what we do have, however, are the texts of ancient commentators, but they are rather difficult to use for this sort of research).

Another avenue of reception studies is closed to classicists as well: we cannot conduct psychological experiments to test and assess the reactions and responses of readers in antiquity. Such experiments have been at the basis of some branches of modern reader-response studies such as Norman N. Holland's research [...], but cf. Jauss's well-founded criticism of this approach in [202]). When we have access to evidence documenting the experience of ancient readers, these are, in general, productive readers, i.e. authors who read and reacted to their predecessors' works. Virgil was a reader of the Homeric epics; Ovid was in turn a reader of Virgil's texts, and we can see their works as witnesses of their reception of classical texts. In general, however, this kind of evidence is rather treated as examples of intertextuality [...].

Aesthetics of Reception

The Constance School, however, was not primarily interested in this empirical approach; instead, they developed a position called "aesthetics of reception." Its main focus is not individual (or collective) historical readers, but rather the ways in which literary texts interact with their recipients, and deploy their potential meanings and the roles they assign to their readers. In his inaugural lecture, Jauss himself had criticized the methods of conventional literary history: without really providing a sustained argument for its choices or writing a continuous historical account, he claimed, it merely produced a hodgepodge of short biographical notices, descriptions of individual works, and literary assessments, which, as Jauss said, quoting a line by the Austrian poet Rainer Maria Rilke, "pop up in some accidental spot here" [203.4]. Jauss himself proposed a new way of writing literary history which ought to take into account that literary works do not magically appear on an empty stage but are framed by the literary context of their period. When a reader opens a new novel, (s)he has already read other novels and developed certain assumptions of what a novel is and should be; the new text will be read and understood against the backdrop of these assumptions. This is what Jauss called the "horizon of expectations," which he defined as "the objectifiable system of expectations that arises for each work in the historical moment of its appearance, from a pre-understanding of the genre, from the form and themes of already familiar works, and from the opposition between poetic and practical language" [203.22]. It is only by comparing an individual work to this historical background that we can judge its position in the poetical, literary, and aesthetical system of its period: what is its relation to these preexisting assumptions? Does it fulfil them, does it contradict them, thus modifying and extending the horizon of expectation for future works?

According to Jauss, it is precisely the horizon of expectation which provides criteria for aesthetical judgments about literature [203.25]: "to the degree that this distance decreases, and no turn toward the horizon of yet unknown experience is demanded of the receiving consciousness, the closer the work comes to the sphere of 'culinary' art or entertainment art [*Unterhaltungskunst*]." Only works which breach and modify the readers' expectations can be considered great literature; texts that merely gratify preexistent assumptions belong to the realm of good workmanship, but not art. Jauss explicitly quotes the contributions of the Russian Formalists whose ideas about the function of parody in the course of literary history are quite similar to his own [...].

This aspect of Jauss's contributions has been discussed intensely; the problems it entails are easy to see. On the one hand, it betrays a marked bias for literature that we might call unconventional, revolutionary, or belonging to the "vanguard." But is it really justified to say that these are the only texts which possess aesthetical value? On the other hand, Jauss remains somewhat vague about the methodology for reconstructing the horizon of expectations which makes such a judgment possible: has not every individual reader made her or his own experiences; can we pretend that there is a way of measuring and assessing the audience's expectations with any degree of objectivity? It may not least be due to such problems that Jauss is considered a great influence on the development of an esthetics of reception but that his calls for a new kind of literary history have not been followed (not even by himself).

Unlike Jauss, his colleague Wolfgang Iser tried to make consistent use of a receptionist approach for the interpretation of individual texts. He also drew up a methodological program in his inaugural lecture at Constance, entitled "Die Appellstruktur der Texte," English translation "Indeterminacy and the Reader's Response in Prose Fiction" [257.1–45]. Moreover, he published two further books ([195] and [196]) which demonstrated a practical use of his ideas. Iser is not interested in individual historical readers either; instead, he establishes the role of the "implied reader" [196.34–8]. This concept describes the role of the reader such as it is inscribed into the text; any individual reader must assume this role in order to realize the potential offered by the text.

Iser is serious in claiming that texts become alive only through being read; before their reception, they are merely black spots on white paper. They need to be concretized in the "act of reading," which, in the case of literary texts, is characterized by the fact that they contain *Leerstellen*, "empty places" which need to be filled by the reader. Hence, readers are motivated into participating and embracing the view produced by the text. Iser has called this aspect of literary texts *Appellstruktur* (the English translation "indeterminacy" does not convey the idea that in Iser's diction, it is the text itself which "appeals" to the reader). Here are some possibilities of what such indeterminacies can be:

- by omitting elements which are self-evident, narratives create gaps which the reader has to fill;
- texts provoke readers to think about possible continuations (this is especially visible in the case of novels which are published in several instalments);
- modern literary works often have an "open" end which does not solve all mysteries and leaves unanswered important questions which readers might have.

It is the interplay between textual elements which provide explicit information and thus lead readers in a certain direction, and such indeterminacies which give them (some degree of) freedom from narratorial constraints that motivate readers to make assumptions about the continuation of the narrative, to revise what they thought they knew about the story and its characters, to accept new perspectives even while they are reading. For Iser, what constitutes a literary text is not "the words on the page," but rather this picture which is constantly changing during the act of reading, this concretization of what is merely hinted at in the text, and the interaction between the reader and the raw data of the text. If, while reading the *Aeneid*, we infer, from clues given in Virgil's text, that Aeneas will not continue his voyage to Italy but stay in Carthage, this assumption (and its final refutation by the text when he does indeed travel on) is part of the text of the *Aeneid* as concretized in our act of reading.

Iser's hypotheses about the ways in which the act of reading works have provoked lively discussions, especially in the USA, and these debates have demonstrated that there are some open questions in his account. Stanley Fish [...] has argued that Iser's concept is based on a distinction between clear, explicit data provided by the text and places where the reader is at greater liberty to react to the text; according to Fish, however, this distinction does not hold water [108.78]: "there can be no category of the 'given' if by given one means what is there before interpretation begins." If Iser were to take seriously his own assumption that texts can be concretized only through reading, i.e. through interpretation, his optimistic belief that there are stable parts which control and govern this interpretation would break down. A related problem can be seen in the fact that Iser's reader is merely a stance that we produce by interpreting the text. But this entails that this reader's role is bare of any claim to be a binding force; if we look closer, we realize that this reader is no more than a construct which allows Iser to bolster his own interpretation. This difficulty has been expressed with special liveliness in Eagleton's words [90.73]: "If one considers the 'text in itself' as a kind of skeleton, a set of 'schemata' waiting to be concretized in various ways by various readers, how can one discuss these schemata at all without having already concretized them? ... It is a version, in other words, of the old problem of how one can know the light in the refrigerator is off when the door is closed." Other critics such as Susan R. Suleiman have criticized Iser for his unclear position with regard to the reader's freedom [343.22–6]: are readers' reactions predetermined by the text and the data it provides or do they have an ample margin in concretizing what is merely hinted at?

American Reader-Response Criticism

This lively discussion of Iser's work in the USA was provoked by the fact that at around the same period when the Constance School was defining its position in Germany, a similar movement in America was pleading for a more prominent role of the act of reading in the interpretation of literature. We have to take a short glimpse at the history of literary criticism in the USA in order to understand why this approach was considered so exciting. From the end of World War II, the practice of literary interpretation in American schools and universities had been dominated by an approach which is called "New Criticism." Its origins date back to the 1920s and 1930s of the last century. New Criticism emphatically claims that a literary work of art must be considered an organic unity whose different parts are in a relation of harmonious tension to each other. It is the interpreter's task to recognize and express this harmony. In order to achieve this aim, the new critics utilize a manner of scrutiny of and immersion in the text that can almost be labeled religious and contemplative in nature; this is the famous "close reading" of New Criticism: the text is isolated from all its surroundings and circumstances, be they historical, biographical, social, or political. This isolation has often been summarized in the slogan "just the words on the page." In this point (and in several other aspects) New Criticism can be compared to the practice of "immanent interpretation" which was dominant in Germany after the end of World War II; its most well-know proponent was the Swiss scholar Emil Staiger (1908–87).

New Criticism firmly believed that unmediated and intense encounters with texts of great poetry can be fruitful and rewarding for our mental life: we are faced with possibilities and experiences that are otherwise inaccessible to us, and by contemplating works of art, we learn to sustain the tension between opposite poles that are irreconcilable in everyday life and to find a balance between such oppositions. In order for this striking and enriching encounter to take place, however, we have to be careful to approach the text itself. Hence, the New Critics caution us against

- attempts to paraphrase a work of art (termed the "heresy of paraphrase" in chapter 11 of Cleanth Brooks's book *The Well Wrought Urn* [47.192–214]),
- making the assumption that a text is identical with its author's intentions (this mistake is called the "intentional fallacy[...],
- failing to distinguish between the text itself and the psychological effects it exerts on its readers ("affective fallacy").

It is this last point which will be of special interest to us here. The essay in which William K. Wimsatt (1907–75) and Monroe Beardsley (1915–85) defined and condemned this "affective fallacy" [379.21–39], became a classic of literary criticism in the USA; it was often read and quoted. Wimsatt and Beardsley write [379.21]: "The Affective Fallacy is a confusion between the poem and its results ... It begins by trying to derive the standard of criticism from the psychological causes of the poem and ends in biography and relativism."

Yet this orthodoxy began to crumble at the end of the 1960s: a number of scholars began to pay more and more attention to the reader's role in literary texts. As an example, we will have a look at an article published in 1980 by Stanley Fish (b. 1938), who was then a young scholar. Fish argues against the positions of Wimsatt and Beardsley, and he develops his own methodology for interpreting literary texts which he provocatively calls "affective stylistics." By analyzing a single sentence in a poem by Thomas Browne (1605–82), Fish demonstrates the ways in which the reader's experience is a result of expectations generated, fulfilled or frustrated, modified and adapted as (s)he meets every single word in this sentence. Fish writes about this sentence [107.25]: "It is no longer an object, a thing-in-itself, but an event, something that happens to, and with the participation of, the reader. And it is this event, this happening ... that is, I would argue, the meaning of the sentence." Fish's methodology consists in an extreme deceleration of this reading process, which is usually imperceptible to readers themselves; in this slow motion, it becomes visible and analyzable.

However, Fish's approach does not escape difficulties that we have already seen in Iser's position: when thus reading in slow motion, can he ever be certain that he is describing more than his own quite subjective impressions that are not valid for other readers? And when he claims that a text's meaning is identical to its reader's experiences in the course of reading it, can he avoid a total relativism in which a text can mean anything any reader sees (or hallucinates) in it? Fish's reply to these objections was not too convincing at this point in time [107.52]: "Most literary quarrels are not disagreements about response, but about a response to a response. What happens to one informed reader will happen, within a range of nonessential variation, to another." In a short while [...], we will see how Fish tried to bolster up this position by developing his concept of interpretive communities.

Overall, the attempts made by Fish and other literary critics to attack the New Critical orthodoxy that the "affective fallacy" must be avoided at all costs, were soon to be successful, and they caused a steady rise in interest for the instance of the reader and the act of reading. However, this development led to different consequences than on the German scene because precisely at the same time, different theoretical positions were monopolizing the public's attention in the USA: instead of advancing a full-blown aesthetics of reception, most American strands of reader-response criticism joined forces with these approaches, as will be seen in some examples: in one of his most well-known contributions, Barthes had written about the "death of the author" and claimed that this death was necessary for liberating the reader [...]; this was at the core of a connection between reader-response criticism and deconstruction (such as has been proposed by Culler [69.31–83]). Feminist strands of literary criticism were interested in examining aspects of a feminine readership [...]. Psychological and psychoanalytical approaches explored connections between reading experience and the creation of personal identity [...]. We have already seen the ways in which Riffaterre combined aspects of a receptionist reading of literary texts with the tenets of intertextuality [...]. Finally, we can briefly mention Culler's attempt to mediate between the extreme opposites of overly subjective interpretation in reader-response criticism and the danger of hypostatizing the "text in itself" to some solid, unmoving object: he tries to define a "literary competence" [...] which is meant to navigate between Scylla and Charybdis.

This development helps us understand why there was not a single unified movement such as the Constance School: "Audience-oriented criticism is not one field but many, not a single widely trodden path but a multiplicity of criss-crossing, often divergent tracks," as Suleiman writes [343.6]. In a paradoxical manner, one could argue that reader-oriented approaches have been killed by their very success: many of their aspects and concepts have been integrated into the frameworks of several different strands of literary criticism; they have become so evidently useful for the daily work of critics that the necessity to have a "school" of its own for these concepts is not felt any longer.

Wheeler's Analysis of Ovid's *Metamorphoses*

The development we have just seen can be observed in classical scholarship as well: concepts such as the "implied reader" or the "horizon of expectations" have become part of the normal analytical toolbox of many scholars, even when they do not explicitly refer to the theories and hypotheses of reader-response criticism. As we have already seen (above, p.86), this adoption of critical terms was facilitated by the fact that in ancient rhetoric and poetics, this orientation toward the reader was quite common. Furthermore, there are a large number of studies which try to utilize the strategies and key concepts of reader-response criticism in a more consistent and systematic manner (to quote just a few examples: Niall W. Slater on Petronius [331]; James Morrison on Homer [268]; Thomas A. Schmitz on Callimachus [320]; in connection with the methodology of narratology, John J. Winkler on Apuleius [380]. Here, we will look at a new interpretation of Ovid's *Metamorphoses* which makes fascinating use of the methodology of reader-response criticism.

When we see Stephen M. Wheeler dedicate the entire first chapter of his study *A Discourse of Wonders* [376] to a detailed examination of the first four lines of Ovid's poem, this can be understood as a clear hint that he is following Fish's lead. In particular, he concentrates on an ambivalence in the first sentence (which had already been noticed before): readers seeing the words *in noua fert animus* will at first tend to regard them as a syntactic unit and understand them as saying "my mind carries me into new, unknown realms." When reading on, however, they will correct this first impression and realize that *noua* is, in fact, an adjective belonging to *corpora* which depends on the participle *mutates*: "My mind wants to tell about forms which have been transformed into new bodies." Yet our first interpretation does not become completely invalidated by this new reading; much rather, it remains part of our reading experience. The first metamorphosis in the *Metamorphoses* is this linguistic game [376.13]: "The experience of reading the sentence thus exemplifies and confirms Ovid's claim: transformation is the innovative incorporation of two statements into one."

In his analysis, Wheeler is careful to distinguish between the real author (the historical person P. Ouidius Naso), the implied author (the authorial instance as we construct it while reading the text), and the narrator of the story in the *Metamorphoses* [376.78]:

> In writing the *Metamorphoses*, the implied author adopts a narratorial persona: in this case, an epic poet "singing" a continuous song. When the Ovidian poet says in the poem that his inspiration moves him to tell of metamorphosis and he prays to the gods for help, this is not meant to be the record of a real event, but rather a fictional rendition, or imitation, of a bard (*vates*) beginning to rhapsodize. This pretense necessitates the involvement of a second type of audience, a narratorial audience, which is the fictional counterpart to the narrator.

Wheeler demonstrates that Ovid is extremely clever at playing with his public's reactions. On the one hand, readers are invited to adopt the role of the fictional audience that is listening to an oral bard improvising stories; on the other, they know that they are reading a book composed by a highly learned and refined poet. Wheeler points out, for instance, that Ovid's narrative contains a number of chronological inconsistencies. The public is thus provoked to compare two points of view: that of the audience who is listening to an oral narrator and is naively giving credence to his story, and that of the cultured reader who has a thorough knowledge of the narrated myths from other sources and is therefore able to recognize anachronism.

Wheeler suggests that Ovid depicted this ambivalence explicitly in the numerous narratives which are inserted into the poem, some of them in complex frames. The reaction of the homodiegetic public [...] often oscillates between acceptance and sceptical rejection. Within the fictional world of the *Metamorphoses*, however, the skeptics are often punished for their behaviour. This becomes especially significant when we take into account that the emperor Augustus himself is depicted as being part of the audience of the *Metamorphoses* (this becomes clear, e.g., when the narrator addresses him with *tibi* "you" in 1.204–5). Thus, the tension between singing and writing, between acceptance and skepticism becomes a question of political ideology [376.185]: "What Ovid represents, in effect, is a model for how dissent is controlled in the early principate: he makes his audience complicit in accepting myths that enshrine the imperatives of a new social order." One could extend Wheeler's idea by pointing out that Ovid is at the same time undermining this process by drawing his public's attention to the fact that only a voluntary action of the audience, the acceptance of a certain point of view, bestows authority on these "noble" myths.

It is a difficult task for interpreters to come to grips with Ovid's ironical way of narrating which constantly wavers between apparent naiveté and superficial credulity on the one hand and tongue-in-cheek sophistication on the other. Wheeler's analysis of the way we read the *Metamorphoses* and of the role of the audience helps us gain a better understanding of these fascinating and important aspects of Ovid's text.

Further Reading

There are a number of excellent collections of articles for those who are interested in the various strands of reader-response criticism. If you read German and want to learn more about the Constance School and the German aesthetics of reception, you will find a collection of the most important programmatic statements as well as a very knowledgeable and helpful introduction by the editor in Rainer Warning's volume [370]. There are two fine collections of articles mainly of American reader-response criticism: the volume edited by Susan R. Suleiman and Inge Crosman [344] as well as the one by Jane P. Tompkins [357]; both also contain immensely useful annotated bibliographies. Harald Weinrich's slim volume *Literature for Readers* [373] is highly recommended, if you read German (no English translation is available). Concerning the application of reader-response criticism to classical literature, one can refer to volume 19.2 (1986) of the journal *Arethusa* which is a special issue on the topic "Audience-Oriented Criticism and the Classics." The German scholar Wilfried Barner has given a number of suggestions to classicists [21] which are still worth consulting. Lowell Edmunds refers explicitly to Jauss and Iser in his interpretation of Horace's Soracte Ode (*carm.* 1.9), but the results are not entirely convincing (see the discussion of Edmunds's approach in Ruurd R. Nauta's contribution [273]), and there is no consistent application or discussion of the methodology of the Constance School.

References

[21] Barner, Wilfried: "Neuphilologische Rezeptionsforschung und die Möglichkeiten der Klassischen Philologie," *Poetica* 9 (1977) 499–521.

[47] Brooks, Cleanth: *The Well Wrought Urn. Studies in the Structure of Poetry*, New York: Harcourt Brace, 1947 [reprint San Diego 1975].

[69] Culler, Jonathan: *The Pursuit of Signs. Semiotics, Literature, Deconstruction*, Ithaca, NY: Cornell University Press, 1981.

[90] Eagleton, Terry: *Literary Theory. An Introduction*, 2nd edn. Oxford: Blackwell, 1996.

[107] Fish, Stanley: *Is There a Text in This Class? The Authority of Interpretive Communities*, Cambridge, MA: Harvard University Press, 1980.

[188] Holub, Robert C.: *Crossing Borders. Reception Theory, Poststructuralism, Deconstruction*, Madison: University of Wisconsin Press, 1992.

[257] Wolfgang Iser, "Die Appellstruktur der Texte" (English translation "Indeterminacy and the Reader's Response in Prose Fiction") in Miller, J. Hillis, ed.: *Aspects of Narrative. Selected Papers from the English Institute*, New York: Columbia University Press, 1971.

[202] Jauss, Hans Robert: "Der Leser als Instanz einer neuen Geschichte der Literatur," *Poetica* 7 (1975) 325–44.

[203] Jauss, Hans Robert: *Toward an Aesthetic of Reception*, Minneapolis: University of Minnesota Press, 1982 [original German edn Frankfurt am Main 1970].

[268] Morrison, James V.: *Homeric Misdirection. False Prediction in the Iliad*, Ann Arbor: University of Michigan Press, 1992.

[271] Mund-Dopchie, Monique: *La Survie d'Eschyle à la Renaissance: éditions, traductions, commentaires et imitations*, Leuven: Peeters, 1984.

[272] Munk-Olsen, Birger: *Les Étude des auteurs classiques latins aux XIe et XIIe siècles* (2 vols), Paris: Éditions du CNRS, 1982–5.

[273] Nauta, Ruurd R.: "Historicizing Reading: The Aesthetics of Reception and Horace's 'Soracte Ode'," in Jong, Irene J.F. de, and Sullivan, John Patrick, eds: *Modern Critical Theory and Classical Literature* (Mnemosyne Suppl. 130), Leiden: Brill, 1994, 207–30.

[320] Schmitz, Thomas A.: "'I Hate All Common Things': The Reader's Role in Callimachus' *Aetia* Prologue," *Harvard Studies in Classical Philology* 99 (1999) 151–78.

[331] Slater, Niall W.: *Reading Petronius*, Baltimore, MD: John Hopkins University Press, 1990.

[343] Suleiman, Susan R.: "Introduction: Varieties of Audience-Oriented Criticism," in Suleiman, Susan R. and Crosman, Inge, eds: *The Reader in the Text. Essays on Audience and Interpretation*, Princeton, NJ: Princeton University Press, 3–45.

[357] Tompkins, Jane P., ed.: *Reader-Response Criticism. From Formalism to Post-Structuralism*, Baltimore, MD: John Hopkins University Press, 1980.

[370] Warning, Rainer, ed.: *Rezeptionsästhetik. Theorie und Praxis* (UTB 303), 2nd edn. Munich: W. Fink, 1979.

[373] Weinrich, Harald: *Literatur für Leser. Essays und Aufsätze zur Literaturwissenschaft*, Stuttgart: W. Kohlhammer, 1971 [reprint Munich 1986].

[376] Wheeler, Stephen M.: *A Discourse of Wonders. Audience and Performance in Ovid's Metamorphoses*, Philadelphia: University of Pennsylvania Press, 1999.

[379] Wimsatt, William Kurtz: *The Verbal Icon. Studies in the Meaning of Poetry*, Lexington: University of Kentucky Press, 1954.

[380] Winkler, John J.: *Auctor & Actor. A Narratological Reading of Apuleius's The Golden Ass*, Berkeley: University of California Press, 1985.

Secondary Source 3.10   Charlotte Higgins, 'If looks could kill ...'

(Source: Higgins, C. (2009) *The Guardian*, 21 March.)

The story of how Actaeon was turned into a stag for glimpsing the naked goddess Diana has inspired artists through the centuries. Charlotte Higgins on a new exhibition that explores the idea of the forbidden gaze.

A grotto in the forest, leafy, dense and dark. Behind is the bright blue and light of a cloud-scudded sky. In the grotto is a fountain and pool, at which the huntress Diana and her nymphs disport themselves, naked. The girls are washing the goddess: she has her foot balanced, in a pose that is ever so slightly undignified, on the edge of the fountain. One of the nymphs rubs her calf with a cloth. Into this intensely intimate and feminine scene blunders Actaeon, a hunter, a prince of the house of Cadmus. He pushes aside an improvised curtain and sees them, in all their fleshy glory. A terrible sin for a man to see a goddess like this – let alone the strict and chaste Diana.

This moment of disaster is captured by Titian in his great canvas *Diana and Actaeon*, part of a suite of works painted for Philip II of Spain in the late 1550s, and based on scenes from Ovid's *Metamorphoses*. The work hangs in the National Gallery of Scotland, which this year, jointly with the National Gallery in London, bought the work from the Duke of Sutherland.

Titian thought of this work as a "poesie", a visual poem, and it is not so much a reconstruction of the scene so carefully made by Ovid as a conversation with it. In Ovid, Actaeon is an innocent, guided by a cruel fate into the cool grove. With typical virtuosity, the author eschews the obvious – which would be to describe the sight of those gorgeous female bodies from the point of view of the inadvertent peeping Tom. Instead he goes for the reaction of the "nudae ... nymphae" as they see the intruder, the hubbub as they scream and scatter and rush to cover up the goddess, but she rises up above the kerfuffle. She blushes deep like the sunset – with anger or shame or both – and looks behind her for her arrows; they aren't there, so instead she grabs the nearest thing, which is a handful of water, and flings it at him. "Now go and tell people you saw me naked," she challenges, as if it's the gossip she's afraid of. He makes a run for it, and he's quicker than normal, suddenly an Olympic runner – then he sees his reflection in a stream. "Oh god!" he wants to groan – except he can't find his voice. He's seen a pair of antlers, he's turning into a stag. His dogs catch sight of him, and hunt him down. As they tear him limb from limb, they call out for their master, wondering why he is missing the fun.

What Titian has done is to insert a moment, or, more like, a freeze-frame, into Ovid's account. We are given the split second of Actaeon's arrival; that minuscule chink of time when everything is on the turn from being perfectly all right to being hideously wrong. Actaeon takes in the scene in one glance, his face is turning scarlet, his hands express shock. Two of the nymphs haven't yet cottoned on; they are still busy with their duties. The one nearest the curtain tries vainly to pull it back, turning to look at her mistress in horror. One girl hides behind a pillar; another, the one sitting atop the fountain, seems to flinch and cower. Only the nymph right next to Diana seems to stare him in the face. As for the goddess, some art historians believe she is looking down and seeing his reflection in the water, while others have called her glare a sidelong glance. Either way, if looks could kill ... And they can. The stag's skull balanced on the pillar reminds us of the gruesome train of events that follows from this moment.

In the *Metamorphoses*, the Diana and Actaeon story is part of a sequence of episodes relating to the house of Cadmus, the mythical founder of Thebes. All of them concern ways of seeing. After Actaeon's sticky end comes the story of his aunt, Semele. She caught the eye of Jupiter, and they slept together. He liked her so much he promised to grant her any wish. She decided she wanted to see him in all his divine glory, stripped of his mortal disguise. He gave in, but he knew where it would end: she was blown to smithereens by the sight of him, and Jupiter whipped out the baby growing in her belly and sowed it into his thigh. The child would grow up to be Bacchus, the great god of wine. Ovid then moves to the Theban seer Tiresias, who is made blind by Juno and given second sight by Jupiter. On the slightest of pretexts, the poet digresses to tell the tale of Narcissus, who fell in love with his own reflection and wasted away as he gazed lovingly at himself. And then it's back to another Theban tale – that of Pentheus, a cousin of Actaeon, who spied on his mother when she was taking part in sacred, Bacchic rites. His bad end is the most gruesome. Because she, out of her mind in a Dionysiac ecstasy, thinks she has seen an animal, not her own son, she rips his limbs from his body. That doubly wrong seeing – he looking at forbidden things, she not seeing straight – is rammed home by Ovid:

> She was the first to see him gazing on the sacred things with profane eyes, she – his mother – was the first to rush at him in frenzy, she was the first to wound him, her own Pentheus, with a thrust of her Bacchic staff.

"Through his own eyes he perishes," says Ovid of Pentheus. There's harm in looking, then – which is the subject of the exhibition opening today at Compton Verney in Warwickshire, called "Fatal Attraction: Diana and Actaeon – the Forbidden Gaze". There will be no Titian, alas – *Diana and Actaeon* will remain at the National Gallery in Edinburgh until September, when it pays a trip to London – but there will be plenty of riffs on the theme. In Jan Brueghel the Elder's version, painted 40 or so years later than Titian's, the picture is unashamedly about the viewer's enjoyment of naked female flesh – it's a sexy, sylvan scene of bathing beauties, with a couple of goofy hounds thrown in and Actaeon a mere speck in the distance. There's none of the sense of doom and drama with which Titian imbues the scene, and plenty of time to enjoy the sight of the nymphs before Actaeon catches up and mayhem breaks out. Charles Joseph Natoire's early 18th-century version is an obvious take on Titian, complete with a red improvised curtain – in this case being hastily shaken out in front of the goddess's face. Lively and fun, the work has a hint of "Carry On" about it – Actaeon, with a particularly witless expression about him, looks as though he may have been peeping from behind the pillar for a while.

A glance can be a dangerous thing in the world of Latin lyric poetry. In Propertius's love elegies, the first line of the first poem reads "Cynthia was the first to capture me with her eyes". "Love," continues the poet, "quelled my look of stubborn pride." Cynthia's look of love is not a dreamy gaze into her beau's eyes, but a fiery glance that, as the ensuing cycle of poems makes clear, completely subjugates him. It reminds me of another Titian in the National Galleries of Scotland, also part of the Duke of Sutherland's collection: *Three Ages of Man* (1513–14). The couple illustrating adulthood, sitting on the grass at the left of the picture, stare deeply into each other's eyes. As Richard Wollheim memorably noted in *Painting as an Art*: "His gaze and her gaze ... ferret each other out. Their eyes copulate."

Titian made another painting of the divine huntress and Cadmus's grandson: *The Death of Actaeon*, which hangs in the National Gallery in London. It was also meant for Philip II, but Titian kept it in his studio until he died in 1576. It is the companion piece to *Diana and Actaeon*, telling the next part of the story. It is also broadly based on Ovid, but brimming over with Titian's own poetic invention. In the *Metamorphoses*, the account of Actaeon's death revolves around the virtuosic catalogue of his dogs, in which each member of the pack is named and briefly characterised. The pathos of the scene is situated in the idea that he is being killed by his own canine companions. There's even a part of Actaeon, as he is mauled and savaged, who can imagine being a spectator at the kill, in all its excitement. Diana has done her work, and she's quite absent.

In the Titian, by contrast, she is there in the foreground, part of the action, the dogs almost seeming to swirl out of her body. Actaeon is halfway through his transformation – his head has become a stag's, but the rest of his features are human. In sympathy with her divine anger, the sky has darkened. The weather is now stormy and brooding, and the placid waters of the fountain have become choppy and angry. In Ovid, the first moment of horror is Actaeon's sight of his metamorphosed body reflected in a stream. In Titian, the important glance is Diana's on her quarry. It's a neat reversal of the first painting, and the point is pressed home by the reversed positions of the characters. Diana's expert hunter's eye fastens fatally on her target. Ready, take aim, fire!

Secondary Source 3.11   Stephen M. Wheeler, 'The danger of disbelief'

(Source: Wheeler, S.M. (1999) *A Discourse of Wonders: Audience and Performance in Ovid's* Metamorphoses, Philadelphia, University of Pennsylvania Press, pp. 162–81, endnotes omitted)

> The emperor said I could write what I liked.
>
> — Alasdair Gray, *Five Letters from an Eastern Empire*

Over the past decade, Ovid's *Metamorphoses* has moved toward the center of Latin literary studies. One of the strengths of recent criticism has been the *pars pro toto* approach to the poem, which has enabled a new generation to read selected passages of the text closely and to pose new questions about poetics, politics, narratology, and gender. One of the shortcomings of this method of reading, however, is that results of local investigation are often isolated and inapplicable to a global interpretation of the poem. This is particularly the case with narratological analysis of the poem. The general purpose of this chapter is to describe an obvious but unpublicized global feature of narrative discourse in the *Metamorphoses* and to explore its implications for our understanding of the narratorial audience's role in the performance of the poem.

Let us begin with the simple question of who speaks in the *Metamorphoses*. Analysis of the distribution of discourse between the primary narrator and character reveals a striking pattern in the poem. In the first three books, the primary narrator is responsible for roughly 70 percent of the narrative; in the middle three books, 46 percent; in the last three books, only 34 percent (figures are based on Avery 1937: 96). If we chart the allocation of discourse by pentad (see graph), the trend of the declining presence of the narrator and the rising involvement of his characters is equally clear. This global pattern of inversion also occurs within individual pentads. In Books 1–5, the narrator speaks by book 77 percent, 71 percent, 63 percent, 48 percent, and 32 percent of the text;

in Books 6–10, the percentages of the primary narrator's discourse are 71, 45, 49, 45, and 17; in the final pentad, 70, 30, 28, 41, and 33. The conclusions to be drawn from these data are: (a) the primary narrator is prominent at the beginning of the poem and each pentad; (b) as the poem continues, he gradually recedes into the background and allows his characters to narrate in his place.

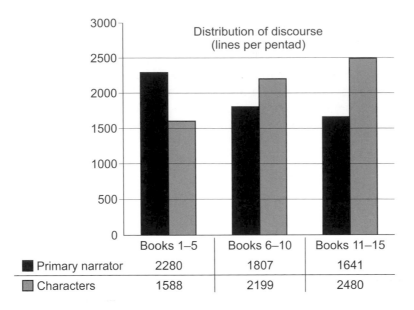

	Books 1–5	Books 6–10	Books 11–15
■ Primary narrator	2280	1807	1641
□ Characters	1588	2199	2480

What are the implications of this structural feature of the *Metamorphoses*? First, it should prompt us to re-examine the common claim the poet's voice and personality dominates, informs, and unifies the whole of the *Metamorphoses*. The importance of the Ovidian narrator, especially in the early books and the beginning of the second and third pentads, is indisputable. However, Solodow's assumption (1988: 37) that the narrator Ovid is "present everywhere ... guiding the reader through the vast confusion of the world" should be qualified. Without counting direct speech (15 percent), more than a third (37 percent) of the *Metamorphoses* is narrated by character-narrators to their audiences. In the last three books of the poem, internal narrators are responsible for 66 percent of the narration. Why then does the poet-narrator gradually yield the stage to his characters, especially as he brings his narrative down to his own times? What effect does the shift of narrative communication have on the external audience's reception of the narrative?

If one focuses on Books 12 to 14, the poet avoids narrating in his own voice the events surrounding the Trojan war, especially those of the *Iliad, Odyssey*, and *Aeneid*. He lets his characters narrate eyewitness accounts instead. Through this technique he presents a series of subjective first person accounts that are not unified by a single authorial vision. The shift from third person to first person narrative in this stretch of the narrative is not simply an Ovidian transformation of his epic models; it reflects a global strategy in the poem, in which the third person narrative of the poet is replaced by the first person narratives of his characters. By speaking less and less in his own voice, Ovid ironically fulfils Aristotle's prescription that the epic poet should be a *mimetes* (*Poetics* 1460 a 7–11). However, instead of acting out a drama, the primary narrator's impersonations lead to the dramatization of storytelling itself. Indeed, the House of Fama (12.39–63), which introduces the epic cycle in the final books of the poems, signifies the fundamental shift away from the poet's own voice to the voices of characters, as the poet effectively becomes a mouthpiece for *fama* (cf. Zumwalt 1977).

Given this global shift in who speaks, let us ask how Ovid represents internal audiences in the *Metamorphoses* and how they mirror the narratorial audience's belief and disbelief in the stories that they hear. In the early books of the poem, the poet-narrator repeatedly demonstrates that skeptical audiences suffer consequences for their disbelief in the stories that they hear. Incredulity is furthermore associated with *impietas* and contempt for the gods. The poet, it appears, is cautioning his own audience against skepticism. Just as tobacco companies are obligated to label a pack of cigarettes with a health warning, so too it would appear that Ovid follows the official line that disbelief in the gods and their authority leads to disaster. Yet, if Ovid were not a disingenuous narrator, such caveats would be unconscionably didactic. For all of the admonitions against skepticism, for all of the skeptics who suffer punishment in the *Metamorphoses*, the narrator seems to push his audience to the brink of disbelief precisely at points when belief is most urgently called for. This kind of play with belief and disbelief may appear harmless, but it takes on a different complexion when the emperor Augustus is invoked as a privileged member of the audience and when the myths told are read as allegories of imperial power. Belief becomes a test of loyalty and disbelief a sign of political opposition. This conflict is introduced programmatically in the poem's first dramatic episode in which Jupiter tells his fellow gods the story of the assassination attempt by Lycaon; the narratorial audience is confronted with the dilemma of believing or disbelieving the story. Before examining this scene in detail, however, it will be helpful to look at how Ovid represents the problem of belief and disbelief in the *Metamorphoses*.

Belief and Disbelief

L.P. Wilkinson reports the story of a lecturer on the *Metamorphoses* who exclaimed: "What an extraordinary thing that such a skeptical man should have believed all this!" (1955: 190). Although Wilkinson lends little credence to the anecdote, he nonetheless cites various passages in Ovid's poetry that prove the poet could not possibly have believed in the fantastic stories of transformation that he tells in the *Metamorphoses*. According to Wilkinson, the astonished lecturer misunderstood Ovid's literary intentions. That is, the poet does not believe in the reality of the mythological gods but accepts them along with the myths because he is playing by the rules of a poetic game. To support his reading, Wilkinson (1955: 192) quotes Heinze (cf. 1960: 315): "The question how this mythical world of the gods should be represented by Ovid in his poetry is not one of belief, but of style, and he answered it differently for the *Metamorphoses* and the *Fasti*." In Heinze's view (1960: 321), the narrator of the *Metamorphoses* does not express genuine disbelief in the marvels he tells, nor does he seek to rationalize them. In the *Fasti*, by contrast, the poet continually questions the credibility of stories that he narrates or rejects responsibility for what he is telling. Heinze concludes that the poet's expressions of astonishment in the *Metamorphoses* elicit wonder appropriate to the epic genre in contrast to the skeptical elegiac narrator of the *Fasti*.

Since the 1960s and 1970s, critics took issue with Heinze's pronouncements about the *Metamorphoses* and *Fasti* (cf. Little 1970). Among other things, Ovid in the *Metamorphoses* came to be read as a skeptical and even irreverent narrator of myth. Galinsky sums up this position well:

> Another ... source of poetic self-irony is Ovid's conviction of the fictitious nature of the myths. For this reason, Ovid likes to distance the reader from the story in order to call attention to what is more important than the substance of the myth, i.e. the way in which it is

told and thus ultimately to the story-teller. But since Ovid essentially
wants to have it both ways — not to believe in the verity of the myths,
but to tell them anyway — the ironies that undermine the credibility of
a given story often are inseparable from the poet's ironic attitude to
himself and his creations. (1975: 175).

Solodow agrees and concludes: "Ovid does retell mythology, with all its
incredible episodes, but at the same time he encourages our skepticism through
the expression of his own" (1988: 71). Given these descriptions of the ironic
narrator in the *Metamorphoses*, Wilkinson's story of the astonished lecturer
makes little sense. How is it that he could have missed the Ovidian narrator's
skepticism, especially when he was predisposed to believe that Ovid was a
skeptic in the first place? A solution to this problem is offered by Graf, who
suggests that the narrator is indeed credulous but the product of an ironic
implied author (1988: 63).

The lack of a clear consensus about the narrator's commitments suggests that
deciding where to stand is a problem in its own right. The source of the problem
seems to be the narrator's pretense of belief in the myths that he tells. The
narratorial audience must decide whether to believe or disbelieve in the
pretense. This does not rule out the narrator's expressions of skepticism or
irony, but the question is whether such skepticism shatters dramatic illusion
or reinforces it. It is becoming increasingly clear, however, that the
Metamorphoses accommodates both belief and disbelief and that the dynamic
interplay between the two responses is what is important. In his essay on
closure in *Metamorphoses* 15 and *Fasti* 1, Barchiesi introduces Ovid's general
poetic strategy with a description of two different roles that the reader can play:

> The poet introduces his audience to a scene full of illusions, and holds
> open a perpetual alternative between naïve participation and
> detachment, credulity and irony. The reader confronted with so many
> tricks one after another gets used to assuming an alias, becoming a
> "duped" reader who is seized by narrative unawares. This credulous
> reader who loses his way seems endowed with a voice of his own, a
> voice that sometimes sounds demanding and official — dare I say,
> imperial? The authoritative voice implies a privileged reader, set apart
> from the anonymous majority and able to make himself heard in the
> poetic text; he pays dearly for his privilege because he is — much
> more than the general reader — a decoy, a "duped" reader.
> (1994: 245 = 1997b: 181).

Barchiesi's description of the dynamics of reading in the M*etamorphoses*
clearly tips the balance in favor of the skeptical reader. Yet it has the advantage
of moving beyond the critical impasse over what the narrator's views of myth,
Augustus, or imperial ideology are. The responsibility for deciding between
belief and disbelief lies squarely with the audience. Barchiesi's analysis of
the "duped" imperial reader raises a question. How can such a reader have a
voice? Barchiesi can assume that the point does not need demonstration in
his analysis of Book 15 of the *Metamorphoses* because it is concerned with
myths that have Augustan implications and can be interpreted from an imperial
perspective. But what about the rest of the poem?

One way that the Ovidian narrator gives a voice to the privileged reader is to
dramatize the participation of such a reader in the story-world of the poem. Two
general types of audience can be discerned: believers and disbelievers. The
tension between a skeptical and a credulous reading of the *Metamorphoses*

[handwritten marginal notes: "perhaps" and "Arachne isn't duped. She retains incredulity, like Lycaon ..."]

receives its fullest exposition during an altercation at the banquet of Achelous, an episode that is generally recognized as the center of the poem. Theseus asks the name of a cluster of islands visible from the river god's seaside grotto (8.573–76). Achelous explains that the islands were associated with five naiads, the Echinades. He washed them out to sea in a flood of anger because they forgot to invite him to a sacrificial festival (8.577–89). Counterbalancing this tale of spite and spate, Achelous tells the story of his love for Perimele, whose maidenhood he once took (8.590–610). Her incensed father threw her off a cliff into the sea, and Achelous caught the girl as she swam and he prayed to Neptune for help. The sea god responded by transforming the girl into an island. Following this denouement, Ovid describes the different reactions of the audience:

> Amnis ab his tacuit; factum mirabile cunctos
> moverat: inridet credentes, utque deorum
> spretor erat mentisque ferox, Ixione natus
> "ficta refers nimiumque putas, Acheloe, potentes
> esse deos" dixit, "si dant adimuntque figuras."
> obstipuere omnes nec talia dicta probarunt,
> ante omnesque Lelex animo maturus et aevo
> sic ait: "inmensa est finemque potentia caeli
> non habet, et quicquid superi voluere, peractum est."

(*Met.* 8.611–19)

[After this the river was quiet. The wondrous event had moved them all. Ixion's son derided the believers, and, as he was a scoffer at the gods with a brash attitude, he said "You tell lies, Achelous, and think that the gods are too powerful, if they give and take away physical forms." All were dumbfounded and disapproved such words, and above all, Lelex, mature both in mind and in age, who spoke thus: "Limitless is the power of heaven and without end; and whatever the gods have willed has come to pass."]

Achelous's tale of love and transformation had moved the audience to wonder. This mood of uncomprehending astonishment, however, is punctured by Pirithous, who derides the credulity of the listeners ("inridet credentes"); he accuses Achelous of telling lies ("ficta refers") and denies that the gods have the power to change forms. Pirithous's critical heresy provokes another stunned reaction and disapproval.

The elder spokesman Lelex, whom Ovid identifies as mature in both mind and age ("animo maturus et aevo") and hence as a figure of authority, answers the objection. He tells the miracle tale of Philemon and Baucis that illustrates at once the metamorphic power of the gods and the theme of piety rewarded and impiety punished (8.620–720). At the end of his tale, Lelex vouches for the reliability of his informants who would not have wished to lie (8.721–22, "'haec mihi non vani (neque erat, cur fallere vellent) / narravere senes,'"). He claims too that he himself saw the trees into which the gods transformed Philemon and Baucis (8.722, "'equidem ... vidi'"). He garlanded them and said the prayer: "'cura deum di sint, et qui coluere, colantur'" (8.724, "'Let those who worship the gods be gods, and let those who have worshipped be worshipped'"). Some readers argue that Lelex too strongly affirms the authenticity of his story and therefore that Ovid implicitly raises our suspicion. But one must also take into account the identity of Lelex's privileged audience — the skeptical Pirithous — who is liable to question the veracity of the report about Philemon and Baucis. The narratorial audience is thus confronted with the choice of whether to side with Pirithous or Lelex; moreover, it must decide how to reconcile these conflicting points of view.

Feeney (1991: 230–32) astutely observes that Ovid dramatizes in Lelex and Pirithous the divided belief that he considers an integral part of entertaining fictions. However, he also notes that most readers of Ovid tend to follow the model of either Lelex or Pirithous. Some focus on Ovid's shattering of dramatic illusion; others emphasize his conviction and credibility. Feeney reframes the whole question to accommodate the views of both Lelex and Pirithous:

> Ovid is not interested in irrevocably exploding our ability to give necessary credence to his fictions, nor is he interested in letting us forget that fictions are his subject. By splitting our response up into these two polarized alternatives he is making us realize that to swim successfully in the sea of the *Metamorphoses* we must be both Lelex and Pirithous. ... The double vision that comes from being both Lelex and Pirithous may indeed be seen as a necessary condition for reading any fictions. (1991: 231)

To make this point, he invokes the useful concept of the duality of belief theorized by Robert Newsom:

> *in entertaining fictions (or making believe) we divide our beliefs between real and fictional worlds* ... an essential part of reading stories or of entertaining any kind of make-believe is "having it both ways." It is insisting on our belief in the fictional world even as we insist also on our belief in the world in which the reading or make-believe takes place. (1988: 134–35, Newsom's emphasis)

Feeney nonetheless concedes the allure of disbelief: "there will always be readers who prefer to side with Pirithous throughout, and I am myself often one of those readers" (1991: 232). He adds, however, that readers who concentrate on authorial manipulation can always talk themselves into a position of skepticism. But disbelief is not always healthy. In antiquity resistance to literary deceptions could be considered a sign of ignorance (cf. Plut. *Quomodo Adul.* 15c–d). Educated readers know how to play by the rules of fiction, so that they may be the wiser for having been deceived.

In the *Metamorphoses*, the Ovidian narrator is clearly aware of the delicate balance between belief and disbelief when entertaining fictions. As a rule, however, he does not represent skepticism as an ideal response. In fact, in a poem noted for its amorality, it is striking how often incredulous characters are singled out as morally dubious. Pirithous is no exception to the rule. The narrator introduces him as "deorum / spretor" (8.612–13, "scoffer at the gods"). The phrase is a variation on Vergil's "contemptor divum" (*Aen.* 7.628), which was applied to the notoriously impious Mezentius. Next the narrator states that Pirithous is "mentisque ferox" (8.613), which means that he possesses the arrogance and boldness typical of those who transgress against the divine. Third, Ovid reminds his audience that Pirithous is "Ixion natus" (8.613), the son of one of the archetypal sinners in Greek myth. Ixion violated the hospitality of Zeus by attempting to rape Hera and was later bound to a spinning wheel in the underworld as punishment (cf. 4.461, 465).

Perhaps most important, Ovid paints Pirithous as a latter-day Lycaon (cf. Otis 1970: 202–3). When Pirithous scoffs at the credulity of his fellow banqueters (8.611–12), "factum mirabile cunctos / moverat: inridet credentes"), he follows a well-established pattern of behaviour in the poem. Jupiter describes a similar outburst of derision when he arrives at Lycaon's house:

> "signa dedi venisse deum, vulgusque precari
> coeperat: inridet primo pia vota Lycaon."

(Met. 1.220–21)

> ["I gave a sign that a god had come, and the common folk had begun to worship me. Lycaon first mocked their pious prayers."]

There are two opposed reactions to Jupiter's advent. On the one hand, the common people, the majority, had begun to pray ("precari / coeperat"); on the other, Lycaon started to mock ("inridet primo") their reverent prayers. Not only is the motif of the different responses to Jupiter's divinity the same as that at the banquet of Achelous, but Lycaon's derision ("inridet...pia vota") prefigures Pirithous's ("inridet credentes"). There can be little doubt that the Ovidian narrator directs his audience to regard Pirithous in the mold of Lycaon.

If Lycaon's disbelief in Jupiter's divinity instigated a flood in Book 1, Pirithous tempts fate with his own skepticism. He is the guest of the river god Achelous, whose own stream is in flood and who claims to have washed away nymphs because they offended his divinity. Lelex draws Pirithous's attention to the danger of flood in his tale about the hospitality that Philemon and Baucis show the gods (8.620–724). Jupiter and Mercury reward the old couple for their piety and punish their inhospitable neighbors with a flood. In Lelex's tale lies a warning to Pirithous not to anger the gods. If Pirithous is a skeptic and skeptics are impious, what implications does this have for Feeney's point that to swim in the sea of the Metamorphoses we must be both Lelex and Pirithous? How is this possible, if to be Pirithous is to be a contemptuous blasphemer of the gods? Is one supposed to identify with such a character? Is one supposed to listen to Lelex with the same skepticism? After Lelex finishes speaking, the narrator says that the tale and the teller had moved them all, especially Theseus (8.725–26, "cunctosque et res et moverat auctor, / Thesea praecipue"). What happened to Pirithous? Was he moved too? The poet does not say. Nor does he say whether Pirithous suffered for his doubt in the power of the gods. However, in the next instalment of Pirithous's story, which is related by Nestor in 12.210–535, the tables are turned. Pirithous hosts unruly centaurs at his wedding who attempt to steal his bride.

Pirithous is the last character in the Metamorphoses to express disbelief in a story told by an internal narrator. His debate with Lelex represents the climax of the dialectic between belief and disbelief that informs the first half of the poem. However, the stories told at the banquet of Achelous recapitulate, above, all, the themes of the first book of the poem (cf. Crabbe 1981: 2315–18). We have already seen that Pirithous is likened to Lycaon, but the similarities run deeper. The issue of the audience's belief and disbelief is foregrounded in the first mythological episode in Book 1: the assembly of the gods (concilium deorum), in which Jupiter decrees the destruction of mankind on account of Lycaon's disbelief in his own divinity (1.163–243). "Firsts" command attention because they establish a pattern that structures the reader's reception of what follows. Furthermore, we might expect that the tale of Lycaon will be authoritative and reliable, coming as it does from the mouth of Jupiter. Finally, it is told within the context of an epic concilium deorum, a device often used for defining the plot of an epic and its moral issues (Anderson 1989: 92).

Jupiter's view.

The beginning of the *Metamorphoses* closely parallels the first book of Homer's *Odyssey*, in which Zeus assembles the gods and defends them from the charge that they cause the suffering of mankind (1.26–43). He claims rather that it is the wickedness of men that is the cause and illustrates his point with the tale of Aegisthus's inhospitable behaviour toward Agamemnon. This story serves as a paradigm for Odysseus's justified punishment of Penelope's suitors. In the *Metamorphoses*, however, Jupiter tells the tale of Lycaon's inhospitality to justify the total destruction of mankind. Ovid's *concilium deorum* thus raises the problem of divine justice all over again. Yet is Lycaon's a tale of divine justice? On the surface it would seem to be. Lycaon sins against Jupiter and pays the penalty. Solodow (1988: 169) contends, however, that Lycaon's transformation into a wolf is not caused by Jupiter and that it is therefore not a punishment. Anderson (1989) argues further that Ovid carefully sets up Lycaon as a paradigm and then fashions the story to sabotage its exemplary status. Ovid manages this dissonance by representing Jupiter as a clumsy and biased narrator of Lycaon's crime and punishment who has little interest in theodicy. There is much to recommend this skeptical reading, but to read this way, is also to risk committing the same error as Lycaon.

The Lycaon episode may not be paradigmatic from the standpoint of truth and justice, but it certainly is from the standpoint of belief and disbelief in the authority of Jupiter. We have already seen that Ovid draws a sharp distinction between two types of audience in the middle of the poem represented by the skeptical Pirithous and the credulous Lelex and that the same distinction is fundamental to the story of Lycaon. In the latter tale, however, Ovid overtly politicizes the setting of the *concilium deorum* and the tale of Lycaon by imposing an analogy between Jupiter and Augustus. More important, the poet-narrator addresses Augustus directly, which suggests that the emperor is a privileged member of the narratorial audience. If this is so, the other members of the audience must consider the political implications of their own responses. To believe in Jupiter's story of the wickedness of Lycaon and the justice of his punishment is to uphold the prerogative of the ruling order; conversely, to doubt Jupiter's authority is to run the risk of treason. What is interesting about his antinomy is that the narrator invites his audience to doubt Jupiter's tale at the same time as he hints that such doubt may be interpreted as disloyalty to the emperor. In short, Ovid places the narratorial audience in a bind; it may either repeat the error of a skeptical Lycaon or acquiesce in accepting an official fiction. In these circumstances, the category of implied audience once again becomes useful, for that audience is in the position to behold the spectacle of the narratorial audience's ambivalence. Nevertheless, if the implied audience is to play the role of the narratorial audience properly, it also must reckon with the consequences of disbelief.

Augustus in the Audience

The memory of Lycaon causes Jupiter to conceive a mighty wrath worthy of himself (1.166, "ingentes animo et dignas Iove concipit iras"). He summons an assembly of the gods: "conciliumque vocat" (1.167). The phrase echoes Vergil (*Aen.* 10.2) and so suggests that Ovid is going to represent an assembly of the gods in the epic tradition. At this point Ovid does not reveal what Jupiter is planning. He leaves it to the audience to surmise that Jupiter intends to make public the story of Lycaon. Next we are told that the gods obeyed at once (1.167, "tenuit mora nulla vocatos"); while they hasten obediently to Jupiter's palace, the poet kills time by giving the audience a guided tour of the city of heaven with an ecphrasis of the *est locus* type. In particular, he develops a witty parallel between the gods who dwell on the Milky Way and the Roman ruling class that lives on the Palatine (1.168–76). The Romanization of architectural, social, religious, and topographical details (1.172, "atria nobelium"; 173, "plebs"; 174, "penates"; 176, "Palatia caeli") literally brings the gods down to earth. The passage is noteworthy above all for introducing an implicit analogy between Jupiter and Augustus, an analogy that is all the more compelling if the audience is aware that Augustus sometimes held impromptu meetings of the Senate on the Palatine. Ovid transforms the divine machinery of epic into an image of contemporary Roman reality, ostensibly paying compliment to the emperor. The insertion of encomium has caused some critics problems because it seems to cast Augustus in a bad light; after all, he is being compared with a violent and angry Jupiter. It is unlikely, however, that the narratorial audience would find Ovid's portrayal of Jupiter questionable or uncomplimentary to Augustus at this point. Furthermore, the analogy to Augustus could have the opposite effect of defusing critical questioning of Jupiter's conduct.

Perhaps more troubling is the change in tone and the anthropomorphic treatment of the gods. What does Ovid's lighthearted and fanciful conceit of a Palatine in heaven have to do with Jupiter's wrath? One could argue that the digression heightens suspense. Yet the humorous portrayal of the gods deflates the atmosphere of serious moral crisis. Anthropomorphism normally is an epic technique to make gods believable characters. Ovid gleefully pushes the techniques to the point of incongruous specificity, making the gods appear all too human — or rather all too Roman — as the *potentes caelicolae* worship their own *penates* (1.172–73). If Lycaon's crime will be to confuse the human and the divine and not to believe that Jupiter is a god, the Ovidian narrator begins to take a step in this direction in his own portrayal of the gods. Ovid's digression on the Milky Way offers the audience an altogether different perspective on the *concilium deorum* than is customary in epic. However, this is not simply burlesque, because it also includes an element of panegyric. Ostensibly, Ovid likens the gods to Romans not to ridicule them, but to compliment the emperor. The audience may play along and accept the conceit at face value, but it also may be inclined to smile in disbelief. Ovid continues to exploit and deepen this ambivalence throughout the episode.

After the detour on the Milky Way, the poet-narrator resumes the story and observes that the gods have taken their seats in an inner chamber faced with marble (1.177, "marmoreo superi sedere recessu"). The parallel with the marble temple-complex of Apollo on the Palatine, in whose library Augustus held Senate meetings, does not seem too far afield (Feeney 1991: 199). Jupiter sits on a throne loftier than the rest "celsior ipse loco"(1.178). This absolute use of the intensive pronoun *ipse* is striking and suggests Augustus *himself.* Even when Jupiter shakes his head of terrifying hair (1.179–80, "terrificam capitis concussit terque quaterque / caesariem"), causing earth, sea, and stars to move, Ovid manages to enjamb the word "caesariem" which alludes punningly (yet once more) to the emperor's presence. Of course, the extended analogy does not entitle one to conclude that Jupiter and Augustus are one and the same; on the contrary, Jupiter's frenzied anger may be contrasted with the image of the emperor's serenity.

Jupiter's ranting speech raises further questions. An impressively orotund opening (cf. 1.182, "non ego pro mundi regno") leads to the incredible proposition that the human race poses a greater threat to Olympus than the giants who assaulted it. The only solution is genocide: "perdendum est mortale genus" (1.188). Anderson (1989: 94) points out that this drastic decision should be of considerable interest to Ovid's human audience. Jupiter counters any objection with an innovative twist on a medical metaphor often used in political discourse: "cuncta prius temptanda, sed inmedicabile corpus / ense recidendum est, ne pars sincera trahatur" (1.190–91, "All means must be tried first, but an incurable body must be cut away by the blade, lest the healthy part becomes infected"). This raises the question of what the uninfected part of the body is. What follows is pure bathos. Jupiter has an obligation to protect his plebeian clients whom he excludes from heaven: "sunt mihi semidei, sunt, rustica numina, nymphae / Faunique Satyrique et monticolae Silvani" (1.192–93, "I have demigods, rustic divinities, nymphs, fauns and satyrs, and sylvan deities upon the mountain-slopes"). Jupiter's paternalistic concern for these gods, who are perhaps best known for their sexually promiscuous and loutish behavior, comes as a surprise. The narratorial audience has been led to believe that the assembly of the gods would be concerned with the rule of the universe, not the political rights of satyrs and fauns. The inconsequentiality of Jupiter's position is all the more striking when one thinks that one hundred lines earlier man had been created to be the crown of creation (1.76–77). Now the human race must be destroyed to protect lower-class gods.

In order to underscore the seriousness of the threat that man poses to these deities, Jupiter, reveals that he himself was the object of a treacherous plot by Lycaon: "struxerit insidias notus feritate Lycaon" (1.198, "Lycaon notorious for his ferocity plotted against me"). The gods greet Jupiter's news with a unanimous uproar (1.199, "confremuere omnes") and make passionate demands to punish the perpetrator (1.199–200, "studiis ardentibus ... deposcunt"), thereby showing their loyalty to Jupiter. Given the degree of Jupiter's indignation, this is a prudent response; however, it also shows that the gods do not have the slightest inkling who Lycaon is, much less what he did or what happened to him. The narratorial audience by contrast, may be expected to know the story of Lycaon. When Jupiter says that Lycaon is notorious for his ferocity ("notus feritate"), the phrase functions as a cue to his fame in mythological tradition. This is a point that deserves closer attention because it raises the issue of what the audience's extra-textual knowledge is.

The poet-narrator begins the whole episode by saying that Lycaon's crime had not yet been made public because of its newness (1.164, "facto nondum vulgata recenti"). At first glance, the phrase "nondum vulgata" appears to be a typical example of a class of phrases by which the poet displays a concern with the relative chronology of the myths he is telling. By saying that Lycaon's crime had not yet been made public, however, Ovid is implying that the tale *is* already well known to his audience. It is also possible that "nondum vulgata" could have a programmatic meaning. Ordinarily, a *fibula* that was *vulgate* was grounds for rejection in the discourse of the Augustan *recusatio*. In the proem to the third *Georgic*, Vergil rejects various mythological themes that have already become commonplace: "omnia iam vulgata" (*G.* 3.4). When Ovid introduces the story of Lycaon, he inverts the *recusatio*-motif when he says that it was "nondum vulgata" and thereby evades the ban on familiar themes by representing the very first telling of this story, from Jupiter's own lips.

Yet if Ovid's audience is already acquainted with Lycaon, it may be struck by a new feature of the story: the unprecedented details of Lycaon's assassination attempt on Jupiter. Given the implicit analogy that Ovid has drawn between Jupiter and Augustus, this would appear to be an extremely topical allusion; Augustus himself was subject to a number of assassination attempts in the years following Actium. Ovid draws attention to this link in his inaugural epic simile, which focuses on reactions to such plots:

> sic, cum manus inpia saevit
> sanguine Caesareo Romanum extinguere nomen,
> attonitum tanto subitae terrore ruinae
> humanum genus est totusque perhorruit orbis;
> nec tibi grata minus pietas, Auguste, tuorum est,
> quam fuit illa Iovi.

(Met. 1.200–205)

> [Just so, when a band of traitors raged to snuff out the Roman state with the blood of Caesar, was the human race shocked by such great terror of the sudden catastrophe, and the whole world shuddered; nor was the piety of your people less gratifying to you Augustus than it was to Jupiter.]

Scholars debate which Caesar's blood (Julius or Augustus) is at issue here, but Ovid is deliberately vague and would seem to admit both possibilities. The close of the simile, nonetheless, points toward plots against the life of Augustus. It seems unlikely, however, that Ovid is referring to a specific conspiracy: this was a chronic, and indeed defining, problem of the principate.

The most surprising part of the simile, in my view, is the apostrophe to Augustus himself. The technique of apostrophe is not itself unusual; it is common for Homer to close a simile with an address to the character with whom the simile is concerned. In Ovid's text, this should be Jupiter. But instead he appeals to Augustus with unblinking directness. First comes the personal pronoun ("tibi"), then the vocative ("Auguste"), and finally the impressive substantival use of the personal adjective ("tuorum"), which neatly equivocates between the *pietas* of family members toward a *paterfamilias* and the *pietas* of Roman citizenry toward the *pater patriae*. This, the first apostrophe in the *Metamorphoses*, gives Augustus a place of honor. Solodow (1988: 56) remarks that Augustus is "not a character within the narrative, but a contemporary figure present only in the simile." Yet is the *princeps* present only in the simile? Why cannot Augustus also be a privileged member of the audience? After all, it is for his benefit that Ovid calls the divine habitation of the Milky Way the "Palatine of heaven" (1.176, "Palatia caeli") and draws the analogy between the *concilium deorum* and the Roman Senate. It should not be surprising that Ovid momentarily singles out the emperor as a privileged member of his audience. We know that Augustus attended poetic recitations. Moreover, we know that he heard Vergil read the *Georgics* after Actium (Donat. *Vita Verg.* 105–9). Indeed, Ovid's appeal to Augustus closely parallels Vergil's invocations of the *princeps* in the *Georgics*. Although the younger Caesar is not expressly an addressee like Maecenas and the *agrestes*, he is arguably a member of Vergil's fictional audience.

If Ovid's apostrophe to Augustus represents him as a privileged member of his audience, it also makes the wider audience aware of the emperor's point of view. Ordinarily, the purpose of an epic simile is to encourage the audience's imaginative participation in the narrative by comparing something in the mythological world with something the audience knows from experience. In Homeric epic, similes most often incorporate events from daily life, assimilating the heroic past to the present world of poet and audience. Ovid's first simile begins in this vein, with a generalized memory of horror at plots against a Caesar, but then shifts apostrophically to the emperor's own gratitude for the *pietas* of his supporters. This movement from a universal shared experience to the response of Augustus defines a model for the reception of Ovid's own poem when the emperor is in the audience. Skepticism about an assassination attempt upon Jupiter or doubts about his justice become politically dangerous; expressions of loyalty and faith are greeted with favor. If Ovid's audience is losing faith in Jupiter's authority, the presence of Augustus forces the audience to reconsider its doubt.

Reading from Lycaon's Perspective

Endowed with the authority of Augustus, Jupiter proceeds to tell the gods of the crime and punishment of Lycaon, a story that illustrates the savagery of mankind and justifies genocide. Far from winning assent, however, Jupiter's narration proves to be both patently manipulative and inconsistent in its details. Jupiter begins by insisting too strenuously on his impartiality and hence the truth of his narrative. He claims to have heard about the infamy of the age (1.211, "infamia temporis"), and desired to prove the rumors false (1.212, "quam cupiens falsam"). To this end he visited earth in human disguise (1.213, "deus humana lustro sub imagine"). Jupiter thus poses as a private investigator to find out the truth. Rather than bore his listeners with a detailed presentation of the evidence for mankind's sin (1.214, "longa mora est, quantum noxae sit ubique repertum, / enumerare"), Jupiter concludes that the infamy itself was far less than the truth (1.215, "minor fuit ipsa infamia vero"). The gods have to take his word for it.

Jupiter next gives a prejudiced account of his travel through Arcadia to the house of Lycaon. The keynotes are savagery and inhospitality. Jupiter begins by saying that he had crossed Maenalon, a mountain bristling with the lairs of wild beasts (1.216, "latebris horrenda ferarum"). This epithet not only suggests the dangerous landscape of Arcadia but also foreshadows the transformation of Lycaon into a wolf. When Jupiter arrives at his destination he once again resorts to evaluative and affective vocabulary. He tells his audience that the house of Lycaon was inhospitable (1.218, "inhospita tecta") and that the king himself is a "tyrannus," a term that conjures up the negative image of political brutality. What is conspicuous here is how heavy handed Jupiter is in his judgments, despite his alleged desire to prove rumors of human wickedness false. He condemns Lycaon before he has even introduced him. Moreover, the narratorial audience, which is familiar with the story, may begin to sense the degree to which the traditional story is being distorted for ideological purposes. Indeed, in some traditions of the myth, Lycaon is not an outrageous villain but a pious king (cf. Forbes Irving 1990: 90–95).

Jupiter next says that he gave a sign that a god had arrived. This would appear to defeat the purpose of his human disguise; however, Jupiter wants to highlight Lycaon's skepticism. He explains that the common people had begun to pray (1.220–21, "vulgusque precari coeperat"), while Lycaon derided their prayers (1.221, "inridet primo pia vota Lycaon"). This scene reprises Ovid's earlier antithesis between the *manus inpia* that attempted to assassinate Caesar and the *pietas* shown by Augustus's supporters. Yet Jupiter's rhetoric leads him into blatant self-contradiction, for in the process of making Lycaon's behavior appear exceptionally bad, he undermines his own claim that all of mankind must be destroyed because of its universal corruption. Here he gives evidence to the contrary: everyone except Lycaon had undertaken *pia vota*. It may be argued that this local inconsistency should not be taken too seriously, but it raises doubts about Jupiter's claims and his impartiality.

Lycaon's disbelief in the divinity of his visitor is clearly motivated by the fact that Jupiter is still disguised as a human. This prompts Lycaon to undertake his own investigation into the truth: "'experiar deus hic discrimine aperto / an sit mortalis: nec erit dubitabile verum'" (1.222–23, "'I will soon find out by a plain test, whether this person is god or mortal: nor will the truth be in doubt'"). Lycaon does not say what his test will be, but Jupiter reports that the tyrant plotted to kill him in his sleep that night (1.224–25, "nocte gravem somno necopina perdere morte / me parat") and comments mordantly that this was Lycaon's method of testing the truth (1.225, "haec illi placet experientia veri"). As I have already noted, this is a new detail in the myth of Lycaon; its mention here clearly fulfills the expectation that Jupiter raised when he said that Lycaon had plotted against him. It was upon this basis that Jupiter argued that mankind should be destroyed for the safety of the satyrs and fauns. However, Lycaon never actually attempts to kill Jupiter in his sleep; Jupiter says he only *prepared* to do so (1.225, "parat").

This non-act is an anticlimactic conclusion to the assassination motif and raises the question of how Jupiter knows that Lycaon plotted to murder him. At this point of his story, Jupiter adopts the position of an omniscient narrator. Yet his omniscience vitiates the danger of the assassination in the first place (Anderson 1989: 96). Jupiter continues his account from an omniscient perspective, explaining that Lycaon was not content with this first plan; he also killed and cooked a Molossian hostage to serve his guest (1.226–30). Here again, Jupiter's version of the story departs from other versions of the cannibal banquet, in which Lycaon kills a child and serves it to the god. One may accordingly ask why Jupiter finds it necessary to make the victim a Molossian hostage. Molossians come from Epirus, which is hardly a geographical neighbor of Arcadia, as any Roman would know. It may be that the Molossian has a special claim to the protection of Jupiter because of the god's oracle at Dodona. In expecting his audience to be horrified at the sacrifice of such a hostage, however, Jupiter once again undercuts his thesis that all men deserve to die.

Jupiter next describes in ghoulish detail the boiling and roasting of the hostage's flesh (1.228–29). However, he does not reveal his identity until Lycaon serves the meal.

> quod simul inposuit mensis, ego vindice flamma
> in domino dignos everti tecta penates.

> (*Met.* 1.230–31)

> [Once he set this on the table, I, with my avenging thunderbolt, brought the house down on its household gods, worthy of their master.]

The effect of this sentence is striking. First, the emphatic change of subject indicated by the juxtaposition of "ego" with "vindice flamma," Jupiter's thunderbolt, marks the god's sudden transformation from a human at Lycaon's table to the god hurling a thunderbolt from on high. There is no point in attempting to assimilate the action to naturalism: this is an example of the *phantasia* that characterizes divine action. The narrative discontinuity, however, is less of a problem than the account of those who suffered from his wrath. As the sentence unfolds, Jupiter takes satisfaction in crushing the household gods, whom he calls worthy of their master (*domino dignos ... penates*). The theological difficulty of the final word *penates* compelled the editor Bentley to emend the text to *ministros*. Bömer explains that *penates* is a metonymy for a part of the house. After Ovid has made a joke about the Olympians having their own *penates*, however, it becomes difficult to avoid the conclusion that Jupiter is directing his anger toward the household gods of Lycaon, who are guilty by association. This vindictiveness stands at odds with his earlier paternalistic concern for the rustic gods.

Lycaon, on the other hand, escapes into the countryside and changes emphasizing the continuity between the man and the wolf. The vividness of the picture is itself a kind of proof of man's savagery. Solodow and Anderson argue, contrary to common opinion, that Jupiter is not the agent of Lycaon's metamorphosis. Solodow (1988: 169) makes his case on the grounds that Jupiter does not say that he actually transformed Lycaon. In a certain sense, this is correct. Jupiter's rhetorical point is that very little separates Lycaon the man from Lycaon the wolf. Yet, why infer that Jupiter was *not* the catalyst of the change? Jupiter's destruction of Lycaon's house (1.230, "everti") recalls the standard punishment of tyrants in Greco-Roman society: razing of the house. Moreover, the razing the house is generally coupled with another punishment — often exile. The destruction of Lycaon's home (a sign of human order) and the end of his kinship line removes the last marker of his humanity, at which point he goes into exile and his wolfish identity takes over. The fact that Jupiter is not *directly* involved in Lycaon's metamorphosis makes it the least prejudicial and most credible part of his story.

Jupiter concludes his speech with a rallying cry against humanity. He paints a picture of the forces of hell ruling on earth (1.241, "qua terra patet, fera regnat Erinys"), sets before the eyes of the gods a conspiracy (1.242, "in facinus iurasse putes"), and calls for summary execution of the criminals. The response of the gods to Jupiter's rhetoric is instructive:

> Dicta Iovis pars voce probant stimulosque frementi
> adiciunt, alii partes adsensibus inplent.

> (*Met.* 2.244–45)

> [Some proclaimed their approval of his words with a shout and goaded his rant, while others played their part in applause.]

Given that one part of the audience (*pars*) approves Jupiter's plan, one might expect that the other part will disapprove. This, in fact, is the normal pattern in the *Metamorphoses*. Moreover, debate amongst the gods is a frequent feature of divine assemblies. The surprise here is that the others (*alii*) do not dissent; they merely express assent in a different way (cf. Feeney 1991: 200). Here Ovid gives a voice to the "duped" reader: the loyal response of the Olympian gods as orchestrated by Jupiter himself.

The narratorial audience, on the other hand, is faced with an impossible choice: respond to Jupiter with disbelief and become the lone wolf opposed to social order; or join the consensus that accepts official fictions without question. This dilemma is exacerbated if the emperor is in the audience watching for signs of loyalty and disloyalty. To make matters worse, Ovid repeatedly pushes the audience to the brink of indecorous laughter with his satirical portrayal of the gods. The audience thus runs the risk of committing an interpretive error similar to Lycaon's and of "conspiring" against Jupiter. Yet if Ovid has a "hermeneutic alibi" in the deliberate ambiguity of his representation of Jupiter and Augustus (cf. Hinds 1988: 26; Bretzigheimer 1993: 23), he also warns his audience of the consequences of disbelieving official myths. In the final analysis, Ovid is not openly mocking Augustus.

Rather he is representing the complex political considerations that shape audience response in a society whose ideological imperatives polarize public discourse. The Lycaon tale illustrates how belief and disbelief — issues that define one's response to fiction — underpin Augustus's authority and legitimate the ideology of imperial order.

Ovid repeatedly returns to the conflict of belief and disbelief after the Lycaon episode. In later examples of the pattern, however, the political repercussions are less explicit. That is, the controlling presence of Augustus fades after the first book and only returns again in the final book. However, Augustus's own quasi-divine power has defined what is at stake in the pull between belief and disbelief. Skeptics of divine power and metamorphosis invariably come to a bad end.

References

Anderson, W.A. (1989). "Lycaon: Ovid's Deceptive Paradigm in *Metamorphoses* I." *ICS* 14:91–101.

Avery, M.M. (1937. *The Use of Direct Speech in Ovid's Metamorphoses*. Ph.D. diss., University of Chicago.

Barchiesi, A. (1994). *Il poeta e il principe*. Rome and Bari.

Bretzigheimer, G. (1993). "Jupiter Tonans in OvidsMetamorphosen." *Gymnasium* 100:19–74.

Crabbe, A. (1981). "Structure and Content in Ovid's *Metamorphoses*." *ANRW* II. 31.4:2274–327.

Feeney, D.C. (1991). *The Gods in Epic: Poets and Critics of the Classical Tradition*. Oxford.

Forbes Irving, P.M.C. (1990). *Metamorphoses in Greek Myths*. Oxford.

Galinsky, G.K. (1975). *Ovid's Metamorphoses: An Introduction to the Basic Aspects*. Berkeley and Los Angeles.

Graf, F. (1988). "Ovid, les Métamorphoses et la véracité du mythe." In *Métamorphoses du mythe en Grèce antique*, ed. C. Calame, 57–70. Religions en perspective IV. Geneva.

Heinze, R. [1919] (1960). "Ovids elegische Erzählung." Berichte der Verhandlungen der Sächsischen Akademie zu Leipzig, Philologische-historische Klasse, 71.7, 1919. Reprinted in *Vom Geist des Römertums*, ed. E. Burck, 3d ed., 308–403. Stuttgart.

Hinds, S.E. (1988). "Genearlising about Ovid." In *The Imperial Muse: Ramus Essays on Roman Literature of the Empire* (= *Ramus* 16 [1987]), ed. A.J. Boyle, 4–31. Victoria.

Little, D.A. (1970). "Richard Heinze: *Ovids elegische Erzählung*." In *Ovids ars Amatoria und Remedia Amoris: Untersuchungen zum Aufbau*, ed. E. Zinn, 64–105. Stuttgart.

Newsom, R. (1988). *A Likely Story: Probability and Play in Fiction*. New Brunswick, N.J.

Otis, B. (1970). *Ovid as an Epic Poet*. 2d ed. Cambridge.

Solodow, J.B. (1988). *The World of Ovid's Metamorphoses*. Chapel Hill.

Wilkinson, L.P. (1955). *Ovid Recalled*. Cambridge.

Zumwalt, N. (1977). "*Fama Subversa*: Theme and Structure in Ovid's *Metamorphoses* 12." *CSCA* 10:209–22.

Secondary Source 3.12   Thomas A. Schmitz, 'Narratology' (summary of Genette's focalisation theory)

(Source: Schmitz, T.A. (2007) *Modern Literary Theory and Ancient Texts: An Introduction*, Malden MA and Oxford, Blackwell Publishing, pp. 57–60)

- In a zero focalization, the narrator assumes the position of an omniscient god: he is in possession of complete knowledge about all emotions, plans, and actions of the characters.

- Internal focalization looks at events in the perspective of one of the narrative's characters, without necessarily using this character's voice. The reader is merely told what this character knows and sees; things that the character did not witness herself or himself need to be told by other characters or added in other ways. This internal focalization becomes especially clear when we read a sentence such as "Bond believed he could see fear in Goldfinger's eyes." Here, the narrative is in the third person, yet this sentence gives us Bond's perspective of the scene: we are certain about Bond's thoughts only and can merely speculate (with Bond) on Goldfinger's feelings. The focalizing character can change in the course of a narrative; the clearest example for this case is the epistolary novel in which events are perceived (and narrated) by various letter writers in turn.

- In external focalization, readers perceive all characters from an external perspective; hence, they have no knowledge of their thoughts and emotions. Some experimental modernist novels have played with this external focalization and used it throughout the text. In "classical" narratives, it is sometimes used to introduce a new character. In this case, we are first given a mere external description ("a young woman of around twenty years, blond, thin," etc.); later, more details that require more than a mere external perspective will be supplied. In this case, it is evident that the narrating voice was already in possession of this supplementary information but that the focalization presupposes a perspective which does not have this information.

The narrative instance (the answer to the question "who is speaking?") is treated in the section on "voice" [133.212–62]. Genette distinguishes different possibilities of the temporal relation between story and narrating:

- The subsequent narrative is the normal case: events are narrated after they have taken place.

- In prior narrative, the relation is exactly opposite: events are narrated before they take place. This is the case, e.g., in prophecies: in the *Aeneid*, 1.267–71, Jupiter predicts that Aeneas's son Ascanius will reign in Alba Longa for 30 years; this is a period of time which exceeds the narrative period presented in the *Aeneid*. However, science fiction does not usually utilize prior narrative: while the narrated events take place in the future as seen from the reader's point of view, the narrator's voice relates them in the past tense because the act of narrating is placed even further into the future and "looks back" on the events.

- As an example of simultaneous narrative, we can think of the live coverage of a baseball match on the radio: everything is narrated exactly at the moment when it is happening. Modern novels (such as the *Nouveau Roman* in France) have sometimes played with this form of narrative.

- In interpolated narrative, narrating and events alternate; good examples for this form would be epistolary novels or diaries: when the narrating begins, the events are not yet finished.

Genette [133.227–62] invents a number of (sometimes rather complicated) terms for the analysis of narrative levels. It is comprehensible that some scholars with a more traditional background have criticized these neologisms as unnecessarily inelegant, yet they have the advantage of being accurate and free from unwanted associations. Genette distinguishes an extradiegetical and an intradiegetic level. Narrative texts tell of events, situations, and characters; all these elements are located *within* the narrative, so they are intradiegetical. The act of narrating, on the other hand, usually takes place *outside of* this narrated universe, so it is extradiegetic: the narrator who, in the first line of the *Aeneid*, announces "Arms and the man I sing," and his "singing" itself do not exist in the same world as Aeneas's wanderings and battles. Of course, such levels can continue and be embedded within a narration; Ovid's *Metamorphoses*, for instance, display a highly complex system of nested narratives within the main narrative.

This fundamental difference between intradiegetical and extradiegetical elements has always been clear to most readers of narrative, even if it was not conscious. Its importance highlighted when narratives, in a parodic or playful manner, break the boundary between the intradiegetical and extradiegetical levels. For example, in Woody Allen's 1997 movie *Deconstructing Harry*, novelist Harry Block one day has an encounter with one of the characters of his novels (and gets an earful about his messed-up life). The joke here lies in the fact that an inviolable border is transgressed: as an author, Block is not on the same level of the narrative as his characters; in regard to the world of his novels, he is extradiegetical. Genette calls such transgressions "metalepses."

Genette then analyzes the relation between the narrator and the narrative. A narrator can either be a character in her or his own narrative and have a minor or a major part in it, or (s)he can relate events in which (s)he had no active role. Genette calls the first case an homodiegetic, the second an heterodiegetic narrator. He makes these terms more understandable by providing a helpful table [133.248] (such tables are typical of his terminological precision). This table is here modified (table 1) so as to use examples from Latin literature.

Table 1   Narrator and narrative according to Genette

Level \ Relationship	Extradiegetic	Intradiegetic
Heterodiegetic	Virgil	Aristaeus
Homodiegetic	Apileius	Aeneas

What follows is a very brief explanation of the items in table 1.

- "Virgil" here means the narrator who enters the stage in the first line of the *Aeneid* and says "I sing" (*cano*); he is also occasionally present in later parts of the epic, e.g. 6.266 "permit me to relate" *sit mihi fas* or 7.41 "I will tell" *dicam*. This narrator is heterodiegetic because he is not present in the events of the epic as a character; he is extradiegetic because his "I will sing" is addressed to the audience and readership of the *Aeneid*, not at characters within the epic text.

- In the fourth book of Virgil's *Georgics* (453–527), the god Proteus narrates the story of Orpheus and Eurydice to his listener Aristaeus. Both are characters within the poem, so the entire narrative is intradiegetic. However,

Proteus himself is not a character in the story he tells, so he is a heterodiegetic narrator.

- The narrator in Apuleius's *Metamorphoses* is homodiegetic because he plays an important role in his own narrative (he relates that he was transformed into an ass and could regain his human features only after long and exciting adventures). On the other hand, his narrative is addressed to the novel's readers, so it is extradiegetic.

- When Aeneas narrates his own adventures in Carthage in the second and third books of the *Aeneid*, he clearly is a homodiegetic narrator. Since his narrative takes place within the *Aeneid* and is addressed to a public in this fictional world (Queen Dido and her court), it is intradiegetic.

If you want to see examples for every imaginable situation and combination, you could analyze the complex and nested narratives in Ovid's *Metamorphoses* (as Stephen M. Wheeler [376.207–10] has done). This section has just presented a small part of Genette's narratological system to give an example of the sensitive methodology he provides for the analysis of narratives. Every critic who has a serious interest in narrative should in any case have a look at Genette's contributions themselves and get an impression of their use, but also of their limitations.

References

[133] Genette, Gérard: *Narrative Discourse. An Essay in Method*, Ithaca, NY: Cornell University Press, 1980 [original French edn Paris 1972].

[376] Wheeler, Stephen M.: *A Discourse of Wonders. Audience and Performance in Ovid's Metamorphoses*, Philadelphia: University of Pennsylvania Press, 1999.

Secondary Source 3.13   D.C. Feeney, 'Ovid's *Metamorphoses*'

(Source: Feeney, D.C. (1991) *The Gods in Epic: Poets and Critics of the Classical Tradition*, Oxford, Oxford University Press, pp. 188–94)

> For given Man, by birth, by education,
> Imago Dei who forgot his station,
> The self-made creature who himself unmakes,
> The only creature ever made who fakes,
> With no more nature in his loving smile
> Than in his theories of a natural style,
> What but tall tales, the luck of verbal playing,
> Can trick his lying nature into saying
> That love, or truth in any serious sense,
> Like orthodoxy, is a reticence?

(W.H. Auden, 'The Truest Poetry is the most Feigning')

Ovid's *Metamorphoses* afford us something of an intermezzo. The very appearance of a chapter on this poem in a book on epic is itself an issue—a fact which the poet would no doubt have found highly diverting. From its first lines the poem continually confronts us with the problem of the extent to which, and the ways in which, it is and is not epic.[1] There is no obligation here to enter into a full account of the poem from the viewpoint of its continually destabilized generic norms, yet by taking this line as a first thread into the poem it may be possible to discover a promising starting-point for our investigation

---

[1]   The entire debate over the epic nature of the *Metamorphoses*, a key issue since Heinze (1919), has been set on a new footing by Hinds (1987); cf. the anticipations of Nicoll (1980).

into what the poem has to say about epic and its gods. As a commentary on the epic view of the gods the poem is priceless, while it will prove to be of the highest importance for the epics which follow it, especially the *Thebaid* and *Argonautica*, where its influence on this aspect of epic form is, if anything, greater even than that of the *Aeneid*.[2] It will emerge that Ovid's emphases are markedly different from those of the poets we have been examining so far, for his range of mythological interest is vast, and his coverage eclectic in the extreme. For all that, his preoccupation with epic modes is pervasive, and highly enlightening.

Novelty is proclaimed in the poem's second word, and paradox follows straight after, as the proem's dense allusions, followed by the opening cosmogony, adumbrate the perspectives we will need in order to read this un-epic epic, an uncategorizable multi-form prodigy:

> In nova fert animus mutatas dicere formas
> corpora; di, coeptis (nam uos mutastis et illa)
> adspirate meis primaque ab origine mundi
> ad mea perpetuum deducite tempora carmen.
>
> My spirit leads me to tell of shapes changed into new bodies; gods, breathe on my undertakings (for you have changed them as well), and, from the first origin of the world, spin out of my poem unbroken down to my own time. (*Met.* 1. 1–4)

In the fourth line, *perpetuum* appears to distance the poet from the non-epic aesthetic of the master, Callimachus, while *deducite* draws him simultaneously nearer.[3] The ensuing cosmogony picks up this tergiversation. Certainly the cosmogony is not serious philosophy for its own sake, but it is concerned with mapping out the terrain of possibility for the poem. It is highly significant that there is a good measure of control and direction behind Ovid's evolving universe, as is very much not the case in, for example, the neoteric universe sung of by Silenus in Vergil's sixth *Eclogue*. Silenus' world is 'essentially fragmented, not ordered, fortuitous, not designed'.[4] Ovid's world, on the other hand, emerges from strife by the work of a god, or nature (21), who organizes the separate locations of the constituent elements (22–31). This world is more epic than neoteric in the very fact of its controlled organization—although, as we shall see shortly, the *mundi fabricator* does not act in a very epic manner. The oddness of the control is caught in a moment of comparison with Vergil's universe: Vergil's Jupiter controls the winds by putting on top of them a mass of high mountains (*Aen.* 1. 61), while Ovid's *mundi fabricator* places above them the *aether*, explicitly 'liquid and lacking weight, containing nothing of earthly sediment' (*liquidum et grauitate carentem / aethera nec quicquam terrenae faecis habentem*, 1. 67–8).

---

[2]   Bibliography on the gods in the *Metamorphoses* in Hofmann (1981), 2188–9; Elliott (1979–80).

[3]   Hinds (1987), 19, with bibliography of the numerous discussions, esp. Kenney (1976): add Hofmann (1985). Such, at least, is the reading imposed by the blunt dichotomies which two generations of Latin poetry had read into the prologue to Callimachus' *Aetia*. A fascinating (as yet unpublished) interpretation by S. J. Heyworth blurs the apparent rigidity of the paradox, yielding a reading of the proem that sees it as true to the spirit of the *Aetia*; see, rather differently, Knox (1986), 9–10. For a restatement of the importance of epic to the definitions of Callimachus and Ovid, see Hinds (1989), Anderson (1988). For the latest and most thorough defence of the reading *illa* in line 2, see Kovacs (1987).

[4]   Hubbard (1975), 61. Note, however, that the *Metamorphoses* begins as if it were an epic ecphrasis (compare Ap. Rhod. *Argon.* 1. 496 ff.).

In many important ways Ovid's cosmogony is redolent of anti-epic allegiances,[5] yet the element of control (however qualified) is indispensable to Ovid's conception of the nature of metamorphosis: as Barkan points out, 'for all its emphasis upon the blurring of clear categories, metamorphosis is as much concerned with reduction and fixity as with variability or complexity'.[6] There is more involved here than acknowledging that agreed categories are necessary for representation of transition. Aristotle's discussion of change, for example, 'insists that in every change (whether movement in space or alteration in quality or size) *something remains the same*'.[7]

The story which most dramatically illustrates the poles of fixity and flux is the weaving-contest between Minerva and Arachne. This story also affords key insights into the poem's conceptions of art, into its ways of talking about the gods and divine power, and will therefore repay some attention.[8] The Arachne story follows on from Book 5, whose last portion is concerned with genre, as Minerva listens to the Muses' account of their singing competition with the mortal Pierides (5. 251–end). Since the issues there have been fully discussed by Hinds (1987), let us analyse the sequel, and follow the goddess as she changes role, becoming herself a competitor in art with a mortal.

Arachne's superlative craftsmanship is described in terms which not only establish her credentials as a mistress of neoteric art, but also (at first) align her with the *mundi fabricator*, and hence with Ovid himself. She begins with rude, unwrought material, as does the demiurge (*rudem ... lanam*, 6. 19; cf. *rudis ... moles*, 1. 7); this she forms into a globe (*glomerabat in orbes*, 6. 19; cf. *magni speciem glomerabat in orbis*, 1. 35). From here on she becomes more and more neoteric. She sets to work the *opus*, making it *soft* by drawing it out to a length, turning the *smooth* spindle with a *light* thumb (*mollibat, leui teretem*, 21–2).[9]

Pallas' work, however, is described first, marked out as artistically and morally weighty, symmetrical and accessible: 'the composition of the goddess' work is flawlessly Classical, perfectly centered, balanced, and framed, highly moral and didactic in content'.[10] Her competition with Neptune at Athens is the first element to be described, occupying the centre of the composition (6. 70–82): self-praise and self-vindication are therefore the subject. The Olympian gods are all there, two times six—with Jupiter in the middle of the assemblage and the line—in all their august weightiness (*augusta grauitate*, 73).[11] Each deity is recognisable by his or her distinctive attributes (73–4); appearance corresponds with actuality.[12] When Pallas 'simulates' an event on her tapestry, it is no dissimulating lie, but the event itself (80–1). Around this

---

[5]   Knox (1986), 10–13.

[6]   Barkan (1986), 66; cf. Coleman (1971), 462, on the cosmogony as a necessary minimum backdrop of order for the metamorphoses to follow.

[7]   Ackrill (1981), 31 (his italics); cf. Anderson (1963), 4–5; Solodow (1988), 183–6.

[8]   The passage is much discussed. See, above all, the extremely valuable article of Leach (1974); also Lateiner (1984); von Albrecht (1984); Hofmann (1985), 230–4; Barkan (1986), 1–18; Brown (1987).

[9]   On the loaded import of such vocabulary, see Cairns (1979), 21; Hinds (1987), 21–2. Ovid also aligns the poetic craft of Orpheus with the action of the demiurge, as they each make a concord out of discordant elements (1. 25, 10. 146–7). On the correspondence between the power of the creator and of the poet, see Lieberg (1982) and (1985).

[10]   Anderson (1972), 160.

[11]   We will return to the resonance of the epithet: Augustus belongs here, if we take him and the gods on their own valuation.

[12]   Barkan (1986), 90 acutely remarks that only the gods can have faith in their form (*fiducia formae*, 2. 731).

satisfying centre are arranged in symmetry four neat scenes showing contests 'between a rash woman and a goddess, all resulting in the metamorphosis of the mortal (83–100)'.[13] The whole is framed by a border of Pallas' own tree, the olive: this is the *modus* (102), a terminus of artistic moderation. The composition is now finished, with the word 'end' at the end in a culminating gesture of decorum (*finem*, 102).

Arachne's work is, by contrast, a neoteric masterpiece, asymmetrical and wilful.[14] The picture it gives of the gods is, correspondingly, far from Pallas' justified order: these gods are swept pell-mell through the currents of natural flux, not static and identifiable by attribute, but bewilderingly mutating in order to work their sexual will upon helpless humans. In the goddess's work, only humans were undergoing change; in the human's work, the humans are a given, while the gods mutate. Jupiter's characteristically regal *imago* on Pallas' tapestry is now the *imago* of a bull, or a satyr (103, 110), adopted for disguise. As the humans in the tapestry are tricked, cheated, duped (*elusam*, 103; *luserit*, 113, 124; *deceperit*, 125), so the spectator is gulled by Arachne's craft: *you* would be tricked, like Europa, into thinking Jupiter's *imago* was a real bull (103–4), even though you have read the story already in the poem and know that the bull is *fallax* and *falsus* (2. 871, 3. 1). The apparently true is an illusion. As Pallas' last lines had capped her stately, measured performance, so Arachne's border is graced with the programmatic *tenui* ('slight', 127).

Pallas and Envy could not pick Arachne's work to pieces (129–30, with yet another weaving/criticism play, on *carpere*). What are *we* to make of it, and of Pallas' own work? This is, after all, a competition, with judgement invited. Most modern readers will instinctively side with Arachne's neoteric vision, and most modern readings, accordingly, offer an Arachnaean version of the poem as a whole.[15] Other important modern readings, however, adopt a Minervan perspective. Otis sees the episode (and the poem) from Minerva's point of view, while Bömer's commentary gives here, as elsewhere, a consistently Minervan reading.[16] A path through these alternatives is offered by Leach, whose fine article demonstrates that if we adhere to one antithesis or the other we will fail to do what justice we can to the complexity of the poem's perspectives.[17] Ovid's pendulum never rests in its oscillation between the poles of Minerva and Arachne, epic and neoteric canons: 'As the creator of the poem, Ovid maintains a vision embracing both points of view.'[18] The episode is a lesson in perspective, with divine and human order and flux, fixity and instability—this is why it comes at a moment which has often been marked as the transition from a predominantly divine perspective to a predominantly human one.[19] Minerva's work is an exaggerated picture of divine epic decorum, Arachne's an exaggerated picture of neoteric divine abandonment. Yet Arachne depicts nothing about the gods that was not already present, however faintly, in epic

---

[13] Anderson (1972), 160.

[14] Anderson (1972), 164–5; Galinsky (1975), 82–3; Hofmann (1985), 230–4.

[15] e.g. Little (1970); Solodow (1988), 196–7.

[16] Otis (1970), 146; Bömer (1969–86), vol. 3. 35–6.

[17] Leach (1974); cf. Brown (1987).

[18] Leach (1974), 104. As Professor Hinds points out to me, the weaving of both contestants is described in markedly neoteric terms in 61–9 (note especially the key *deducitur* of 69: cf. Hofmann (1985), 231). As he puts it, 'the two contestants have more in common than they are prepared to admit; neotericism depends on what it subverts'.

[19] Otis (1970), 166, 315; Wilkinson (1955), 148.

tradition. Minerva's reading is *too* epic, glossing over the difficulties of divine action which had been present in epic from the beginning.[20]

This is not to say that Arachne's craft might not be, in the end, closer to the poem's dominant mode.[21] In the last resort, Ovid is a human artist, like Arachne, and not a god.[22] Arachne corresponds to one commonly available archetype of the artist: obsessive, naïve, destroyed (like Ovid) by direct encounter with the power of the world she is trying to describe. Her metamorphosis into a spider is a sickeningly appropriate punishment for Minerva to devise. The perpetual weaver of webs that are proverbially easy to destroy,[23] her qualities of fine grace are exaggerated into parody as she becomes simply small, tiny (142), her fingers programmatically *exiles*, embodying the stylistic thinness which is the fate of failed small-scale composition (143). The celebrator of beautiful disorder is now doomed to the spider's weaving of utter symmetry.[24] Worst of all, as Seneca tells us in a fascinating disquisition on animal instinct, a spider's work is not art. All spiders produce the same, none is more skilled than the next:

> Nascitur ars ista, non discitur. itaque nullum est animal altero doctius: uidebis araneorum pares telas ... incertum est et inaequabile quidquid ars tradit: ex aequo uenit quod natura distribuit.

> That art is innate, not learnt. And so no animal is more learned than the next: you'll see that spiders' webs are all equal ... Whatever art bestows is uncertain and uneven; what nature distributes issues from an even source. (Sen. *Ep.* 121. 23)

At the end, it really is true that you would know she was taught by Minerva (*scires a Pallade doctam*, 23).

References

Ackrill, J. L. (1981). *Aristotle the Philosopher* (Oxford).

Anderson, W. S. (1963). 'Multiple Change in the *Metamorphoses*', *TAPhA* 94. 1–27.

Anderson, W. S. (ed.) (1972) *Ovid's Metamorphoses: Books 6–10* (Norman, Okla.).

Anderson, W. S. (1988). Review of Knox (1986), *AJPh* 109. 459–61.

Barkan, L. (1986). *The Gods Made Flesh: Metamorphosis and the Pursuit of Paganism* (New Haven).

Bömer, F. (ed.) (1958). *P. Ovidius Naso: Die Fasten* (Heidelberg).

Brown, R. (1987). 'The Palace of the Sun in Ovid's *Metamorphoses*', in Whitby–Hardie–Whitby (1987). 211–20.

Cairns, F. (1979). *Tibullus: A Hellenistic Poet at Rome* (Cambridge).

Coleman, R. G. (1971). 'Structure and Intention in the *Metamorphoses*', *CQ*, NS 21. 461–77.

---

[20] Ovid delights in resensitizing us to epic's evasions. It has been objected, for example, that his battle descriptions are too distant: 'Urbane hexameters and pointed conceits adorn the violence and gore of the battle of the Lapiths and Centaurs' (Lyne (1984), 13). Yet these tactics may jolt us into seeing Homer and Vergil as being themselves merchants of beautiful descriptions of the horrific and macabre.

[21] So Brown (1987), 219–20, and (one suspects) Leach (1974).

[22] Leach's discussion is extremely valuable here as well.

[23] Otto (1890), 34.

[24] Plin. *HN* 11. 80–2; Philostr. *Imag.* 2. 28.3; Plut. *Mor.* 966 e–f.

Elliott, A. G. (1979–80). 'Ovid's *Metamorphoses:* A Bibliography 1968–1978', *CW* 73. 385–412.

Galinsky, G. K. (1975). *Ovid's* Metamorphoses: *An Introduction to the Basic Aspects* (Berkeley and Los Angeles).

Heinze, R. (1919). *Ovids elegische Erzählung* (Leipzig).

Hinds, S. E. (1987). *The Metamorphosis of Persephone: Ovid and the Self-Conscious Muse* (Cambridge).

Hofmann, H. (1981). 'Ovids "Metamorphosen" in der Forschung der letzten 30 Jahre (1950–1979)', *ANRW* 2. 31. 4. 2161–273.

Hofmann, H. (1985). 'Ovid's *Metamorphoses*: *carmen perpetuum, carmen deductum*', *PLLS* 5. 223–41.

Hubbard, M. (1975). 'The Capture of Silenus', *PCPhS*, NS 21. 53–62.

Kenney, E. J. (1976). 'Ovidius Prooemians', *PCPhS,* NS 22. 46–53.

Knox, P. E. (1986). *Ovid's* Metamorphoses *and the Traditions of Augustan Poetry* (Cambridge).

Kovacs, D. (1987). 'Ovid, *Metamorphoses* 1. 2', *CQ*, NS 37. 458–65.

Lateiner, D. (1984). 'Mythic and Non-mythic Artists in Ovid's *Metamorphoses*', *Ramus* 13. 1–30.

Leach, E. W. (1974). 'Ekphrasis and the Theme of Artistic Failure in Ovid's *Metamorphoses*', *Ramus* 3. 102–42.

Lieberg, G. (1982). *Poeta Creator: Studien zu einer Figur der antiken Dichtung* (Amsterdam).

Lieberg, G. (1985). '*Poeta Creator*: Some "Religious" Aspects', *PLLS* 5. 23–32.

Little, D. A. (1970). 'Richard Heinze: Ovids elegische Erzählung', in E. Zinn (ed.), *Ovids Ars amatoria und Remedia amoris: Untersuchungen zum Aufbau* (Stuttgart). 64–105.

Nicoll, W. S. M. (1980). 'Cupid, Apollo, and Daphne (Ovid, *Met.* 1. 452 ff.)', *CQ*, NS 38. 174–82.

Otis, B. (1970). *Ovid as an Epic Poet* (Cambridge).

Solodow, J. B. (1988). *The World of Ovid's* Metamorphoses (Chapel Hill, N.C.).

von Albrecht, M. (1984). 'Ovids Arachne-Erzählung', in Harmatta (1984). 1. 457–64.

Secondary Source 3.14 Paul Barolsky, 'Ovid's Protean Epic of Art'

(Source: *Arion*, Winter 2007, vol, 14, no. 3)

I know of no work of literature more wonderful than *Metamorphoses*. Even those who have never read Ovid or have read but fragments of his poem are familiar with many of his stories: Apollo and Daphne, Echo and Narcissus, Pyramus and Thisbe, Icarus and Daedalus, Orpheus and Eurydice, Venus and Adonis. Ovid's book may be popular but it is also radically searching: it is about the causes of things, about how birds, beasts, trees, flowers, and rocks came to be, a book about why things are the way they are. His poem is nothing less than a history of the world from its creation out of chaos through the writing of *Metamorphoses* itself in the age of Augustus Caesar. History, we might say, culminates with Ovid's poem, which is the artful mirror image of the cosmos in the multiplicity of all its forms.

When we read Ovid, we become part of a wide community, a community that embraces artists of various types in the modern European tradition who have responded to *Metamorphoses*—from the authors who forged the Roman de la Rose to the poets of our own day inspired by the Augustan bard. If Ovid has been read by great artists, he is also read by those who like a good story, a story told well, a story that gives pleasure. In that respect, Ovid belongs to everybody.

Metamorphoses is a poem about nature, both its physical beauty and the natural catastrophes that mark the world: flood, conflagration, famine, plague. In this respect, Ovid is a realist. *Metamorphoses* is also a history of desire, a multitude of stories of love, lust, passion and affection, a reminder that the intertwined histories of Western art and literature, enriched by Ovid, are the aggregation of such stories of desire.

As a sustained and radical exploration of form and transformation, *Metamorphoses* is a work about art, about artistic form. Although Ovid's acute attention to artifice of various kinds has often been discussed over the years, often incisively, there is still more to be said about Ovid's sense of art. The sum of Ovid's allusions to art in *Metamorphoses* is greater than the parts, and the full implications of his vision of art are still, I believe, only dimly surmised.

In order to clarify our understanding of Ovid's conception of art, let us recall a crucial, well-known fact about *Metamorphoses*. As a poem inspired in part by Homer and Virgil, by the *Iliad*, *Odyssey*, and *Aeneid*, *Metamorphoses* is an epic or, as some would say, a mock-epic, which, toward the end, braids the myths of Achilles, Odysseus, and Aeneas, all men of arms and great deeds—in a word, heroes. Yet Ovid's epic is an epic of a different kind, what I wish to call the "epic of art," in which artists of various types, not warriors, are the principal heroes and heroines. Ovid's understanding of mythic artists has its roots in Homer and Virgil—for example, their celebration of the prodigious artistic skill of Vulcan. But magnifying the theme of art in his own epic, giving it a far more extensive role in his poem than in previous epics, Ovid transforms the epic hero from soldier into artist.

Ovid's poem is a *carmen*, a song. In *Metamorphoses*, songs tell stories, and stories are sometimes rendered pictorially in woven images. In his work, Ovid achieves an even greater unity of the arts. Sculpture, architecture, painting, weaving, handicraft, poetry, song, storytelling, and rhetoric are brought together in *Metamorphoses* in a prodigious synthetic art, of which Ovid is the ultimate author, the artist who embodies and unifies all of the arts. In short, Ovid as artist is the supreme hero of his own epic.

In book one, Ovid makes it abundantly clear that his opus differs from previous epics, for unlike the poems of Homer and Virgil, Ovid's focuses attention on the central theme of his own epic—art. With a great flourish of stories about art, Ovid introduces the theme of artifice in its many forms. After an unknown god molded the earth in the beginning, the son of Iapetus, Prometheus, made images of man out of the clay of the earth, whence the origins of sculpture. Ovid pursues this thread in the story of the son of Prometheus, Deucalion, and his wife Pyrrha, who, after the flood, toss behind them the stones that turn into human beings. Likening the human forms within stone to unfinished statues during this metamorphosis, Ovid thereby places Deucalion in the line of descent from his father, Prometheus. This genealogy of art reaches its apex later in book ten in the story of Pygmalion, whose statue made from ivory softens eventually to the sculptor's touch and comes to life.

As a sculptor in words, Ovid also describes the reverse effect of people in the flesh transformed into stone—Battus, Aglauros, Niobe and all the adversaries of Perseus subjected to Medusa's gaze. For Ovid, sculpture is neither the hard substance that softens and comes alive nor the living flesh transformed into stone. Rather, compounded both of the myths of Pygmalion and Medusa, sculpture in Ovid is ambiguously and more fully than in one myth or the other both a living presence in hard stone and the petrification of the flesh. Ovid gives us the fullest and deepest understanding in all of literature of the existential doubleness of sculpture, forever poised ambiguously between life and death.

In book one, Ovid also begins his sustained celebration of architecture, for example in his evocation of the marble halls of the gods. Although the builder of such sublime architecture is unnamed, we might well attribute it to the gods themselves, of whom Vulcan is the premier figure. Vulcan is the author of the Sun-god's dazzling palace made of bronze, gold, and ivory and adorned with an illustrated silver door—a work pictured by Ovid at the beginning of book two as he pursues one thread from a story in the first book.

The other principal architect of Ovid's poem is of course Daedalus, designer of the great labyrinth, a work of astonishing ingenuity that deceives the eye in its winding passages, which are likened in their ambiguities to those of the Meander River as it flows back and forth, out to the sea but also, at times, back to its source. Daedalus's ambiguous structure is a fitting simile for the complexity of Ovid's poem, which is plotted with comparable complexity as its fables both foretell and echo each other—for example, the myth of Prometheus foreshadows the tale of Pygmalion, the sculptor whose art echoes in turn that of Prometheus. As sculpture is ambiguous in its play between life and death, so is daedalic architecture, which, like Ovid's poem, is ambiguous as it moves in two directions at once.

In book one again, Ovid introduces another principal art, painting, which emerges in the myth of Argus, whose head is cut off by the murderous Mercury, after which Juno adorns the peacock's feathers with the dead shepherd's one hundred eyes. When Juno reappears in book two, mounting her chariot borne aloft by peacocks, Ovid refers not once but twice to the fact that their pinions were *pictis*, "painted." Juno is for Ovid an originary painter.

Ovid also evokes the art of painting in the myth of Arachne's weaving contest with Minerva, especially when he uses the verb *pingere* to describe what the goddess depicts. By analogy, we can construe Arachne's woven stories as pictorial, for example, the myth she pictures of Jupiter's rape of Europa—a cunning revision of Ovid's own version of the story in book two in which the maiden was deceived by the "image of a bull." In other words, Arachne, picturing Jupiter as a bull, renders an image of an image. When Arachne weaves with one thousand colors, she stands for Ovid himself, whose richly chromatic text is shot through with colored threads. Blacks, whites, grays, silvers, golds, yellows, reds, purples, pinks, blues, and greens abound in the author's pictorial poetry. Ovid's identity with Arachne is often observed, for the poet, speaking of his text as something woven, thus identifies with the consummate weaver among mortals.

When Arachne weaves the story of Europa, which visually echoes Ovid's telling of the tale in book two, she alludes to the horns of Jupiter, who appears in the image of a bull, are so perfect in form that they seem to have been made by hand. Seeing the beauty of natural form here (as elsewhere in his poem), Ovid transforms a detail in nature into the artifice of craftsmanship.

Ovid's image of Jupiter as a beautiful snow-white bull at the end of book two resonates with the similar image of the beautiful, snow-white heifer into which Jupiter transforms Io in the final myth of book one. In the story of Jupiter and Io we come to one of the most delightful examples of art in the first book of Ovid's poem, the art of storytelling. After the Olympian god takes his pleasure with Io, he transforms the nymph into a cow in order to conceal her from his wife. No fool she, however, Juno is on to his little game and descends to ask, "where did the cow come from?" Quick to respond, Jupiter tells a very brief story; he says that the heifer sprang from the earth fully grown. Close readers of Ovid's poem will recognize a little joke in Jupiter's story. The god imitates Ovid, since one of the threads of book one is the series of stories of beings born of the earth: Prometheus' humans are formed out of the earth, the off-spring of the giants take on human form when they emerge from the earth, humans are born from the stones of the earth after the flood, and the Python is born from the earth at the same time. In this context, Jupiter's story of yet another earth-born creature reads like farce.

Imitating Ovid, Jupiter in effect becomes a poet and, although his story of a cow emerging from the ground is preposterous, its conformity to Ovid's series of stories of comparable births gives it, in context, a kind of verisimilitude. Nevertheless, as Ovid says elsewhere in a self-mocking manner, all poets are liars. In the style of Ovid, Jupiter is such a poet-liar. Jupiter's short story within Ovid's poetry is exemplary of the art of storytelling so prominent throughout *Metamorphoses*. It sometimes seems as if there are as many storytellers in Ovid's poem as there are stories. In book ten, for example, Ovid tells the story of Orpheus, who tells the story of Venus and Adonis, within which Venus tells the story of Atalanta and Hippomenes—another example of Ovid's weaving.

In book one, we meet the consummate storyteller, Mercury, who is dispatched by Juno to assassinate Argus and thus liberate Jupiter's beloved Io from captivity. Disguised as a shepherd, Mercury tells Argus the wonderful story of the origins of Pan's pipes, and after his victim falls asleep during the story, the god dispatches him with a blow of the sword. Like all the other storytellers in *Metamorphoses*, Mercury stands for Ovid himself, since it is through the god's lips that he tells the story of the origins of the sweet new music of the pipes. With delicious, often-observed irony, Ovid mocks his own storytelling, since Mercury's story of Pan and Syrinx is obviously a version of Ovid's tale of Apollo and Daphne. Mercury's narrative, which is ultimately Ovid's own, should arouse interest, but it does not prevent Argus from nodding off. Ovid's capacity to laugh at himself is exemplary—a model to us all.

As verbal art, storytelling is not only linked to the art of poetry, it is also related to the art of rhetoric, the art of speaking well, indeed persuasively. Ovid exhibits this art in the story of the debate between Ulysses and Ajax over the arms of Achilles, in which the former is an exemplar of eloquence or *facunditas*. Ulysses argues ever so skillfully that Ajax is not worthy of the shield of Achilles because he is unable to appreciate its heavenly art, its virtuoso depiction of sea, sky, and cities. Here the art of rhetoric celebrates the art of craftsmanship.

The intertwined stories of sculpture, architecture, weaving, painting, poetry, storytelling and rhetoric in *Metamorphoses* grow out of the emphatic celebration of art in book one of the poem, as we have seen; but, of all the arts with which Ovid identifies, we have left to last the central art, that of music. Ovid's poem, his carmen or song, is a song about music and begins with Apollo, the god of the lyre, whose beloved Daphne is transformed into the laurel with which his instrument will always be entwined. A little later on in book one, Ovid rewrites this myth, again as we have seen, transforming it into the similar story told by Mercury of Pan's pursuit of Syrinx, who is (in turn) transformed into reeds, which is then the origin of the sweet new music of the pipes. In what is arguably the single most beautiful sonority in all of *Metamorphoses*, Ovid evokes the phonic beauty of music as Syrinx prays to her sisters for assistance, *orasse sorores*, a sonorous suggestion of the sweet sussurations of the whispering reeds into which she will be transformed.

Many are the singers of whom Ovid sings throughout his symphonic work: Ochyroe, the singer of prophetic songs, the Pierides who compete in song with the Muses, Medea, whose songs, like those of Circe, are incantations, enchantments, Canens, whose name speaks of her role as singer, monstrous Polyphemus who seeks to woo his beloved by playing his Pan pipes; and let us not forget within this great chorus of singers at the very end of Ovid's song, Pythagoras, who gives voice to the poet's view of the world in flux. Ovid's use of the verb *cano* here tells us that Pythagoras' eloquent world-picture is more than speech; it is song. At bottom, it is Ovid's song.

All of the songsters in *Metamorphoses* are but a chorus to the great soloist who dominates Ovid's own work of music: Orpheus, the son of Apollo, who gives mythic meaning to the often-used phrase, "the power of music." With his lyre Orpheus casts a spell over all of nature. The stones of the earth follow in his path, and trees draw near as he plays his lyre.

After his beloved Eurydice is bitten by a snake and dies, Orpheus's grief is so stunningly intense that everything stops. Even Ovid's perpetual poem, which captures the continuous motion of nature, the pulsating flux of life itself, is now suddenly arrested, and Sisyphus sits still upon his rock to listen. For an unforgettably enduring moment, Ovid's poem is itself still—the ultimate rest in the poet's score.

When the world resumes and Orpheus plays his lyre in grief, all the birds and beasts draw near to listen. He sings many songs, among them that of Pygmalion. It should not escape our attention that the story of a hard statue that comes alive is sung by a singer who is himself seemingly turned to stone in grief at the death of his beloved. Ovid's song about Orpheus' music is not about life or death but about the rhythms of life and death, about how life defines death, about how death gives definition to life.

Ovid sustains his story of stone when he sings of Orpheus' own death, for he is stoned to death by Ciconian women. Whereas stones had previously fallen under the spell of Orpheus, such stones are now the instruments of his demise. But the story of stone does not end here, since stones also mourn the bard's death. When the limbs of the dead Orpheus are scattered, his head and lyre float upon the river Hebrus. His instrument makes mournful sounds, his tongue murmurs in doleful harmony with the lyre. When a serpent strikes at Orpheus' head, Apollo intervenes and petrifies the creature's open jaws. Thus ends another of Ovid's stories of stone, in this case a tale of stone interwoven with music.

Stone and song are also closely interwoven in another story, which is a myth of the transformation of one form of art into another. In the tale of the treacherous Scylla who seeks to betray her father Nisus, architecture is metamorphosed into music. The palace of the king rose from walls that sang, because Apollo had once placed his lyre upon its stones, which still resonated with the sound of the god's instrument. Imagine that!

Even the form of a musical instrument provides Ovid with the opportunity to intertwine the arts. Describing the wings Daedalus fashions for Icarus and thus moving beyond "the fine arts" as they have been called, the poet likens their form to that of the pipes of Pan. Through form Ovid unites the art of aviation with the art of music. It would almost seem that Ovid, long before Walter Pater, saw all art aspiring to the condition of music.

No less does art aspire in Ovid, as is often observed, to the condition of weaving. The threads of Ovid are woven into the daughters of Minyas who in fact spin yarn as they tell tales, in other words, spin yarns. They tell the story of Mars and Venus in which Vulcan makes a net to capture his adulterous wife and her lover, a net so finely spun that it is like the delicate, gracile threads with which Arachne weaves and thus tells her stories. Arachne's weaving is as subtle, Ovid suggests, as the labyrinth of Daedalus, which is threaded by Ariadne. Her golden thread is the clue to the building's form—a form mirrored in the labyrinthian structure of Ovid's own poem. The threads of Ovid's text are also implicitly tied to the strings of the lyres of Apollo and Orpheus, through whom Ovid makes his own music.

Although Ovid's poem is filled with artistic contests, those of Apollo and Pan, Apollo and Marsyas, the Pierides and the Muses, Arachne and Minerva, Ulysses and Ajax, the poet nevertheless achieves a unity or concord of all the arts out of such discord. Ovid in a sense competes with Orpheus in song, with Pygmalion and Medusa in sculptural effects, with Daedalus in plotting, with Arachne in the weaving of pictures, but he ultimately achieves an implicit identity with all of these artists who, in a sense, are his own personae. In the end, all of the arts are united in the poet himself. The poet is a kind of superartist who presides over his magnum opus of all the arts.

Neither Wagner's *Gesamtkunstwerk* nor Baudelaire's *correspondances* of the arts, Ovid's synthesis of the arts in *Metamorphoses* is nevertheless an ancient antecedent to all modern explorations of the unity of the arts, just as the poet's self-conscious celebration of himself as a prodigious and multifaceted artist in many forms foreshadows the modern idea of the artist as hero.

Ovid's unified embodiment of all the arts is itself mythic, for the poet is the Protean artist par excellence. Ovid thinks in no uncertain terms of Proteus' capacity to transform himself into a lion, boar, bull, stone, tree, river, or flame as art. Ovid embellishes this art of self-transformation by surrounding Proteus with a cluster of other characters who similarly practice the art of self-transformation: the daughter of Erysichthon transforms herself into a mare, a

[handwritten in left margin: Book 5 ends with the Golden Fleece.]

heifer, and a bull; the river god Achelous transforms himself into a serpent and a bull; the mother of Achilles, Thetis, transforms herself into a bird, a tree, and a tiger; and the sons of Sleep assume the forms of beast, bird and serpent—among these children, Phantasos wears the forms of earth, rocks, water, and trees. Like Proteus and other Protean figures, ever changing their form, Ovid is himself a type of Proteus. He appears now in one form, now in another, as he elusively assumes the masks of Pygmalion, Orpheus, Daedalus, Arachne, and the other artists whose stories he tells.

When Ovid transforms himself into a type of Proteus he does so with extraordinary subtlety. The poet's artful self-transformation thus evokes his definition of art in the story of Pygmalion where he says that the sculptor's artifice conceals his very art. We can therefore read *Metamorphoses* over and over again without ever seeing that in his extensive celebration of art the core myth is that of Proteus. As Proteus transforms himself into a bull, lion, or serpent, for example, so Ovid transforms himself into an architect, sculptor, or painter.

Of the various metamorphoses in Ovid's poem, the most exalted is that of apotheosis or deification. *Metamorphoses* rises to a series of such transformations towards its conclusion. In the wake of the deification of Hercules, who put off his mortal body and rose beyond the clouds to the stars in a chariot drawn by four heavenly horses, Ovid turns in the final books of the poem to those apotheoses that address the glory of Rome. When Aeneas was purged of his mortal body he was made a god, as was Romulus, who similarly rose as Quirinus to heaven and took on a new and more beautiful form worthy of the gods, after which his wife also soared heavenward to the stars. These apotheoses, metamorphoses of mortals into gods, are the preparation for the deification of Caesar, whose soul rose to heaven where he too became a star.

As a prophetic singer, Ovid speaks next of the day when his patron Augustus, who now rules the world, will ascend to the heavens. But this series of metamorphoses as deification, both historical and prophetic, is not yet complete. For in the last lines of his poem or song, which are no mere epilogue, Ovid makes a poetic prophecy of his own fame and glory. He imagines a future when his work will transcend the wrath of Jupiter or time's capacity to consume, a future where the better part of himself will be borne beyond the stars and, if the prophecies of poets are truthful, he will live forever. Thus, the ultimate metamorphosis of *Metamorphoses*, the final transformation of the Protean poet.

The story of Ovid's ascent to the stars does not end with his poem, however, for over a millennium later Dante would metamorphose Ovid's ascent into the epic of his own heavenward journey in the *Divine Comedy*. Although ostensibly guided toward the stars by Virgil, Dante, as the poet-hero of his own poem, also writes under the star of Ovid's "epic of art," which provided the modern poet with an example of extreme artistic self-consciousness. In other words, Ovid's self-formation as artist, his identity with various mythic artists whose personae he assumes, inspired Dante to shape his own self-reflexive persona as poet. Whereas Ovid appears in multiple guises in *Metamorphoses*, Dante portrays himself as the singular subject of his own "epic of art," which becomes a foundational text for the modern celebration of the artist as hero.

Dante's great epic was in turn important for Vasari's *Lives* of the artists, a work of epic proportions that traces the rise of art from Giotto, who is glorified by association with Dante, to its perfection in the work of Michelangelo, who is portrayed as a new Dante. Vasari's history of art is grounded in one of

Ovid's central myths, the story of Narcissus, whose self-reflection in a pool of water the poet likens to a work of art. As Vasari suggests over and over throughout the *Lives*, works of art are, in a sense, reflections of their makers. The paintings of Piero di Cosimo, for example, which portray a primordial humanity, are the reflection of an artist who is a savage or wild man, whereas, antithetically, the works of Leonardo, marked by extraordinary grace, are reflections of an artist who was said to be exceedingly graceful.

Vasari's biography of Leonardo is a crucial source for what is arguably the central fable of art in the world of what is called "modernism"—Balzac's "The Unknown Masterpiece." Building on Vasari's portrayal of a painter who, aspiring to a perfection beyond perfection, cannot bring his paintings to completion, Balzac metamorphoses Leonardo into Frenhofer, a painter, who, seeking to achieve a great masterpiece, is unable to realize his ambition. Although Balzac's tale is a short story, it is epic in scope and in its portrayal of an artist's heroic struggle. For when the painter lays siege to his canvas over a period of ten years, his mighty attempt to achieve greatness evokes the duration of the siege of Troy.

Balzac's story, which was to haunt the imagination of countless modern artists and writers, including Zola, Henry James, Cézanne and Picasso, to name only a few, turns the heroic battle of the artist into a tragic tale of failure. Ultimately unable to realize his elusive masterpiece, the artist destroys his failed painting and commits suicide. The glory of the artist from Ovid to Dante, from Dante to Michelangelo, from Michelangelo to Balzac, is here transformed into the story of defeat—a plot that still echoes in all the recent claims of the death of the artist, the end of art history, or the failure of modernism.

When we read Balzac's story today, dwelling on it as it pertains to the high modernism of the final centuries of the last millennium, we do so with an excessively narrow focus if we fail to see also its taproots in the tradition of the "epic of art"—a tradition that brings us full circle to Ovid's *Metamorphoses*. Although Balzac's Frenhofer is indeed a paradigmatic figure in the story of modern art, he is also a mythic figure who assumes the same Protean personae as Ovid.

Frenhofer aspires to be a type of Pygmalion. Whereas his fellow painter, Pourbus, paints a figure in which the blood does not flow beneath the skin (as it does in Pygmalion's creation), Frenhofer expressly compares himself to the mythic artist when, after all the years of his epic quest in art, he contemplates how long it must have taken Pygmalion to realize his masterpiece. Condemning the work of Pourbus for its lack of the life-giving fire of Prometheus, Frenhofer proclaims his own Promethean aspirations and identity. With an ultimate ironic twist, however, the very fire of Prometheus which provides the heat that animates his figures becomes in Frenhofer's hands the instrument of destruction when he burns his paintings. Art for Frenhofer is a struggle between life and death, and he boldly states that, like Orpheus, he would descend into the Hades of art to bring the ancient ideal of beauty back to life.

The myths of Prometheus, Pygmalion, and Orpheus essential to Ovid's shifting artistic personae are thus essential to Balzac's modern but still mythic hero of art. Although none of his heroes is particularly Ovidian, what is Ovidian about Balzac's painter in general is the way in which, like Ovid, he assumes the multiple personae of mythic artists. Doing so, he is himself a Protean hero in the epic quest of his own art. Not surprisingly, Frenhofer in fact invokes Proteus in his long discourse on art, but there is a peculiarly ambiguous turn in his mythic allusion.

Although Balzac's painter as a type of Prometheus, Pygmalion, and Orpheus is a Protean figure like Ovid, Frenhofer nevertheless does not compare himself to Proteus, the mythic artist of self-transformation. Rather, pursuing the implications of Ovid, he says that Proteus stands for the multiplicity of forms with which the artist struggles in order to realize a great work of art—a struggle that still evokes, for example, Menelaos wrestling with the elusive Proteus or Peleus attempting to grasp the evasive Thetis. The struggle of Frenhofer, the embattled modern artist par excellence, who wrestles with the multiple forms of his art, not only transforms ancient myth into a parable of modern art history, it also simultaneously leads us back to *Metamorphoses*—a book about transformation, where Ovid gave form in the first place to the "epic of art" in which the poet himself is the supreme, transformative hero.

Secondary Source 3.15   Lorna Hardwick, 'From the classical tradition to reception studies'

(Source: Hardwick, L. (2003) *Reception Studies: New Surveys in the Classics*, Greece & Rome, New Surveys in the Classics, no. 33, Oxford, Oxford University Press, pp. 1–11, illustrations omitted)

On 30th January 1943, Adolf Hitler's close associate Goering made a radio broadcast to the beleaguered Sixth Army at Stalingrad on the eastern front. He compared the German army to the Spartan soldiers at Thermopylae in 480 BCE when they stood, fought and died to prevent the advance of the Persians ('the barbarians') into Greece. Goering's broadcast was not well received. The dispirited and starving listeners described it as 'our own Funeral Speech' and some officers joked ironically that 'the suicide of the Jews', besieged by the Roman army on the top of Masada in 73 or 74 CE was a more apt comparison.[1] This episode raises a host of questions about the reception of classical texts and ideas in later cultures. In this instance, not only was the classical allusion used as model to sanction expectations of behaviour but further allusions were used as a counter-text to challenge the rhetoric of the high command.

At the turn of the twentieth and twenty-first centuries, a translation by Edwin Morgan of Racine's *Phèdre* into modern Scots was staged at the Royal Lyceum Theatre Edinburgh.[2] Morgan's translation into a Glaswegian-based Scots was part of a move to give status to the Scots language as part of the emerging classical theatre in Scotland. He also wanted to find out what it was about the play which would survive and transcend what he described as 'a jolt into an alien register'. The translation and the staging represented the latest point in a continuing commentary on the migration through successive languages and theatrical traditions of the story of Phaedra – Euripides' *Hippolytus*, Seneca's *Phaedra* and Racine's *Phèdre*. The function of reception studies is to analyse and compare the linguistic, theatrical and contextual aspects of this kind of migration.[3]

These examples demonstrate the extraordinary diversity in the range of classical receptions. Each has its own reception history and requires appropriate methods of investigation. Each yields insights into the texts and contexts of

---

[1]   The broadcast and reactions to it are described by Antony Beevor, *Stalingrad* (London, 1998), 380. Beevor comments drily, 'They did not realise how accurate they were. Hitler was indeed counting on a mass suicide, above all of senior officers.'

[2]   Published text, E. Morgan, *Phaedra* (Manchester, 2000).

[3]   See for example Amy Wygant, *Towards a Cultural Philology: Phèdre and the Construction of Racine* (Oxford, 1999).

ancient works, their subsequent interpretation and their situation in the modern context of reception. The aim of this book is to engage with this rich cultural field by outlining the main features of current work in reception studies and discussing in more detail some of the most significant recent developments. This chapter sets out the conceptual and critical framework which the rest of the volume will use in the discussion of specific examples.

The increasing prominence of reception studies in relation to Greek and Roman texts, images, ideas and material culture is a fairly recent development. Although *Rezeptionsgeschichte* (reception history) or study of *Nachlebung* (afterlife) has been an important strand in German scholarship, its development in the international field and especially its adaptation in Anglophone scholarship has involved significant reshaping of the scope of reception studies and of the sources and methods used. In particular, the emergence of this specialism signals a move away from previous ways of looking at the relationship between ancient culture and its subsequent interpretation and adaptation. One strand in classical scholarship has been what was called 'the classical tradition'. This studied the transmission and dissemination of classical culture through the ages, usually with the emphasis on the influence of classical writers, artists and thinkers on subsequent intellectual movements and individual works.[4] In this context, the language which was used to describe this influence tended to include terms like 'legacy'. This rather implied that ancient culture was dead but might be retrieved and reapplied provided that one had the necessary learning. More recent research has tended to move away from the study of a linear progression of 'influence'.

The notion of some great chain of influence which linked great works of the Greeks and Romans to their counterparts in Renaissance, Enlightenment, Victorian and modern 'high culture' has fallen out of fashion. This is partly to be regretted since studies of transmission of texts and canon formulation and adaptation are valuable adjuncts to other aspects of classical study and help to explain how and why classical texts have been interpreted in particular times and contexts. However, one good reason for the replacement of the methods of 'the classical tradition' as the sole means of studying classical texts through time is that such an approach was based on a rather narrow range of perspectives. Furthermore, it could carry an assumption, sometimes tacit sometimes explicit, that these works yielded a 'meaning' which was unproblematic, there to be grasped and to be applied in all kinds of situation far removed from the ancient one. Thus the associations of value carried with it were narrow and sometimes undervalued diversity, both within ancient culture and subsequently.

The diversity of ancient culture itself is now more widely recognized and interest has focused on ways in which some aspects were selected and used ('appropriated') in order to give value and status to subsequent cultures and societies and to inspire new creative work. This kind of study has proved valuable in that it has enabled people to distinguish more readily between the ancient texts, ideas and values and those of the societies that appropriated them. So, for example, we are less likely to simply confuse Greek and Roman cultural practices with those of the Victorians who filtered their appropriations

[4]   Among outstanding works of this kind are G. Highet, *The Classical Tradition: Greek and Roman Influences on Western Literature* (Oxford, 1949); R.R. Bolgar, *The Classical Heritage and its Beneficiaries* (Cambridge, 1954); M.I. Finley (ed.), *The Legacy of Greece* (Oxford 1981); R. Jenkyns, *The Legacy of Rome: a New Appraisal* (Oxford, 1992). It is interesting to compare their scope and methods with a recent study such as T.P. Wiseman (ed.), *Classics in Progress: Essays on Ancient Greece and Rome* (Oxford, 2002), which contains chapters on 'Contemporary Poetry and Classics' (Oliver Taplin) and 'Socrates on trial in the USA' (Malcolm Schofield).

of the ancient world into education, the arts and social values.[5] This increased sense of discrimination in examining the interfaces between cultures has had the further valuable effect of liberating the ancient texts for re-appropriation and reworking ('refiguration') by new generations of writers and artists. It is of course true that 'guilt by association' has sometimes remained a potent factor in causing rejection of the societies and values of Greeks and Romans as part of modern cultural studies. It can hardly be denied, for instance, that Athenian society in the fifth century, BCE, a society which saw a flowering of the arts, was based on slavery of various kinds (in common with most of the ancient world and much of the modern) nor that the material improvements associated with Roman culture were disseminated as a result of the success of its imperial war machine. Appropriation of the practices, attitudes and values of Greek peasant society by the modern far right or of the public buildings, emblems and propaganda of the Romans by empire-builders and totalitarian regimes acts as an awful warning of the unlovely effects of uncritical adulation of any culture.[6] Such issues are of particular concern in reception studies, where the focus is on the two-way relationship between the source text or culture and the new work and receiving culture. Analysis of the principles and assumptions underlying selectivity and contextual comparisons between source and receiving conditions are vital tools.

It is important also to be aware that interest in reception of classical texts is not just a modern phenomenon. Greek and Roman poets, dramatists, philosophers, artists and architects were also engaged in this type of activity – refiguration of myth, meta-theatrical allusion, creation of dialogue with and critique of entrenched cultural practices and assumptions, selection and refashioning in the context of current concerns. Reception within antiquity is an important mediating factor between classical and modern cultures. Greek drama, for instance, did not cease in the fifth century BCE. There were important fourth-century and Hellenistic activities and the Romans, too, selected and adapted in order to create their own cultural traditions of comedy, of distinctive tragedies by Seneca and others, and of pantomime.[7]

Because reception is concerned with the relationship between ancient and modern texts and contexts, as well as those separated by time within antiquity, it has implications for the critical analysis of both. It used sometimes to be said that reception studies only yield insights into the receiving society. Of course they do this, but they also focus critical attention back towards the ancient source and sometimes frame new questions or retrieve aspects of the source which have now been marginalized or forgotten.[8] Reasons for such marginalizations are often significant. This means that reception studies have to be concerned with investigating the routes by which a text has moved and the cultural focus which

[5]   Particularly important in recent scholarship in this field are R. Jenkyns, *The Victorians and Ancient Greece* (Oxford, 1980); F.M. Turner, *The Greek Heritgae in Victorian Britain* (New Haven, CT, 1981); G.W. Clarke (ed.), *Rediscovering Hellenism: The Hellenic Inheritance and the English Imagination* (Cambridge, 1989).

[6]   For discussion of appropriation of Greek civic values by extremists in the USA see Page du Bois, *Trojan Horses: Saving the Classics from Conservatives* (New York and London, 2001). For discussion of the institution of slavery in Greece and its effect on scholarship see most recently Paul Cartledge, 'Greek civilisation and slavery' in T.P. Wiseman (ed.), *Classics in Progress: Essays on Ancient Greece and Rome* (Oxford, 2002), 247–62.

[7]   For discussion of this aspect see D. Wiles, *The Oxford Illustrated History of Theatre* (Oxford, 1995), ch. 2.

[8]   See the discussion and references in L. Hardwick, 'Convergence and divergence in reading Homer' in C. Emlyn-Jones, L. Hardwick and J. Purkis (edd.), *Homer: Readings and Images* (London, 1992), 227–48.

shaped or filtered the ways in which the text was regarded.[9] Reception studies therefore participate in the continuous dialogue between the past and the present and also require some 'lateral' dialogue in which crossing boundaries of place or language or genre is as important as crossing those of time.

Reception studies, therefore, are concerned not only with individual texts and their relationship with one another but also with the broader cultural processes which shape and make up those relationships. The discussions in this volume will be concerned with two main aspects of reception studies:

1. *The reception itself*

(i)   The artistic or intellectual processes involved in selecting, imitating or adapting ancient works – how the text was 'received' and 'refigured' by artist, writer or designer; how the later work relates to the source.

In relation to this it is necessary to consider

(ii)   The relationship between this process and the contexts in which it takes place. These contexts may include: the receiver's knowledge of the source and how this knowledge was obtained; a writer's or artist's works as a whole; collaboration between writer/translator or director and designer and actor; the role of the patron or financiers; the role of the audience/reader/public (both actual and imagined). In other words, factors outside the ancient source contribute to its reception and sometimes introduce new dimensions.

(iii) The purpose or function for which the new work or appropriation of ideas or values is made – for instance, its use as an authority to legitimate something, or someone, in the present (whether political, artistic, social, or educational or cultural in the broadest sense).

2. *How the reception is described, analysed, evaluated*

No description is neutral and the forms, concepts and categories used by reception critics need clearly to indicate the extent to which they are using ancient categories to analyse and judge modern receptions. For example, discussion of a modern production of Greek drama would almost certainly consider how the chorus was represented and staged and whether masks were used. It might, but frequently does not, include assessment of the degree of equivalence to other ancient practices such as how the chorus was awarded and financed, i.e. the social and economic values underlying the staging of the play.

Equally, reception studies at all periods have been shaped by current conceptual and theoretical frameworks that shape and define 'knowledge'. Trends in modern literary and cultural theory, for instance, have stressed ambivalence and indeterminacy in the meaning attributed to texts, and disjunction and fissure in what might earlier have been seen as broader cultural certainties. For those reasons, reception of classical texts is playing an increasingly important part in studies of the cultural politics associated with change – for instance in the emancipation of Eastern Europe in the last part of the twentieth century and in post-colonial drama and literature. The appropriations and refiguring of classical texts in these contexts provides a yardstick of comparison between writing in independent and in colonized societies and the nature of the receptions is a significant indicator of cultural change.

---

[9] 'Text' is used in its broadest sense throughout this discussion to include oral sources, written documents and works of material culture such as buildings or sculpture. Each type of text of course makes particular demands in terms of description and analysis of its form and content.

In addition to the general influence of literary and cultural theory there are some theoretical approaches which impact directly on reception issues. Three have been particularly influential. In the 1960s Hans Robert Jauss developed a theory of the 'aesthetics of reception' (*Rezeptions- ästhetik*).[10] This asserted that the historical character of an artwork could not be captured merely by describing it (as did the Formalists) or examining its production (as did the Marxists). Instead Jauss developed a theory of the interaction of production and reception. This involved dialogue between producer/artist and reader/audience/consumer. To frame this dialogue Jauss used the notion of a 'horizon of expectation'.[11] Jauss's adaptation of the concept focused on a horizon of experience of life and thus rooted the receiver's mind-set in his or her social and cultural context. This was what could be said to shape expectations and interpretations of texts.

A related theoretical response was that of Wolfgang Iser. Iser's main theoretical work appeared in the mid 1970s. Jauss's background was in literary history, Iser's is in English literature and his work focuses on reader-response as a trigger for the construction of meaning in literary texts (and by extension in drama, although comparable theoretical work on audience response is still lacking).[12] Iser's work covers the input to interpretation of a literary text by both the 'actual' reader and the 'implied' reader, that is the reader to whom the structure and language of the text speaks.

The third major theorist whose work has influenced reception studies is Hans-Georg Gadamer. His major work was published in the 1960s and 1970s.[13] Gadamer's main, although indirect, contribution to reception studies was his theory that the meaning to be attributed to a text is not 'essential', i.e. waiting to be drawn out, but constructed as part of the historical nature of understanding ('a fusion of horizons between past and present'). The implications for the study of classical texts are important since they suggest that the meaning attributed to an ancient text is shaped by the historical impact of its subsequent receptions. Even if one modifies Gadamer's theory to the weaker position that subsequent receptions have at least a contributory effect on the interpretation of ancient texts, this alone would justify a major scholarly role for the study of the histories of aesthetics of reception.

This possibility leads to a fourth theoretical approach which is sometimes used in reception analysis. This is the concept of 'critical distance' which uses the distance in time, place and culture that exists between ancient and modern versions of a text in order to enable the reader/spectator to move outside the limits of his or her own society and cultural horizons and thus to see these more clearly and more critically. This concept is important both for envisaging the possibility of the individual group enlarging horizons of expectation or even transforming them and for its potential when classical texts are used as critical devices for outwitting censors and enabling current social and political

[10]   H.R. Jauss, *Towards on Aesthetic of Reception*, tr. T. Bahti (Minneapolis, 1982).

[11]   This was based on the work of Karl Popper, the philosopher of science and Karl Mannheim, the sociologist and had been elaborated by Ernst Gombrich in *Art and Illusion* (Princeton, 1960). For discussion see Robert C. Holub, *Reception Theory: a Critical Introduction* (London, 1984).

[12]   W. Iser, *The Act of Reading: a Theory of Aesthetic Response* (Baltimore and London, 1978). On drama and the audience see S. Bennett, *Theatre Audiences: a Theory of Production and Reception* (London and New York, 1990). On the Audience as potential 'translator' see L. Hardwick, 'Who owns the plays? Issues in the Translation and Performance of Greek Drama on the Modern Stage', *Eirene* 37 (2001), Special Edition *Theatralia*, 23–39.

[13]   H-G. Gadamer, *Truth and Method*, first published 1960; the translators G. Barden and J. Cumming (New York, 1975) used the second edition (1965).

concerns to be addressed through the apparently neutral, 'distant' (and safe) medium of classical culture.

Towards a working vocabulary for reception studies

The vocabulary used in this study is centred around the central questions of how the reception in question and its context relate to the classical source and its content.

Acculturation	assimilation into a cultural context (through nurturing or education or domestication or sometimes by force)
Adaptation	a version of the source developed for a different purpose or insufficiently close to count as a translation
Analogue	a comparable aspect of source and reception
Appropriation	taking an ancient image or text and using it to sanction subsequent ideas or practices (explicitly or implicitly)
Authentic	close approximation to the supposed form and meaning of the course. At the opposite end of the spectrum from invention (i.e. a new work)
Correspondences	aspects of a new work which directly relate to a characteristic of the source
Dialogue	mutual relevance of source and receiving texts and contexts
Equivalent	fulfilling an analogous role in source and reception but not necessarily identical in form or content
Foreignization	translating or representing in such a way that *difference* between source and reception is emphasized
Hybrid	a fusion of material from classical and other cultures
Intervention	reworking the source to create a political, social or aesthetic critique of the receiving society
Migration	movement through time or across place; may involve dispersal and diaspora and acquisition of new characteristics
Refiguration	selecting and reworking material from a previous or contrasting tradition
Translation	literally from one language to another. Literal, close, free are words used to pin down the relationship to the source as are phrases like 'in the spirit rather than the letter'. Translation can also be used metaphorically as in 'translation to the stage' or 'translation across cultures'. Free translations sometimes merge into adaptations or versions
Transplant	to take a text or image into another context and allow it to develop
Version	a refiguration of a source (usually literary or dramatic) which is too free and selective to rank as a translation

The approach adopted in this study is not limited by any one of the theoretical positions outlined above, although it is informed by them all. My discussion is framed by these key assumptions:

(i)   Receptions do in practice affect perceptions of and judgements about the ancient world and therefore need to be analysed.

(ii)   Receptions within antiquity need to be considered within the same framework of enquiry as subsequent receptions so that the diversity of ancient culture is more fully recognized and the impact of ancient reception approaches on intervening interpretations is investigated.

(iii) Reception studies require us to look closely at the source text and context as well as at the receiving ones. This does not imply that the source is a yardstick of value but rather that a 'critical distance' between source and reception illuminates both. The traditional practices of classical philology have an important part to play in developing the broader cultural philology that reception studies needs.

(iv)   The concept of cultural horizon (with its ancient analogue *paideia*) provides a useful but not constraining framework for reception studies. How cultural horizons, with their assumptions, expectations, aspirations and transformations, relate to classical material is a crucial area in modern reception studies which also have to take into account the impact of new technologies and art forms (such as film).

(v)   Reception practice and its analysis reveals both commonalities and differences between ancient and modern. The shifting balance between commonalities and differences undermines the crudely polarized positions that classical texts either address universal and unchanging aspects of human nature or that they are remote and alien with nothing of value to offer to post-classical experience.

(vi)   Reception of classical materials is an index of cultural continuity and change and therefore has a value beyond its role in classical studies.

(vii) Reception is and always has been a field for the practice and study of contest about values and their relationship to knowledge and power.

The examples discussed in this volume are necessarily selective. Where possible I have focused on material which is widely available and to which readers can develop their own critical response. Art and architecture are mentioned only in passing as they would require a separate and extensively illustrated study. Similarly philosophy and historiography are only briefly discussed [...]. Film gets a fuller discussion, partly because it presents issues of analysis and evaluation which are of particular interest in reception studies and partly because it represents a new aspect not only of classical receptions but also of the *paideia* in which they are embedded.

Secondary Source 3.16   Eleanor Winsor Leach, 'Ekphrasis and the theme of artistic failure in Ovid's *Metamorphoses*'

(Source: Winsor Leach, E. (1974) 'Ekphrasis and the theme of artistic failure in Ovid's *Metamorphoses*', *Ramus*, no. 3, pp. 102–42)

I

In his review of the first edition of Brooks Otis's *Ovid as an Epic Poet*, William Anderson challenges the notion that structural symmetry is the principle that governs Ovid's narrative design.[1] To propose an alternative view of Ovidian

---

[1]   *A.J.P.* 89 (1968) 93–104. Anderson has developed the remarks made in this review into more extensive interpretive comments in his edition, *Ovid's Metamorphoses: Books 6–10* (Norman, Oklahoma) 151–171.

aesthetics, he takes for his example the weaving contest of Arachne and Minerva in Book 6. Minerva's tapestry which depicts her own victory in the contest for the naming of Athens is arranged in a completely symmetrical design. The judging gods stand six on either side of Jupiter; the disputants likewise stand on opposite sides. Each corner of the tapestry contains a panel showing the punishment of mortals who in one way or another have challenged the gods, and the whole is framed with an ornamental border of olive leaves. "The goddess," as Anderson says, "produced a perfect piece of Classicistic art, structurally balanced and thematically grandiose, in support of the established order." With this monumental and authoritarian piece of work, the tapestry of Minerva's rival Arachne contrasts in every way. It is flagrantly asymmetrical and lifelike:

> a swirl of divine figures in unedifying situations ... one god after another gratifying his lust for a human woman. There is no apparent structure to the tapestry which consists of nine affairs of Jupiter; six of Neptune; four of Apollo and one each of Liber and Saturn. Juxtaposed as they apparently are, they have a cumulative effect, much as Baroque paintings do by contrast with the neatly arranged masterpieces of Raphael.

As Anderson points out, Minerva is unable to achieve a genuine triumph in the contest. Arachne was not deluded in her claims to equal the goddess in skill (6.129–130): *non illud Pallas, non illud carpere Livor / possit opus*; "Neither Pallas, nor Envy could find any fault in this work."). Inflamed by jealousy and indignation, the goddess destroys by force that work of art that her divine talents could not surpass (6.130–131: *doluit successu flava virago/et rupit pictas, caelestia crimina, vestes*; "The golden haired warrior maiden smarted at her success and tore apart the many colored tapestry, the sky-dwellers' crimes."). The implication, Anderson suggests, of the tale for the *Metamorphoses* as a whole is that symmetrical design is "no prerequisite to Ovidian art; a set of loosely ordered tales can form a masterpiece."

The more one agreed with this suggestion that the style of the Arachne's mythological representation is somehow paradigmatic for the *Metamorphoses*, the more one wants to question further. How far should one press the identification of the poet's own aesthetic principles with those of the doomed tapestry? What are the implications of Minerva's action for Ovid's own art?[2]

It has often been remarked that Ovid shows a particular interest in artists and in their works of art, an interest that often manifests itself in the use of words from the vocabulary of the graphic arts but is also apparent in the precise descriptions that allow the postures of his characters to be visualized as clearly as those of statues[3] and his scenes to be envisioned with all the detail of

---

[2]   In *Ovid's Metamorphoses*, note 1 above, 169, Anderson implies some conclusions by comparing Minerva's tapestry with "certain surviving examples of Augustan classicistic art," while he assimilates Arachne's work more closely to Ovid's own style by calling it, "freer, more mannered, more dramatic and distorted, less specifically detailed." He conjectures that Minerva would have won a clear-out victory in the original version of the contest story and thus Ovid would have "changed the story to produce this ambivalent result."

[3]   Douglas F. Bauer, "The Function of Pygmalion in Ovid's *Metamorphoses*," *T.A.P.A.* 99 (1962) 1–21, catalogues the figures turned into stone in each book and includes references to statues and the materials of sculpture. The topic is also treated by the authors listed in note 4 below.

actual paintings.[4] From these points it is further conjectured that he saw the poet and the graphic artist approaching their common task of mimesis with a similar concern for reproducing actual impressions of the real world. Such ideas make his vision seem especially close to that of Arachne whose woven figures are so lifelike as to deceive the spectator (104): *verum taurum, freta vera putares* ("You would think the bull was a real one, that the sea was real"). The story of Europa which provides the context for these words is, of course, one that Ovid has already told in his poem (2.833–875). By his translation of the subject from descriptive narrative into an explicitly visual medium, Ovid seems to be making some self-conscious commentary upon his own artistic methods, but the point, I think, is more than a distinction between symmetrical and asymmetrical principles of organization and style.

The styles of the tapestries are inseparable from their subjects. Minerva's angry response makes this point. On their surface the two tapestries appear to present incompatible views of the gods. The vision of Arachne's tapestry is perfectly in keeping with the world vision of the *Metamorphoses* whose first five books have presented numerous examples of the free and energetic loves of the gods. The reader who is sympathetic to Arachne cannot help but think that Minerva's formal and high-minded depiction of divine power and justice embodies some hypocritical misrepresentation. But of course the goddess's work is also perfectly faithful to the theological ethos of the poem, and her images of divine vengeance have their analogies in such stories as that of Aglauros, Battus, Semele, Actaeon and Pentheus. Both Minerva's and Arachne's versions of mythology and metamorphosis assert the power of the gods: the one as a force of order, the other as a force participating in the flux of nature. As the creator of the poem, Ovid maintains a vision embracing both points of view. A balance between them is essential to the temper of the poem. Thus it is impossible to identify Ovid's perspective entirely with Arachne's, even when he serves as sympathetic champion of her aesthetics of verisimilitude. All the same, the poet's apparent sympathy is not pointless. Arachne's vision is personal, limited and rebellious; it represents the human artist's determination to assert his version of truth in the face of an uncertain

[4] N. Laslo, "Riflessi d'arte figurata nelle Metamorfosi di Ovidio," *Ephemeris Dacromania* 6 (1935) 368–440, and Heinrich Bartholomé. *Ovid und die antike Kunst* (Leipzig, 1935), are concerned with Greek and Roman art as an "influence" on Ovid's descriptive style and much of their discussion has to do with specific works of art, although the latter deals with Ovid's general interest in art as a reflection of his Augustan environment. Pierre Grimal, "Les Métamorphoses d'Ovide et la peinture paysagiste à l'époque d'Auguste," *R.E.L.* 16 (1938) 145–161, deals more theoretically with parallels between Ovid's descriptive and atmospheric effects and those of the paintings of his time and speaks of a general tendency towards a kind of naturalism, a point echoed by Christopher Dawson in his extensive study of the paintings, *Romano-Campanian Mythological Landscape Painting, Y.C.S.* 9 (1944: rep. Rome, 1965) 177: "Ovid is the literary counterpart of the landscape and mythological landscape painters; both are at once the products and creators of the artistic taste of their times." H. Herter, "Ovids verhältnis zur bildenden Kunst" in N.I. Herescu. ed., *Ovidiana: Recherches sur Ovide, Publiées à l'occasion du bimillénaire de la naissance du poète* (Paris, 1958) 49–74, concludes that Ovid's pictorial grasp of "die echte oder die mythische Wirklichkeit" need acknowledge no debt to the visual arts, while H. Bardon, "Ovide et le baroque," *Ovidiana*, 74–100, speaks of an imagination that makes the poet's world tangible to the reader. Simone Viarre, *L'image et la pensée dans les Métamorphoses d'Ovide* (Paris, 1964), treats the subject of visual imagination extensively in her first four chapters (1–96), then, after summarizing: "Ovide sculpte des formes et utilise la matière comme un sculpteur; il fait voir les couleurs des lignes, des paysages dignes d'un peintre; il découpe et monte le film mouvementé de sa vision à la manière d'un cinéaste," she goes on to show how Ovid exceeds the techniques of the visual arts in his portrayal of motion and the dynamic life of nature. See also Antonio Menzione, *Ovidio: Le Metamorfosi:sintesi critica e contributo per una rivalutazione* (Turin, 1964) 265–268.

is Ovid talking about himself?

and authoritarian world. And her self-assertion is a failure even as she produces the masterpiece of her work. Both the partial vision of Arachne and her defeat are typical of Ovid's unusual treatment of artists and works of art in the poem.

Stories in which artists figure play an important role in the *Metamorphoses*. Insofar as we can determine from Ovid's existing sources, the poet has made major changes to bring out new themes in these stories and draw them closely into the context of the poem. Some he has virtually invented himself. The full implications of the Arachne incident can best be seen as a part of the continuously problematic relationship of the artist figure to his world in the whole context of the *Metamorphoses*.

The fact that artists and their artifacts are a traditional element of classical literature makes Ovid's unusual treatment of them the more striking. As I shall briefly show, the general background for this subject gives no hint of his individualistic approach. The tapestries of Minerva and Arachne stand in the rhetorical tradition of *ekphrasis* – poetic description of works of art – which had not by Ovid's time achieved its ultimate form as a self-limited rhetorical exercise, but was very much a feature of epic and other forms of hexameter poetry.[5] Shields, cups, woven garments and architectural sculpture all provide conventional *loci* [places] for *ekphrasis*, but this categorical list of visual objects may be expanded to include passages where the song of a bard is summarized in its essential detail.[6] All *ekphraseis* have something about them of the bravura piece, the ornamental digression, but their very conspicuousness prompts the reader to reflect upon their potential relationship to the main current of the poem. Although one could remove these passages

[5]   P. Friedlander, *Johannes von Gaza und Paulus Silentiarus und Procopius von Gaza, Einleitung über die beschreibung von kunstwerken in der antiken literatur* (Leipzig, 1912: rep. Hildesheim, 1969) 1–23, discusses the tradition as a series of variations on Homer; A. W. Fairbanks, Introduction to *Philostratus Imagines* (Cambridge, 1931) xvii–xix, remarks on the intermingling of literary and visual perspectives; Bartholomé, note 4 above, analyses the visual composition of Ovidian *ekphraseis* with reference to literary models and ancient works of art. Friedlander's remark that Ovidian *ekphraseis* have nothing new to contribute to the tradition epitomizes the somewhat negative attitude that scholars have often taken towards this phenomenon. The importance of these passages as a vehicle for serious literary statement has suffered considerable damage from the rather conspicuous function of *ekphrasis* as ornamental and recreational digression in oratory. See E. Norden, *Die antike Kunstprosa* (Leipzig, 1909) 285–286; S. F. Bonner, *Roman Declamation* (Berkeley, 1949) 58–59. Although imitation within the declamatory schools is a token of the admiration with which *ekphrasis* in poetry was regarded, it should not be taken to indicate that the purposes of the poets and orators were precisely the same. In recent years the best contributions to our understanding of the literary function of *ekphrasis* have been made within the context of practical criticism (e.g. M. C. J. Putnam, *The Poetry of the Aeneid* [Cambridge, Mass., 1964] 147–150; Gilbert Lawall, *Theocritus' Coan Pastorals: A Poetry Book* [Cambridge, Mass., 1967] 27–31; Leo Curran, "Catullus 64 and the Heroic Age," *Y.C.S.* 21 [1969] 171–192; A. J. Boyle, "The Meaning of the Aeneid: A Critical Inquiry, Part II: *Homo Immemor*, Book VI and its Thematic Ramifications," *Ramus* 1 [1972] 116–119). Some interesting theoretical points have recently been added by George Kurman, "Ecphrasis in Epic Poetry," *Comparative Literature* 26 (1974) 1–13, who stresses the non-rhetorical elements of the tradition: the link with the theme of creation; the power of art to illustrate history, create life and frustrate time; the similarity between *ekphrasis* and the epic simile, and its relationship with prophecy. Only his concluding remarks, that *ekphraseis* may be regarded as "miniature dramas" interjected into the larger frame of the epic poem, seem to me off the point.

[6]   The similarity between these two kinds of "epic device" has scarcely been given adequate theoretical notice although the modern critic habitually uses the same technique of symbolic interpretation for both. However, L. Castiglione, *Studi intorno alle fonte e alle compozione delle Metamorfosi di Ovidio* (Pisa, 1906: rep. Rome, 1964) 329–331, does compare the episodes of Arachne, the Pierides and Orpheus with the bard songs of Demodocus in the *Odyssey* and Orpheus in the *Argonautica*.

from the narrative without doing violence to its continuity, they offer the artist an opportunity to speak *in propria persona* and to make us aware of the self-consciousness of his art through his attention to the fictional artistry of some other creator. With their ability to perceive the relevance of almost all digressions, modern critics have consistently demonstrated that the purely ornamental qualities of ekphrastic passages are subordinate to their thematic importance. Thus the shield of Achilles in whose forging the ancient commentators saw an allegory of creation[7] presents in shining bronze images of cities at war and peace. It is fitting that Achilles should win his supreme victory in this armor which embodies, as fully as any explicit statement in the poem, the fated alternatives of his own destiny: brief glory in war or a homely, peaceful old age. The shield of Aeneas presents no alternatives. Its images of Roman history chart the course of destiny in which the hero must play his inevitable role and illumine the similarity between his own deeds of violence and those of his descendants. The figured cloak that Athena weaves for Jason in the *Argonautica*, as Gilbert Lawall has shown, bears mythological scenes whose common denominator is their foreshadowing of the devious strategies by which the hero will gain the golden fleece.[8] The coverlet on the marriage bed of Peleus and Thetis shows the grimly foreboding story of Theseus' betrayal of Ariadne and emphasizes dark undertones in the joyous wedding scene whose final consequences are to be the destruction of Troy and the decline of man from his pristine heroic stature.

The significance of such descriptions lies in their ability to enlarge the perspectives of the poem by introducing some object that belongs naturally to its own closed world and yet incorporates external material that could not, save through the medium of *ekphrasis*, be admitted into the framework of this world. One might compare them to windows opening upon a world beyond the poem. The cities and men on the shield of Achilles present a cosmic overview, a generalization unavailable to Homer's single-minded characters. These scenes are only symbolically related to the dramatic foreground of the *Iliad*. The cities are not Troy; the warriors not Hector nor Agamemnon. The very anonymity of the shield figures is what makes them serve so effectively as a universalization of the epic's own themes of peace and war. The significance of the figures on Jason's cloak is actually so cryptic that no critic before Lawall had even thought to investigate their meaning. In bucolic poetry the subjects introduced by *ekphrasis* are even more obliquely related to their contexts. The scenes on the decorated cup in Theocritus' first *Idyll* are not really pastoral scenes as all, yet the frozen postures of their figures exemplify the timeless, changeless world created by art in the same idealizing manner as the poems themselves. The figures of Orpheus and the unknown scientist on the prize cups offered by Damoetas and Menalcas in Vergil's third *Eclogue* are even further removed from the rustic world of pastoral, but symbolize the complementary orders of art and agriculture that shape the vision of the pastoral poet. The same obliqueness of subject matter characterizes the verbal works described. The bard at Alcinoös' court in the *Odyssey* tells the tale of the adultery of Mars and Venus, but neither Homer nor Odysseus interprets this story of the gods as a reflection of the hero's own adventures, and Odysseus is

[7]   Heraclitus, *Quaestiones Homericae*, excerpted in G. Dindorf ed., *Scholia Graeca in Homeri Iliadem*, 4 vols. (Oxford, 1877) vol. 4, 187–191.

[8]   Gilbert Lawall, "Apollonius' *Argonautica*: Jason as Anti-Hero," *Y.C.S.* 19 (1966) 154–158. The scenes advise Jason to depend upon the power of the gods; make use of magical charms; rely upon the power of Aphrodite; avoid war and utilize his resources of intelligence and trickery.

hardly able to understand its foreshadowing of his future triumph over the potentially adulterous situation at home. In the *Aeneid*, Iopas sings of the separate course of the wandering sun and moon.[9] The figures of Dido and Aeneas are symbolically illuminated, but only the reader can sense the implication that these two monarchs who have known lives of wandering should, like sun and moon, have remained forever apart. *Ekphraseis* of this kind have the function of extended metaphor and are full of possible analogies that the reader explores for himself.

But the tapestries of Arachne and Minerva have no such metaphorical subtlety. They are not, as it were, windows looking towards a world outside of the poem but mirrors of the poem itself. In their miniature, self-contained panoramas of metamorphosis they reiterate the very themes that the poem has already made explicit. A similar kind of internal reflection is produced by those passages where verbal artists make extensive contributions to Ovid's poetic scheme. Both the daughters of Minyas in the fourth book and Orpheus in the tenth are the fictive authors of carefully composed groups of tales and another pair of tales is provided by the contest of the Muses and the nine daughters of Pieros in Book Five. In their artistic self-consciousness these persons stand apart from Ovid's other fictional storytellers who generally contribute only one tale apiece and that of an autobiographical nature.[10] The artist's recitals comprise eclectic combinations of tales that stand out from their narrative framework in their apparent digressiveness from the chronological organization of the poem.[11] But the subject chosen by these self-conscious storytellers is again metamorphosis and their productions are again miniatures of the larger poem. The song of Orpheus imitates Ovid's own organization insofar as it has its own little chronology centered about the inhabitants of Paphos[12] and its own tale within a tale. Ovid makes no perceptible stylistic distinction between these stories related by other poets and those he tells *in propria persona*. Their wit, their descriptive techniques and their narrative pacing are the same as that of the larger poem, and thus many critics have assumed that their speakers are introduced as a mere device for creating variety in the potentially monotonous sequence of transitions from story to story.

But all these episodes have one common element that they share with the episode of Arachne and that is their emphasis upon the personality of the artist,

[9] An extensive analysis of the relationships of the song to its context is given by C. P. Segal, "The Song of Iopas in the *Aeneid*," *Hermes* 99 (1971) 336–349.

[10] J. M. Frécaut, "Les transitions dans les Métamorphoses d'Ovide," *R.E.L.* 46 (1968) 261–263, observes that the typical situation involves the curiosity of a person who questions, more or less directly, a friend, a host, a passing traveller. Curiosity is often aroused by a chance allusion and the tale-teller is eager to relate to another a marvelous history in which he has participated or which he has witnessed.

[11] For the chronological pattern see Pierre Grimal, "La chronologie légendaire des Métamorphoses," *Ovidiana*, 245–252; R. Coleman, "Structure and Intention in the *Metamorphoses*," *C.Q.* 65 (1971) 461–476. Grimal, 253, points out that the tales of the Muses and Minerva form a kind of entr'acte: legends looking back to former times, while Coleman remarks on Ovid's balancing of straightforward chronological progress against "inset patterns," i.e., groups of stories bound together by thematic associations of similarity or contrast. "In themselves" he observes "these patterns tend to work against the *perpetuitas carminis* (continuousness of the song) by marking off an internally close-knit unit."

[12] Simone Viarre, "Pygmalion et Orphée chez Ovide (*Met.* X. 243–297)", *R.E.L.* 46 (1968) 235–236, observes that the stories from Pygmalion through Adonis trace the history of a family associated with the Cypriot Venus as a vegetation goddess.

the reasons for this performance and his ultimate fate.[13] In all four cases, the fate of the human artist, regardless of his talents, is disastrous. Here again is a major difference between Ovid's treatment of artists and art-works and that in previous poems where, without exception, the work of art is reverenced for its beauty, the poet's song heard with appreciation and the person of the artist held in honor. Traditionally, the artists associated with *ekphrasis* stand out from their fellow men as possessors of unusual powers of perception or prefiguration. But the daughters of Minyas are destroyed by Bacchus; the Pierides overwhelmed by the scornful Muses and Orpheus' tales of unfortunate love provoke the wrath of the Thracian women. All are reduced to the level of ordinary men. In the course of the poem the hard fate and failure of the artists stands in particular contrast with the better luck of the heroes that begins with Perseus' triumph over the Gorgon and culminates in the apotheosis of Hercules and a string of subsequent deifications. While the heroes grow more and more capable of holding their own against the powers of the gods and of nature, the position of art grows more and more tentative and the artist becomes a helpless figure at odds with nature and the authority of the gods. One wonders at Ovid's purpose in treating his fictional counterparts so harshly when he has made such an effort to draw them closely into the context of his work.

The combination of Ovid's ekphrastic mirroring of the poem with his attention to the personal history of the artist (that is to say his role within the metamorphic world of the poem) give the reader a particular vantage point from which to observe the artist's struggle to reproduce and interpret his own world in his work. Since Ovid seldom speaks in a personal voice throughout the poem, but only indirectly through his style, tone and perspective,[14] these artistic figures who are themselves the creators of miniature metamorphoses provide his only major opportunities for explicit reflection upon the problems of creative vision that underlie the shaping of the work as a whole. They are sufficient, I think, to challenge the still persistent image of Ovid as a supremely self-confident artist whose words flowed with careless ease,[15] and even the more recent pictures of him as the sympathetic spokesman for the pathos of love or the spinner of psychologically gratifying fantasies of a Utopian world of nature.

[13] Although various structural and functional parallels between these stories have often been observed, e.g., Castiglione, note 6 above, 329–331, Grimal note 11 above, 253–254, they have never been linked as stories of artists. One reason is that the Pierides and Arachne episodes have been taken at their face value as examples of the gods' righteous punishment of impiety. Thus Brooks Otis, *Ovid as an Epic Poet*, 2nd ed. (Cambridge, 1970) 146, sees the dominant themes of the incidents to be determined by the kinds of stories told in the frames. The tales of the Minyeides, Pierides and Arachne are all examples of human offense and divine *ira* (the Pierides and Arachne in their "positive impiety, deliberate *hybris*" offer very serious offenses indeed) while the story of Orpheus is primarily told as a love story. The insert tales in these four episodes do, Otis observes, have something in common. They are all love stories which Ovid inserted primarily for the sake of balancing his amatory theme against the theme of divine anger.

[14] The various modes of authorial intervention that M. von Albrecht has discussed in *Die Parenthese in Ovids Metamorphoses und ibre dichterische Funktion, Spudasmata* 7 (Hildesheim, 1964), give myriad insights into the minds of the characters and the frequently paradoxical nature of the situations, yet betray remarkably little of the author's own thoughts or purposes. By addressing both reader and character, he creates a direct relationship between them, while he, as it were, steps aside (see also, Otis, note 13 above, 335–338). Thus Otis, quite accurately remarks (343): "Ovid is not to be ticketed on the basis of any one part of the poem. His own identity is as elusive as that of his characters."

[15] E.g., J. M. Frécaut, *L'esprit et l'hunor chez Ovide* (Grenoble, 1972) 269: "Le charme des *Métamorphoses* auquel ont été sensibles la plupart des lecteurs, consiste dans un style aux mille nuances que ne se plie aux lois d'aucun genre littéraire, sans être désordonné, dans un jeu aux mille reflets qui ne s'interdit d'aborder aucun des grands thèmes poétiques sans être prétentieux, destructeur ou grotesque."

As they are adumbrated by the Ovidian artists, the problems of the
Metamorphoses are those of reconciling personal vision with the nature of
reality and of preserving integrity of artistic expression within an authoritarian
and uncertain world.

II

In the fourth book of the poem, following the tales of conflict between the
gods and the House of Cadmus, Ovid introduces the first human artists: the
daughters of Minyas. In their refusal to acknowledge the divine lineage of
Bacchus, the girls are doomed from the outset. As the episode of Pentheus has
just shown, Bacchus has many qualities that are unsettling to those who
cherish the civilized life: the dangerously seductive beauty of the *puer aeternus*
and a power to draw man into nature against his reason and will. His festival
appears as a hiatus in the order of social activity as his dishevelled, thyrsus-
bearing followers run wild with the ecstatic noise (28–30):[16]

> quacumque ingrederis, clamor iuvenalis et una
> femineae voces impulsaque tympana palmis
> concavaque aera sonant longoque foramine buxus.
>
> (Wherever you approach, the clamor of young men and voices of
> women unite and the cymbals struck with the palms and the hollow
> brass resound and the box-wood flute with its long mouthpiece.)

Against this clamorous background, the three young women give their
allegiance to the quiet and rational arts of Minerva (32–35):

> solae Minyeides intus
> intempestiva turbantes festa Minerva
> aut ducunt lanas aut stamina pollice versant
> aut haerent telae famulasque laboribus urgent.
>
> (Only the daughters of Minyas remained within disturbing the festival
> with untimely work of Minerva; either they spin the wool or twist the
> spindles with their thumbs or stick close to the loom and urge their
> serving maids to work.)

In Aelian's version of the story the sisters pursue their domestic arts because of
their fidelity to their husbands. Nicander seems merely to have suggested that
they were somewhat compulsively dedicated to industry for its own sake.[17]
Neither account offers any hint of a parallel to Ovid's treatment of the story as a
framework for a group of tales. Although they apply themselves to their work
like Roman matrons, the sisters decide to shorten the long hours of their
isolation from society (37–41):

> "dum cessant aliae commentaque sacra frequentant,
> nos quoque, quas Pallas, melior dea, detinet," inquit,

[16]   Quotations are from *P. Ovidius Naso Metamorphosen*, M. Haupt, ed., 10 *Auflage*, M. von
Albrecht, ed. (Zurich, 1969).

[17]   Aelian *Varia Historia* 3.42. Nicander Book 4 in Antoninus Liberalis, *Metamorphoses* 10,
ed. M. Papathomopoulos (Paris, 1968). The description here is ἐκτόπως φιλεργοί (10.4–5:
unusually devoted to work). In both versions, the sisters are married. Ovid, by making no mention of
husbands, puts a stronger emphasis on their similarity to Minerva herself and makes their dedication
to the civilized life seem a matter of personal preference rather than duty. In Nicander's version,
Bacchus approaches the sisters in the guise of a young girl and urges them to join in the rites. Ovid
makes their defiance less direct.

"utile opus manuum vario sermone levemus
perque vices aliquid, quod tempora longa videri
non sinat, in medium vacuas referamus ad aures!"

("While others are idle and flock to these fictitious rites, let us also,
whom Pallas, a better goddess, holds back, lighten the useful work of
our hands," she said, "with diverting speech. Let each by turns make
some contribution for idle ears at the time should not be
allowed to seem long.")

Although the Minyeides regard their fellow women as derelict of duty, the *nos quoque* suggests that they intend to allow themselves a bit of a holiday. Their storytelling thus serves as a legitimized approximation of the escape from everyday life that others find in the rites of Bacchus.[18]

The three sisters are connoisseurs of metamorphic mythology seeking in their choice of stories after the recherché, the *fabula non vulgaris* ("story not commonly known"). The section of the poem containing their narrative is carefully designed as a kind of bravura piece:[19] four tales dealing with the complications and frustrations of secret love and forming among themselves a pattern of contrasts and similarities. Two tragic – or pathetic – stories involving mortals alternate with two comic stories involving gods. The ill-starred Pyramus and Thisbe destroy themselves in their innocence and folly while Leucothoe is buried alive in consequence of her yielding to the sun-god. Mars and Venus are held fast in Vulcan's golden net, but their apprehension provokes no worse consequence than the laughter of the gods. The lustful nymph Salmacis struggles ludicrously to capture Hermaphrodite until the two merge together into one sexually ambiguous form, a permanent image of erotic frustration. As lover and love-object man appears helpless and vulnerable while the powerful gods love guiltily but go unscathed. The emphasis upon divine power and human frailty makes love appear as a forbidden experience for man.

In their attitude towards their subject the storytellers combine a kind of moral primness with a strongly romantic fixation on love. *Tantus dolor urit amantes* (278: "Such sharp indignation singes lovers"), moralizes Alcithoe and her words might be applied to all of the stories told. Passion appears an ambivalent force, both fascinating and fearful, that leads man outside the secure boundaries of civilizations into a dangerously uncontrollable world of nature. The naïve Pyramus and Thisbe, as Segal has put it, "leave behind

[18]   The association between weaving and love stories seems to be borrowed directly from Vergil, *G.* 4. 333–346, where Cyrene and her nymphs listen to Clymene's song of the loves of the gods from the beginning of time. From this model, Ovid also takes the suggestion for his inclusion of the adultery of Mars and Venus (*G.* 4. 345–346: *curam ... inanem/ Volcani, Martisque dolos et dulcia furta;* "the barren love of Vulcan, and the wiles and sweet thefts of Mars"). In its context, Clymene's song contrasts with the unhappy love of Orpheus. Ovid has incorporated the contrast between carefree divine and pathetic mortal love into the structure of the four tales.

[19]   For various observations on thematic links between the tales see Haupt-von Albrecht, note 16 above, *ad* v. 36, 199 (erotic-aetiological character of metamorphoses and Asian settings in first and third tales); V. Pöschl, "L'arte narrative di Ovidio nelle Metamorfosi," *Atti del Convegno Internazionale Ovidiano,* 2 vols. (Rome, 1959) 2. 295–305 (symbolic shadings of individual tales); Otis, note 13 above (three different types of amatory pathos in first, third and fourth); Charles P. Segal, *Landscape in Ovid's Metamorphoses, Hermes, Einzelschriften* 23 (Wiesbaden, 1969) 49–53 (use of landscape in first and fourth).

the shelteredness of childhood innocence for the dark night of adult life and adult sexuality".[20] The lion that frightens Thisbe and leaves her bloody cloak for Pyramus to discover represents a threatening wildness in this new realm of experience that neither lover is prepared to encounter. Nature in the Salmacis tale takes on strongly sexual overtones when the lustful nymph of the pool turns her beautiful glade into a forest brothel. For her submission to the sun Leucothoe lies buried beneath a mound of earth while her envious sister Clytie becomes a part of the vegetable world always instinctively turning to follow the course of the sun. Destructive metamorphoses are the consequence of the human lovers' yielding to nature, yet even Mars and Venus are unable to conceal their adultery from the all-seeing eyes of the sun.

The thematic cast of the stories is psychologically appropriate to the circumstances in which they are told. Such reservations about love are precisely what might be expected from devotees of the virgin goddess. At one and the same time the stories provide a vicarious experience of passion and a justification of withdrawal. As artists the Minyeides are observers of love, nature and the power of the gods; both in their weaving and in their narrative they express their resistance to the chaotic force of nature.

Such an escape is not permitted. No sooner are the stories concluded than the influence of the neglected Bacchus falls upon the tellers. As the dissonance of the wild rout draws nearer the Minyeides see their domestic instruments come alive, growing into a tangle of Bacchic vegetation (394–398):

> coepere virescere telae
> inque hederae faciem pendens frondescere vestis;
> pars abit in vites et, quae modo fila fuerent,
> palmite mutantur; de stamine pampinus exit;
> purpura fulgorem pictis adcommodat uvis.

> (The looms begin to turn green and the hanging tapestry starts to leaf out with the appearance of ivy. Part meanders off into vine shoots, and the erstwhile threads are changed into leaves and the tendrils spring forth from the loom warp. The purple colors fit their sheen to the painted grapes.)

The late day now poised between light and darkness is suddenly ablaze with torches. The voices of wild animals echo in the darkness, but still the girls resist and flee, hiding themselves in shadow. Bacchus still cannot compel them to participate in the wild enthusiasm of his festival, but instead he punishes them by intensifying their instinct to withdrawal. The Minyeides are changed into bats, natural creatures who shrink from nature's light and cling to the shelter of the civilized world (414–415):

> tectaque, non silvas celebrant, lucemque perosae
> nocte volant seroque tenent a vespere nomen.

> (They congregate in houses, not forests, and full of hatred for the light they flit by night, and take their name from the late evening.)

---

[20]   Segal, note 19 above, 50.

The conclusion that Ovid has given the story is much gentler than that of Nicander and Aelian where the sisters are maddened with Bacchic fury like that of Agave and tear apart Leucippe's own child.[21] Ovid's new ending is precisely suited to his recasting of the tale as a parable of art. Bacchus has paid no attention to the contents of the Minyeides' stories; it is their independence that he cannot tolerate. Yet by allowing them to preserve their instinct for withdrawal as the last vestige of their human identity he implicitly mocks their adherence to a civilized order. Personal autonomy and the freedom to maintain an orderly vision from a position of personal detachment: these prerogatives of art are denied to the artists of the *Metamorphoses* whose very attempts to control their world leave them the more open to the violence of uncontrolled experience. In this respect the story provides a programmatic introduction to the theme of artistic failure. The artist's struggle for autonomy occurs again in the stories of the Pierides and Arachne; his futile quest for order is the chief theme of the tale of Orpheus.

The art of the Minyeides is a personal pastime that offers only a passive resistance to divine power. In the fifth and sixth books where the human artists have emboldened themselves to the point of measuring their skills against those of the gods, Ovid draws a stronger contrast between human limitations and the authority of the gods. By allowing the gods to act as narrators in this section of the poem, he places the human artist in a disadvantaged position that makes his struggle seem the more futile. The stories told by the Muses and Minerva present the human artist as a pretentious rebel pointlessly mocking and vilifying his betters while they boast of themselves as proprietors of a divine art that embodies a truly superior and authoritative vision of the world.

In book five Pegasus creates the fountain on Helicon, as idyllic home for the daughters of memory. As the Muses lead Minerva to their sacred spring she marvels at the charms of the remote *locus amoenus* (263–268):

> ad latices deduxit Pallada sacros.
> quae mirata diu factas pedis ictibus undas
> silvarum lucos circumspicit antiquarum
> antraque et innumeris distinctas floribus herbas
> felicesque vocat pariter studioque locoque
> Mnemonidas.

> (She led Pallas to the sacred springs where, marvelling long at the waters made by the blows of a foot, she surveys the groves of ancient trees and the caverns and the grasses brightened by countless flowers and she calls the daughters of Memory equally blessed in their zeal and in their place.)

This fertile grove is easily recognizable as that same arch-symbol of poetic inspiration that poets have long celebrated,[22] yet Ovid's Muses give no indication that human poets are welcome to come drinking and cutting the flowers. The goddesses have withdrawn to their lofty paradise with professions of fear for their safety in the greater world. Their gesture indicates an indifference to human affairs and a refusal of sympathetic commerce with men. Although they are goddesses, they picture themselves as helpless maidens frightened of all things (273–274: *omnia terrent/virgineas mentes*; "everything

---

[21] Castiglione, note 6 above, 362–363, comments on Ovid's refinement of the story.
[22] Callimachus, *Hymns* 2. 110–112; Lucretius, *D.R.N.*, 1. 117–118; 927;' Propertius 3.3.5; 3.1.3.

frightens virgin minds"). Yet the story they tell to Minerva as an explanation of their fears does not show weakness, but the avenging power typical of gods. They speak of King Pyreneus whom they scornfully term *durus* and *ferox*, a conqueror and an unjust tyrant who deceived them with a promise of shelter from the rain. His invitation was gracious enough (282–283: *subiere minores/ saepe casas superi*; "Superior beings have often entered humble houses"), yet the Muses see nothing in it but base flattery to which they yielded primarily because it was raining. A gracious return for the king's hospitality does not seem to enter their minds. When the rain stops they are eager to get on their way (285–288):

> desierant imbres, victoque aquilonibus Austro
> fusca repurgato fugiebant nubila caelo;
> impetus ire fuit: claudit sua tecta Pyreneus
> vimque parat.

> (The rain had departed, and with the south winds driven off by the west wind the dark clouds fled from the purified sky. There was a move to go; Pyreneus closed up his house and got ready to use force.)

Certain that they are on the verge of rape, the Muses all the same escape easily and take flight from the rooftop with Pyreneus in pursuit (289–293):

> ipse secuturo similis stetit arduus arce
> "qua" aue "via est vobis, erit et mihi," dixit, "eadem,"
> seque iacit vecors e summae culmine turris
> et cadit in vultus discussisque ossibus oris
> tundit humum moriens scelerato sanguine tinctam.

> (He, like one about to follow, stood high on the roof-top. "Whatever path you take," he said, "mine will be the same," and he cast himself, that madman, from the topmost peak of the tower and fell onto his face and, his bones all shaken apart, dying, he beat the ground tinged with his scoundrel's blood.)

The swift and facile escape indicates that the Muses had no real cause for fear. They knew their powers and could afford to mock their enemy's folly. But the king's final words: *qua via est vobis erit et mihi eadem* ("Whatever path you take, mine will be the same"), in which the muses find an insinuating leer, actually point to a meaning in the story that they refuse to acknowledge.[23] From their point of view, Pyreneus is *vecors* ("out of his mind"); he has tried to imitate their divine flight. Indignation and scorn cloud the picture of a mortal man seeking poetic inspiration. Rough and uncultivated as he may be (we have only the Muses' word for his character), Pyreneus longs for the society of the Muses. Even his attempt to shut them up in his house suggests his eagerness to capture the grace of art. Such a man must fall on his face. The Muses

---

[23]   The incident has now known source and the usual conjectures have been made: Pauly-Wissowa vol. 24, 19, *s.v.* Pyreneus, either a Phocian regional tale or the invention of a Hellenistic poet; Röscher, *s.v.* Pyreneus, 3345, the lost original must have been a kind of *Wielandsage* involving the creation of a means of flight. The incident, however, is so perfectly contrived to display the character of the Muses, that there seems no reason at all why Ovid could not have invented it. We can then see in it an inversion of the gracious commerce between the Muses and men to be found in such passages as Hesiod, *Theogony* 80–97 (the Muses' counsel to the rulers of men) or Pindar, *Olympian* 14 (invocation to the Graces of Orchomenos). The only critic who shows any sympathy for Pyreneus' point of view is Viarre, note 4 above, 385, who sees the psychological import of the desire for flight as a manifestation of subconscious impulse.

snatch their delicate persons away and rejoice most indelicately in the bloody details of their enemy's death. For them Pyreneus exemplifies all the crude insensitivity that makes man undeserving of art and thus they justify their retreat from the world.

This story, so heavily colored by the divine point of view that we cannot see the human side of it, clearly forms a prelude to two tales of human artists who challenge the gods. The nine daughters of Pieros whom the goddesses have transformed into magpies will not remain silent in their punishment and invade the very sanctuary of Helicon complaining of their fate. As the Muses explain this intrusion to Minerva with an account of their recent victory over these women, they once more show their scorn of human pretension. The Pierides were *stolidae sorores* who accused the Muses of deceiving the unlearned masses *vana dulcedine* ("with empty sweetness"). In the eyes of the Muses the contest was no real challenge but a mere formality recollected with scorn (315–316):

> turpe quidem contendere erat, sed cedere visum
> turpius.

> (Shameful indeed it was to compete, but to yield seemed more shameful.)

The origins of the Pierian story are obscure, but Ovid would once again seem to have his most immediate model in Nicander. If Antonius' sketch is reliable, Nicander's account was factual and unambiguous.[24] The song of the false Muses clouded the world with darkness and left nature inattentive, but the true Muses held nature spellbound and made the summit of Helicon rise up almost as high as the sky. Whatever songs the contestants may have sung, the Pierides were inferior artists and Nicander was on the side of the divine skill. But in place of any such abstract judgment upon the talents of the competitors, Ovid lets the songs form their own contrast. The songs should be regarded as a pair of short epic compositions: a gigantomachy and a tale of the rape of Persephone. Since the Muses are giving the account, they compress the song of the Pierides into a hasty, distasteful summary while their own lengthy contribution is unfolded in all its detail.

The gigantomachy is overtly insulting to the dignity of the gods. According to the Muses, the sisters placed the giants in a false position of honor while extenuating the deeds of the greater gods. Fleeing from the earthborn monster Typhoeus, the terrified Olympians take refuge in Egypt concealing their persons in animal form (325–331). Jupiter turns himself into a goat; Apollo a ram; Semele a kid; Juno a cow; Diana a cat; Venus a fish and Cyllene an ibis. Since there is no other extensive treatment of this same subject in the *Metamorphoses*, the truth of this picture of cowardice and debasement cannot be assessed in terms of Ovid's own mythology.[25] Even the comments of the Muses give no real evidence as to whether this portion of the story should be taken as fabrication or fact. All the same, its contents are very much in keeping with the Pierides' contention that the Muses

[24]   Nicander (Antoninus Liberalis, *Metamorphoses* 9). This version places the birth of the Heliconian spring at the very moment of this triumph of the Muses.

[25]   Nicander (Antoninus Liberalis, *Metamorphoses* 28) is the oldest extant version, and the myth can perhaps be safely called an obscure one although Porphyry *De Abstinentia* 3.16 alleges that it was told by Pindar. J. Gwyn Griffiths, "The Flight of the Gods before Typhon: An Unrecognized Myth," *Hermes* 88 (1960) 374–376, proposes that it involved an assimilation of the Greek gods to the animal-formed gods of Egypt.

have deceived man by their *vana dulcedo* ("empty sweetness"), and the song should probably be thought of as a satirical mock-epic intended to expose the hollow nature of divine authority. Its vision of the mutability of the gods is one that the reader of the *Metamorphoses* cannot find wholly surprising or unfamiliar.

To this image of instability among the powers that govern the universe, the song of the Muses provides an assertive answer, a justification of the ways of the gods.[26] It begins where the other concluded, defending divine power by a celebration of the Olympian's final crushing defeat of the giants. Where the gigantomachy showed the world turned to chaos, this tale shows its return to order. Order comes in strongly in the conclusion where all the threads are tied up in a series of metamorphoses.

The Muses explain the affairs of the gods with an understanding available only to divine minds. Under the influence of a goddess, Pluto falls in love with a goddess and provokes a goddess's anger and grief. The emotions and motives of the divine figures in the tale are never communicated to men. Nymphs and mortals appear only as the faithful, unquestioning helpers of the gods. Those who do not know their place are duly punished: the rude boy who laughs at Ceres' hunger and Ascalaphus who betrays Persephone's eating of the pomegranate in the underworld. Justice comes about through Jupiter's arbitration. The tale begins with an invocation to Ceres the bestower of *fruges* and *leges* and closes on the same note with Ceres' rewarding of the pious and her gift of the agricultural arts to man. Its obvious moral is that the private affairs of the gods have no lasting detrimental effect upon their provisions for human welfare. In this respect it is a perfect piece of authoritarian art, and quite obviously an example of that *dulcedo* which, in the Muses' eyes, is not *vana*. In its separation of divine and human affairs, it is no more accurate a reflection of the mythological ethos of the *Metamorphoses* than the debased gigantomachy, yet, like the earlier poem, it does not ring wholly false. The nymphs, as might be expected from the honorific treatment given to their kind in the tale, vote in favor of the Muses, but the Pierides clamor for the victory. Perhaps the reader might second them had he been allowed to hear their song in its entirety. Ovid leaves the situation ambiguous. The Muses claim to have punished their rivals less for the impiety of their work than for refusing to accept their inevitable inferiority as human artists.

The ensuing contest of Minerva and Arachne in Book Six makes the discrepancy between human and divine viewpoints clearer by the very fact that its art works present a more recognizable reflection of the nature of metamorphosis within the poem, and, at the same time, a clearer expression of the thoughts and intentions of their creators.

---

[26]   Anderson, *A.J.P.*, 102–103, seems to share Heinze's favorable opinion of the tale, suggesting that Ovid has given it certain literary qualities that make it, on his own terms, deserving of victory, namely, a "desultory, asymmetrical structure" similar to "the kind of epic structure which Ovid himself chose for the *Metamorphoses*." But Otis, note 13 above, 153–154, noting ironic undercurrents in the tale is not sure that the reader should accept it soberly: "It is rather disconcerting to witness the respectable Muses relating to the respectable Minerva the tale of Pluto's unpremeditated *amor*. Ovid, of course, preserves appearances by an epic tone and decorum ... but he certainly brings out the humor of the action; the gods who are at such pains to punish criticism are, in fact, only too vulnerable to it. The story of Prosperpina is far more akin to the impious stories of the Pieriae than the somewhat unsophisticated Muses can readily understand."

From Minerva's point of view, Arachne is the very epitome of the rebellious upstart, a woman with neither position nor background to recommend her, but only her skill (7–8; *non illa loco nec origine gentis/clara, sed arte fuit*). As the child of a humble wool-dyer, reared in a small cottage, she comes to cherish ambitions of making her name famous throughout all Lydia (8–12). Her hopes were not ill-founded, for her work compels universal admiration and, like the legendary bards whose songs dazzle nature, she draws the nymphs from grove and stream to marvel at her grace in weaving and the beautiful painting of her needle (15–20). It is in keeping with her pride in her self-made success, that the girl denies any obligation to Minerva's teaching and is ready to prove her autonomy by participating in a contest with the goddess (25). Minerva tricks her in the most appropriate way by disguising herself as a very old woman to speak for the authoritarian point of view. Arachne must confess her dependence upon Minerva and rest content with mortal fame. Such admonitions are precisely calculated to make the ambitious young woman go further in staking her modernity and independence against tradition (37–41).

As the narrator prepares to describe the pictures — for Ovid's voice now supersedes that of Minerva — he pauses for a moment to abstract an overview of the scene. The rival artists and their tapestries blend harmoniously into one continuous panorama of beauty and color. The colors shimmer on the surface of the webs like the hues of the rainbow (63–67):

> qualis ab imbre solet percussis solibus arcus
> inficere ingenti longum curvamine caelum,
> in quo diversi niteant cum mille colores,
> transitus ipse tamen spectantia lumina fallit:
> usque adeo, quod tangit, idem est; tamen ultima distant.

> (Just as the bow, when the sun's rays have been struck by the rain, is accustomed to paint the long expanse of the sky with its monumental arch in which, since a thousand diverse colors sparkle, the point where the hues overlap deceives onlooking eyes so completely that each is the same as what it touches and yet the far edges are wholly different.)

In the classical tradition, the rainbow is an ominous sign, and the image of transitory beauty in the simile seems to foreshadow the short life of Arachne's tapestry. Yet Ovid's emphasis upon the intermingled shades of the spectrum gives a hint of the thematic contingency of the tapestries. His description of the subtly overlapping colors whose differences are apparent only at the outside extremes of the arch (*quod tangit, idem est; tamen ultima distant*) could easily refer to the artists' two versions of metamorphosis.[27] Only after this point has been made do the pictures spring into separate focus (69): *vetus in tela deducitur argumentum* ("an ancient scenario is drawn forth from the loom"). *Argumentum* has a double meaning, suggesting both the plots of the stories and their function as expressions of opposing points of view. Each weaver has her own ideas to demonstrate.

---

[27]   Menzione, note 4 above, 139: "E un'immagine che potrebbe essere simbolicamente applicata al trascolorante monde fiabesco delle *Metamorfosi*."

The contradictory visions of the tapestries as *argumenta* is sharpened by the recurrence of the same gods in each. Minerva lays claim to her inevitable victory by depicting herself as victor in another contest and she portrays her fellow divinities as they wish to appear in the eyes of man. They are arranged in formal postures, impressive in their dignity (72–73): *sedibus altis/augusta gravitate sedent;* "they sit on their lofty thrones with august gravity"). The image of Jove is regal and even the defeated Neptune appears in a gesture of majestic power striking the rock with his trident. With their gifts of sacred spring and olive, he and Minerva are benefactors of man. The subject, as Anderson has pointed out, is that of the Parthenon frieze.[28] In his outline of the composition, Ovid has captured the cold aloofness of that same monumental pediment that places the gods so far above the reach of man. But the moral, for Arachne's benefit, has to do with divine order and justice. Only the arguments of gods, Minerva seems to say, can be settled by peaceable contention. Thus the four corner panels of the tapestry present a facet of divine justice, showing metamorphosis as the god's punishment of those mortals who challenge their superiority.

But Arachne presents metamorphosis as it serves the erotic whims of the gods. In place of the stationary, regal Jove is the bull who abducts Europa. The lifelike quality of the tapestry suggests truth in the art. Arachne sees through human eyes the shapes in which the gods have been seen by those whom they wished to deceive. The verbs: *elatus; luserit; visus; fallis; luserit; deceperit* underscore the insistent theme. The illusion Arachne creates is that which the gods themselves have perpetrated. One recalls that, only a moment before, she herself has been tricked by a goddess in an impenetrable disguise.

It is hard to imagine the composition of this tapestry. Ovid has deliberately blurred the boundaries of its scenes to give the impression of a cosmic panorama of shifting forms, natural objects set in natural backgrounds (121–122): *omnibus his faciemque suam faciemque locorum/reddidit;*[29] she rendered for each thing its proper appearance and the appearances of the places"). Such a spectacle of motion and energy evokes a spirit of artistic play. The fact is that Arachne does not, by her representation, make a moral judgment upon the loves of the gods.[30] It is Minerva's interpretation that makes the subject immoral and trivializes this vast panorama of desire and generation as *caelestia crimina.* By her violent reaction to the success of her rival the goddess

28   Anderson, *Ovid's Metamorphoses,* ad. 6.72.

29   Laslo, note 4 above, 391, calls it a little gallery. The separate events need not necessarily be imagined as run together; the phrase *suam faciemque locorum* ("the proper appearance of the places") suggests that each incident had its distinctive background. Ovid is probably thinking of a series of pictures like that in the Odyssey frieze. *Suam faciemque locorum* is somewhat suggestive of the language Vitruvius uses to indicate the topographical verisimilitude of the landscape painter's art (*De Architectura* 7.5.2: *ab certis locorum proprietatibus imagines exprimentes*; "forming images in accordance with the peculiar characteristics of places").

30   Ovid clearly makes the point that the artist's intentions are at the mercy of his interpreter. The degree of misunderstanding involved may be illuminated by W. R. Johnson's remarks on the erotic character of the *Metamorphoses,* "The Problem of the Counter-Classical Sensibility and its Critics," *California Studies in Classical Antiquity* 3 (1970) 123–152: "It seems to me not improbable ... that the *Metamorphoses* is an attack on Augustus' efforts to reform society by means of an artificial religious revival and the imposition of stringent and inhuman moral codes. From this point of view, the *Metamorphoses*' beautiful and original treatment of eroticism, so far from being merely another indication of Ovidian shallowness, constitutes a bold and powerful defense of human nature, human dignity and human individuality in the face of ferocious and arbitrary attempts to control human nature and finally to enslave it."

betrays the very principle of just and rational triumph that she has illuminated in the center of her own tapestry. Her divine dignity is diminished by her own crime against art.

In its awareness of supernatural power concentrated towards the furthering of the most natural instincts, Arachne's tapestry captures the spirit of the "divine comedy" that forms so large a part of the early books of the *Metamorphoses*.[31] The destruction of the piece invites the reader to look questioningly backwards upon the poem. Should it now be seen through Minerva's eyes as an impious spectacle of *caelestia crimina?* Has Ovid deliberately spun an image that implies the vulnerability of his own work? One can easily be tempted to carry the moral of the story beyond the immediate confines of the situation and to read into this incident a reflection of the rebelliousness and concomitant apprehensiveness of the poet whose own forthright portrayal of human nature constantly pushed at the boundaries of social propriety and dared the tolerance of official moral sanction. Seen in this manner, the incident serves as an example of Ovid's anti-Augustanism. But these external resonances of the tapestries are nowhere near so important as their embodiment of conflicts within the poem itself. As I earlier remarked, it is not Arachne's tapestry alone, but the two scenes in combination that form a mirror of the *Metamorphoses*. Ovid's linking of the two in the rainbow simile suggests their intrinsic interassociation. That is to say, the poem itself contains principles and perspectives that simultaneously complement and contradict one another, divine vengeance and divine comedy, visions of order and chaos intermingled. Only in the tapestries are these perspectives drawn apart as if for momentary clarification. The very act of separation divides the poem against itself and shows, in consequence, how easily the authoritarian point of view with its demands for reason and order can overwhelm the human perspective. The tapestry of Minerva shows what the poem would be like if the human perspective were excluded: a strangely stiff tale of the god's control of the universe. The limited and fragile human vision is what gives the poem its vitality and its fidelity to the actual life of the world. Arachne's vision is bound to an uncertain and unpredictable world of appearances and her limitation is at once the source of her artistic strength and her fatal weakness. Yet only such an artist as she, doggedly asserting her autonomy and the truth of her vision, can reveal the ironic injustice of divine order. Having been deceived by a goddess in disguise, she has undergone the same experience as the figures in her tapestry and her subsequent death identifies her even more closely with the fate of her work. Her desperate suicide reveals her dedication to her art, and Minerva, professing a questionable pity, transforms her into a spider, a compulsive weaver whose work is always liable to sudden destruction.

In the central portion of Book 6, the brief tale of the flaying of Marsyas provides a grisly reprise of the stories of Arachne and the Pierides with the cruelty of the gods' suppression of the lesser artist carried to a new extreme. In Book 8, Daedalus helps Minos to conceal the shame of his house by constructing a labyrinth so complex that he can scarcely find his own way back to the door

---

[31]   G. Lafaye, *Les Métamorphoses d'Ovide et leur modèles grecs* (Paris, 1904; rep. Hildesheim, 1971) 102: "ce qu'il aime c'est précisément cette galanterie, dont les auteurs de métamorphoses lui donnaient l'exemple." Otis' remark, note 13 above, 153, that Arachne is to be distinguished from Ovid because her intentions are deliberately blasphemous is not very convincing. The subject is also treated by Leo Curran in "Transformation and Anti-Augustanism in Ovid's Metamorphoses," *Arethusa* 5 (1972) 83–84, where Arachne's work is said to represent Ovid's Alexandrianism.

(167–168: *vixque ipse reverti/ ad limen potuit*),[32] and then, in his longing for freedom, creates the wings that cause the death of his son. Both stories suggest the artist's inability to predict or control the consequences of his own art. But in this central portion of the narrative (Books 7–9) these artists are overshadowed by the more prominent figures of the heroes whose successes are gained through divine favor. The series of their adventures reaches its culmination when Hercules is admitted to the heavens after his fiery death. Preceded as it is by a short divine council that harks back to the scene on Minerva's tapestry, the apotheosis of Hercules is linked with the themes of divine justice and order insofar as it shows that the gods can be as capricious in their benevolence as in their vengeance.[33]

The long section dealing with Hercules is followed by an equally lengthy study of Orpheus, the chief of legendary artist heroes. The lives and accomplishments of the two have certain points of similarity. Each has achieved a measure of

---

[32]   The short description of the labyrinth (8. 160–168) constitutes a kind of *ekphrasis*. In an interesting paragraph, Bartholomé, note 4 above, 79–80, points to a curious contradiction where the *error variarum viarum* ("wandering of the various paths", 161) is compared with the windings of the River Meander, something far less complicated than the labyrinth itself. In the light of this comparison he finds it strange that Daedalus should lose himself inside. From another point of view, one might see the craftsman as having transformed a natural model into something fantastic and baffling. Ovid may be thinking of the fact that the Meander pattern, as developed in artistic decoration, is far more contorted than the natural figure from which it takes its name, yet this concept of transformation through complication has its relevance to the general picture of art in the poem. Daedalus' self-confusion within the labyrinth is a symbolic detail that foreshadows the fatal consequences of his next attempt to imitate nature: the wings. His artistic failure thus falls in the general pattern being unfolded in the poem, but Ovid greatly undercuts the pathos of his story by appending the tale of his jealous murder of his nephew Perdix (8.236–259) directly after the death of Icarus. He is thus not only unable to control the consequences of his art, but also unable to control himself. In the *Aeneid*, Daedalus' creation of the temple doors at Cumae (6.14–33) makes him a true artist, and, as A. J. Boyle has observed, note 5 above, 118–119, his history and his failure are closely analogous to Aeneas' own experience. In the *Metamorphoses* Daedalus is no more than a craftsman and is far less sympathetic than other artists, perhaps because he has served a king, perhaps because Ovid wishes to undercut the dignity of the Vergilian figure.

[33]   The significance of the apotheosis is still one of the most controversial points in the poem. Hermann Fränkel, *Ovid: A Poet between Two Worlds* (Berkeley, 1945) 211–213, and L. P. Wilkinson, *Ovid Recalled* (Cambridge, 1953) 193, take the apotheosis quite seriously as a token of man's triumph over nature and mortality, but Otis, above note 13, 167, 329–330, is unable to find the clear symbolic significance that he would like to see: "[apotheosis] comes as an oddly perfunctory conclusion to his amatory tragedy ... how can the gods who caused the suffering now assume an attitude of justice and mercy — no longer amorous and spitefully or rightfully, if mercilessly, avenging but actually benevolent? There is an evident shift of point of view." In the long run, Otis attributes this ambivalence to Ovid's own ambivalence towards his heroic subject, his lack of sympathy with the Augustan world, all of which seems to him to create unresolved problems in the poem. More recent studies are putting the case for Ovid's negativism more strongly. An insight into the peculiarly half-hearted impression given by Ovid's treatment of apotheosis is supplied indirectly by Wade Stephens' point in "Two stoic Heroes in the *Metamorphoses:* Hercules and Ulysses," *Ovidiana*, 273–282, that the tradition of Stoic apotheosis as recorded by Cicero involves a deification by human gratitude rather than by divine intervention. It is just this nobler, more humane perspective that Ovid excludes, making apotheosis a token of the capriciousness of the gods even in their so-called justice. Thus Karl Galinsky, "Hercules Ovidianus (Metamorphoses 9, 1–272),"*Wiener Studien* 85 (1972) 93–116, brings out all the details that undercut the dignity of Hercules' last moments. This Hercules is the comic strongman, dying in the posture of a banqueter on the pyre. Even as he is en route to join the gods, he denies their existence. After Hercules' death, the succeeding apotheoses become more and more wooden and comic. Galinsky bolsters this point by remarking on the Vergilian identification of Hercules with Aeneas: another vestige of Augustanism that Ovid attacks through his parody. The case is also put by Coleman, note 11 above, 476: "Caesar's translation to the heavens, while it links him with Hercules, Aeneas and Romulus, is after all, no more glorious a consummation than had been granted to Callisto and Arcas. Deification — astrification — what are these but two more varieties of metamorphosis to be treated with as much or as little suspension of disbelief as the rest?"

control over nature, the one by deeds of strength, the other by his gentler appeal to nature's instinct for harmony. In spite of their achievements, each is undone by human passions and meets a violent death at the hands of women. The background created by the apotheosis of Hercules would seem to create an appropriate context for an artist's similar triumph over the vagaries of his fate. Yet the ultimate achievements of the artist hero, here portrayed with rueful irony, is far less than that of the hero of force. Where the former is allowed to escape the consequences of his personality, the latter is submerged by his.

The story of Orpheus' failure differs greatly from those of the artists who have preceded him. There is no contest of human and divine skills and no question of defamation of the gods. Rather, Ovid focuses upon the artist's search for order and the relationship between his articulation of emotion and fantasy and the internal order of his experience. It is not, of course, the mere fact of Orpheus' death that constitutes his failure, but rather the manner in which Ovid portrays it. If he had kept to the model set by Vergil in the *Georgics*, the musical glory of the singer would have transcended the vicissitudes of his emotional life. Instead he uses the pattern of Vergil's story humorously — at times in a spirit of parody — to demythologize the magic of Orphic song and illuminate the human personality and limitations of the artist.[34] The songs that Orpheus sings reflect the cast of his mind, an area that Vergil leaves unexplored, and the story moves towards a fatal confusion of art and life. The ancient synthesis of artistic order and natural harmony loses its meaning and the content of Orpheus' poetry becomes the immediate cause of his destruction.

At the outset Ovid makes it clear that the musical genius of Orpheus cannot secure the happiness of his private life. Although he summons Hymen to his wedding, the invocation is futile (10.3: *Orphea nequiquam voce vocatur*; "he is called all in vain by the Orphic voice"). The god comes with bad omens; the smoke of the marriage torch elicits foreboding tears. Upon losing Eurydice, Orpheus weeps as an ordinary mortal; the phrase *vates deflevit* ("the bard wept") suggests the dissolution of musical power in emotion. One recalls that the Vergilian Orpheus mourned his loss in elegiac song. Likewise Orpheus' descent into the underworld is an act of human bravery, yet devoid of the magic that characterizes Vergil's account of the journey. There is none of the continual plaintive music that renders hostile demons motionless and captivates the unfeeling shades. Only when Orpheus has reached the throne of Persephone does he touch the chords of his lyre and begin to sing. Even then Ovid uses the prosaic *ait* ("he said") to introduce his utterance and appropriately enough. Where Vergil has clouded this scene in elliptical mystery, not venturing to find words for the supreme moment of Orphic inspiration, Ovid spells out the lover's plea. The song, which begins with the famous declaration that the singer has not come to visit the realms of the dead as a curious tourist, is prosy and argumentative (32–39):

> omnia debemur vobis, paulumque morati
> serius aut citius sedem properamus ad unam.
> tendimus huc omnes, haec est domus ultima, vosque
> humani generis longissima regna tenetis.
> haec quoque, cum iustos matura peregerit annos;
> iuris erit vestry: pro munere poscimus usum;
> quodsi fata negant veniam pro coniuge, certum est
> nolle redire mihi: leto gaudete duorum.

---

[34] The tone is aptly interpreted by Charles Segal in "Ovid's Orpheus and Ovidian Ideology," *T.A.P. A.* 103 (1972) 473–494. While Otis, note 13 above, 351, considers the parody chiefly as an undercutting of Vergil's Augustanism, Segal regards it as the means to a new and more individualistic characterization.

(We are in all things owed to you, and, though we tarry a little while, sooner or later we hasten to a single abode. Hither we all make our way; this is our final home and you rule the longest enduring kingdom of the human race. She also when, in old age, she will have lived through her fair span of years will be under your law. I ask the use of her as a kind of gift. But if the fates deny grace for my wife, it is certain that I have no wish to return. Rejoice in the death of two.)

At the conclusion of this most effective argument, it is strange to hear that the bloodless shades wept and Ixion stayed his wheel. While Vergil posits that the rulers of the dead have no human emotions, Ovid contrives the kind of arguments that might appeal to the emotionless. It would be impossible, he seems to imply, for the pure harmony of music to achieve any victory without persuasive content in the song. The singer's art becomes a mere vehicle for his discourse on love. By this emphasis, Ovid has already suggested the fatal power by which the here and now of human desire for affection can overwhelm the potential glory of art for its own sake.

In the *Georgics* it is difficult to separate the human identity of Eurydice from her involvement in Orpheus' music. She is a function of his mythical power, at once the ideal towards which art aspires and the muse that draws it forth. The loss of Eurydice upon the very threshold of the upper world suggests the imperfection that haunts all labors of the human spirit when they are called from realms of imagination into a harsh real world. When *dementia* turns the singer's head backwards to confront the real shade of Eurydice, we see the fallible human nature of the poet overmastering the abstract ideals of his art. But since Ovid's Orpheus is a lover who is also a musician, his Eurydice is a wife as well as a muse. She is not a projection of his artistic spirit, but a separate human creature whose actions remain unpredictable and uncertain. Ovid rationalizes the fatal backward glance. Orpheus was *avidus videndi* ("greedy for a look"), yet also apprehensive that Eurydice might fail him or fall behind (56: *hic, ne deficiat metuens*). Where Vergil makes the lover's passion betray the artist, Ovid presents the more common human situation in which the successful lover betrays himself by lingering doubts and fears.

After his second loss of Eurydice, Orpheus remains silent on the banks of the underground river feeding his mind on despondent emotion (75) for seven days, while Vergil's Orpheus sings like a sad nightingale robbed of her young. Turning his back on other women, the Vergilian Orpheus sings of his grief for Eurydice, his dedication to love and to art remaining inseparable until his death. Ovid observes that the cause of Orpheus' rejection of *femineam Venerem* ("female love") is uncertain (80–81): *seu quod male cesserat illi,/ sive fidem dederat* ("either because he had had a bad experience or because he had given his faith"). With the argumentative energy that by now has come to appear typical of his personality, he undertakes a campaign against women (83–85):

> ille etiam Thracum populis fuit auctor amorem
> in teneros transferre mares citraque iuventam
> aetatis breve ver et primos carpere flores.

> (Indeed he was among the people of Thrace the exponent of transferring
> love to immature boys and of snatching the brief spring of their youth
> and its first flowers.)

In this context Orpheus remembers his art and uses it as a kind of argument to justify his rejection of unsettling feminine love. Retiring to a mountain top, he makes himself quite comfortable by calling up a little grove of trees with his song. He informs his mute audience of a deliberate change in his artistic identity (149–154):[35]

> Iovis est mihi saepe potestas
> dicta prius: cecini plectro graviore Gigantas
> sparsaque Phlegraeis victricia fulmina campis.
> nunc opus est leviore lyra, puerosque canamus
> dilectos superis inconcessisque puellas
> ignibus attonitas meruisse libidine poenam.

> (Often before I have sung the power of Jove. With stronger chord I have sung the giants and the conquering thunderbolts scattered over the Phlegraean fields. Now I have need of a lesser lyre and would sing of the boys cherished by the gods and girls overcome by forbidden flames who merited the penalty of their lust.)

As Anderson has pointed out, the actual songs do not precisely conform to the outline, for the only tales of homosexual love are those of Hyacinthus and Ganymede while Myrrha is the chief example of forbidden love.[36] This puzzling discrepancy suggests that Orpheus' thoughts and purpose wander as he sings. The relationship of the tales to the mind of the singer becomes much closer and more intricate than the simple outline suggests.

Like the tales of the Minyeides those of Orpheus form symbolic and thematic parallels within a patter of off-set symmetry.[37] Three short tales at the beginning lead up to the story of Pygmalion which is followed by the interwoven stories of Myrrha and Adonis, the latter interrupted by Venus' tale of Atalanta. The tragic conclusion of the Adonis story ends the recital. In all of the tales save that of Pygmalion, love is presented as a fatal impulse verging on death. The Pygmalion story stands out by contrast for it is the least closely related to Orpheus' two categories, but rather, as a tale of love and an artist, comes closest to the experiences of the teller himself.

The tales of Hyacinthus and Adonis that open and close the sequence are similar vegetation myths in which the human figures who are objects of the gods' passions are too frail to survive their experience of divine power. Their ultimate transformation into delicate flowers is a final token of their frailty. Apollo

[35] Orpheus creates a grove of trees to shade his mountain-top retreat. Pöschl, note 19 above, 297–298, shows how the trees in Ovid's catalogue, with their reminiscenes of bucolic, epic and elegiac poetry, are an externalization of Orpheus' poetic identity: a summary of the artist's career.

[36] Anderson, *Ovid's Metamorphoses*, 493, 501, 517, shows that it is possible to fit the stories to the declared theme, but only through careful interpretation.

[37] The varied facets of this interassociation have now been illuminated by many critics. See *inter al.* Fränkel, note 33 above, 96–97; Bauer, note 3 above, 9–21; Otis, note 13 above, 370–372; Anderson, *Ovid's Metamorphoses*, 484–535. Coleman, note 11 above, 466–470, provides a representative summary saying, "Each seems to focus on one or more aspects of the plight of Orpheus himself, the death of a loved one, the punishment of impiety, conversion to homosexuality with its concomitant attribution of depravity to women's love, and transformations that exhibit a special relationship between life and death."

mourns guiltily over the dead Hyacinthus whom his healing arts cannot revive. His supernatural energy has been too strong (199–201):

> ego sum tibi funeris auctor.
> quae mea culpa tamen, nisi si lusisse vocari
> culpa potest, nisi culpa potest et amasse vocari?
>
> (I am the author of your death, but what, all the same, is my fault? Unless it can be called a fault to have played, unless it can be called a fault to have loved.)

Adonis, whose boyish beauty resembles Cupid's, is urged to effeminacy by the maternal Venus. He must, she warns him, seek only *tutae praedae* ("safe quarry"); he must be neither brave nor bold. Such repressive solicitude goes contrary to the young man's nature (709: *sed stat monitis contraria virtus*; "but his heroism stood opposed to her warnings") and seems only to stir up the adventurous instinct that sends him in pursuit of the boar. In both of these stories the sorrow of the divine lover who ruefully ponders his own guilt is a vicarious expression of Orpheus' own self-recrimination. Unrestrained passion destroys its own object and robs the beloved of his identity.

In the story of Atalanta and Hippomenes, which Venus tells to Adonis to describe her power, love is also a destroyer of individuality. When Atalanta attempts to preserve her identity as an independent virgin, Venus opposes her and gives Hippomenes the golden apples, an erotic token, to break down her resistance. Yet in the end, Venus' anger destroys the identity of both lovers, for she causes them to mate as wild animals with no resistance to passion. In contrast to Atalanta's self-determination is the weakness of Myrrha, the daughter who loves her father and thus never gains an identity separate from that of her creator. The fact that Cinyras and Myrrha are descendants of Pygmalion and his self-created bride is one indication of dark overtones in this seemingly optimistic central tale. The incestuous love of child for father is only a reversal of Pygmalion's passion for the woman he has created by his art.[38]

The story of Pygmalion is directly preceded by a short account of the impious Propoetides who are punished by unchastity and finally turned to stone. With these women Pygmalion's ideally chaste woman brought forth out of ivory is contrasted. Although the snowy whiteness of the material may rouse all manner of ideal associations, one may recall that gleaming white ivory (*candens elephantum*) in the *Aeneid* is the substance of the gate of false dreams.[39] With the aid of Venus, Pygmalion further transforms his beloved from a lifeless statue into a living woman. The parallel with Orpheus' leading of Eurydice from the underworld is clear. Both in his piety and in his art Pygmalion is similar to Orpheus, and the story appears to serve as Orpheus' own wish-projection as the one love story that he finds ideal in its embodiment of the final lover's triumph that he himself failed to sustain. His apparent identification with his own protagonist shows how his inclinations are tending from a dissatisfying dedication to art towards a gratifying love.

---

[38]   As Viarre, note 12 above, 239, points out, Pygmalion asks for a wife *similis eburnae* (276: "like the ivory woman"), while Myrrha declares to her father that she wishes to marry a man *similem tibi* (364: "like you"), and wishes that her father felt a *similis furor* (355: "passion like her own").

[39]   Viarre, note 12 above, 243–244, points to an association between statues and corpses; the association with Vergil's gates of the underworld would be very much to the point, and as Bauer, note 4 above, 16, remarks, Ovid uses *ebur* 6 times in this short tale as if to be sure the reader noticed what the material of the statue was. Anne Amory Parry's remarks on the association of ivory "with deceptive truth and with Penelope" in the *Odyssey*, "The Gates of Horn and Ivory," *Y.C.S.* 20 (1966) 3–57, might also be taken into account.

Taking the stony Propoetides as his exemplar of feminine conduct, Pygmalion believes that women are naturally tainted with intellectual vice. Art gives him a refuge from reality and the ivory woman he creates is such a one as nature could never produce (248–249: *qua femina nasci/nulla potest*). Even as he creates her, he begins to love his work (249: *operisque sui concepit amorem*; "he conceived a love for his own work"). The love, at this point, however, is not clearly to be distinguished from any artist's dedication to his skills and to the artifacts he produces.

Pygmalion is an idealist who believes in the superiority of art over nature; yet at the same time the kind of skilled craftsman whose work has a deceptive appearance of actual life (250–252):

> virginis est verae facies, quam vivere credas
> et, si non obstet reverentia, velle moveri:
> ars adeo latet arte sua.

> (The face is that of a real maiden whom you would think to be living, and, if delicacy did not interpose some scruple, wanting to move: so skilfully does art conceal itself by its own art.)

So skilfully has Pygmalion's art concealed itself that the art itself soon begins to disappear. The simple *amor operis* ("love of his work") changes to fervent passion (252–253: *miratur et haurit/ pectore Pygmalion simulati corporis ignes*; "Pygmalion marvelled and breathed into his breast passionate flames for the pretended body"). Soon he is thoroughly confused by the nature of his own work (254–255):

> saepe manus operi temptantes admovet, an sit
> corpus an illud ebur, nec adhuc ebur esse fatetur.

> (Often he moved his hands towards the work, testing whether it might be a body or whether it was ivory, nor yet would he say that it was ivory.)

At this point ivory has indeed become the stuff of false dreams. As he touches and pokes at his statue, Pygmalion feels guilty for his boldness, and in his confusion woos his lady with presents like a pastoral swain: simple shells and stones at first, then rings, clothes, necklace and earrings. The very gesture, which indeed makes a *meretrix* [prostitute] of the ivory lady, indicates that Pygmalion has lost all sense of the self-sufficiency of his art. Unable at last to find any solution to the stasis created by the conflict between his art and his personal emotions, he places himself in the hands of Venus.

More than one critic has spoken of the transformation of the ivory statue into a living woman as a sanctification of the powers of art.[40] Anderson, in his edition,

---

[40]   With each critic building upon the remarks of his predecessors, there is a kind of inevitable progression in the interpretations of the story. Hermann Fränkel, note 33 above, 96, associated Pygmalion directly with Ovid as a symbol of "the artist's boundless liberty to represent such perfection as nature could never produce." Bauer, note 3 above, 12–14, developed this idea even further, seeing in the transformation of the statue a paradigm of "the poet's resurrection of the heritage of antiquity for the benefit of posterity; a miracle of art." Neither gave much attention to the more obvious and immediate link between Pygmalion and Orpheus which Viarre, note 12 above, 235–246, developed in detail with the indisputable conclusion that "Pygmalion in reanimating the corpse of a loved woman realizes the dream of Orpheus in bringing Eurydice to life." Segal, note 34 above, synthesizes and reinterprets the observations of all three of his predecessors, understanding the intertwinement of the Pygmalion and Orpheus stories as "a metaphorical reflection of the creative and restorative power of his own [Ovid's] art" (491). But it is hard to think that Ovid could imagine himself in Pygmalion's role, begging a goddess to give life to the work he has so proudly created.

observes that Pygmalion reaches the point where he cannot remain content with
lifeless loveliness, while Segal speaks of Pygmalion's miracle as a perfect
fusion of love and art. But the fact is that when Pygmalion becomes a lover he
sacrifices his identity as an artist. The most, I think, that can be said for the story
is that Orpheus considers it ideal. To the detached reader the courtship scene
with its echoes of bucolic and elegiac passion, its extravagant rituals played out
before an unyielding, inanimate object can hardly be other than burlesque.
Although Ovid's story is certainly more delicate than that older version in
which the Pygmalion figure makes love to the statue of Venus, still the erotic
overtones are so strong as to suggest that Pygmalion is very close to this pass.[41]
The portrayal of his humorless obsession with Ovid's typical comic perspective
reveals the limitations of his love.

Pygmalion's passion is only such a version of love as might appeal to the
despondent mind of a lover who has failed and in consequence envisions an
ideal love as one that is completely secure. Unlike the real Eurydice whom
Orpheus has twice lost, the ivory woman has no identity separate from that of
her creator. When Pygmalion prays to Venus for a *coniunx ... similis mea
eburnae* (275–276: "a wife resembling my ivory image"), he secretly hopes that
the two might be the same. *Similis* suggests not merely the likeness of a woman,
but her likeness to Pygmalion himself. The love for a self-reflecting image
recalls the passion of Narcissus and it is clear that Pygmalion would fare no
better if Venus did not grant his wish. The element of magic that makes the story
a perfect fantasy of gratification also makes it irrelevant to the complexities of
lover in the real world. When the ivory woman awakens, her lover may be
satisfied that he is the center of her new universe, the sun, as it were, in her
vision of the sky (292–294):

> dataque oscula virgo
> sensit et erubuit timidumque ad lumina lumen
> attollens pariter cum caelo vidit amantem.
>
> (The maiden felt the kisses given, and she blushed and raising her
> timid eyes to the light saw her lover equally with the sky.)

The story has no setting, no images of the natural or the civilized world to fill
out its background. Pygmalion has created a private love object and realized a
private love within a world wholly isolated from reality. Although he seems to
succeed where Orpheus failed, his singular, escapist love is analogous to
Orpheus' own withdrawal from the world of experience into an imaginary
world of art where love is treated vicariously.

The last scenes of Orpheus' life call attention to the frailty of the artist's
imaginary world. In his withdrawal he still cannot shield himself from the
sexual aggression of the Maenads and ironically falls victim to the violent side
of that very passion whose violence he had sought to escape. For a moment
Ovid shows him again in his traditional role (11. 1–2):

> Carmine dum tali silvas animosque ferarum
> Threicius vates et saxa sequentia ducit ...
>
> (With such song the Thracian artist drew the forests and the spirits of
> the wild beasts and the rocks that followed him.)

[41]   The most detailed discussion of the sources is in Otis, above note 13, 418–419. Otis himself does
not stress the art theme but associates the story with that of Iphis as a "miraculous reward for human
love and piety."

In this ideal picture the singer's power is abstracted from the specific content of his songs, yet, ironically, it is only irrational beings who are capable of a pure appreciation of art for its own sake. Even during the violent scene of his death, the music of Orpheus retains vestiges of its influential magic. The first weapons hurled by the Maenads are enchanted by the singer's art and fall harmlessly, like suppliants, before his feet (11. 10–13). Only when their discordant voices have drowned out his music, can the Bacchae make the stones obey their hostile purpose. Then, the spell of his art becomes fatal to the charmed circle he has created (20–22):

> ac primum attonitas etiamnum voce canentis
> innumeras volucres anguesque agmenque ferarum
> maenades Orphei titulum rapuere theatri.

> (But first of all the Maenads tore to pieces the glory of Orpheus'
> theatre, the countless birds and snakes and the line of wild beasts even
> now held spellbound by his singing.)

The artist is isolated amidst nature. The order he has created is ultimately powerless to defend him. Nature in its fullest sense includes not only the enchanted circle of beasts and trees, but also the Maenads and the violent passions Orpheus has attempted to deny by his art. In the hands of the raging women, nature becomes a means of destruction, for their weapons are their leafy *thyrsii* (28: *non haec in munera factos*; "not created for such duties"), clods of earth, branches ripped from the trees, and finally the tools abandoned by frightened farmers in a nearby field. This last, wholly Ovidian detail is of course an ironic recollection of Vergil's persistent analogy of farmer and singer as the makers of order in nature. For the first time Orpheus speaks in vain (40: *nec quicquam voce moventem*; "not influencing anything by his voice"). As his lyre floats down the river its song has faded to an indeterminate murmur (*flebile nescio quid*; 52) and no vestige of his enchanting power remains when a wild serpent rises to strike at the severed head cast upon the Lesbian shore.

Thus at last united with Eurydice in the underworld, Orpheus becomes nothing more than an ordinary human lover. Ovid's comic, demythologizing tone returns (61–66):

> Umbra subit terras et, quae loca viderat ante,
> cuncta recognoscit quaerensque per arva piorum
> invenit Eurydicen cupidisque amplectitur ulnis;
> hic modo coniunctis spatiantur passibus ambo,
> nunc praecedentem sequitur, nunc praevius anteit
> Eurydicenque suam iam tutus respicit Orpheus.

> (His shade passes into the underworld and recognizes all the places he
> had seen before, and seeking through the fields of the pious discovers
> Eurydice and grasps her with desirous arms. Here now they stroll
> together with their steps conjoined; now he follows her
> lead, now as leader he goes before her and Orpheus looks back in all
> security upon his Eurydice.)

The fateful journey that once seemed so full of symbolic implications for the power of the artist has now turned into a lover's game and the fateful backward glance becomes a simple domestic sport. The picture is charming, but hardly representative of a successful union of love and art.[42] Ovid says nothing more of Orpheus' music; he has not, it would seem, brought his lyre on this second journey. Personal satisfaction for the artist seems only to be obtained in a withdrawal from art into love.

III

The picture of artistic failure that emerges from these major ekphrastic episodes[43] is echoed in other minor incidents throughout the poem. In the brutal tale of the flaying of Marsyas, Ovid increases the sense of divine cruelty by omitting the details of the satyr's actual contest with Apollo.[44] All that he shows is the helpless victim crying out in agony that no music was worth such great pain (6.386: "*a! piget, a! non est,*" clamabat, "*tibia tanti*"). With more than his usual grotesque horror, Ovid pictures the trembling veins, the ribs and sinews laid raw. It is all, one senses, a graphic metaphor for stripping the artist of his pretensions and baring the sensitive inner man. Thus Marsyas' desperate protest (385): *Quid me mihi detrahis?* ("Why do you tear me away from myself?").

Throughout the poem love is invariably fatal to the power of the artist. Canens, the wife of Picus, is an Orphic musician said to move rocks and forests and hold the rivers and swift birds spellbound by her voice (14.337–340). Yet her gentle power is useless when her faithful husband falls victim to the passion of Circe, the sophisticated creator of magical *carmina*. Although Circe cannot prevail over Picus' mind, she can destroy his person. Singing one last grieving song, Canens melts away into nature, knowing nothing in her innocence of the powerful counterforce that has overwhelmed her own magic and broken the order of her world.

Yet if some artists are destroyed for the sake of reciprocal love, others cannot gain love. Even Apollo, the most sympathetic, perhaps, of all the gods in the poem, cannot make his divine art serve his love for Daphne. Under the influence of Cupid's arrows, the god is reduced to utter bafflement, unable to control either himself or the object of his passion. His very confidence in his oracular powers deceives him, for he cannot imagine his own failure (1.491). Although he proclaims himself the fount of poetic inspiration (1.518: *per me*

---

[42]   Segal, note 34 above, 490–494, regards the entire Orpheus story as a "fairy-tale" that Ovid has made truer and more real than the contemporary myths of Augustan ideology, but this conclusion necessitates one's reading of the reunion of Orpheus and Eurydice in the underworld as a wholly fortuitous event and overlooking the disappearance of Orpheus' art.

[43]   One other extensive ekphrastic passage in the poem, the description of the doors of Apollo's palace (2.1–19), differs from those I have been discussing in that it is a work of divine art, forged by Vulcan, with no piece of human art-work for contrast, and also in that it is not shown in the process of creation. Its debt to the Homeric shield of Achilles and the "Hellenistic" asymmetry by which earth and sea are treated in unequal detail are discussed by Bartholomé, note 4 above, 74–80, who remarks also on its symbolic relationship to the narrative as a foreshadowing of the world that Phaethon will see in his journey and fall. In this context, one may add, its function can be considered ironic. I cannot entirely agree with Herter, note 4 above, 57, that the sculpture has no psychological effect upon Phaethon, even though he does not stop to study it on his way into the palace. The doors present the view of the universe that appears to the minds of the gods, far off, highly systematized, making the course of the sun appear simple with no sense of the perils of the journey. The constellations of the zodiac are neatly arranged, six on each door. The symmetry is unnatural and gives Phaethon no warning of that moment when he will see the great arms and trail of the Scorpion, stretching across the space of three constellations (195–200), the final terror that will cause him to lose all control of the fiery chariot. From the human point of view, the work of divine art presents that same over-exaggerated image of order that characterizes other "official" self-presentations of the gods.

[44]   Otis, above note 13, 315, sees Marsyas' tale as the last of the sequence of divine vengeance tales that include the stories of the Pierides, Arachne, and Niobe.

concordant carmina nervis; "by my power songs make harmony with the strings"), his lyric performance here is an impromptu plea panted out as he speeds along in pursuit (503–524) and left unfinished for lack of breath (525–526). Daphne belongs wholly to herself and to nature. She will never appear as the god's artful eye imagines her, with her scattered locks neatly combed (497–498), but can only be glimpsed at a distance, beautiful in motion, her natural grace augmented by the swirl of drapery that flutters behind her in her flight. In her elusive independence Daphne embodies many of the intractable qualities that place real nature beyond the artist's power of control.

When art cannot win love, the artist's creative power is sometimes perverted by jealousy into destructive violence. Such is always the case with Circe, whose *carmina* work her will over nature but never bring her the lovers she desires.[45] But the artist-lover whose failure most strongly exemplifies the futility of art as a civilizing influence is Polyphemus, whose disastrous courtship of Galatea is related by the nymph herself in Book 13. In part the episode is a rather broad parody of its source in Theocritus *Idyll* 11. Ovid makes humorous capital out of a scale enlargement of details to bring out the awkwardness of the Cyclops' gigantic size. Not only does he comb his hair with a rake and play on a pipe of a hundred reeds in place of the usual seven, but also the sound of his singing is so forceful that its physical impact is felt by the mountains and waves. Accordingly, Ovid has also increased Polyphemus' verbosity. At the point where the Theocritean singer has four complimentary similes ("soften than the lamb," etc.) the Ovidian Polyphemus has twenty-three. In this manner all the details of the episode go to create the image of a massive and forceful creature restrained by his dedication to love and a temporary faith in music, and here is where Ovid's Theocritean burlesque begins to serve his portrayal of the personality of the artist.

The Theocritean Polyphemus poem exemplifies the way in which song can temper the emotional torment of love. The solitary Cyclops sings wistfully; yet his song is its own satisfaction. His vision of Galatea is perhaps no more than a fantasy, a woman who appears to him in his dreams; yet even if she can never be won by singing, the lover can keep his fantasy alive by his song. ἐποίμαινεν τὸν ἔρωτα / μουσίσδων (80–81: "by singing he shepherded his love") says Theocritus in conclusion; that is to say he nourished and tended it as one of the facts of his daily life.[46]

---

[45]   The sinister and negative qualities of the Ovidian Circe in Books 13 and 14 are brought out by C. P. Segal in two papers: "Myth and Philosophy in the *Metamorphoses*: Ovid's Augustanism and the Augustan Conclusion of Book XV," *A.J.P.* 90 (1969) 269–274; "Circean Temptations: Homer, Vergil, Ovid," *T.A.P.A.* 99 (1968) 419–442. In his opinion, the "Augustan" themes that begin to develop with Aeneas' journey towards Italy are seriously undercut by the depiction of Italy as "Circe's realm of violence and magic." One might add that Circe in her section of the poem functions as an anti-artist, far more powerful than the true artist Canens, and thus gives the impression that Italy, far more than Greece in the earlier parts of the poem, is a country where natural and supernatural forces are wholly hostile to the fragile strivings of art.

[46]   The more serious aspects of this piece as a poem about the function of poetry are discussed by Helmut Erbst, "Dichtkunst und Medezin in Theokrits 11. Idyll," *M.H.* 22 (1965) 232–236; E. B. Holtsmark, "Poetry as Self-Enlightenment in Theocritus," *T.A.P.A.* 97 (1966) 253–260; Edward W. Spofford, "Theocritus and Polyphemus," *A.J.P.* 90 (1969) 22–35; Anne Brooke, "Theocritus' *Idyll* 11: A Study in Pastoral," *Arethusa* 4 (1971) 73–82. In observing that "Ovid has converted the light comedy of Theocritus into farce," Otis, note 13 above, 287, somewhat underestimates the thematic complexity of both poems, but especially Ovid's total inversion of the Theocritean celebration of art. For such a reversal to take place, it is necessary, as Heinrich, Dörrie argues, *Die Schöne Galatea* (Munich, 1968) 54–57, to break the stasis of the Cyclops' continual and futile illusion by introducing a new figure, Acis, to create through jealousy "einen psychischen Ablauf in die Secle des Kyklopen." Thus Dörrie very plausibly suggests that Acis must be Ovid's original invention.

But Ovid's Galatea is no fantasy, but a real woman with a real lover, Acis, whom she greatly prefers to the ridiculous Cyclops. The violence that figures in this new version of the story is not merely that of emotion, but rather stems from the savagery of the Cyclops.[47] At first love appears to have reformed his wild nature and prompted an awkward effort to acquire the grace of a civilized man (764–769):

> iamque tibi formae, iamque est tibi cura placendi,
> iam rigidos pectis rastris, Polypheme, capillos,
> iam libet hirsutam tibi falce recidere barbam
> et spectare feros in aqua et conponere vultus;
> caedis amor feritasque sitisque inmensa cruoris
> cessant, et tutae veniunt abeuntque carinae.

> (Now you have a care for looks and now a care for pleasing and now, Polyphemus, you comb your stiff locks with a rake and now you are pleased to cut back your shaggy beard with a pruning hook, and look into a pool and compose your wild countenance. Your love of slaughter, your savagery and your immense thirst for blood disappear and ships come and depart in safety.)

In the opening portions of the song, the parody strikes a note of pathos. The awkwardness of the Cyclops' fulsome verses can even rouse the reader's sympathy as he thinks of Galatea laughing in Acis' arms. In its central portions, the poetry comes near to the beauty of its Theocritean original as Polyphemus spins his lovely description of the deep mountain cave that knows no season, the fruits, the flowers and the animals that belong to his pastoral realm. He is quite caught up in a dream of innocent love that is wholly a part of the natural paradise that surrounds him. Towards the end, however, the song breaks away from its model as the Cyclops begins to draw his own portrait in his verse. He boasts of his physical appearance, of the size and strength that give him freedom from the power of Jove. All this is intended for an elaborate compliment. In place of Jove, he worships Galatea whose anger is more cruel than the thunderbolt of the king of the gods. The thought of her anger brings thoughts of her scorn, and accordingly of the lover Acis for whom he well knows he has been spurned. Suddenly the song goes out of control. The pretty compliments are marred by a savage boast (863–866):

> modo copia detur,
> sentiet esse mihi tanto pro corpore vires!
> viscera viva traham divisaque membra per agros
> perque tuas spargam – sic se tibi misceat! – undas.

> (Let only the chance be given me, he'll feel what strength goes with my great size. I shall drag out his living entrails and scatter his torn limbs over the fields and on the surface of your own waves – let him thus intermingle himself with you.)

With these words the taming influence of love upon the Cyclops is undone. The fault of the song is not its harmless exaggerations and improbabilities, but its inability to sustain its own fantasy. By a series of associations, the Cyclops has allowed his dream world to dissolve into real life.

---

[47]   Menzione, note 4 above, 159, sees the hyperbolic qualities of the episode clearly: "Polyphemus is no longer the immature young giant of Theocritus' eleventh *Idyll*, but the dreadful monster of tradition, his song grotesque and absurdly hyperbolic."

Suddenly the songs ends. It has in no manner tempered the lover's passion, for he rises from his seat and paces frantically along the forested shore. In a moment the reality he feared is before him. He has spied Galatea with Acis, and his savage boast likewise becomes a reality as he hurls a chunk of the mountain at the hapless lover, turning the peaceful shore into a pool of blood. Instead of taming the Cyclops' wild nature, song has elicited and inflamed his savage fury and destroyed even such a vision of beauty as the Cyclops can enjoy.

With its fatalistic view of the most traditionally idealized form of human endeavor the theme of artistic failure is a sombre element in the *Metamorphoses*, yet Ovid would scarcely have been himself if he did not at least once treat the subject with his characteristic self-parody. In his recent remarks on the structure of the poem, R. Coleman has already pointed out a thematic link between Orpheus' recital and the story of King Midas in Book 11 which follows immediately upon Orpheus' death.[48] The King's gift of making living things inanimate is the reverse of Pygmalion's animation of ivory. But the implications of the story considered as a whole go beyond this limited parallel and the fate of Midas may be linked with that of Orpheus as a humorously metaphorical recapitulation of the artist's dilemma. The story is based upon incidents in other sources where Midas was variously renowned for his wealth, for his capture of Silenus from whom he learned the wisdom of nature, and for his asses' ears.[49] From the combination of these somewhat incompatible details Ovid has woven one of the most innovative tales in the entire poem whose very originality suggests its deliberate thematic relevance to its context.

King Midas is not a creative artist but a kind of hanger-on of the arts, who can boast of having studied Bacchic rituals under Orpheus. As an amateur and an enthusiast, he is delighted to play host to Silenus and return him safely to the company of Bacchus. But instead of a request for natural wisdom, the traditional feature of the story, he naively conceives the notion of the golden touch (11. 102–103: *effice, quidquid / corpore contigero, fulvum vertatur in aurum*; "let it happen that whatever I touch with my body be turned into tawny gold"). Ovid does not seem to indicate that greed is Midas' chief motivation. *Fulvum aurum* suggests as much of an aesthetic as a pecuniary craving for gold. When the gift has been granted, Midas can scarcely believe his powers and with child-like joy sets out to prove them upon every object in sight. As leaves, earth, corn, water, door-posts turn to shining gold, Midas seems to see his new power as a form of art capable of transmuting the entire universe (118–119):

> vix spes ipse suas animo capit aurea fingens
> omnia.

> (He scarcely grasps his own hopes in his mind, imagining everything golden.)

---

[48]   Coleman, note 11 above, 470. Otis, note 13 above, 192–193, also suggests a comparison between the two stories, calling the tale of Midas a story of aesthetic insensitivity: "Pygmalion is the artist rewarded; Midas is the philistine punished or stigmatized; a reverse miracle. The true artist does not want to turn his world into gold." But of course, metaphorically speaking, the Augustan artist *does* attempt to turn his world into gold.

[49]   Asses ears: Aristophanes, *Plutos* 287; capture of Silenus: Herodotus 8.138; Xenophon, *Anabasis* 1.2.13; Aelian, *Varia Historia* 3.18; Cicero, *Tusc.* 1.48. Hyginus, 191, gives the same two parts to the story as Ovid does, but reverses their order, thus destroying the thematic progression from art to nature so important to Ovid's tale.

In creating a world of static, precious objects whose new substance preserves the outlines of their old forms, Midas carries out a travesty of artistic transformation. Quite literally he renders nature immobile. But like his old teacher, Orpheus, the king soon discovers his personal isolation within the world of his own fabrication, for nature transmuted has become an unnatural nature incapable of sustaining human life. In the midst of abundance, Midas encounters famine. There is a touch of pathos in Ovid's picture of the happy, hungry king at the table, discovering with every mouthful of the precious metal the full implications of his transforming powers. The art he longed for proves capable of destroying its practitioner.

When Bacchus has allowed Midas to dissolve his power into nature leaving no more remnant of his perverse dream than a glint of gold in the sands of the River Pactolus, the king veers towards a second extreme. Leaving his world of artifice he goes in search of an exaggerated artlessness (146–147):

> Ille perosus opes silvas et rura colebat
> Panaque mountanis habitantem semper in antris.

> (He, full of hatred for wealth, affected the life of the forests and the countryside and of Pan living always in the caverns on the mountains.)

In cultivating a Pan-like primitivism, Midas has not improved in judgment and discrimination (148–149):

> pingue sed ingenium mansit, nocituraque, ut ante,
> rursus errant domino stultae praecordia mentis.

> (His nature remained doltish, and just as before, his thick wits were again ready to do their master harm.)

As eaves-dropper and would-be judge in the music contest of Pan and Apollo, he aspires to an honest expression of his taste and commits still another error of discrimination – not to mention diplomacy – in acclaiming Pan's rude piping over the learned strains that pour forth from Apollo's gilded lyre. While even Mt. Tmolus confesses the superiority of the civilized divine artist, Midas must needs be more natural than nature. Once more his simple-minded enthusiasm is his doom. His asses' ears symbolize his solecism and his bondage to the sub-human world.

Midas' comical flight from the golden palace to the wilderness is only a debased version of Orpheus' taking refuge in nature. His stubborn preference for Pan makes him a sympathetic champion of artistic independence in the face of divine authority. Thus his amateurish search for aesthetic pleasure reflects the plight of the genuine artists. Beyond this, Ovid's intention of the "golden touch" gives this story a theme that elsewhere in the *Metamorphoses* is conspicuous by its absence: that of the artist as the recreator of a lost golden age. Once his material golden age has proven a failure, he turns, as many poets have done, to seek a new innocence in the forest. It is symptomatic of Ovid's ironic treatment of the powers of art that this metaphorical focus for artistic idealism should appear only in a burlesque association with the most foolish character in the poem. W. R. Johnson has commented on the way in which the topos *ab auro ad ferrum* (from gold to iron) – the sense of a declining universe – pervades the fabric of the poem.[50] Unlike his predecessor Vergil, Ovid has no bright visions of the way in which the lost ideal might be recaptured. As Pythagoras points out in his philosophical discourse (15. 259–261) the *aurea saecula* [golden eras] are useful primarily as a measure of mutability. Only such a false golden age as the deluded Midas can capture through borrowed magic is possible.

In order to believe in the recoverability of a golden age, it is necessary to believe in man's power to create order in nature, to harmonize society with its natural environment and to impose some pattern on mutability. The human artists of the *Metamorphoses* show that art can have many effects other than that of creating order. It can provide a perilous, self-destructive isolation from reality; it can stir up jealous passions or provoke the anger of the gods. Indeed, the artist is unable to predict or govern the consequences of his own work. No longer can he assume an instinctive harmony with nature, for its chaos of passions and unpredictable forces baffles his intellectual control. Even when his traditional kinship with nature seems to survive – as in the case of Orpheus or Canens – it is no longer a sign of his superior vision, but rather of his helpless innocence, and the nature that responds to his harmonizing spells is all the same at the mercy of the same forces that threaten his own person. It seems hardly accidental that so many of Ovid's artists are women, for this unprecedented characterization emphasizes their frailty and their liability to become the victims of a harsh world. In the midst of capricious gods and irrational forces, unexpected transformation over-rides deliberate artistic creation. Metamorphosis, the physical interaction of force and form, leaves no place for permanent monuments of human intellect or skill. As the order of art slips into the chaos of reality, the artists themselves achieve their only vestige of immortality as birds, beasts and weeping springs: permanent features of a subhuman world. Arachne and the Pierian magpies mindlessly and mechanically carry out the activities by which they had once attempted to achieve autonomy as individual creators.

As I suggested in the opening section of this paper, the images created by Ovid's artists depart from the traditional metaphorical function of ekphrastic description in their mirroring of Ovid's own picture of metamorphosis. The reader who looks to these passages for some assurance of the power and permanence of artistic creation is answered only by a glimpse of the limited perspectives of the poem itself with all its emphasis upon dissatisfaction, uncertainty and mutability. Yet by this very token, the descriptions achieve some of the traditional enlightening function of *ekphrasis*, for they show that even the artist can conceive no better world than that in which he exists.

As the maker of the poem, Ovid does not necessarily share the limitations of his characters and his artistic identity is never so frail. He is the ultimate controller of their destinies, illuminating their errors and foreseeing their inevitable destruction. Yet in this omniscient role he operates under a self-imposed limitation because his vision of nature and human nature allows him to give no better or more satisfying order to his world. He cannot find solutions for the impasse of man and nature; he cannot reconcile human and divine viewpoints for the benefit of man. The humane creative vision can live with authority and uncertainty only so long as it hardens itself to the necessity of keeping multiple viewpoints in suspension.

[50]   Johnson, note 30 above, 142–144. Noting Ovid's development of the *topos* in 1.107–115, he observes: "Presiding over the deterioration is Jupiter himself, and under his rule the rest of the poem will unfold, a mirroring of the disintegration of reality, of the illusion of classical order, and of the viciousness of gods and men to man."

Unlike Vergil, Ovid does not attempt to perceive sense and ultimate purpose in the motivations and events he portrays,[51] but rather, uses his wit to elicit the contradictions and improbabilities inherent in the nature of things. In the manner of the visual artist he fixes his reader's attention upon the varied and shifting surfaces that meet the eye. *Facies* and *forma* – the tangible and perceptible – dominate the poem. Its only consistent motivation is unchanging change. No other single thematic pattern governs the world's history from its beginning to the poet's own time. As many scholars have now observed, the sequence of the mythological narratives is recognizably chronological, yet lacks a sense of teleological progress. History unfolds as a series of accidents within a loosely perceived continuum of time. Over and over these accidents repeat themselves as the primal forces of love and anger are released by men and the gods. There are no clues to guide man in his wanderings through the maze of nature, only a constant recycling of forces, the accumulation and release of emotions and tensions.

At the conclusion of the poem, even the poet's formal claim to immortality is stated in terms of these forces that have governed the world of metamorphosis (15.871–879):

> Iamque opus exegi, quod nec Iovis ira nec ignis
> nec poterit ferrum nex edax abolere vetustas.
> cum volet, illa dies, quae nil nisi corporis huius
> ius habet, incerti spatium mihi finiat aevi:
> parte tamen meliore mei super alta perennis
> astra ferar, nomenque erit indelebile nostrum,
> quaque patet domitis Romana potentia terris,
> ore legar populi, perque omnia saecula fama,
> siquid habent veri vatum praesagia, vivam.

> (And now I have completed a work that neither the wrath of Jove nor fire nor steel nor devouring time will have power to destroy. When it will, let that day which has power over nothing but my body end the space of my uncertain life; still I shall be lifted in my better part eternally above the lofty stars, and my name will be incapable of destruction. Wherever Roman power extends over conquered lands, my

---

[51] The failure of Ovid's commitment to an "Augustan" purpose in his amatory epic that disturbed Otis so greatly that he considered it a flaw in the poem has been taken up by Segal, note 19 above, 71–94; note 45 above; Coleman, note 11 above; Johnson, note 30 above; Curran, note 31 above. In various ways all these critics argue that Ovid's deliberate purpose from the very beginning of the poem included the creation of a negative picture of divine authority – as a kind of allegory of human political authority – and of official mythologies. (Douglas Little's alternative proposition, "The Non-Augustanism of Ovid's *Metamorphoses*," *Mnemosyne* 25 (1972) 389–401, that Ovid was a pleasure seeking poet of Greek fantasy who was simply indifferent to politics, does not take full account of the political consciousness of such episodes as that of Arachne.) In accordance with the several critics who have written on the baroque or mannerist vision of the poem, Bardon, note 4 above, Pöschl, note 19 above, R. Crahay, "La vision poétique d'Ovide et l'esthetique baroque," *Atti del Convegno internazionale ovidiano*, Vol. 1, 91–110, and also Viarre, note 4 above, these exponents of Ovid's anti-Augustanism tend to stress the dynamic and sensuous image of Ovid's "continuum of nature" as the major creative achievement of the *Metamorphoses*. Viarre, 357–444, regards the poem as a celebration of the dynamic inter-relationship of nature and man; Segal, 86–88, places particular emphasis on the moral ambivalence of nature; Curran, 82–88, remarks on Ovid's flaunting of the traditionally Roman desire to keep nature under human control. Johnson's concluding statement on the literary value of "counter-classical" poems captures the general perspective of these new approaches (150–151): "But if we need poems that celebrate the human spirit and the place of man in the goodness of existence and in the beauty of universal order, we need no less poems that warn of the enemies of that order which are within us and that remind us that great virtues can degenerate greatly. We need, that is, not only a poetry of celebration but a poetry of disenchantment."

words will be on the mouths of the people and through all generations, if poets' prophecies contain anything of the truth, in my fame I will live.)

The language of apotheosis is unmistakable. Ovid does not identify himself with the fragile artists who have fared so poorly in his mythical world, but rather boasts of a power of survival like that of Hercules, Aeneas and the Caesars: the god-favored heroes of force. By this very gesture, he reminds us that they are all persons in a mythical world that his own imagination has created. As *ira Iovis*, even Augustus' own displeasure is relegated to the world of myth. In its final verses the poem stands poised between myth and history. In the real world the poet gains independently that status that the mythical heroes could not achieve without the aid of the gods, and indeed the aid of the poet himself.[52]

Wesleyan University, Connecticut[53]

---

[52] For the *ira Iovis* and the inter-relationship of myth and reality in these stanzas, see Segal note 45 above, 288–292; Johnson, note 30 above, 147–148. In similar fashion, A. W. J. Hollemin, "Ovidii Metamorphoseon Liber XV 622–870 (*Carmen et error*)," *Latomus* 28 (1969) 460, observes, "Ovid aimed at deprecating the legalized immortality of dynasts as contrasted with the true *gloria immortalis* of free poetry".

[53] This paper was composed during my term as a Senior Visiting Fellow at the Center for the Humanities, Wesleyan University, Spring 1974. I wish to express my thanks to Prof. Hayden White, Director of the Center and to Wesleyan University for the highly congenial atmosphere afforded by the Center.

Block 4   Myth and reason in classical Greece

Secondary Source 4.1   K. Algra, 'The beginnings of cosmology'

(Source: Long, A.A. (ed.) (1999) *The Cambridge Companion to Early Greek Philosophy*, Cambridge, Cambridge University Press, pp. 45–65; footnotes edited)

1   INTRODUCTION: MYTH AND COSMOLOGY

Greek philosophical cosmology did not originate completely out of the blue. The first philosophical cosmologists – usually referred to as Ionian or Milesian cosmologists because they worked in Miletus, in Ionia – could react against, or sometimes build upon, popular conceptions that had existed in the Greek world for a long time. Some of these popular conceptions can be gleaned from the poetry of Homer and Hesiod (eighth century B.C.). In Homer the cosmos is conceived as a flat earth, surrounded by the Ocean (Okeanos), and overlooked by a hemispherical sky, with sun, moon, and stars. In the eighth century the annual course of the sun and the rising and setting of some constellations were integrated into a primitive seasonal calendar. Lunations were used for small-scale calendrical purposes ("the twenty-seventh of the month is best for opening a wine-jar," Hesiod *Works and Days* 814) and at some point – although there are no traces of this in Homer or Hesiod – some form of lunisolar calendar was established.[1]

Traditionally such cosmic protagonists as earth, sun, and moon were thought of, and worshipped, as gods, even if their cult in Greece does not appear to have acquired the status of the cult of the Olympians, well-known from myth and poetry.[2] But even in Homer, when Zeus calls a meeting of the gods (*Iliad* XX.1–18), the rivers, except for Okeanos, and the nymphs also come along. Sun, earth, heaven, rivers, and winds could be addressed in prayers and called to witness oaths. Some Olympians too were connected – and in some contexts even identified – with particular cosmic phenomena (Zeus the cloud gatherer as god of the sky, Poseidon as god of the sea, and so on).

In addition, both within the Greek world and in the cultures of their near-Eastern neighbours mythical stories circulated about the *origin* of the world conceived as the successive birth of such cosmic deities.[3] In such a context, speaking about the cosmos meant speaking about the gods, and theories about the origin of the cosmos (cosmogonies) were actually stories relating the genealogy of the gods (theogonies). The classic early Greek example of the latter category is Hesiod's *Theogony* (second half of the eighth century B.C.).[4] In this work the first stages of the history of the cosmos are depicted as follows (*Theog.* 116–33):

> First of all Chaos came into being, and the broad-bosomed Earth (*Gaia*), a firm seat of all things for ever, and misty Tartaros, deep down in broadpathed earth, and Eros, the most beautiful among the immortal gods, he who loosens our limbs, and subdues the mind and thoughtful counsel of all gods and men. From Chaos, Erebos and black

---

[1]   On early calendars and chronology, see Bickerman [83] 27–34.

[2]   See Burkert [85] 174–76.

[3]   Some of the main texts have been conveniently collected and translated by Pritchard [125].

[4]   For the remnants of other early cosmogonies ascribed to Orpheus and Musaeus, see DK 1 [H. Diels and W. Kranz (1961), *Die Fragmente de Vorsokratiker*, Weidmann, Berlin] and 2; a survey in KRS [G.S. Kirk, J.E. Raven and M. Schofield (1983) *The Presocratic Philosophers* (2nd edn), Cambridge, Cambridge University Press] 21–33.

Night came into being, and from Night, again, came Aither and Day, whom she conceived and bore after having mingled in love with Erebos. Now Earth first of all brought forth starry Ouranos, equal to herself, so that it would cover her on all sides, to be a firm seat for the blessed gods forever. She also brought forth large mountains, the beautiful abode of divine Nymphs who dwell in the woody mountains. She also bore the unharvested sea, seething with its swell, Pontos, without an act of delightful love. Then she slept with Ouranos and bore Okeanos with his deep eddies [...].

In the paratactic way characteristics of (Greek) polytheism, this story depicts the cosmos as a plurality of distinct divine entities: each god has his or her own province. The familiar Olympian gods emerge later on in the story and are even more fully anthropomorphic in character. But also the more "abstract" deities of these first stages, such as Night and Earth, who play their roles just shortly after the first beginnings from primeval Chaos, behave in an anthropomorphic fashion: they make love and beget offspring.

As a story (*mythos*) this may be attractive, but it is only an explanation of sorts. Why precisely god A comes to love god B remains as obscure as are the ways of love in the world of mortals. Readers or listeners may accept these elements of the story as true, but in an important sense they do not really *understand* what happens. Moreover, the explanatory mechanism of gods begetting other gods by making love apparently allows exceptions. The sea, for example, springs forth from Earth without an act of love. Nor is it in all cases clear why god Y is born from god X: the various stages of the story are not linked in a very perspicuous way. True, in many cases some sort of rationale beyond the birth of one god from another may be thought up, but this is always a matter of *interpretation*, and the sort of connections that such an interpretation may bring to light could be rather diverse. Night, for example, is said to have brought forth Day, and we may surmise that this is because Day follows Night. But elsewhere Night is also the mother of Death (212), perhaps because Night and Death share the same negative characteristics. Again, elsewhere (224) Night is also said to be the mother of Deceit, and some interpreters suggest that this may be because deceptions generally occur at night.[5] But such links are at best associative and vague, and they do not add up to a clear and coherent account.

It is illuminating to compare all this to the first philosophical cosmogony of which the outlines are more or less clear. It was devised by Anaximander a good century after Hesiod's poem. Its outlines have to be reconstructed from various pieces of indirect evidence (in particular ps.-Plutarch and Hippolytus, DK 12 A10 and 11) and opinions differ about a number of the details of this reconstruction. However, the main features of the following account should be fairly uncontroversial.

According to Anaximander (DK 12 A10), the cosmos as we know it originated from an eternal, and eternally moving, qualitatively and quantitatively indefinite primary stuff, the "boundless" (*apeiron*), through a process of successive stages. At the first stage a finite germ (*gonimon*),[6] is separated off from the boundless. It is said to "produce hot and cold," presumably because in some sense these opposites are already contained in it. At the second stage, the hot

---

[5]   More examples of such interpretations are in West [135] 35–36.

[6]   The idea is certainly Anaximandrean, although we do not know whether he actually used the term *gonimon*. [...]

(apparently flame) and the cold (apparently a kind of moisture or mist) are actually separated, and the flame grows as a kind of fiery bark around the moist centre, part of which dries up and becomes earth. At the third stage, the tension between the opposite "elements" becomes so strong that the whole structure explodes. The fiery bark bursts open and its parts are flung outwards to form fiery rings at various distances around the centre, which still consists of earth and mist (from now on we follow DK 12 A11). Some mist is flung along and envelops the fiery heavenly circles, leaving open only some holes through which fire shines out. The result is the basic structure of the familiar cosmos: earth, water, and air (three manifestations of the "cold") at the centre, and "wheels" (Aetius II.20.1) of fire enveloped in mist around it at various distances. The fire which blazes through the holes are what we perceive as the heavenly bodies. In the rings of the heavenly bodies the battle between fire and mist continues to play its role: at times the holes are partly or fully closed by mist, at other times fire "regains" them, which accounts for various astronomical phenomena, such as the phases of the moon and eclipses of both sun and moon.

In the course of the process of the earth's drying up, living creatures are generated spontaneously from slime or mud. As fish or fishlike creatures, they are born in the wet parts and surrounded by thorny barks. When they reach the dryer parts, the barks break off and the creatures now live on land for a while. Finally, there is a picturesque account of the generation of the first human beings. Human infants could not have sprung forth in the same way as other creatures, for they are notoriously helpless during the first years of their existence. Hence, we are told, they started out as fetuses in large fish, and only emerged from these when they were strong enough to nurture themselves.

In comparison with Hesiod's account much has changed. Instead of Hesiod's whole range of independent cosmic factors, we now find a more *reductive approach*: various stages of the cosmogony, including the account of the generation of living beings (zoögony), as well as some phenomena in the world as it presently is, are explained by reference to the interaction of only two factors (the hot and the cold), which have separated off right at the beginning from the boundless origin of everything. Furthermore, these basic explanatory factors are no longer more or less anthropomorphic gods. Instead, the genesis of the cosmos is explained in terms of recognizable elements of nature – in other words, the approach is *naturalistic*. Moreover, we can now understand the way the various stages of the process are connected. We know how the cold (in the form of the watery) and the hot interact and tend to destroy each other. Also the introduction of *analogy* adds to the intelligibility of the story.[7] The "germ" that the boundless produces at the beginning and from which the cosmos will grow is presented as a spermlike mass, and at the second stage fire is said to surround the wet kernel as a kind of bark. Indeed there is a striking similarity between the description of the "birth" of the cosmos and those of the generation of living beings (and humans who are at first "enveloped" in fish). It is perhaps not too bold to speak of the application of a rudimentary biological model of generation.

There is a further difference between the mythical cosmogonies and their philosophical counterparts – a difference of context rather than content, which accordingly is often overlooked. Hesiod's *Theogony* presents itself as a *hymn*.[8]

---

[7] On the use of analogy, see Lloyd [108].

[8] Cf. *Theog.* 11; 33; 37; 51; and *Works and Days* 654–59, which may refer back to the *Theogony*.

The contents of hymns were not usually original. They tended to articulate and embellish what was already given by tradition.[9] Hence they were particularly fit to be recited at important social or ritual events.[10] This also applied to theogonies, whose main function was to connect the existing pantheon to a supposed origin of the cosmos, and so they were often connected with ritual and cult.[11] No such connections to tradition and ritual are attested (nor are they plausible) for the early Ionian cosmologists. They appear to have indulged in theoretical activity for its own sake, they felt free to speculate, and as we shall see, they had no scruples about devising theories that were in crucial respects radically different from those of their predecessors.

2   THALES AND THE BEGINNINGS OF GREEK COSMOLOGY

The first of the three great cosmologists from Miletus was Thales. In antiquity he counted as the archetypical *uomo universale* ['Renaissance man']: well versed in engineering as well as in mathematics and astronomy, and also involved in the politics of his time. For all that, he probably wrote nothing, and he was a shadowy figure already by the time of Plato and Aristotle. His geometrical activities appear to have been largely of a practical nature, and his astronomical work – most famously, his allegedly successful prediction of a solar eclipse[12] – seems to have been primarily a matter of description and measurement, with no clear connection to his more general cosmological views.

The difficulty of determining what these views were becomes apparent when we examine our earliest and most important piece of evidence, a passage in Aristotle's *Metaphysics* (I.3 983b6.984a4; DK 11 A12):

(1)   Most of the first philosophers thought that principles in the form of matter (*hylê*) were the only principles of all things. For that from which all things are, and out of which all things come to be in the first place and into which they are destroyed in the end – while the substance persists, but the qualities change – this, they say, is the element and first principle of things. And this is why they say that nothing comes to be and nothing perishes, because such a nature is always preserved. [...] For there has to be some natural substance, either one or more than one, from which the other things come to be, while it is preserved.

(2)   However they do not all agree on the number of first principles and on their form, but Thales, the founding father of this kind of philosophy, claims that it is water – that is also why he declared that the earth rests on water – possibly deriving this view from seeing that the nutriment of all things is moist and that even heat comes to be from this and lives by this; and that from which they come to be is the principle of all things. So this is why he developed his view, and also because he saw that the

---

[9]   It is probably against this background that one should interpret Herodotus' claim (II.53) that Homer and Hesiod basically "gave to the gods their titles and clarified their provinces (τιμάς τε καὶ τέχνας διελόντες) and made clear their various kinds" (εἴδεα αὐτῶν σημήναντες).

[10]   Hesiod may well have recited his own *Theogony* at the funeral games of Amphidamas in Chalcis. See West [135] 43–46; J.P. Barron and P.E. Easterling "Hesiod," in Easterling and Knox [95] 52–54.

[11]   For examples, see Pritchard [125] 1 (on an Egyptian creation myth); 60–61 and 332 (on the Babylonian Enuma Elish and its recitation). For a judicious treatment of various views on the connection between myth and ritual, see Kirk [106] 8–31.

[12]   A controversial issue: Dicks [170] is extremely sceptical on the astronomical achievements of the Milesians; for a clear and balanced review of the evidence on Thales and the eclipse, see Panchenko [180].

seeds of all things have a moist nature, and that water is the natural principle of moist things.

(3)   There are some who think that also the very early writers, who, long before our present generation, were the first to write about the gods (*theologêsantes*), had this view of nature. For they made Okeanos and Tethys the parents of generation [cf. Homer, *Iliad* XIV.201, 246], and they claimed that that by which the gods swear is water [cf. *Iliad* II.755, XIV.271], namely what the poets themselves call the river Styx. For what is oldest is the most honourable, and one swears by what is most honourable. But it may be considered uncertain whether this view about nature is old and time-honoured. However, Thales is said to have explicitly stated this opinion on the first cause.

This passage is part of a larger context in which Aristotle investigates whether and to what extent earlier thinkers anticipated his own theory about the factors (or "causes" as he labels them) that determine the nature of physical bodies and the way they change. Here he is dealing with "matter" (*hylê* or *hypokeimenon*), which he claims to be the only explanatory factor adduced by the earliest thinkers. In (1) he ascribes to this category of philosophers the main features of his own conception of matter, according to which the material principle of a thing (x) is not just that "out of which" (x) has come to be, but also that which persists in the process of (x)'s changing and thus constitutes its "basic stuff". In other words, the material principle is both that *from* which and that *of* which a particular thing is made.

If we were to map this general scheme onto the view ascribed to Thales in (2), namely that the material principle of all things is water, we would have to conclude that Thales claimed not only that all things come *from* water, but also that in some sense they really still *are* water. However, if we take a closer look at what exactly Aristotle ascribes to Thales in (2) and (3), that is, in the passages specifically devoted to him, we get a slightly different picture. Here there is no talk of water as a persisting basic stuff (nor, for that matter, of water as that into which all things will finally dissolve). Instead, the focus is on water as the *origin* of things. According to Aristotle, Thales may have drawn on the analogous cases of nutriment and seed, and these are both things from which something may be said to grow. Further, the explicit link between the idea that the earth rests on water and the claim that water is the principle (*archê*) of things makes good sense only when water is thought of as that *out of which* things such as the earth have arisen – the earth, having emerged from the water, is naturally represented as still resting on it. However, it does *not* make good sense if the assumption is that the earth still *is* water. In addition, we know that the comparison (alluded to in (3)) between Thales' tenet and the mythical views to be found in some poets was in fact made by the sophist Hippias. He is probably Aristotle's source here, in a work in which he grouped together opinions of both philosophers and poets on the basis of similarity (DK 86 B6).[13] Now the particular examples from the poets that Aristotle here provides definitely speak of the *origin* of things: Okeanos and Tethys are described as *parents*, and the point of swearing by the Styx was presumably that it was the oldest, that is, the first, of all things.

It is therefore safest to assume that Thales merely claimed that water was the *origin* of all things, not that all things *are* water. That this was sufficient for Aristotle to include him among the class of earlier philosophers who anticipated

13   On Hippias as Aristotle's source, see Snell [183] and Mansfeld [29].

his own theory of matter is not as odd as it may seem. Elsewhere Aristotle is ready to submit that the earlier thinkers conceived of the Aristotelian causes in a rather vague and unclear way,[14] and after all, Thales is here said only to be the "founding father" of this kind of approach. So he may well have anticipated only one aspect of Aristotle's conception of matter.[15] His thesis about water, in that case, was cosmogonical rather than cosmological.

Two further observations on our text. First, the problem of the stability of the earth, which Thales is said to have solved by supposing that the earth rests on water, was to be a recurring problem in early Greek cosmology. However inadequate we may judge Thales' solution to be (because it invites the question on what then does water rest), we may charitably claim that it does reveal a rudimentary degree of systematization insofar as it constitutes a link between his cosmology and his cosmogony. The reductive strategy of using one explanatory factor to account for different *explananda* may be regarded as prefiguring what we find in the more elaborate system of Anaximander.

Secondly, part (3) indicates that Aristotle was unwilling to go along with those, like Hippias, who had claimed that Thales and poets like Homer were basically talking about the same thing. He argues that it is unclear whether Thales' view of nature is really as old as Homer and other poets. Whatever they may have *meant*, they did not *say* the same thing as Thales. They were talking about mythological entities (Okeanos, Tethys, and Styx), not about nature. In order to be juxtaposed to Thales, their words have to be *interpreted*. Thales however, is said to have explicitly stated (*apophênasthai*) his view about water as a first cause of nature. A similar view is expressed by Aristotle's pupil Theophrastus (*ap.* Simplicius *In phys.* 23, 29) who claims that Thales was really the first to "reveal the investigation of nature (*physiologia*) to the Greeks and that, though he had many predecessors, he was so much their superior as to outshine them all." Accordingly, Theophrastus' collection of *Physical opinions*, which is at the basis of much of our sources for early Greek thought, did not include the opinions of the poets. Eudemus, another pupil of Aristotle, treated the history of "theological" views of the early poets in a separate treatise, as a subject in its own right, distinct from the history of philosophy proper (Eudemus fr. 150 Wehrli).

So much for Thales' cosmogony. The information preserved about his conception of the world in its present state, that is, his cosmology, is equally scanty, and here again our main evidence is furnished by Aristotle (*De an.* I 411a7; DK 11 A22):

> Some say that it [i.e., soul] is intermingled in the universe. That, perhaps, was why Thales thought that all things are full of gods.

Aristotle's source, probably Hippias again, told him that Thales had said that all things are full of gods, and he conjectures that this probably meant that everything is somehow ensouled. In another passage, he also conjectures what being ensouled must have meant according to Thales (*De an.* I 405a19; DK 11 A22):

> From what people say about him, it seems that also Thales supposed that soul is some kind of moving principle – if, that is, he said that the [magnetic] stone has a soul because it moves iron.

---

[14] Cf. *Metaph.* I. 4 985a11–15 on Anaxagoras and Empedocles.

[15] Cf. Mansfeld [32] 143.

Aristotle was apparently unsure about what exactly Thales had said or thought; but if the way he reconstructs his views in these two passages, on the basis of what he himself found in his source, is correct we may assume Thales claimed that there is some principle of motion in the whole of the physical world, even in apparently inanimate objects and that we may call this "soul" and even "god" or "gods." Some notion of the divine, then, was retained in Thales' cosmology. The same holds true of the theory of Anaximander, who is said to have described the "boundless" as immortal and indestructible. These epithets were traditionally associated with the divine (cf. Aristotle *Phys.* III 203b13–15). Also Anaximenes, the third Milesian in line, called *his* basic stuff air, divine (cf. the texts printed as DK 13 A10). Even if this shows that the world picture of the early Milesians was not fully "secularized," it should be stressed that instead of the more or less anthropomorphically conceived cosmic deities of Hesiod we now have a more depersonalized or "physicalized" conception of divinity that does not readily allow for a description in wholly theistic terms.[16]

From the fact that the Milesians considered their first principle – be it water, air, or the boundless – to be divine, we may infer that they thought of it as somehow alive. As we saw, the evidence suggests that they also considered the cosmos, as the offspring of this first principle, to be in some sense alive. Such a view of the cosmos has been labeled "hylozoïsm" (from *hylê* = matter, and *zoê* = life). The term as such is anachronistic: it was first devised by Ralph Cudworth in the seventeenth century,[17] and strictly speaking, the Milesians had no conception of matter as such.[18] Nevertheless, as a descriptive label it usefully captures a feature of Milesian physics that sets it apart from both Aristotelian physics (according to which matter without form was incapable of producing change), and the cosmologies of the post-Parmenidean generation of early Greek philosophers, that is the atomists and pluralists. The atomists and pluralists took over the Eleatic thesis that Being (in their case transformed into the atoms of Democritus, the elements of Empedocles, and the seeds of Anaxagoras) is itself immutable, and they accordingly denied that matter contains an internal principle of change. Hence, Anaxagoras and Empedocles introduced what Aristotle called external "moving causes" (Mind, or Love and Strife), whereas Democritus reduced all substantial and qualitative change to the rearrangement of eternally moving (but not living) and intrinsically immutable atoms. Contrary to these later views, the Milesians indeed appear to have assumed that matter had an intrinsic principle of change.

For all that, hylozoïsm was probably a tacit presupposition rather than an explicitly defended thesis, and it may well be for this very reason that it appears in various guises.[19] At any rate, it was not recognized as a position *sui generis*

[16] Cf. Babut [164] 22. [...] It is possible (i.e., it might be inferred from Aristotle, *Phys.* III.4 203b7) that Anaximander claimed that the *apeiron* in fact "steers" (*kubernan*) all things. But *pace* Solmsen [184] and Babut [164], there is no reason to take this otherwise than as claiming that the *apeiron* is somehow at the basis of the cosmogonical process.

[17] R. Cudworth, *The True Intellectual System of the Universe*, published in 1678, esp. Book I, ch. III. In this work, Cudworth takes issue with various forms of atheism, arguing that they can be reduced to two main kinds: "atomick atheism" and "hylozoical atheism."

[18] Burnet [6] 12, n.3 used this as an argument against the application of the term hylozoïsm. I would object that for us to be allowed to use the term it suffices that the Milesians' theories were "materialist" in the broad sense that Aristotle recognized, that is, that in explaining the physical world they did not invoke any other causes (whether incorporeal forms or any other kind of separate moving cause) apart from corporeal entities.

[19] Cf. KRS, 98. The kind of materialism posited appears not to have been very strict; the material world, or its *archê*, are sometimes said to be *themselves* alive or divine, sometimes to *contain* soul or god (Thales). A similar ambiguity characterized the mythical world view, where the gods could be either *identified with* or said to *reside in* the elements of the cosmos.

by Aristotle. As we noted, he did claim that Thales and his successors had only accepted material causes, but he was apparently unable to see matter as anything but inert.[20] That is why he objected against the Milesians that "wood does not make a bed, nor bronze a statue, but something else is the cause of the change" (*Metaph.* I 984a23–26). In his view the early materialist theories easily revealed their own shortcomings in this respect, so that "the very circumstances of the case led people on and compelled them to seek further" (984a18–20) and to discover what Aristotle himself would call the moving cause.[21] In other words, Aristotle had no patience with the idea that water, air, or the boundless can of its own accord change into a cosmos. Yet, this appears to have been precisely what the early Ionian philosophers believed. As an unreflective presupposition, this hylozoïsm was probably a remnant of the mythical world view that saw the elements of the cosmos as living and divine entities. After all, such a world picture was unlikely to be replaced overnight by a full-blown mechanistic materialism in which the cosmos was simply made up of blind and dead matter.

3   THE COSMOLOGIES OF ANAXIMANDER, ANAXIMENES, AND XENOPHANES

We shall now examine some further details of the cosmologies of Thales' successors. Like Thales, whose conception of a flat earth supported by water was probably indebted to earlier mythological world pictures, Anaximander stuck to the concept of a flat earth, which he thought of as drum-shaped, with its diameter three times its height (DK 12 A10). However, his account of the shape and position of the earth was crucially different. First of all, he dropped the entire idea that the earth needs support. This is Aristotle's report (*De caelo* II 295b10–16; DK 12 A26):

> There are some who claim its equilibrium to be the cause of its remaining at rest – among the ancients, for example, Anaximander. They argue that that which is situated at the centre and equally related to the extremes has no impulse to move in one direction – be it upwards, downwards, or sideways – rather than in another; and since it is impossible for it to move in opposite directions at the same time, it must remain at rest.

It has been claimed that even if we knew nothing else about Anaximander, this theory alone should guarantee him a place among the creators of a rational science of the world.[22] After all, he is credited with two important innovations: the (implicit) introduction of the Principle of Sufficient Reason, and the application of mathematical arguments to a cosmological question. The former claim is no doubt correct: the earth remains in position because it does not have a sufficient reason to move one way rather than another. But the second claim appears to be in need of qualification. It is true that our text refers to an argument from "equilibrium," but it is not clear why we should conceive of

[20]   Note that when he tries to elucidate the role of matter in his own system, he usually resorts to the analogy of the production of artifacts from some inanimate stuff. In such cases it is quite obvious that matter cannot initiate the required process of change. It is telling that, by contrast, the Milesians appear to have preferred the use of *biological* analogies.

[21]   Interestingly Cudworth, who does leave room for hylozoïsm as a position *sui generis*, follows Aristotle's account of the Milesians in this particular respect, and claims (op. cit., 113) that they recognized only "senseless and stupid matter, devoid of all understanding and life." According to Cudworth (ibid.) the first hylozoïst was Strato of Lampsacus, Theophrastus' pupil and successor as head of the Peripatos.

[22]   Cf. Kahn [162] 77.

this equilibrium in purely mathematical terms. Indeed, elsewhere in Anaximander's cosmology, equilibrium appears to be a matter of opposing forces or elements (the hot and the wet), and it is plausible to assume that it is such a physical equilibrium that is at issue here as well. One might think, for example, of the mutual repulsion of warring opposites, which could explain the tendency of the earth to remain as far away from fire as possible, hence at the centre of the fiery rings of the heavenly bodies.

It may be that a similar conception of physical equilibrium was at the basis of Anaximander's puzzling claim that the ring of the sun is furthest from the earth, and that the rings of the stars (which may or may not include the planets) were closest, with the ring of the moon in between (DK 12 A11). After all, the ring of the sun obviously contains the greatest mass of fire, and given the opposition between fire and earth, it is not implausible that in the course of the process of cosmology such a mass of fire should have been flung furthest from the centre.[23] It is also possible that this part of Anaximander's story was simply introduced to account for the apparent fact that the lower rings do not obscure the more remote ones. He may, in other words, have argued that the brighter light of the outer rings simply shines through the comparatively modest amount of mist surrounding the lower rings of fire. Whereas the commonly accepted sequence, with the stars at the greatest distance, would have led to the objection that the sun's ring should blot out part of the ring of the stars at those places where they intersect when seen from the earth.[24] On the former interpretation, we shall have to assume that Anaximander was ready to ignore the appearances (according to which the moon is nearer than the stars) for the sake of the overall system of his cosmology; on the latter, he provided an alternative account of these phenomena. On any account, the particular sequence he plumped for appears to have been closely connected with his idiosyncratic conception of the heavenly bodies as concentric rings of fire enveloped in mist. It was not taken over by any other Greek cosmologist.

Anaximander's attempt to specify the relative distances of these cosmic rings (DK 12 A11 and 18) has also been heralded as the first attempt to describe (part of) the orderly structure of the cosmos in mathematical terms. However, the details are very controversial and a modicum of scepticism is appropriate.[25] Most importantly, we do not really know Anaximander's arguments for choosing the numbers he put forward, and there are no indications that empirical measurements played any role.

Whether the orderly structure of Anaximander's cosmology does or does not involve its being inherently *stable*, is a moot point. The context in Simplicius (deriving from Theophrastus) where the only literal fragment has been preserved allows for different interpretations. It says that Anaximander claimed that:

> ... the source of coming-to-be for existing things is that into which destruction too happens "according to necessity; for they pay penalty and retribution to each other for their injustice according to the assessment of time," as he describes it in these rather poetical terms (Simplicius *In phys.* 24, 17; DK 12 A9; B1).

[23]   This has been suggested by Mansfeld [12] vol. 1, 59.

[24]   This interpretation has been defended by Bodnár [165], following a suggestion of Von Fritz referred to in Kahn [162] 90, n. 5. For other suggestions, see Guthrie [15] 95 with n.1.

[25]   In fact it is not certain whether Anaximander specified the size (and hence the distance) of any ring other than that of the sun; the text of the relevant source Hippolytus (DK 12 A11) is corrupt at the crucial point. Cf. Kahn [162] 94–97; KRS, 134–37.

What is probably the verbatim quotation – here placed between inverted commas – describes what is going on in what indeed are "poetical" and anthropomorphic terms. Nevertheless, the idea of time presiding like a judge over warring opposites that pay penalty and retribution for their injustice may plausibly be taken to refer to the orderly sequence of what are basically physical processes. We appear then to be told that processes of physical change, such as the gradual destruction (drying out) of moisture by fire, are reversible and will in fact be reversed. In principle this might simply mean that the predominance of one of the elements is followed by the predominance of the other, and that this process goes on *ad infinitum*.

However, Anaximander may also have believed that his cosmos would eventually resolve back into the boundless, and the text just quoted may accordingly be taken to refer to some sort of cosmic cycle: as soon as fire has "won" and dried out the entire cosmos, it is itself extinguished for lack of nourishment.[26] Such a conception would fit in well with his conception of the cosmos as a living and generated being, for such a being would normally be bound to die and disappear again. On the other hand, it remains unclear how we should envisage the details of the process. Thus one wonders how the cosmos in its final state (either as fire or as moisture) was supposed to be taken up by the quality-less *apeiron*.

According to the Greek biographical tradition, Anaximander's fellow Milesian Anaximenes was his pupil. This is how Theophrastus' account, preserved by Simplicius, presents him (Simplicius *In phys.* 24, 26–30; DK 13 A5):

> Anaximenes, son on Eurystratus, of Miletus, a companion of Anaximander, also says like him that the underlying nature is one and infinite, but not undefined as Anaximander said, but definite, for he identifies it as air; and it differs in its substantial nature by rarity and density. Being made finer it becomes fire, being made thicker it becomes wind, then cloud, then (when thickened still more) water, then earth, then stones, and the rest come into being from these. He, too makes motion eternal, and says that change, also, comes about through it.

In this report, "the underlying nature" is an Aristotelian term, equivalent to "the material cause." Our discussion thus far has enabled us to see that the application of this term, by Aristotle or Theophrastus, to Thales' water or Anaximander's boundless is misleading because these cover only one aspect of the Aristotelian material cause: water and the boundless are that-from-which things are, not that *of which* they still consist. In the case of Anaximenes, the application is more appropriate, for not only does he have the cosmos originate *from* air (which is testified elsewhere, DK 13 A6), but he also claims that everything in our world still *is* air.

For the rest there are some obvious similarities with Anaximander: the basic stuff is one and infinite (or quantitatively boundless) and also divine (DK 13 A10). Moreover, of all the then known physical "elements," air comes closest to the qualitative indefiniteness of Anaximander's *apeiron*. It is a fair guess that the particular series of rarefied and compressed forms of the air of which our text speaks is based on a rough pattern of common experience: we see air turn into fire or into wind, wind into clouds, clouds into water, water into mud (earth), and mud into stone.[27] However, we do not see a stone or even

---

[26]   See for example Mansfeld [12] vol. 1, 62.

[27]   In view of the fact that it is not just air, water, and earth that we are dealing with, it is unlikely that this is simply a philosophical reformulation of the primacy of Ouranos, Gaia, and Okeanos in mythical cosmogonies, as Guthrie [15] 123 suggests.

water turn into a plant. In these cases presumably, some kind of mixture (the sources are silent on the details of the mechanism at work) of primary elements (e.g., earth and water) is required. There is no need to assume that Theophrastus is here projecting back the later (Empedoclean or Aristotelian) conception of elements onto Anaximenes' system.[28] On the contrary, we may note that the basic model that is at stake here can be traced back to Anaximander, whose system implies that *nothing* in our cosmos comes *directly* from the originative boundless, but that all cosmic entities are the result of the joint workings of the opposites which have in their turn come from the *apeiron*.

it comes from somewhere

Some further remarks on Anaximenes' application of compression and rarefaction as an explanatory mechanism. Insofar as we are dealing with a basic stuff whose quantitative changes are observed to account for alterations that are (or appear to be) qualitative, we may give Anaximenes the credit for the brilliant intuition that qualitative differences can be reduced to quantitative factors. All the same, we should note that the basic stuff at issue is not itself quality-less (as are, for example, the atoms of Democritus, which differ only in shape, size, and position), but is air. Moreover, what made later quantitative physics so successful was the application of mathematics to specify and explain the quantitative elements of the theory, and there is no trace of this in Anaximenes.

It was noted earlier that Anaximander used an element of common experience – the way water and fire interact – as the basis of his cosmogonical and cosmological explanations. Anaximenes continued on the same path and supported his claim that qualitative differences can be reduced to the quantitative process of condensation and rarefaction – and hence that air could turn into other elements when compressed or rarefied – by referring to the phenomenon that our breath is chilled when we compress it with our lips, and warm when we loosen our mouth (DK 13 B1). Anaximenes also resembles Anaximander in his use of analogy to shore up the main features of his cosmology. For he appears to have argued that just as air in the form of the breath-soul (*pneuma*) holds us together, so air surrounds and steers (*periechei*) the cosmos (B2; however, the authenticity of this 'fragment' has been doubted by some scholars).

Like Thales and Anaximander, Anaximenes addressed the problem of the earth's stability: it rides on air like a leaf floating in the wind (A20). The same goes for the heavenly bodies, which are fiery but are supported by air (A7). Their turnings are explained by reference to currents of condensed and opposing air (A15). In abandoning Anaximander's conception of the heavenly bodies as rings, Anaximenes returned to the traditional hemispherical conception of the (cosmos and the) sky, which he compared to a felt cap turning around our head. He accordingly rejected the idea that the sun and the other heavenly bodies move under the earth; instead, he claimed that they are carried round the earth, being obscured part of the time by the higher northern parts of the earth (A7).

We cannot here deal at length with the various detailed explanations of meteorological phenomena, or the basis of the mechanisms of evaporation and condensation, which our sources ascribe to both Anaximander and Anaximenes. Suffice it to say that the views at issue found their way into the Greek meteorological tradition: a number of them recur, for example in Epicurus' *Letter to Pythocles*. The more general outlines of early Ionian

[28] Anaximenes' "elements" are not just the quartet "fire, air, water, earth" familiar from Empedocles and Aristotle, nor are they immutable, as in Empedocles.

cosmology did not have such a lasting impact. In the short run, however, they do appear to have influenced Heraclitus of Ephesus, [...] as well as the enigmatic philosopher-poet Xenophanes, who as a young man left his native town Colophon in Ionia in 546 B.C., when it was captured by the Medes, to settle in southern Italy.

It is indeed more than likely that the latter's critique of the traditional Greek anthropomorphic conception of the gods (DK 21 B5, 14, 15, 16) was partly prompted by the demythologizing of the physical world by the Milesians. In addition, as was pointed out above, the Milesians did not abandon the notion of divinity altogether, but introduced a reformed and "physicalized" conception of it. It is conceivable and even plausible that this helped Xenophanes to conceive of his "one god" in what may be called pantheistic terms, as a cosmetic entity (this appears to be suggested by Aristotle *Metaph.* I986b21–24; DK 21 A30).[29] Finally, and most importantly from the perspective of this chapter, the ancient testimonies on Xenophanes' general cosmology show that he was in many details indebted to the Ionian tradition. Like the Milesians, he defined that from which all things are, and plumped for earth and water (B29 and 33). Rather like Anaximenes he claimed that clouds are exhalations from the sea, and that the heavenly bodies are ignited clouds (B30 and 32; A32 and 40). He conceived of sea and earth as opposites, engaged in a cyclical process between droughts and floods (A33), an idea that reminds one of Anaximander. He supported this claim by pointing to the existence of fossils in stones in Syracuse, Malta, and Paros, a remarkable example of the use of empirical evidence in support of a cosmological claim.

4 MILESIAN COSMOLOGY AND THE HISTORY OF PHILOSOPHY AND SCIENCE

The picture that emerges from the previous sections shows us that despite an undeniable debt to the tradition of mythical cosmology and cosmogony, the Milesians introduced a way of explaining the physical world that was new in a number of significant respects. Nevertheless their contribution has been assessed in fairly different terms. As we noted, Aristotle thought of their materialistic cosmologies and cosmogonies as the beginning of physics, which he regarded as part of philosophy. This view is still endorsed by the majority of modern scholars, but it has had its critics.

Hegel played down the more strictly physical or scientific importance of these early theories, claiming that their main point was of a more general philosophical character.[30] On the other hand, it has been argued more recently that, although we may be dealing with the beginnings of physics of science, we are not allowed to speak of the beginning of *philosophy*, for the simple reason that nowadays cosmology and physics no longer belong to philosophy.[31] However, one wonders whether this exclusive application of the term "philosophy" in its narrow twentieth-century sense sits comfortably with the very historicity of the concept of philosophy on the one hand and the conception of the history of philosophy as a discipline *sui generis* on the other.

[29] This, admittedly, is a controversial point. For a judicious defence of the view I here follow see Barnes [14] 94–99 [...].

[30] See Hegel [22] 179: "The proposition of Thales, that water is the Absolute ... is the beginning of Philosophy, because with it the consciousness is arrived at that essence, truth, that which is alone in and for itself, are one." On the other hand, Hegel [22] 187–88, finds the details of Anaximander's cosmology "a mere succession in time" containing "no real necessity , no thought, no Notion," and hence philosophically insignificant.

[31] This position has been defended by Mansfeld [116].

Indeed, one may argue that it would amount to a relapse into the basically unhistorical practice – familiar for example, from Aristotle – of studying the philosophers of the past from the point of view of, and only insofar as they are relevant to, one's own philosophical views (or, more broadly, the views of the tradition or era one belongs to). Historians of philosophy, by contrast, should be able to bracket their own philosophical views where appropriate. In the present case this would amount to using the term "philosophy" not in any specific sense, but in a sense broad enough to cover what in different ages people (Aristotle, for example) were prepared to regard as philosophy.[32]

Also the label "science" has sometimes been denied to these early cosmologies because they were supposedly still too heavily indebted to the mythical tradition,[33] or too weakly supported by observational data. The latter point is an important one that raises the question of the *method* applied by these early thinkers. If we adhere to what is usually called the "Baconian" picture of science – the idea that science should take its starting point through a series of controlled observations – the theories of the Milesians can hardly if at all be called scientific, for they did not practise detailed and systematic observation. At the same time, it should be acknowledged that the questions that they addressed were for the most part very general ones, such as how the cosmos came into existence. It is hard to imagine how they could have coped with such questions along Baconian lines, that is, without resorting to a fair amount of speculation. Moreover, even their more specific theories were mostly concerned with what Epicurus was later to call *adêla* (nonevident things), that is objects that could not be observed clearly and directly, such as (the nature of) the celestial bodies. As a matter of course their theories about such objects were speculative, as indeed were those of later Greek physicists.

In our century the Baconian theory of science has been attacked forcefully by Karl Popper, who claimed that in general science does not proceed by such simple inductive processes, and that moreover the whole question of how scientific theories originate is of no importance. Science, in his view, is a matter of daring and interesting hypotheses that are to be judged by their explanatory power and, most importantly, by whether they stand up to criticism and to tests. Popper saw the early Greek philosophers, in particular Thales and Anaximander, as the founding fathers of this kind of scientific approach. Accordingly, he presented early Greek cosmology as a critical tradition to which each philosopher made his own contribution by testing the theories of his predecessors and by coming up with alternative hypotheses. Thales, he suggests, "founded the new tradition of freedom [...] the tradition that one ought to tolerate criticism."[34]

But this "Popperian" picture of early Greek cosmology is as hard to defend as its Baconian counterpart. For one thing, we do not know anything about the alleged tolerance of the Milesians, whereas the evidence on their immediate successors (cf. Xenophanes DK 21 B7 on Pythagoras; Heraclitus DK 22 B40 on Pythagoras and Xenophanes) suggests a self-conscious, scornful, and satirizing attitude towards the work of others, a far cry from the gentlemanly and constructive criticism presupposed by Popper. More importantly, precisely

[32]   The fact that the Milesians did not call *themselves* "philosophers" – Pythagoras is said to have been the first to use the term – is immaterial in this connection. They did not call themselves "scientists" either, and once the term "philosophy" had been coined, others used it to describe the activities of the Milesians.

[33]   This position appears to have been rather overstated by Cornford [88] [90] and Jaeger [481]. On this, see Vlastos [187].

[34]   Popper [122] 150.

because the theories of the Milesian philosophers were mainly concerned with quite general questions and with objects that were not clearly and directly observable, and because such observational data as were available were of a rough and general kind, we can hardly speak of hypotheses that could be *tested* and *falsified* by any kind of observational evidence.[35]

Where, then, does all this leave us with respect to the "method" of the early cosmologists? We may well acknowledge that they made *some* use of observational data to support their theories (e.g., Xenophanes on fossils) and that they often used familiar phenomena or observable processes as an analogy, and thus as an explanatory model. It is true that this does not amount to a systematic and methodical use of observation, and it is also true that the observational data at issue in the analogies are of the same general kind as the theories themselves.[36] But the introduction of observational features as such should not therefore be pooh-poohed or disparaged. It was new, it helped to make the theories more intelligible, and as such it contributed to the development of a more "rational" world view.

Perhaps we may conclude as follows. Just as the activities of the Milesians cannot be labeled "philosophical" in any specifically *modern* sense of the word, so they are not to be called "scientific" in a specifically Baconian or Popperian sense either. Yet, to do justice to what they initiated and to their position in Greek intellectual history, we might regard them at least as protoscientists, standing at the gateway of the history of that part of ancient philosophy that was called physics.

References

[6] Burnet, J. *Early Greek Philosophy*, 4th ed. (London, 1930; 1st ed. 1892).

[12] Mansfeld, J. *Die Vorsokratiker: Auswahl der Fragmente, Übersetzung und Erläuterungen* (Stuttgart, 1987).

[14] Barnes, J. *The Presocratic Philosophers*, 2nd ed. [1st ed. 1979 in 2 vols.] (London, 1982).

[15] Guthrie, W. K. C. *A History of Greek Philosophy*, vol. 1, *The Earlier Presocratics and the Pythagoreans* (Cambridge, 1962).

[22] Hegel, G. W. F. *Lectures on the History of Philosophy*, vol. 1 (London, 1892), trans. E. S. Haldane/F. H. Simson of *Vorlesungen über die Geschichte der Philosophie* (first publ. 1825/6).

[29] Mansfeld, J. "Aristotle, Plato and the Preplatonic doxography and chronography," in G. Cambiano, ed. *Storiografia e dossografia nella filosofia antica* (Turin, 1986), 1–59 = Mansfeld [32] 22–83.

[32] Mansfeld, J. *Studies in the Historiography of Greek Philosophy* (Assen/Maastricht, 1990).

[83] Bickerman, E. J. *Chronology of the Ancient World* (London, 1968).

---

[35] This point was already made by Vlastos [187] before Popper published his views on the Presocratics. In a way the point was also made by the author of the fifth-century Hippocratic treatise *On ancient medicine*, who claimed that concerning the subjects studied by cosmology "it would not be clear to the speaker himself or to his audience whether what was said was true or not, since there is no criterion to which one should refer to obtain clear knowledge." See Lloyd [124] 113.

[36] Thus the Anaximandrean idea that the cosmos grows out of a spermlike substance as if it were a living organism only presupposes a very rough observation of how living beings are generated. The fact that the analogy is not very detailed entails that the cosmic process is only described and explained in its bare outlines.

[85] Burkett, W. *Greek Religion* (Cambridge, Mass., 1985), trans. J. Raffan of *Griechische Religion der archaischen und klassischen Epoche* (Stuttgart, 1977).

[88] Cornford, F. M. *From Religion to Philosophy: A Study in the Origins of Western Speculation* (London, 1912; repr. New York, 1957).

[90] Cornford, F. M. *Principium Sapientiae* (Cambridge, 1952).

[95] Easterling, P. E. and B. M. W. Knox, eds. *The Cambridge History of Classical Literature*, vol. 1 *Greek Literature* (Cambridge, 1985).

[106] Kirk, G. S. *Myth: Its Meaning and Function in Ancient and Other Cultures* (Cambridge, 1970).

[108] Lloyd, G. E. R. *Polarity and Analogy: Two Types of Argumentation in Early Greek Thought* (Cambridge, 1966).

[116] Mansfeld, J. "Myth science philosophy: a question of origins," in W. M. Calder III, U. K. Goldsmith, and P. B. Kenevan, eds. *Hypatia. Festschrift Hazel E. Barnes* (Boulder, Colo., 1985) 45–65 = Mansfeld [32] 1–21.

[122] Popper, Sir Karl "Back to the Presocratics," in Furley/Allen [148] 130–53, first publ. in *PAS* 59 (1958–59) 1—24.

[124] Lloyd, G. E. R. "Popper versus Kirk: a controversy in the interpretation of Greek science," in Lloyd [154] (1991) 100–20.

[125] Pritchard, J. B., ed. *Ancient Near Eastern Texts Relating to the Old Testament*, 3rd ed. (Princeton, 1969).

[135] West, M. L. *Hesiod, Theogony* (Oxford, 1966).

[148] Furley, D. J. and R. E. Allen, eds. *Studies in Presocratic Philosophy*, vol. 1: *The Beginnings of Philosophy* (London, 1970).

[154] Lloyd, G. E. R. *Methods and Problems in Greek Science. Selected Papers* (Cambridge, 1991).

[162] Kahn, C. H. *Anaximander and the Origins of Greek Cosmology* (New York, 1960; repr. Indianapolis, 1995).

[164] Babut, D. "Le divin et les dieux dans la pensée d'Anaximandre," *REG* 88 (1972) 1–32.

[165] Bodnár, I. M. "Anaximander's rings," *CQ* 38 (1988) 49–51.

[170] Dicks, D. R. "Solstices, equinoxes, & the Presocratics," *JHS* 86 (1966) 26–40.

[180] Panchenko, D. "Thales' prediction of a solar eclipse," *Journal for the History of Astronomy* 24 (1994) 275–88.

[183] Snell, B. "Die Nachrichten über die Lehre des Thales und die Anfänge der griechischen Philosophie- und Literaturgeschichte," *Philologus* 96 (1944) 170–82 = B. Snell *Gesammelte Schriften* (Göttingen, 1966) 119–28.

[184] Solmsen, F. "Anaximander's infinite: traces and influences," *AGP* 44 (1962) 109–131.

[187] Vlastos, G. "Cornford's *Principium Sapientiae*," in Furley/Allen [148] 42–55 = Vlastos [160] 112–23, first publ. in *Gnomon* 27 (1955) 65–76.

[481] Jaeger, W. *The Theology of the Early Greek Philosophers* (Oxford, 1947).

Secondary Source 4.2   P. Murray, 'What is a *muthos* for Plato?'

(Source: Buxton, R. (ed.) (1999) *From Myth to Reason? Studies in the Development of Greek Thought*, Oxford, Oxford University Press, pp. 251–62)

'We cannot tell (nor could Plato himself have told) where the figure or myth ends and the philosophical truth begins.'[1] This comment of Benjamin Jowett's on the *Timaeus* encapsulates the problem which I shall be considering in this paper: what constitutes *muthos* for Plato, and how far we can speak of Platonic myth as something separable from Platonic philosophy?

I shall begin by summarizing the discussion of myth in *Republic* book 2, where the question is raised as to what kind of education the young guardians should receive in the ideal state. The educators begin with *mousikē*, and *mousikē* includes *logoi*—stories (or discourse perhaps). There are two kinds of *logoi*, says Socrates at 377a1, one true, the other false (*to men alēthes, pseudos d'heteron*).

> 'Should children be educated in both, or only in the false ones?

> 'I don't know what you mean.' [Adeimantus' comment is a sure sign that what follows is not going to be totally familiar to Socrates' audience, or, by implication, to his readers.]

> 'Don't you know that we tell *muthoi* to children first of all? And myth is in general false, but also contains some truth' [*hōs to holon eipein pseudos, eni de kai alēthē*].[2]

Problematic truth status is here presented as a defining characteristic myth. And myth is by implication contrasted with a form of discourse that is true. But *muthos* we should note, is nevertheless a kind of *logos*. I should say here that I am not going to focus on problems associated with the difficult question of how we should translate *pseudos*, which of course has a wide semantic range covering lies, falsehood, deceit, and fiction. The question of how far Plato (and the Greeks in general) distinguished between these different modern categories is highly debatable, as several recent studies have shown. Christopher Gill in particular has written extensively on this subject,[3] and I am inclined to agree with him that the distinction between lies and fiction was not a primary concern of Plato's even though the concept of fiction is clearly discernible to us in Plato's writing. So I shall stick with 'lies' or 'falsehood' as a translation of *pseudos* and its cognates.

Myth, Socrates continues, has a vital part to play in the education of the young, since it is through myth that the values of society are handed down. Children must not listen to myths made up by anyone that they happen to come across, because, if they do, they run the risk of absorbing beliefs which are the opposite of those that they should have when they grow up. Hence the first task of the founders of the state must be to supervise the production of stories (377b11) by laying down *tupoi* (patterns or guidelines) which mothers and nurses must follow in order that they may mould the souls of children by means of *muthoi*. Poets too are to be constrained by these same *tupoi*, and indeed poets in particular need to be controlled since it is they who have been responsible for the perpetuation of myths which are false (377d5–6). When Adeimantus asks for clarification on this point, Socrates replies that Hesiod, Homer, and the

---

[1]   Jowett (1953), iii. 698, quoted by Guthrie (1962–81), v. 253.

[2]   All translations are my own unless otherwise stated.

[3]   See his essay 'Plato on Falsehood—Not Fiction', in Gill and Wiseman (1993), 38–87.

other poets are guilty of the greatest wrong, namely that which occurs 'if someone doesn't lie well or finely' (*ean tis mē kalōs pseudētai*), that is 'when someone makes a bad likeness in words about the nature of gods and heroes, like a painter whose portrait bears no resemblance to the things he wants to portray' (377d9–e3). For example, the story of Cronos and what Zeus did to him is an ugly lie and should not be repeated, *even if it were true* (378a2), because it would encourage young men to commit horrible crimes against their fathers. So the objection to a myth such as this is not that it is untrue in terms of factual accuracy, but that it would set the wrong ethical example. The question of whether the story happened or not is irrelevant to Plato's purpose: he is not concerned with the factual veracity of history here, but with the ethical truth that should be expressed through myth. If they are going to persuade prospective guardians that no citizen has ever quarrelled with any other, all stories of gods and heroes quarrelling must be suppressed, and story-tellers and poets must be compelled to make up stories which foster excellence of character and the cohesion of society.

Plato does not object to myth as such; on the contrary myth, defined as a form of discourse which is 'in general false, but also contains some truth', is seen as an essential instrument of persuasion.[4] But myth has traditionally been the province of poets, and the problem with poetic myth in Plato's eyes is that it is wholly false. 'What sort of *muthoi* should we tell, then?', asks Adeimantus at 378e5, to which Socrates replies: 'You and I are not poets at the moment, but founders of a city. And founders need to know the patterns according to which poets are to compose their stories, but they don't need to compose the stories themselves.' 'We are not poets *at the moment*'. At this point in the dialogue Socrates is more interested in controlling poets than in appropriating their function for himself, but that will change later on. The *tupoi* or patterns which Socrates proceeds to lay down concerning gods and heroes are all designed to promote the values which the founders of the state require in their society. And once again the discussion focuses on the problematic truth status of myth: no one wants to be deceived about the real nature of the most important things, we are told (382a–b), but spoken falsehood (382c6) can be useful as a kind of medicine (a *pharmakon*) provided it is used by experts, that is, by the rulers of the state (389b). In the case of stories about the gods such as they have been discussing—and Plato uses the term *muthologia* here—human beings, unlike the gods, *cannot* know the truth about the past; all we can do is to make our falsehood as like the truth as possible (382d2) so as to make it useful.[5] As before, 'truth' here clearly means something other than factual knowledge of events: the truth of myth has to be distinguished from the truth of history.

The myths of the poets are severely criticized by Plato, but it is not long before we are provided with an example of the kind of myth that should be promulgated in the ideal state. The so-called 'noble lie' is introduced at 414b8 with an explicit reference back to the earlier discussion:

> Can we devise one of those lies—the kind which arise as the occasion demands, which we were talking about just now—so that with a single noble lie [*gennaion ti hen pseudomenous*] we can persuade the rulers themselves, if possible, but at least the rest of the community? [It would be nothing new], but a Phoenician sort of tale like those the poets tell

[4] On this topic see Brisson (1994), 144–51; Detienne (1981), 160, 173–82; Cerri (1996), 53–74.

[5] Adam (1963) ad loc. rather tartly remarks that 'Plato seems to have supposed that ancient history and mythology could be manufactured to order'.

and have persuaded people to believe about the sort of thing that often happened 'once upon a time', but doesn't happen now and is not likely to: indeed it would take a lot of persuasion to get people to believe it.

The noble lie, that the citizens of the ideal state sprang up from mother earth, and that god put gold, silver, iron, and bronze into the different categories of people when they were made—this *pseudos* is explicitly introduced as a fantastic tale, and one which has much in common with the myths of the poets. Plato takes care to assimilate his myth as far as possible to traditional tales by skilfully combining the motif of autochthony with the familiar association of different metals with different degrees of worth. As Adam points out the reference to a 'Phoenician' sort of tale recalls Cadmus, the Phoenician, who sowed the dragon's teeth from which the Spartoi or earth-born men sprang, a myth to which Plato refers in the *Laws* (663e) as an example of the incredible stories that people will believe. But the difference between Plato's noble lie and the false myths of the poets rests in the fact that the former is specifically designed to foster noble ends: patriotism, brotherly love, and social cohesion. As a charter myth it also legitimizes the practice of promoting or demoting citizens to their appropriate class. The story with all its circumstantial detail is avowedly false; what matters is the moral and social purpose which the myth is designed to achieve, and it is this which makes the difference between a *pseudos* which is good or fine and one which is not.

The noble lie is constructed in accordance with the principles laid down in the earlier discussion; but what of Plato's other myths? The narratives which we commonly designate as Plato's myths characteristically deal with non-verifiable aspects of experience that are beyond ordinary mortal knowledge: the distant past, the life of the soul after death, the divine creation of the universe, and so on.[6] When a myth is introduced there is generally some kind of break in the dramatic dialogue, signalling that we are moving into a different register, and some reference is usually made to the truth status of the myth that is to follow. For example, in the *Protagoras* (320c) the sophist prefaces his myth with words that highlight the mythical nature of his narrative:

> 'Would you rather that I showed you [that virtue is teachable] by telling a story (as an older man speaking to his juniors) or by going through a systematic exposition [*muthon legōn epideixō ē logōi diexelthōn*]?' Several of those who were sitting around asked him to proceed in whichever way he preferred. 'Well,' he said, 'I think that it will be more enjoyable to tell you a story,' [which he then proceeds to do]. 'Once upon a time [*ēn gar pote chronos*] ...'.[7]

This is a typical way of beginning a myth, the *pote* ['once'] setting the story in some distant and timeless past.[8] When he has finished his story Protagoras once again explicitly draws attention to the distinction between *muthos* and *logos* which he had made at the beginning: on the question of why good men cannot make their sons better he says, 'I shan't tell you any more stories,

---

[6] See e.g. Brisson (1994), 109–38.

[7] Trans. Taylor (1991). It makes no difference for my purposes whether this myth is based on Protagoras' own work or not (on which see Taylor, 78–9), since what interests me is the way in which *Plato* incorporates the myth into his dialogue. Nevertheless Plato's portrayal of Protagoras suggests that he chooses to use myth for the wrong reason—purely for entertainment value (Taylor, 76). This impression is confirmed by Socrates' reaction to the sophist's display—he is spellbound, but remains unconvinced by the message that the myth is designed to convey. Could it be that this is an example of how *not* to use myth?

[8] For timelessness in myth see Brisson (1994), 30.

but rather give a literal exposition' (*ouketi muthon soi erō alla logon*, 324d6). The Atlantis myth which Critias tells at the beginning of the *Timaeus* [...] is given a very elaborate introduction, beginning with the words (20e):

> Listen then [a very typical opening] ... the story [and this time it is a *logos*] is a strange one, yet wholly true, as Solon, the wisest of the Seven Wise Men declared. He was a relation and close friend of my great-grandfather ... and he told the story to my grandfather ... who in turn repeated it to us when he was an old man.

In the *Gorgias*, before the myth of the judgement of the dead, Socrates signals that he is about to launch into a story with some highly teasing words: 'Listen, then ... to a very fine story [*kalou logou*], which will, I suppose, seem to be myth [*muthon*] to you, but is fact [*logon*] to me; what I'm going to tell you I tell you as the truth' (523a). He then tells his story about the judgement that awaits us after death, which he says he has heard from some unnamed source, and believes to be true (524a8–b1). Similarly in the *Phaedo* Socrates, who is in any case filled with prophetic powers like a dying swan (84e ff.), says that he has heard about what happens to the soul after death, again from some unnamed source (108c7–8). In this case Socrates does not insist on the truth of his account, indeed he explicitly refuses to commit himself, saying at 114d:

> To insist that these things are exactly as I have described them would not befit a man of intelligence. But to think that this or something like it is true ... is fitting and worth risking ... one should repeat such things to oneself like a spell, which is why I myself have been spinning out my story [*muthon*] for so long.[9]

The effect of this kind of strategy, and particularly the practice of attributing the myth to a source other than the narrator,[10] is to distance the protagonist (Socrates, Critias, or whoever) from the story he is telling and to mark off the myths from the dialogues in which they are embedded in such a way as to draw attention to their problematic status, particularly through the playing around with the notions of *muthos* and *logos*. What, after all, is the difference between the *logos* of the *Gorgias* and the *muthos* of the *Phaedo*? It is as if Plato sets up a distinction between *muthos* and *logos* only to confound it. There is, to be sure, a reason why Socrates' *logos* will seem to be *muthos* to Callicles, since Callicles has insisted throughout the dialogue that philosophy is merely child's play.[11] But the fact that an eschatological myth can be labelled as *logos* in one dialogue and *muthos* in another suggests that the meanings attached to these words depend to a large extent on context. What we have here is an example of the polemical use of the *muthos/logos* distinction[12] [...].

Plato's concern is not so much to free the mind from myth, but rather to appropriate myth from the hands of the poets and construct new myths that will serve the interests of philosophy. This is nowhere more apparent than in the

---

[9] Cf. *Phdr.* 265b–c; *Tim* 29d1, 72d4–8. This is one respect in which the noble lie differs from Plato's other myths. For the recipients of the noble lie are apparently expected to believe the story just as it is given, and there is nothing tentative about the 'truth' which the lie is designed to promote. See further Gill in Gill and Wiseman (1993), 56–7.

[10] Cf. e.g. Diotima at *Smp* 201d. Also relevant here is Burkett's observation (1979: 3) that myth is 'non-factual story telling—the telling of a tale while disclaiming responsibility'.

[11] See especially *Grg.* 485a4–e2. For the notion of philosophy as play in Plato, see Guthrie (1962–81), iv. 56–65.

[12] [...] On the differences between the eschatological myths in the *Gorgias, Phaedo*, and *Republic* in terms of their philosophical content, see Annas (1982).

myth of Er, which is introduced (at 614b2) with words which implicitly contrast it with traditional poetic myth: 'What I am going to tell you won't be like Odysseus' tale to Alcinous, but the story of a brave man, Er, son of Armenius, a native of Pamphylia, who once upon a time died in battle [*hos pote en polemōi*] ...' Odysseus' tale to Alcinous in books 9–12 of the *Odyssey* includes, of course, the visit to Hades, with which Plato's vision of the afterlife will be starkly contrasted. But at a deeper level Plato is highlighting the difference between his own philosophical myth and the false myths of the poets which he had so vehemently criticized earlier on in book 10.[13] The myth with which the dialogue closes, takes on a poignant urgency if we look back to the words of the aged Cephalus in book 1 (330d):

> You know, Socrates, when a man faces the thought that he will die, fear and anxiety about things that did not trouble him before come upon him. The stories [*muthoi*] about Hades, and about the punishment to be suffered there for wrongs done here, at which he once used to laugh, torment his soul with the fear that they may be true. And ... he becomes full of doubts and fears.

The *Republic* is very far from being an abstract discussion of the nature of *dikaiosunē*, framed as it is between the realistic setting of book 1, and the mythical narrative at the end of book 10, itself surely the prime example of the kind of *muthos* an old man on the threshold of death should be contemplating. I cannot agree with the view that the myth of Er is merely an appendage to the argument, or that Plato uses myth either here or elsewhere as a last resort, as if *logos*, rational discourse, were his primary concern, and *muthos* somehow second best. Plato recognizes that myths are necessary for human beings, even for philosophers; hence the importance of appropriating myth from the domination of the poets.

I have spoken about Plato's myths as if they were easily separable from their contexts, and indeed the famous myths are signposted and set apart as mythical narratives in ways which I have indicated. But the notion of myth in Plato's dialogues is rather more pervasive than my analysis so far has suggested. This is certainly the case in the *Republic*, where Plato repeatedly draws attention to the quasi-mythical status of his own text. He even prefaces the discussion of myth in book 2 with words which liken his own activity to that of a myth-maker: 'Come now, let us educate our guardians as if we were at leisure and telling a story' (*hōsper en muthōi muthologountes ... logōi paideuōmen ...* 376d). Again, at 501e he uses the term *muthologein* of his own activity (*hē politeia hēn muthologoumen logōi*) and at 536c he apologizes for getting carried away and speaking too seriously: 'I was forgetting that we are amusing ourselves [*epaizomen*].'[14] When he is asked to explain how the ideal state will degenerate, Socrates invokes the Muses:

> How will Auxiliaries and Rulers begin to quarrel with each other or among themselves? Shall we, like Homer, invoke the Muses to tell us 'how the quarrel first began'? Let us suppose that they address us in a

---

[13]   See Halliwell (1988) on 614b2.

[14]   For other such comments see e.g. 369c, 378e, and 588b–c, where Socrates suggests that they mould (*plattein*) an image of the soul in words, like the traditional mythological images of Chimaera, or Scylla, or Cerberus. The language here recalls Socrates' earlier words at 377b–c (quoted above) about the necessity of moulding children's souls by means of myths. It is also significant that the process of constructing the ideal state is frequently described in terms of artistic metaphors. See e.g. 472d–e, 488a, 540c and, for further references, Rutherford (1995), 224.

tragic and lofty style as if they were speaking seriously, though they
are really only playing with us and teasing us as if we were children.
(545d5–e3)

There then follows an account of how the breeding arrangements in the state
go wrong, which includes some obscure mathematics[15] and makes reference to
the metals of the noble lie. This explanation must be right, says Socrates,
because it comes from the Muses (547b). The myth of the noble lie is thus
balanced by an equally mythical account of the degeneration of society. It is
precisely because Socrates has no rational explanation to offer that he draws
attention to the poetic nature of his discourse at this point.

I would argue therefore that the mythical element in Plato's writing is
evident not only in the so-called Platonic myths, but also in his general
mode of narration. Imagery of one sort or another pervades the *Republic*:
the ship of state, the sun, the line, the cave, the tyranny of desire, the soul as
a many-headed beast and so on. Socrates is teased for his habitual use of
images (*eikones*, 487e), and the provisional nature of his explanations is
repeatedly made explicit.[16] So how much of the dialogue should we regard
as *muthos* and how much as *logos*? The closer we look the more difficult
it becomes to maintain a clear-cut distinction between the two, for the
'philosophy' of the *Republic* cannot be separated from the mode in which it
is expressed.[17]

Socrates' highlighting of his own activity as narrator relates to one of the central
questions of the *Republic*, the question of whether the ideal state can ever be
realized. When it is chided for not tackling this issue, he replies (472d–e):
'Would you think a painter any the less good if he were to paint a picture of the
most beautiful man ... but be unable to show that such a man could exist ...
Haven't we been making a word-picture of an ideal state [*paradeigma ...
logōi*]?' What is a *paradeigma logōi* if it is not a myth?[18] Even when Socrates
suggests that the ideal state *is* realizable he does so in language which
emphasizes the impossibility of what he is saying:

> If those who are pre-eminent in philosophy are compelled to take
> charge of the city, whether it has happened in the infinity of past time,
> or is happening now in some foreign place far away from our
> sight,[19] or whether it will happen in the future, we are ready to insist
> that the society we have described has existed, does exist, or will exist,
> whenever the Muse of philosophy herself gains control of the city.
> (499c–d)[20]

As Charles Segal has put it, 'The critical ambiguity of the *Republic* is
ultimately a question about the status of myth: is the ideal state capable of
realisation or is it only a metaphor for the soul's self discovery in truth and

---

[15]   On this see Ehrhardt (1986), and Annas (1982: 296) on the problem with the argument here.

[16]   See e.g. 472c–d, 504b–c, 506d–e, 517b, 533a, and Rutherford (1995), 235–6.

[17]   On the integral relationship between the arguments of the dialogues and their literary frame, see
M. Frede, 'Plato's Arguments and the Dialogue Form', in Klagge and Smith (1992), 201–19; and, on
the whole question of what constitutes philosophic discourse, see Nightingale (1995), 148, 163–71.

[18]   Christopher Rowe has pointed out to me that strictly speaking it is an analogy, like that between
statesmanship and weaving in the *Politicus* (279b), which is referred to as a *paradeigma*. But I would
describe the ideal state as a mythical kind of analogy.

[19]   ἔν τινι βαρβαρικῷ τόπῳ, πόρρω που ἐκτὸς ὄντι τῆς ἡμετέρας ἐπόψεως. The
alliteration in the Greek reinforces the point.

[20]   Cf. 471c–473b, 540d, 592b.

justice?' As he sees it the *Republic* has 'two planes of organisation, one philosophical and analogical (the relation between microcosm and macrocosm, soul and state), the other mythical (descent, journey, vision). It is surely no accident that "I descended" (*katebēn*) is the first word of the dialogue.'[21]

But I wonder how easy it is to make the distinction between the philosophical and the mythical. At the beginning of the *Timaeus* the *Republic* itself is referred to as a city which was described as it were in myth (*hōs en muthōi*, 26c9) and contrasted with the true story (*alēthinon logon*, 26e5) of Atlantis and its inhabitants which forms the subject of the present dialogue. But this distinction between *muthos* and *logos* appears to have little validity. If the *Republic* is a *muthos*, so is the *Timaeus*, which takes me back to the quotation of Benjamin Jowett's with which I began: 'We cannot tell (nor could Plato himself have told) where the figure or myth ends and the philosophical truth begins.' Myth is essential to Plato's conception of philosophy.

But what is a *muthos* for Plato? A falsehood containing some truth, a story which aims at truth but which is not in itself true. Myth can have different functions.[22] It can, as in the case of the noble lie, be used as a *pharmakon*, a medicine or drug, to promote very specific social and political ends. Or it can be a 'likely story', an approximation to the truth. Human beings, not being gods, can never know the truth,[23] hence myth-making is an essential human activity. But for Plato the difference between poetic and philosophical myths is that the philosopher is aware of the approximate status of his myths, whereas the poet is not. Plato tells stories, and not only in those parts of his work which we commonly call his myths. The dialogues themselves are stories, stories which, of course, contain rational argument, but which also share some of the characteristics of his mythical narratives. I am thinking, for example, of the elaborate settings of many of the dialogues, so full of authenticating detail, but which often serve to distance the teller from his tale (I heard it from X who heard it from Y, etc.). The most perfect example of this is the *Phaedo*, where the usually invisible author, Plato himself, is mentioned. 'Plato, I think, was ill' (*Platōn de oimai ēsthenei*), says Phaedo at 59b10. By distancing himself from the narrative being reported, Plato can have it both ways: the account can appear to be utterly realistic, but there is no guarantee of its veracity. So the *Phaedo* is not presented as an exact report, but becomes, rather, a message about Socrates' true nature, an invitation to engage in the kind of philosophy that Socrates himself practised.[24] Story-telling, imagery, myth are fundamental to Plato's meaning.

---

[21]   Segal (1978), 329 and 323. On the significance of *katebēn*, see also Clay (1992).

[22]   See J.E. Smith (1985), with bibliography of previous treatments of the subject.

[23]   See e.g. *Rep.* 517b–c, cf. 382d; *Phdr.* 246a3–6, 278d; *Tim.* 27c–29d, 68d3–4, 72d4–8. On myths as 'likely accounts' see J.E. Smith (1985) [...].

[24]   See L. Kosman, 'Silence and Imitation in the Platonic Dialogues', in Klagge and Smith (1992), 73–92. The difficulty that Phaedo's remark has generated amongst commentators can be exemplified by Burnet's note: 'Of course it is an advantage from a dramatic point of view for Plato to keep himself out of his dialogues ... At the same time it is hardly credible that he should represent himself as absent on this occasion unless he had actually been so. It has been said that, had Plato really been ill, he would have had no occasion to make the reservation implied by οἶμαι [I think]. He must have known whether he was ill or not. That is so; but it does not follow that Phaedo was equally well informed, and he is the speaker, not Plato' (Burnet (1911) on 59b10).

If we look in Plato's work for a consistent distinction between *muthos* (myth) and *logos* (reason), let alone a development from one to the other, we look in vain.[25] Even if we were to restrict the meaning of *logos* to rational argument or dialectic, dialectic is always embedded in dialogue. And though it operates in a different way from myth (whether in the narrower sense of the set-piece narratives like the myth of Er, or in the broader sense of story-telling), dialectic is never enough: it supplements rather than replaces myth. Dialectic and myth may be viewed as different modes of explanation, but Plato does not present the one as being superior to the other, and neither mode is self sufficient. Myth is not simply the expression of a primitive form of mentality; it is, in Claude Calame's words, 'a mode of discourse rather than a way of thinking'. Hence *muthos* and *logos* exist side by side, and indeed are often indistinguishable, since both are in essence types of discourse.

To think about the place of myth in Plato's work is ultimately to think about how we should read his texts. I was struck by the comments of Julia Annas on the account of the decline of state and individual through the four stages of timocracy, oligarchy, democracy, and tyranny (*Rep.* 543–80). 'The resulting eight vignettes of state and individual', she says, 'have been admired for their literary power, but they leave a reader who is intent on the argument unsatisfied and irritated.'[26] If the passages which demonstrate Plato's literary powers merely get in the way of the argument, what are they there for? I shall end with a quotation from Martha Nussbauam:

> The tendency to regard arguments as expressing the content of a philosophy, image, story, and conversation as giving it a pleasing, decorative surface goes very deep in our entire philosophical tradition. Philosophy has developed a style for itself that powerfully expresses its claim to have separated out the rational from the irrational, to have purified itself of the confusions of emotion and sense, which are the stuff of poetic discourse. The deductive argument keeps these messy irrational elements at bay, protecting reason's structures against them. It is evident that the question of philosophical style is connected at a very deep level with a conception of the rational and the relations between 'rational' and 'irrational'. Plato's writing tells us, in its multifaceted progress, that these questions need to be reopened, these polarities re-examined.[27]

References

ADAM, J. (1963), *The Republic of Plato*, 2nd edn. (Cambridge).

ANNAS, J. (1982), 'Plato's Myths of Judgement', *Phronesis*, 27: 119–43.

BRISSON, L. (1994), *Platon: Les Mots et les myths*, 2nd edn. (Paris).

BURKERT, W. (1979), *Structure and History in Greek Mythology and Ritual* (Berkeley and Los Angeles).

BURNET, J. (1911), *Plato's Phaedo, Edited with Introduction and Notes* (Oxford).

CERRI, G. (1996), *Platone sociologo della comunicazione*, 2nd edn. (Lecce).

CLAY, D. (1992), 'Plato's First Words', *YCS* 29: 113–29.

---

25   See e.g. Annas (1982), 199–22; Brisson (1994), 109–43; Detienne (1981), 91 ff.; and above all the works of J.-P. Vernant. The *muthos/logos* issue is addressed most recently in Vernant (1996), 237–64, 352–6.

26   (1981), 294.

27   The quotation is taken from p. 91 of '"This Story Isn't True": Poetry, Goodness and Understanding in Plato's *Phaedrus*', in Moravcsik and Temko (1982).

DETIENNE, M. (1981), *L'Invention de la mythologie* (Paris). (The Eng. trans. is not recommended.)

EHRHARDT, E. (1986), 'The Word of the Muses (Plato, *Rep.* 8.546)', *CQ* 36/2: 407–20.

GILL, C. and WISEMAN, T. P. (1993) (eds.), *Lies and Fiction in the Ancient World* (Exeter).

GUTHRIE, W. K. C. (1962–81), *A History of Greek Philosophy*, 6 vols. (Cambridge).

HALLIWELL, S. (1988), *Plato: Republic* 10 (Warminster).

JOWETT, B. (1953), *The Dialogues of Plato Translated into English with Analyses and Introductions*, 4th edn. (Oxford).

KLAGGE, J. C, and SMITH, N. D. (1992) (eds.), *Methods of Interpreting Plato and the Dialogues* (Oxford).

MORAVCSIK, J. and TEMKO, P. (1982) (eds.), *Plato on Beauty, Wisdom and the Arts* (Totowa, NJ).

NIGHTINGALE, A. (1995), *Genres in Dialogue: Plato and the Construct of Philosophy* (Cambridge).

RUTHERFORD, R. (1995), *The Art of Plato: Ten Essays in Platonic Interpretation* (London).

SEGAL, C. (1978), '"The Myth Was Saved": Reflections on Homer and the Mythology of Plato's *Republic*', *Hermes*, 106: 315–36.

SMITH, J. E. (1985), 'Plato's Myths as "Likely Accounts", Worthy of Belief', *Apeiron*, 19: 24–42.

TAYLOR, C. (1991), *Plato: Protagoras,* 2nd edn. (Oxford).

VERNANT, J.-P. (1996), *Entre mythe et politique* (Paris).

Secondary Source 4.3   Tim Chappell, '*Logos* and *muthos* in Plato'

(Source: Written for the Open University (2009) by Professor Tim Chappell, Department of Philosophy)

The natural assumption is that *logos* means 'reason' and *muthos* means 'myth'. That is not altogether wrong, but it is too simple. The Greek words *logos* and *muthos* have a long history already by the time they reach Plato. Not every part of that history suggests a reason/myth antithesis between *logos* and *muthos*. Both are quite common words in Greek; like most common words in any language, both are multiply ambiguous for anyone who uses them, including Plato. Alongside the reason/myth antithesis, we might also suggest that the ambiguities of *logos* in Plato's time roughly parallel those of the English word 'account', while the ambiguities of *muthos* roughly parallel the ambiguities of 'story'.[1]

It was not always so. For the archaic poets Homer and Hesiod (eighth century BCE), *logos* and *muthos* were nearly synonyms, and both meant roughly 'thing said', as opposed to *epos*, 'way of saying it' (Homer, *Odyssey* 1.96, 3.94, 4.324, 11.561 and *Iliad* 15.392; Hesiod, *Works and Days* 106, 194 and *Theogony* 24). Likewise, two or three centuries later, the early Greek philosopher Xenophanes (*c.*570–470 BCE) takes *logos* and *muthos* as close enough in sense to pair them in poetic duplication: he exhorts us to speak of the gods *euphēmois mythois katharoisi te logois*, 'with well-omened speeches and pure words'

---

[1] Luc Brisson has argued that Plato himself is the first to use *mythos* to mean 'fictional story' (1998, p. x). The history of ambiguities that I describe here seems to me the main obstacle to his thesis.

(DK21, B1.13–14). Even more strikingly, perhaps the greatest Presocratic philosopher, Parmenides (520–450 BCE), can describe his own argument as a *muthos* (DK28, B2.1, B8.1–2) despite its rigorously rational nature.

But some of the archaic evidence does suggest something like the reason/myth distinction. So far as we can ascertain it[2], the origin of the words themselves points that way. *Logos* comes from the same root as *legein*, a verb which means not only 'to speak' but also 'to arrange' or 'lay out' (it may even be cognate with the English 'lay' and the German *lagen*). *Muthos*, by contrast, apparently connects with *muein*, a verb that means 'to close the mouth' (*muein* may even be cognate with our word 'mouth'). A *muthos*, then, is a *completed* story – one on which you can close your mouth having completed it. But because *muein* has the root meaning 'to *close* the mouth', it just as easily generates words meaning 'to keep silence' as 'to finish a tale'; for instance *mustērion*, 'mystery', a secret of religion that none may speak of openly. It seems that, like other esoteric cults, the Greek mystery religions had special stories known only to them. If so, there would be nothing more natural than the name *muthos* for these stories – and nothing more natural than the appropriation of this word by outsiders to the cult to mean the sort of thing that we in English denote by 'hocus-pocus' or 'mumbo-jumbo'. Hence by Plato's time *muthos* has come to mean not just 'story', but also, very easily, '*unlikely* story'; and *logos* has come to mean not just 'account', but also, equally easily, '*rational* account' or even 'theory'. Greek speakers of the fourth century BCE would not have heard an opposition between the words *muthos* and *logos* as *inevitable*, but it would have come quite naturally to them.

Something like this seems to have been at least part of the process that made it possible for Socrates' contemporary Thucydides (460–400 BCE) to take for granted the category of *to muthōdes* 'the legendary', as something to be lumped together with poetic exaggeration and lazily believing whatever is convenient: all of which he contrasts sharply with his own strenuous search for truth (*hē zētēsis tēs alētheias*), the only method that befits a scientific historiography (*A History of the Peloponnesian War* 1.21). Plato himself makes a rather similar complaint at *Sophist* 242c8–9, where he says of the Presocratic philosophers that *muthon tina hekastos phainetai moi diēgeisthai paisin hōs ousin hēmin*, 'each of them seems to me to tell us some story as if we were children'. Here it is tempting to translate *muthon tina* not just as 'some story', but as 'some fairy-story'.

Another source of the *muthos/logos* contrast surely brings us back to Xenophanes and Parmenides. Xenophanes' central thesis is the difference between (on the one side) the inaccessible ideal of 'clear truth' (*to saphes*)[3] about the gods, which he argues would have to be based upon reasoned argument like his own, and (on the other) the irrational and fantastical fables about the gods that were standard in the classical Greek paganism of his time, and which he dismisses, along with much else, as mere 'seeming' (*dokos*):

> The clear truth no man knows, nor ever will know,
> About the gods, or what I say about the world.

[2] My own primary method of ascertaining it (I am no more a trained etymologist than Heidegger) was to consult Liddell and Scott (sixth edition), the standard ancient Greek dictionary for English-speaking scholarship.

[3] The idea behind the term *to saphes* is strikingly rationalistic: Xenophanes' theology must be true *because* it is 'clear', i.e. rationally ordered. A similar thought makes Descartes claim, in the *Discourse on the Method*, that 'whatever we clearly and distinctly perceive is true' (Descartes, 2006 [1637], 4.43). Algernon in *The Importance of Being Earnest* has something like the opposite idea: 'The truth is never pure, and rarely simple' (Wilde, 2000 [1895], Act 1, line 241).

> Even he who chanced to speak complete reality
> Would not know he had done it. Seeming is crafted over all.

(DK21, B34)

What about Parmenides? What is notable about Parmenides is the ruthless austerity of his logic. He is the first thinker in the Greek tradition to do what Socrates later recommended, and follow his argument *exactly* where it leads him, even if that is to somewhere very strange indeed. Parmenides presented his views in a long narrative poem, written in Homer's heroic metre. Today we have inherited some parts of this poem, in fragments that other ancient authors including Plato quote, not always very accurately.

In the fragments of Parmenides' poem that we have, one division is more striking than any other. This is the division that he makes between the first and the second parts of his poem. The first part of his poem is an astonishing tour de force of a priori argument.[4] In this part of the poem a goddess (*thea*) who addresses him purports to prove, from the logical properties of the verb 'is' alone, that nothing can coherently be thought to exist except one perfect, uncreated, unchanging, indivisible and undifferentiated reality. This extraordinary exposition of monistic idealism is quite unprecedented in the Greek tradition, though there are parallels in Indian thought.[5] It forms a violent contrast with the second part of Parmenides' poem, in which 'the goddess' apparently developed (here the fragments are fragmentary indeed) some much less unusual views for Parmenides' time about all the processes of creation, division, and differentiation that we normally take to characterise the world around us – cosmology, physiology, biology and so on. This stark division between two quite different sorts of discourse is marked by Parmenides when he has his goddess say:

> And now – see – I cease from my trustworthy word and thought
> About the truth; from now on, learn about mortal opinions
> By hearing the deceitful ordering of my words.

(DK28, B8.50–2)

Even if neither Xenophanes nor Parmenides uses the *words logos* and *muthos* to mark the distinction that later authors such as Thucydides and Plato take for granted, nonetheless the *idea* of a *muthos/logos* distinction, or something very like it, is surely present in both. It is there in Xenophanes' contrast between *to saphes* and *to dokos*, 'clear truth' and 'seeming'. And it is there in Parmenides' contrast between 'truth' and 'mortal opinions' (*doxas broteias*). Parmenides' goddess is confident that her report of 'the truth' is trustworthy, but about 'mortal opinions', she paradoxically admits, even her own words will form a 'deceitful ordering' (*kosmon apatēlon*).

This is the historical and cultural background against which there appears the strange figure of Socrates (469–399 BCE). Pretty well the first and securest testimony we have about him is that he took no interest in speculative theology. According to Plato, when Socrates was put on trial he defended himself against the charge that he 'busied himself investigating the things below the earth and in the heavens' (*Apology* 19b5) by simply denying it: 'men of Athens, I take no interest at all in these questions' (19c9). Later in Plato's *Apology*, Socrates even

---

[4] 'A priori' means arguing from first principles which are 'given' rather than themselves established by argument.

[5] The tradition of *Advaita Vedanta* (the non-duality interpretation of the Vedas, going back perhaps to 1000 BCE) includes strikingly Parmenidean conclusions, though these tend to be proclaimed rather than argued for.

wonders (26d) whether his prosecutors have confused him with another philosopher whom the Athenians had also impeached – the early scientist Anaxagoras (500–428 BCE), whose claim that the sun and the moon are not divinities, but made of rock, Socrates describes as 'absurd' (26e2). Socrates contrasts Anaxogoras' interests very sharply with his own preoccupations, which focus on a crucial ethical question: the question of what kind of human life can bear philosophical examination as the life most worth living (38a5–6).

Sources as various as the comic poet Aristophanes and Plato himself make it quite clear that there were plenty of people around in Socrates' time who were concerned with the cosmological, metaphysical and theological questions that interested Anaxagoras. So why did Socrates, unlike all of them, restrict his inquiries so strictly to ethics? In brief, because he thought that this was all that could be justified, by the standards of *logos*, as anything better than *muthos*.

Some of Socrates' contemporaries, such as the famous sophist Protagoras (490–420 BCE), may have found one or another way of being fairly relaxed about the *muthos/logos* distinction. For example, there is a well-known passage in Plato (*Protagoras* 320c3) in which Protagoras himself, while clearly recognising that distinction, also implies the surprisingly modern idea that *muthos* can be an allegorical or figurative way of saying the very same thing as can also be said in *logos*.[6] That is not to say, of course, that Protagoras did not share Socrates' qualms about metaphysical speculation. Such qualms are well-expressed in the famous words with which Protagoras began his book *On the gods*:

> Concerning gods, I have no way of knowing either that they are or that they are not, nor what they are like in their form; for there are many things preventing knowledge, both obscurity and the brevity of human life.

> (DK80, B4)

Like Protagoras, Socrates steadfastly refused to inquire into any questions for which he thought we lacked a credible method of inquiry. And Socrates clearly influenced Plato in this. There is a discernible echo of Protagoras' words in a heavily ironical passage from Plato's middle-to-late dialogue the *Timaeus*:

> Concerning the other divinities, to speak and know their coming-to-be is more than we have powers for. So we should put our faith in those who spoke of it in the olden days, since they were themselves offspring of the gods – as they claimed, and no doubt they knew all about their own family background. Obviously there can be no doubting the children of the gods, even those whose accounts lack the evidence of proof or even likelihood.

> (40d7–e3; trans. T. Chappell)

This reluctance to engage in mere speculation is evident too in a famous passage in Plato's *Phaedo*, where Socrates explains his rejection of Anaxagorean science by saying how much of an intellectual disappointment it was to him. He had hoped, he tells us, for a comprehensive explanation of the teleological ordering of the universe, of how the mind of God, *nous* ('mind' or 'intelligence') 'orders everything as it is best for it to be' (*Phaedo* 97c5). But instead:

> My friend, I was cast down most violently from this wonderful hope. For as I go on with my reading I find out that the man makes no real

---

[6]   Plato presents the same idea via an Egyptian priest at *Timaeus* 22c9: 'this is said in the form of a myth, but the truth is ...' (*touto muthou men schemaa echon legetai, to d' alēthes esti ...*).

use of *nous* at all, and finds no genuine causes for the ordering of things. His 'causes' are Airs and Ethers and Waters – all sorts of absurdities like that ...

(*Phaedo* 98b7–c2; trans. T. Chappell)

Socrates will not engage in a cosmological enterprise like Anaxagoras', because it is merely speculative. It falls the wrong side of the *muthos/logos* distinction, because it simply does not have enough logical rigour. Socrates' rule is the one that Sir Isaac Newton expressed with such masterly disdain: 'It is not my business to make up hypotheses' (*hypotheses non fingo*).

Then what is Socrates' business? What kind of logical rigour would satisfy him? We get one partial answer to that by reading the 'Socratic' dialogues, the early works of Plato, in which Socrates addresses a series of ethical topics using his 'elenchus' (*elegkhos*), the question-and-answer method of close and careful logical reasoning – taking one step at a time, and avoiding *makrologia* or long-winded speechifying – which he describes, and then gives us an example of, in the *Apology* (21c–22e, 24d–27e). And we get another partial answer by recalling what we have just seen Socrates say he hoped would be the upshot of Anaxagoras' theory. Anaxagoras *would* have presented an adequate theory of the universe, says Socrates in the *Phaedo*, if he had shown how the divine Mind arranges everything 'as it is best for it to be'. A fully worked-out teleological account of the universe, one that explains the way each and every thing is by explaining with full and irresistible cogency how it is *best* for each and every thing to be just that way and no other: that, by Socrates' estimation, is what we need to expunge every trace of *muthos* from our picture of the world, and give us an understanding of how things are that fully deserves to be called a *logos*.

The trouble is that there is a tension between these two partial answers. It is just this tension that determines Socrates' restriction of his own inquiries to ethical questions. And it is the very same tension that gives its characteristic shape and orientation to much of Plato's own philosophical work – including his political masterpiece the *Republic*, and his own attempt, in the *Timaeus*, to provide an account of the cosmos that meets Socrates' requirements in the *Phaedo*.

This is the tension between the negative and positive roles that Socrates sees for *logos*. It is a point familiar to every reader of the Socratic dialogues[7] that their results are usually destructive. In those dialogues Socrates offers no account of his own: all he does there is apply his elenchus to the questioning, and usually the destruction, of the accounts that others offer.

> I am sterile in wisdom, and the reproach that many have made of me – that I ask other people questions, but have nothing to bring to light about anything myself, because I have hold of nothing wise – that reproach is true.

(*Theaetetus* 150c4–7; cf. Aristotle, *On Sophistical Refutations* 183b7)

In its negative role, Socratic reasoning is not a sticky mortar, holding constructions together; it is a corrosive acid, dissolving them into their component pieces. So much so that Plato comes to doubt that Socratic reasoning could have a positive role to play as well. He comes to think that it is not just that Anaxagoras' positive cosmology, or Protagoras' positive political

---

[7]   The Socratic dialogues of (generally) unquestioned authenticity are *Euthyphro, Crito, Charmides, Laches, Lysis* and *Euthydemus*. Besides these the *Apology* is certainly Socratic, but only marginally a dialogue. *Protagoras, Gorgias, Meno, Ion, Menexenus, Cratylus, Republic* Book I and *Theaetetus* have many of the features of Socratic dialogues, but in various ways resist straightforward classification as such.

philosophy, is too lacking in logical rigour to pass the test set by Socrates' elenchus. It is rather that no possible cosmology or political philosophy could conceivably pass that test. There simply is no way to give an account of the ordering of the cosmos, or of the best ordering of the polis (city state), which satisfies the standards of logical rigour that Socrates is determined to apply. By those standards, Socrates is entirely justified in doing what he does: in refusing to engage in any kind of philosophical speculation that takes us beyond the limited and negative task of exploding human misconceptions about the nature of the good life. For there is nothing more that the standards of *logos* itself can allow.[8]

This tension between the negative and positive functions of Socratic *logos* could have been resolved two ways. It could have led Plato to renounce the positive conception of *logos* altogether, and follow Socrates in 'asking questions but not answering them' – in taking a largely sceptical and destructive conception of what reason could do. Or Plato could have resolved the tension the other way, in favour of a positive conception of *logos*: that is, he could have gone in for constructive theory-building about polis and cosmos, and simply renounced the rigorous standards of Socrates' negative rationality.

Plato does neither of these things. He abandons neither Socrates' 'wonderful hope' of a constructive political and metaphysical philosophy, nor the strict and rigorous conception of the critical demands of *logos* that cast Socrates down from this hope, leaving him disillusioned with Anaxagoras in particular and speculative philosophy in general. Rather, instead of trying to resolve the tension between the positive and negative conceptions of *logos*, between theory-construction and *elenchus*, Plato tries to find a way of living with that tension.

In this Plato follows Parmenides. We have already seen how Parmenides' poem distinguishes between the purely rational truth and the opinions of mortals. It is not for nothing that 'the goddess' describes this second part of her discourse, about mortal opinions concerning cosmology, biology, physiology and so on, as a 'deceitful ordering of words'. For if the first part of her discourse is correct, the second part of it cannot even be thinkable. If pure reason itself requires that we recognise nothing as existing except the one perfect and unchanging transcendent reality, there is nothing left for studies of an imperfect and changing natural world to be except 'deceitful orderings of words'. For that world is itself no more than a deceit.

Does that mean that true philosophy can have nothing to say about the natural world, and must restrict itself to the severe logic of transcendent reality? Parmenides apparently thought not. After all, his philosophy *does* have things to say about the natural world – his poem does have a second part as well as a first. True, Parmenides' natural philosophy is deeply compromised by his transcendent philosophy, since the latter implies that the former can have no role except to lead understanding astray. On the other hand, Parmenides'

---

[8]   From our standpoint in history, it is of course rather striking that what Socrates thought hopelessly speculative was *science*, and what he thought rigorously logical was *ethics*. Many people today would see things exactly the other way round. A first line of defence might lie in pointing out that Socratic ethics is all about the human world, and in quoting that very Socratic couplet in Pope's *Essay on Man*: 'Know then thyself, presume not God to scan; / The proper study of mankind is man' (1732, Epistle 2, 1.1–12). A second and securer defence is to note that it is only a certain sort of science that Socrates condemns as lacking rigour – the speculative cosmology of his time (he seems, so far as we can tell, to have been a great admirer of the other major kind of science that he knew about, namely mathematics); and it is only a certain sort of ethics that he thinks has this rigour – namely his own negative project of exposing fallacies, confusions and prejudices.

transcendent philosophy is equally deeply compromised by his natural philosophy. The 'opinions of mortals' may be full of deception; but there again Parmenides himself is a mortal. The natural world of particular events, movement, change and process may be a tissue of illusion; but there again it is only within this natural world that Parmenides can claim to experience the particular event of his chariot journey to the house of the goddess, to undergo the process of being taught by her so as to change from ignorance to understanding. And the goddess's 'truth' may be a piece of pure, divine and timelessly general reasoning; but there again Parmenides is not divine, and he presents this 'truth' in the very human and culturally particular form of a mythical poem.

Parmenides' paradox is that he cannot speak about the purely rational world of transcendent reality except in the impure and sub-rational language of the natural world: for mortals like us, to get at *logos* we must go via *muthos*. And Plato inherits this paradox. He too accepts that, in order for mortals like us to say anything positive at all about the nature of the cosmos or the polis, we will have to go beyond what *logos*, pure reason itself, can justify. Given our own rational infirmities, we will often have to accept 'a probable story' (*eikōs muthos*) as a substitute for a fully cogent proof.[9] Certainly Socrates is ready to forecast at *Timaeus* 26e4–5 that the long narrative that Timaeus will unfold about the origin of the cosmos will be no 'made-up story' (*plasthenta muthon*) but a 'true account' (*alēthinon logon*). But if Socrates meant any more than 'account' by *logos* here, that would be over-optimistic, as Timaeus apologetically admits at the beginning of his speech. It is appropriate in more than one way that he addresses his apologies to Socrates:

> And if, Socrates, in much of what we say about many of these matters – about the gods and how everything has come to be – we turn out to be unable to give you arguments which are always in every way consistent with themselves, and completely rigorous, do not be surprised. If we can provide likelihoods that are as good as any that could be provided, we must settle for that. For we should remember that I the speaker and you the judges of my speech are human in nature, so that on these questions we should accept the probable story, and look for nothing beyond it.

(*Timaeus* 29c4–d3; trans. T. Chappell)

The Socrates of the Socratic dialogues would have rejected the content of Timaeus' cosmological narrative as uncontrolled and unproved speculation – just as he would have rejected the form of it as *makrologia*. It is not that Plato in the *Timaeus* rejects this rejection. Socrates' standards of logical cogency are endorsed by Timaeus and the other characters of the dialogue just as assuredly as they were by Socrates himself. The point is not that Plato no longer feels any pressure to meet those standards. It is rather that he has come to think, paradoxically perhaps, that there is something to be gained by flouting them sometimes. Flouting them cannot of course deliver us the full truth, completely proved by fully cogent arguments. But it can deliver us a second-best approach to the full truth. The *Timaeus* tells us more than once (e.g. 47e6–48a6) that the only correct way to understand the visible universe is to realise that good order

---

[9]   The *Timaeus* cosmology as a whole is called both an *eikōs muthos* (29d, 59c, 68d) and an *eikōs logos* (30b, 48d, 53d, 55d, 56a, 57d, 90e) (Partenie, 2009). Cf. *Theaetetus* 164d9, where Protagoras' main doctrine is 'the *mythos* of Protagoras', and Theaetetus' defence of the identity of knowledge and perception is also a *mythos*. Earlier, at *Theaetetus* 156c4, the flux theory of perception was also a *mythos*.

for it means being as much like the rational universe as it can be. 'Accounts, and what they are accounts of, should be of the same nature' (*Timaeus* 29b5): it is no accident that good order for a discourse about the visible world, such as the *Timaeus* itself, means being as much like a fully rational discourse as it can be – even if that is not very like.

When we turn from the philosophy of the cosmos to the philosophy of the polis, we see that the character who comes closest to making the same point in the *Republic* is Socrates himself:

> 'What then?' I said, 'do you think it justice for someone to speak about what he doesn't know, as if he did know? ... Have you not noticed that all opinions without knowledge are things of shame? The best of them are blind. Or can you see any difference between blind men who take the right road [surely an allusion to *Meno* 96e ff.], and those who have a true belief without *nous*?'
>
> (*Republic* 506c)

The *Republic* offers us the highest and most metaphysically ambitious doctrine in all of Plato's works: a theory of the perfect city, based on a vision of the perfect good. And it offers us this through the mouth of the wisest of all men, Socrates. Yet even here, Plato makes it quite clear that the most that can be offered is not knowledge, but only true belief *without* an account: merely an image (*ton eikona*, 509b1) – a comparison or analogy (*apeikasia,* 514a1) – of reality. It is not the good itself that Socrates' discourse offers us, but only an *interest-payment* on the good. (*Republic* 507a2: the Greek word for 'interest-payment' is *tokos*, literally 'child'. Plato means something derived from the good, by way of the good's own generative powers, which shares its properties and reveals them in small compass.) At *Republic* 501e2–5 Socrates explicitly tells us what he is doing in describing the perfect city as *mythologia*: even at his highest pitch, what Socrates deals in is not *logos* strictly speaking, but only *muthos*.

This is most obvious of all when Socrates attempts to speak about the Forms[10] (which is what he is just beginning to do at 506c, as quoted above). The Forms are the centrepiece of Plato's whole metaphysics – the very metaphysics that is to take us beyond every kind of *muthos* and into the pure rationality of *logos*. And yet at the dramatic heart of the *Republic* we discover that the only way to speak about the Forms is by way of analogies – namely the three famous analogies that are known as the *images* of the Sun and the Line, and the *myth* of the Cave. The very awareness that is supposed to take us decisively beyond mere guesswork and opinion, into the realm of knowledge, turns out to be something we can only guess at; the very route to a world of pure reasoned argument turns out to be a route that we cannot manage by reasoned argument alone. The theory of Forms, the key to all logical cogency everywhere, is itself an example of the kind of speculative metaphysics that the Socrates of the early dialogues would have rejected for a lack of logical cogency. Perhaps it is no accident that, in the dialogues where the theory of Forms begins to be introduced, we never see it introduced for the *first* time, but always as 'nothing new' and as 'what I have been saying all along in all our other conversations' (*Phaedo* 100b1–2). Perhaps Plato found it impossible to write an argument that would serve as a fully cogent direct and frontal introduction of the Forms.

---

[10]   Forms are ideal, perfect entities, of which objects and values in the concrete world are imperfect copies.

This is one of the reasons why we need to do more than pick out of the text of the *Republic* only such patently mythical passages as the myth of Er (*Republic* 614a–621d), compare them with other examples of Platonic myths,[11] and offer only the comment that these myths are meant to adorn Plato's literary style, or, 'among other things, to make philosophy more accessible' (Partenie, 2009). Such comments are, no doubt, not mistaken: Plato himself says something like this in, for example, *Laws* 903b. But what they miss is the sense in which Plato sees *every* attempt at positive and constructive philosophical theorising as inevitably partaking of the quality of *muthos* as well as of *logos*. No philosophical theorising can avoid speculation, analogy and imitation, not just because (as Socrates suspected) positive theorising can never be completely logically cogent, but also because language is itself a kind of imitative speculation: as Plato suggests in the *Cratylus*, words themselves encapsulate their makers' view of the world. Writing too is a kind of imitation – the imitation of the thoughts that went into the writing (*Phaedrus* 275d ff.). To take up Plato's book the *Republic*, and be confident thereby that you are getting direct access to Plato's own *logoi* (plural of *logos*), is therefore at least a triply hazardous enterprise.

But if Plato believes, as he says in the *Phaedrus*, that no *written* philosophy can ever be fully serious, then isn't he doing something paradoxical in *writing* the *Phaedrus*? And if Plato's own works, the *Republic* among them, not only include but actually *are* only imitations and analogies, then don't they fall under Plato's own ban on imitation in *Republic* Book X? The answers are yes, and yes. Plato is well aware of the paradox, and fully serious about the ban. The justification for his intellectual enterprise is only that, since mortals are (as Socrates quite rightly argued) incapable of the divine truth of *logos*, the next best thing to that is the 'golden lie' (*Republic* 414b–415d) of *muthos*. For even if imitations and myths are forbidden, not all imitations or myths are equally forbidden: some are better for the soul than others. Notice how bad for the soul the myths of Homer and Hesiod are according to *Republic* Books II–III. (Plato's objection to these myths is not that they're false and therefore shouldn't be taught to children; it's that they shouldn't be taught to children and therefore are false.) Notice too Plato's clear desire, evident throughout the *Republic*, to replace those bad myths with better ones. It should strike us as no accident that what Socrates has just been doing at the beginning of the *Republic* is the very thing that the Athenian court eventually convicted him of – introducing a new goddess to the city (*Republic* 327a1–4; *Timaeus* 26e3).

References

Aristotle, *On Sophistical Refutations* in Barnes, J. (ed.) *The Complete Works of Aristotle* (revised translation), vol. 1, pp. 278–314.

Brisson, L. (1998) *Plato the Myth-Maker* (trans. G. Naddaf), Chicago, IL, University of Chicago Press.

Descartes, R. (2006 [1637]) *Discourse on the Method* (trans. I. MacLean), Oxford, Oxford University Press.

Hesiod, *Theogony* in Wender, D. (trans.) (1986) *Hesiod: Theogony and Works and Days*, Harmondsworth, Penguin.

Hesiod, *Works and Days* in Wender, D. (trans.) (1986) *Hesiod: Theogony and Works and Days*, Harmondsworth, Penguin.

---

[11]   E.g. the myths of the afterlife in *Gorgias* 523a–527a, *Laws* 903b–905b and *Phaedo* 107c–115a; the myth of the winged soul in *Phaedrus* 246a–249d; the myth of Theuth at *Phaedrus* 274c–275e; the cosmological myth of *Statesman* 268–274e; the Atlantis myth in *Timaeus* 21e–26d and *Critias*; and the myth of the androgyne in *Symposium* 189d–193d.

Homer, *Iliad* in Lattimore, R. (trans.) (1951) *The Iliad of Homer*, Chicago, IL and London, University of Chicago Press.

Homer, *Odyssey* in Lattimore, R. (trans.) (1967) *The Odyssey of Homer*, New York, Harper Row.

Liddell, H.G. and Scott, R. (1968) *A Greek-English Lexicon* (ninth edn), Oxford, Oxford University Press.

Newton, Sir Isaac (1726) 'General scholium' in *Philosophiae Naturalis Principia Mathematica* (3rd edn).

Parmenides (28) in Diels, H. and Kranz, W. (1961) *Die Fragmente der Vorsokratiker* (7th edn), 3 vols, Berlin, Weidmannsche Verlagsbuchhandlung.

Partenie, C. (2009) 'Plato's myths' in Zalta, E.N. (ed.) *The Stanford Encyclopedia of Philosophy* [online], http://plato.stanford.edu/archives/fall2009/entries/plato-myths/ (Accessed 21 January 2010).

Plato, *Apology* (trans. T. Chappell) from Hamilton, E. and Cairns, H. (1989) *Plato: Collected Dialogues* (fourteenth edn), Princeton, NJ, Princeton University Press, pp. 3–26.

Plato, *Cratylus* (trans. T. Chappell) from Hamilton, E. and Cairns, H. (1989) *Plato: Collected Dialogues* (fourteenth edn), Princeton, NJ, Princeton University Press, pp. 421–74.

Plato, *Laws* (trans. T. Chappell) from Hamilton, E. and Cairns, H. (1989) *Plato: Collected Dialogues* (fourteenth edn), Princeton, NJ, Princeton University Press, pp. 1225–513.

Plato, *Phaedo* (trans. T. Chappell) from Hamilton, E. and Cairns, H. (1989) *Plato: Collected Dialogues* (fourteenth edn), Princeton, NJ, Princeton University Press, pp. 40–98.

Plato, *Phaedrus* (trans. T. Chappell) from Hamilton, E. and Cairns, H. (1989) *Plato: Collected Dialogues* (fourteenth edn), Princeton, NJ, Princeton University Press, pp. 475–525.

Plato, *Protagoras* (trans. T. Chappell) from Hamilton, E. and Cairns, H. (1989) *Plato: Collected Dialogues* (fourteenth edn), Princeton, NJ, Princeton University Press, pp. 308–52.

Plato, *Republic* (trans. T. Chappell) from Hamilton, E. and Cairns, H. (1989) *Plato: Collected Dialogues* (fourteenth edn), Princeton, NJ, Princeton University Press, pp. 575–844.

Plato, *Sophist* (trans. T. Chappell) from Hamilton, E. and Cairns, H. (1989) *Plato: Collected Dialogues* (fourteenth edn), Princeton, NJ, Princeton University Press, pp. 957–1018.

Plato, *Theaetetus* (trans. T. Chappell) from Hamilton, E. and Cairns, H. (1989) *Plato: Collected Dialogues* (fourteenth edn), Princeton, NJ, Princeton University Press, pp. 845–919.

Plato, *Timaeus* (trans. T. Chappell) from Hamilton, E. and Cairns, H. (1989) *Plato: Collected Dialogues* (fourteenth edn), Princeton, NJ, Princeton University Press, pp. 1151–211.

Pope, A. (1732) *An Essay on Man* in Butt, J. (ed.) (1963) *The Poems of Alexander Pope*, London, Methuen.

Protagoras, *On the gods* (80) in Diels, H. and Kranz, W. (1961) *Die Fragmente der Vorsokratiker* (7th edn), 3 vols, Berlin, Weidmannsche Verlagsbuchhandlung.

Thucydides, *A History of the Peloponnesian War* in Warner, R. (trans.) (1972) *Thucydides: A History of the Peloponnesian War* (introduction and notes by M.I. Finley), Harmondsworth, Penguin.

Wilde, O. (2000) *The Importance of Being Earnest* in *The Plays of Oscar Wilde* (introduction and notes by A. Varty), Ware, Wordsworth Editions.

Xenophanes (21) in Diels, H. and Kranz, W. (1961) *Die Fragmente der Vorsokratiker* (7th edn), 3 vols, Berlin, Weidmannsche Verlagsbuchhandlung.

Secondary Source 4.4   Glenn W. Most, 'From logos to mythos'

(Source: Buxton, R. (ed.) (1999) *From Myth to Reason? Studies in the Development of Greek Thought*, Oxford, Oxford University Press, pp. 25–36; footnotes edited)

Some readers, perhaps, will be startled by my title. And understandably: after all, they will long have been familiar with the idea that the development of mankind as a whole has tended to follow a trajectory leading from Mythos to Logos, and will have learned that a development of this sort not only took place in ancient Greece but has also been one of the most important parts of the legacy of the Classical world to Western civilization. Such an idea is expounded in numerous works of scholarship and, even more, in countless popular presentations;[1] and indeed there is much to be said for it, not least that it enlists the Greeks in the service of modern impulses towards Enlightenment whose benefits many of us have come to count upon (and thereby legitimates at one stroke both the ancients and the moderns). Hence my present purpose is not to call into doubt the fact, and the value, of some kind of evolution—in at least certain parts of the history of Europe and of those countries influenced by Europe—away from a traditional, narrative, anthropocentric view of the structure and meaning of things (which I shall call here Mythos) and towards a more progressive, logical, mechanical kind of account (let us call this Logos) —indeed, even brief reflection upon the news reports coming from those parts of our world today in which such an evolution has been delayed, halted, or reversed is enough to make one glad for its even sporadic appearances. Nor would I wish to deny that, among the turbulent innovations characteristic of Greek culture in the first millennium before Christ, there were also a number of sustained critiques of traditional myths in the name of something much like our own version of rationality—after all, considering how much delight the Greeks took in putting things into question, it would have been quite strange if it had not occurred to at least some of them to criticize their myths too.

Rather, I would like to suggest that more has been involved, both in this familiar evolution from Mythos to Logos in ancient Greece and above all in the discovery of this evolution by the modern historiography of ancient Greece, than a simple and self-evident movement of spiritual progress on the one hand—what Leopardi derided as '*dell'umana gente | Le magnifiche sorti e progressive*'[2] [progressive and splendid destinies of the human race]—and its inevitable recognition by a value-free modern scholarship on the other. Matters were—matters always are—infinitely more complex, and hence more interesting. Perhaps the most convenient entrance into these unfamiliar complexities is provided by a book whose very title announces its programmatic adherence to these familiar notions: Wilhelm Nestle's *From Mythos to Logos: The Self-Development of Greek Thought from Homer to the*

---

[1]   Three examples chosen not quite at random: Burkert (1985), 312; West (1986), e.g. 116; Wilamowitz-Moellendorff (1959), 40f.

[2]   G. Leopardi, 'La ginestra o il fiore del desorto' [The broom, or flower of the desert], lines 50–1. The italicized words are a citation, as Leopardi himself indicates in an ironic note: 'Parole di un moderno, al quale è dovuta tutta la loro eleganza.' [Words of a modern writer, to whom all their elegance is owed.] They come from his cousin, Terenzio Mamiani. As often, Leopardi deploys citationality in order to undermine facilely optimistic notions of human progress.

Sophists and Socrates.[3] For widespread though these notions may be, Nestle's version of them remains one of their most eloquent, and stubbornly influential, formulations; and below the superficial clarity and simplicity of his conception lie significant tensions and surprising paradoxes which can tell us much not only about this single scholar but also about this whole set of issues in modern scholarship.

Consider the following passage, taken from its very first page:

> Just as the surface of the earth was originally completely covered by water, which only gradually withdrew and let islands and continents appear, so too for primitive man the world surrounding him and his own nature were covered over by a mythical layer of beliefs, which only over a long period of time gradually retreated enough for larger and larger areas to be uncovered and illuminated by rational thought.[4]

As mythical images go, this one is certainly quite striking; but what Nestle evidently intended was in fact to use it to illustrate the inevitable *decline* of Mythos. For this scholar, Mythos and Logos were above all two contradictory ways in which humans can establish meaning in their world: as he put it in the book's opening words,

> Mythos and Logos—with these terms we denote the two poles between which man's mental life oscillates. Mythic imagination and logical thought are opposites. The former is imagistic and involuntary, and creates and forms on the basis of the unconscious, while the latter is conceptual and intentional, and analyses and synthesizes by means of consciousness.[5]

Put in these terms, one might suppose that these two modes of consciousness could be connected with one another in any one of a number of ways, that they could operate simultaneously at different levels or upon different objects, or could follow upon one another in the one direction or the other at any time. But, at least for Nestle, this is far from being the case. He claims instead that a unidirectional, necessary sequence determines both modes temporally in such a way that at a first stage we find Mythos, and only at a second one, derived from it, Logos. In his eyes, the paradigmatic example of this fundamental process of human history is provided by ancient Greece, and above all by the sixth and fifth centuries BCE, when 'the mythic thought of the Greeks was replaced step by step by rational thought, one domain after another was conquered for natural explanation and research, and the consequences for practical life were drawn'.[6] To linger for a moment upon Nestle's oceanic analogy: once upon a time—let

---

[3]   W. Nestle (1940).

[4]   Ibid. 1: 'Wie die Erdoberfläche ursprünglich ganz mit Wasser bedeckt war, das erst allmählich zurückwich und Inseln und Kontinente hervortreten ließ, so war auch dem primitiven Menschen die ihn umgebende Welt und sein eigenes Wesen von einer mythischen Vorstellungschicht überdeckt, die erst in längeren Zeiträumen allmählich soweit zurücktrat, daß immer größere Gebiete vom denkenden Verstande bloßgelegt und erhellt wurden.'

[5]   W. Nestle (1940), 1: 'Mythos und Logos—damit bezeichnen wir die zwei Pole, zwischen denen das menschliche Geistesleben schwingt. *Mythisches Vorstellen* und logisches Denken sind Gegensätze. Jenes ist—unwillkürlich und aus dem Unbewußten schaffend und gestaltend—bildhaft, dieses—absichtlich und bewußt zergliedernd und verbindend—begrifflich.' (Italics in original.)

[6]   This is how Nestle (1940: p.v) defines the fundamental aim of his book: 'Denn das ist sein eigentliches Ziel: zu zeigen, wie in einer überraschend kurzer Zeitspanne, im 6. und 5. Jahrhundert v. Chr., das mythologische Denken der Grierchen Schritt für Schritt durch das rationale Denken ersetzt, ein Gebiet um das andere für eine natürliche Erklärung und Erforschung erobert und daraus die Folgerungen für das praktische Leben gezogen wurden.'

us say, at the time of Homer—reality was covered over by mythical hallucinations as though by a primeval layer of water and slime; but in the following centuries—let us say, by the time of Plato—the blazing force of the sunlight of reason gradually evaporated the oozy habitat of the imagination's insubstantial creatures and allowed the contours of the real world to appear. From the sixth century BCE to our own time, the mythic primal ooze has apparently retreated even further—indeed, if only there were no greenhouse effect to melt the polar ice, we might be able to imagine it vanishing once and for all one day. It is only on the basis of mythical notions like this that Nestle could ever have come up with the title for his book, a title which may seem innocuous at first glance, but which becomes more bizarre the more one reflects upon it.

What is so problematic in this title and in the ideas underlying it? Not so much that Nestle's interpretation distorts the meaning of many individual texts and authors of earlier Greek literature—after all, doing just this is our own profession and favourite pastime. Nor is it simply that he has constructed a framework which brightly illuminates some developments that may well have been taking place in the period he is considering but which leaves many others in the shadows—for such disadvantages are the inevitable consequence of any approach, and no hermeneutics [study of the principles of interpretation] can avoid thematizing some phenomena at the cost of turning others into foil or context for them. Nor shall I insist here upon the obvious objection that in the period of Greek literature Nestle is investigating there is much of Logos in Mythos and much of Mythos in Logos—for example, that already Homer betrays unmistakable traces of familiarity with the rationalizing allegorical interpretation of traditional legends[7] and attempts wherever possible to suppress or play down the more monstrous or irrational elements of Greek mythology, while Plato still introduces what he calls, and what we recognize, as myths, in order to communicate what he says is incapable of being revealed by logical means alone: for Nestle's teleological model [relating to design or purpose], as he himself points out,[8] is certainly flexible enough to be able to deal with such hybrids.

All the objections listed and, by *praeteritio* [omission, passing over], not posed in these sentences, can, and indeed should, be directed against Nestle's project and against the many like it for which Nestle may be taken as a particularly helpful example. But here I should like instead to place the emphasis upon a feature of Nestle's approach which is much more fundamentally problematic than these particular issues or results and which resides, instead, in the basic structure of this model. What I have in mind is Nestle's basic premises of a strict teleological development from Mythos to Logos, from a starting point measured as defective by unalterable criteria towards a necessary goal identified with the knowledge of an absolute and unchanging reality which must, inevitably, one day be attained. When we are asleep, says Heraclitus, everyone dreams his own world, but once we awaken we all share the same world;[9] Nestle replies that in Mythos the world is always distorted, and in a potentially infinite number of different ways, but that in Logos there is only one world and we all inhabit it. If this were not so, the Greek achievement could not claim any validity for us: for, in Nestle's view, the Mythos of the Greeks, entertaining as it is, must in the end remain foreign to us, while the Logos of the Greeks is identical with our Logos

---

[7]   See Most (1993).

[8]   e.g. (1940), 17–18, 21.

[9]   Heraclit. B 89 DK.

too. For Nestle, if the myths of Greek Mythos seem familiar to us, it is only because, and to the extent that, particular historical traditions have chosen, for whatever reasons, to transmit them to us; but the law of non-contradiction and the syllogism [deductive scheme, of argument], towards which Nestle's book points at the horizon like an Aristotelian Promised Land which Plato could see but not yet enter, are ours not because of specific historical contingencies but because of the essential nature of our minds and of the reality surrounding us. Hence for Nestle the Greek development from Mythos to Logos in fact amounts to a process of dehellenization, a transformation which begins with the Greeks as being merely Greeks and ends up with the Greeks as being universal, unconditioned specimens of humanity in the abstract (a condition to which Germans, too, can aspire).

It should be clear by now that Nestle's concept of Logos is—within his very own terms—deeply implicated in Mythos: his fundamental construction of a necessary development from Mythos to Logos corresponds not to what he himself could ever describe as Logos, but rather to impulses which he too would have no choice but to assign to the realm of Mythos. Indeed, there is scarcely a single symptom of Mythos listed by Nestle which could not be diagnosed throughout his own text. Does Mythos make rich use of personifications? But Nestle too personifies his two basic concepts and permits them to enter into lively relations with one another and to become involved in complicated dramatic plots, seemingly without the decisive contribution or the active participation of concrete human beings. Does Mythos translate mental contents into reified material terms? But Nestle too conceives the mental development he is describing as being identical with the bodily maturation of a child towards adulthood, as though the one process were just as continuous, irreversible, and natural as the other. Does Mythos believe in the magical effect of cult practices? But Nestle too ascribes to the great geniuses of human history supernatural capabilities which are necessary for his model as the motors of historical evolution and which he emphatically indicates, but which in the end he cannot explain, but only revere. And any lingering traces of doubt about the status as Mythos (in Nestle's sense) of Nestle's Logos can perhaps be banished by a sentence, a place, and a date. The sentence reads:

> To go on this path from Mythos to Logos, to grow up from the immaturity of the mind to its maturity, seems to have been reserved for the Aryan peoples since these are the ones that belong to the most highly talented race, and among these there is in turn no other people in whom this development can be traced so clearly as among the Greeks.[10]

And the place and date: Stuttgart 1940, the city and year in which Nestle's book was first published.

Nestle was apparently not at all a Nazi himself and seems to have thought, oddly, that by means of this book he could help to increase the amount of rationality in the troubled world around him.[11] But it is hard to work with pitch without blackening one's hands; and no pitch is blacker, or stickier, than the

---

[10]   W. Nestle (1940), 6: 'Diesen Weg vom Mythos zum Logos zu gehen, aus der Unmündigkeit zur Mündigkeit des Geistes emporzuwachsen, scheint den arischen Völkern als denen der höchstbegabten Rasse vorbehalten geblieben zu sein, und unter ihnen läßt sich wieder bei keinem diese Entwicklung so klar verfolgen wie bei den Griechen.' The peculiar mixture, in this sentence, of the cosmopolitan language of Kant's Enlightenment with the racist vocabulary of Hitler's Germany has a markedly distasteful effect.

[11]   Cf. (1940), p. vi.

opposition between Mythos and Logos. It would not have been worth spending so much time on Nestle if he had been only a little confused, or if he had merely intended to secure for his book a greater success in the local markets of his day by introducing into it a few poetical interludes and topical remarks. On the contrary, Nestle's book is significant enough to justify my recalling, but at the same time revising, his title with my own. For it is not merely the case that his work is still widely known and astonishingly influential, above all, but not only, in Germany; what is more important is the evident fact that the teleological, developmental program formulated so strikingly in its title is familiar even today to many people who otherwise, when they hear the name Nestle, think only of chocolate.

So fascinated is this program by the questions (which I deliberately set aside here), whether, and if so for what reasons and in what ways, the Greeks actually did undergo some sort of development from Mythos to Logos in the sixth and fifth centuries BCE, that it seems entirely to fail to recognize the existence of another, no less important development, namely the decisive evolution since the eighteenth century in modern Western culture's understanding of rationality from Logos to Mythos—hence my title. During this latter period, philosophers have developed the concept of rationality in such a way that they have created from within it a new concept of the mythic which has put into question any simple opposition between Mythos and Logos and has revealed Mythos to be in fact nothing other than an especially interesting category of Logos. The momentous consequence of this process is that Logos itself, so far from remaining unaffected by this development, has been fundamentally altered by it, and has turned out not to be so completely different from Mythos as earlier generations had sometimes supposed. In other words: the concept of Logos presupposed by Nestle has been hopelessly out of date for over two centuries, and what has above all demonstrated its inadequacy has been precisely the modern study of myths, especially Greek myths.[12]

Until the eighteenth century, myths were understood entirely on the basis of the rational structure of a Logos which was itself not put into question by them. Whether this Logos was conceived as philosophical or religious, pagan, Jewish or Christian, in antiquity, the Middle Ages, or the Renaissance, was of course of decisive importance for the specific results, but mattered surprisingly little for the methodological question of the way in which this Logos had to deal with those myths. The myths never put the Logos into question; only the Logos put the myths into question, and never failed to find the right answer for every question. This could happen in one or the other of two ways.

On the one hand, the Logos could simply exclude the myths, by demoting them to the status of being an error, a lie, a sacrilege, or a mere entertainment. Plato took over, extended systematically, and grounded philosophically Xenophanes' polemic claim that the myths of the poets had nothing to do with true religion;[13] the rest of Western culture went on to inherit as a central topos Plato's anguished contempt for the poets (but without Plato's anguish). When Plutarch writes, 'muthos means a false logos similar to a true one',[14] or when Crates distinguishes muthos from historical truth (historia) and fiction (plasma) and

[12] The secondary bibliography on the history of modern studies of ancient myth is enormous. I have found most useful the following general works: Bäumler (1926): Burkert (1980); Burkert and Horstmann (1984); Feldman and Richardson (1972); Fuhrmann (1971); Graf (1993a); Gruppe (1921); Horstmann (1979).

[13] Xenoph. B 11 DK; Pl. *Rep.* 377e–383c.

[14] Plu. *De glor. Ath.* 4 = *Mor.* 348a: ὁ δὲ μῦθος εἶναι βούλεται λόγος ψευδὴς ἐοικὼς ἀληθινῷ.

defines it as 'a representation of what has not happened and is not true',[15] or when St Paul contrasts Jesus' message of salvation as the truth (*alētheia*) with the *muthoi* of the unbelieving heathens,[16] the Logos, whatever it happens to be in each case, remains untouched by the Mythos: the definitive rejection of the Mythos as insubstantial cathartically reinforces the Logos.

Or on the other hand, the Mythos could be integrated into the Logos—but only according to the rules of Logos' game and only if the Mythos were thereby entirely denatured. For this purpose the indispensable tool for many centuries was allegorical interpretation; indeed, there are worse ways to define our own modern age than to call it the first largely post-allegorical period. The duty and the achievement of allegorical interpretation was always to corroborate the Logos by demonstrating that the Mythos, which had at first seemed so alien to it, had in fact always already been entirely contained within it. Certainly, defending the Mythos, protecting it from total condemnation, was sometimes the allegorist's conscious intention, sometimes an unexpected by-product he readily welcomed; but the fundamental asymmetry of allegorical interpretation is immediately revealed by the fact that the allegorists never looked for traces of Mythos in their Logos, but only for traces of their Logos in the Mythos. Allegorical interpretation always started with a Logos and returned to it after a detour which passed through Mythos but which did not change the Logos in any way whatsoever.

In every regard, allegorical interpretation confirmed the correctness of the Logos and saved the Mythos only in so far as it proved that the latter's intelligibility rested upon its identification with the former. *Objectively* the doctrinal content of the Mythos was always unmasked at the end as being identical with the already quite familiar contents of whichever Logos was involved—whether these contents were historical or physical, moral or psychological, cosmological or medical, theological or astrological, seems to be of considerable interest to some modern historians of allegoresis but was in fact of no importance at all as far as the methodological principles themselves were concerned. There was no kind of doctrinal content whatsoever that could be transmitted *only* by means of myths: for each particular content, a purely conceptual version could readily be found that was both possible as a paraphrase and plausible as a premiss.

Subjectively the allegorist presupposed that the person who spoke in terms of Mythos was himself already entirely familiar with this Logos and had deposited it as his authentic message within the myths he invented—in other words, that he had cloaked the Logos in Mythos in order to protect it from the ignorant masses, or to guarantee that only a few elect would have access to it, or to save himself from being misunderstood, or to attract children and challenge the curious, or for whatever reason the allegorist could invent. In any case, the poet told the people myths, but at the same time he himself knew the Logos perfectly well: had he wished to, he would have been entirely capable of uttering forth the Logos unconcealed, like Protagoras in Plato's dialogue, who offers his listeners the choice whether they would prefer that he deliver his speech as a *muthos* or as a *logos*.[17] In this way the contrast between Logos and Mythos is distributed between the two opposite roles of the *sophos* and the *polloi*, the wise (male) individual and the ignorant masses: the trajectory of the Logos through the

---

[15]   Crates fr. 18 Mette = Sext. Emp. *Adv. math.* 1. 264: μῦθος δὲ πραγμάτων ἀγενήτων καὶ ψευδῶν ἔκθεσις.

[16]   2 Tim. 4: 4; Titus 1: 14; cf. also 1 Tim. 4: 7; 2 Pet 1: 16.

[17]   Pl. *Prt.* 320c.

Mythos corresponds to a communicative path which begins with the author and finally reaches the allegorical interpreter unaltered, but only via the detour of the benighted masses, who, like an idiot entourage, surround the royal Logos in its intentionally transparent mythical incognito, celebrating its fame and completely misunderstanding its meaning. Even Nestle still locates the Logos in the endangered individual genius and the Mythos in the indolent, suspicious masses.[18] Hence allegorical exegesis cannot, strictly speaking, have any awareness of the kinds of historical problems modern hermeneutics was created to deal with, since the allegorist supposes that he is merely rediscovering a postulated identity: what he thinks he finds in the myths is the very same Logos which the wise author had concealed within them; the transparent community of a few enlightened individuals over the course of centuries provides a last instance and guarantee for the universal intelligibility and eternal self-identity of the Logos contained within the Mythos.

But there is always a fly in the allegorist's soup: for even if the *content* of the Mythos always reveals itself in the allegorist's hands to be nothing other than the Logos, none the less the *conversion mechanisms* which transform that Mythos into his Logos remain resolutely arbitrary and cannot themselves ever be successfully subsumed into the Logos. In other words, the soberly edifying content of the Logos remains the goal of allegorical interpretation, but in the capricious techniques of allegorical interpretation the Mythos' whimsical vivacity lives on to avenge itself on its dry, learned mockers. The whole rhetorical toolbox of tropes and figures of speech is emptied out and put to use so as to transform the characters of Mythos into the concepts of Logos, by metaphor and synecdoche [figure of speech: part stands for whole], by metonymy [use of the name of one thing for that of another] and synonymy [use of words of the same meaning], by homonymy [use of words identical in form, but different in meaning], and antonymy [use of words of opposite meaning], etc.: in the end even the dustiest philosophy is rescued by a suavely unscrupulous rhetoric, and however rational, expectable, and edifying the tenets finally revealed turn out to be, the means that had to be used in order to attain them are always irrational, astonishing, and entertaining. Consider Proclus' replies to Socrates' criticisms of some traditional Greek myths:

> the ejection of Hephaestus from Olympus signifies the procession of the divine from the top down to the last creatures in the sensible world, a procession begun, ended, and guided by the Demiurge and the universal Father; the chaining of Cronos represents the union of all creation with the intellectual and paternal transcendence of Cronos; the castration of Ouranos suggests in hidden language the separation out of the Titanic chain from the order which maintains the whole ...[19]

What I wish to emphasize here is not so much the evident discrepancy between the poets' colourful stories and the philosopher's technical doctrines, but rather the apparent lack of any sense on Proclus' part that he needs to explain to us just why he has chosen the specific figural transformations he has in order to create these philosophical meanings: for him, clearly, the doctrinal ends entirely justify the rhetorical means. *We*, who at long last have managed with some difficulty to take up a position outside the allegorical tradition, may well be able to enjoy such colourful feats of sleight of hand aesthetically, as a form of literary play within the Logos, by means of which the enchanting techniques of poetic texts manage to live on in the philosophical treatises which were supposed after all to

---

[18] (1940), 18.

[19] Procl. *in Rem publ.* i, p. 82, 10–18 Kroll.

demystify and replace them; but the conceptuality of the Logos, which was supposed to be guaranteed by allegorical interpretation, certainly ends up in the long run being undermined by it instead. How can the Logos possibly tolerate Proclus' frank admission, just a few lines later, that philosophical allegorical interpretation sometimes asserts the exegetical equivalence of something not only with what is similar to it, but even with what is exactly opposite to it?[20] It is hardly surprising that different allegorists—or indeed even the same one—can present a multiplicity of entirely different interpretations for the very same mythic story without almost ever comparing them, let alone criticizing or refuting them. A procedure which does not allow the rational instance of intersubjective control to set any limit to the potentially infinite multiplication of mutually incompatible but not mutually competitive interpretations must sooner or later suffer a crisis. For allegorical interpretation, that crisis came in the eighteenth century.[21]

But scholars are stubborn, and many variants of the traditional allegorical approach to myths managed to survive well beyond the end of that century. Karl Philipp Moritz performed an aesthetic exclusion of Mythos from Logos,[22] Walter F. Otto an ontological [relating to being or existence] one;[23] the unmasking of Mythos as an error in the name of Logos was the ambition of Max Müller, for whom myths were a childhood illness of language, and of Jane Ellen Harrison, for whom they were ritual misunderstood.[24] And anyone who subscribes even today to a global hermeneutic strategy that prides itself on imagining that it is the science which holds the keys to all mysteries—so for example the Freudians, the Jungians, and the Marxists—inevitably ends up resurrecting old techniques in new forms.

References

BÄUMLER, A. (1926), *Das mythische Weltaltar: Bachofens romantische Deutung des Altertums* (Munich).

BURKERT, W. (1980), 'Griechische Mythologie und die Geistesgeschichte der Moderne', in W. den Boer *et al., Les Études classiques aux XIXe et XXe siècles: Leur place dans l'histoire des idées* (Entretiens sur l'Antiquité Classique, 26; Vandœuvres-Geneva), 159–207.

BURKERT, W. (1985), *Greek Religion, Archaic and Classical* (Oxford; orig. *Griechische Religion der archaischen und klassischen Epoche* (Stuttgart, 1977)).

BURKERT, W. and HORSTMANN, A. (1984) 'Mythos, Mythologie', in J. Ritter and K. Gründer (eds.), *Historiches Wörterbuch der Philosophie*, vi (Basle), 282–318.

FELDMAN, B., and RICHARDSON, R. D. (1972), *The Rise of Modern Mythology* 1680–1860 (Bloomington, Ind.).

FUHRMANN, M. (1971) (ed.), *Terror und Spiel: Probleme der Mythenrezeption* (Poetik und Hermeneutik, 4; Munich).

GRAF, F. (1993a), *Greek Mythology: An Introduction* (Baltimore; orig. *Griechische Mythologie: Eine Einführung* (Munich, 1985)).

GRUPPE, O. (1921), *Geschichte der klassischen Mythologie und Religionsgeschichte während des Mittelalters im Abendland und während der Neuzeit* (= W. H. Roscher, *Ausführliches Lexikon der griechischen und römischen Mythologie,* Suppl. 4; Leipzig).

---

[20] Ibid. 20–3.

[21] I have discussed the crisis of allegorical interpretation in the 18th cent. in Most (1989).

[22] Moritz (1791).

[23] Otto (1929); (1955); (1963).

[24] (1890), pp. iii, xxxiii; (1903); (1912); (1921).

HARRISON, J. E. (1890), *Mythology and Monuments of Ancient Athens* (London).

HARRISON, J. E. (1903), *Prolegomena to the Study of Greek Religion* (Cambridge).

HARRISON, J. E. (1912), *Themis: A Study of the Social Origins of Greek Religion* (Cambridge).

HARRISON, J. E. (1921), *Epilegomena to the Study of Greek Religion* (Cambridge).

HORSTMANN, A. E. A. (1979), 'Der Mythos-Begriff vom frühen Christentum bis zur Gegenwart', *ABG* 23: 7–54, 197–245.

MORITZ, K. P. (1791), *Götterlehre oder mytholgische Dichtungen der Alten* (Berlin).

MOST, G. W. (1989), 'The Second Homeric Renaissance: Allegoresis and Genius in Early Modern Poetics', in P. Murray (ed.), *Genius: The History of an Idea* (Oxford), 54–75.

MOST, G. W. (1993), 'Die früheste erhaltene griechische Dichterallegorese', *RhM* 136: 209–12.

NESTLE, W. (1940), *Vom Mythos zum Logos: Die Selbstentfaltung des griechischen Denkens von Homer bis auf die Sophistik und Sokrates* (Stuttgart).

OTTO, W. F. (1929), *Die Götter Griechenlands* (Bonn).

OTTO, W. F. (1955), *Die Gestalt und das Sein: Gesammelte Abhandlungen über den Mythos und seine Bedeutung für die Menschheit* (Darmstadt).

OTTO, W. F. (1963), *Mythos und Welt* (Darmstadt).

WEST, M. L. (1986), 'Early Greek Philosophy', in J. Boardman, J. Griffin, and O. Murray (eds.), *The Oxford History of the Classical World* (Oxford), 113–23.

WILAMOWITZ-MOELLENDORFF, U. VON (1959), *Der Glaube der Hellenen*, i, 3rd edn. (Darmstadt).

Secondary Source 4.5   Graham Harvey, 'Myth: a Religious Studies approach'

(Source: Written for the Open University (2009) by Dr Graham Harvey, Department of Religious Studies)

Introduction

Myth and ritual have been topics of perennial debate and research in the academic study of religion. In concert with other disciplines, particularly Classics, Religious Studies has devoted considerable attention to the relation between myth and ritual. Additionally, definitional questions have been asked about the relation between myth and other kinds of narrative, and between ritual and other kinds of activity. The inherently multi-disciplinary project of Religious Studies makes it possible to lay studies of classical texts and scriptures alongside data drawn from ethnological observation of myth-telling among diverse communities. The result is a fresh perspective inspiring further debate in relation to historical and contemporary myths as well as contributing to critical debates about myth as an academic category. The underlying assumption of this article is that myth should be approached as *performance*. It is inspired by the statement of the Māori scholar Te Pakaka Tawhai that:

Our *korero tahito* ['ancient explanations' or, perhaps, myths] have in the telling more or less depended in the past upon such factors as the appropriateness of the emotional climate in which it is told, the messages stated by the surroundings on the occasion, the body language of the narrator and the attributes that the human voice lends to words.

(Tawhai, 1988, p. 99)

'In the past' here does not mean that such practices have been abandoned; Tawhai clearly demonstrates that this is not the case. Rather, he is pointing to the change caused by the publication of Māori traditional knowledge and its subsequent treatment as something rigid, inapplicable to new situations or superseded. Performed myth, to the contrary, is vital and performative: acting on people and changing the world.

In part this article's focus on myth-telling is a deliberate attempt to collapse the dichotomy between myth and ritual, motivated by a revaluation of religious action and, indeed, a definition of religion as something people *do* rather than something people *believe*. The article uses research among indigenous communities and self-identified Pagans to engage with tales about 'tricksters' (deity-like but morally ambiguous beings whose selfishness can, strangely, have positive results for others); myth-inspired novels arising from 'animist realism' (a narrative device based on an understanding that the world is full of life); and tales about mimicry (mimesis) and what happens when hunters take it too far.

By discussing some contemporary ways of telling inherited and borrowed myths, the article contributes to consideration of myth as enchantment (understanding the world differently, even counter-intuitively) and empowerment (acting differently in the enchanted world). It also seeks a way to incorporate redundancy and entertainment into definitions of myth and religion. It suggests (and perhaps no more than that) some ways of engaging with myth that arise from attending to contemporary oral and literary performances and may cast new light on material more commonly approached by scholars of myth.

Segal and Smith on myth and ritual

The thoughts of two leading Religious Studies scholars provide two foundations for this argument about performative myth. The first is best known for his studies of myth but encourages the treatment of myth as ritual. The second is best known for his studies of ritual but reflects on the historical divorce between academic studies of myth and ritual.

Robert Segal is among the most devoted scholars of the history of myth-ritualist theories. He has written extensively (e.g. 1998, 2005, 2006, 2008) about debates concerning the relationship between myth and ritual initiated by William Robertson Smith's *Lectures on the Religion of the Semites* (1889). Anthropologists, biblical scholars, classicists, literary critics, medievalists and scholars of religion, among others, have pondered whether myths interpret rituals or provide their preparatory scripts, or whether rituals perform myths or require explanation by them. Conflicting positions have been taken about whether myth or ritual precedes and/or takes precedence over the other. Segal does more than survey such arguments. His critical interventions point toward areas in which myth–ritualist arguments generate understanding – in relation to myths and rituals that are integrally linked in particular ways; and other areas where they do not – in relation to those myths and rituals which operate separately from one another (Segal, 2008, p. 120). He is less interested in the interpretation of the content of myths – what they seem to say about the world – and more interested in myth's functions and effects. Drawing on the work of American classicist Gregory Nagy (2002), Segal anticipates that future research will emphasise the performative nature of myth. Even when myths have no connection with rituals, the key fact is that myths are told, spoken and performed in other (verbal and non-verbal) ways. Segal invites us to consider myths or myth-tellings as rituals and not only as aspects of or occasions for rituals (Segal, 2008, pp. 120–1).

Following Segal along this route is timely in part because it coincides with growing interests among Religious Studies scholars in the 'doing' of religion, especially in everyday rather than elite contexts. Religion has for too long been defined in accordance with the canons of official teachings of beliefs about sacred persons or activities as scripted by texts and hierarchies (a peculiarly Christian approach, it turns out). Paying so much attention to authorities has privileged texts and their authorised interpreters over speakers, readers, hearers, performers, doers, doubters, resisters, transgressors and others. An indicator of the currency of a performative turn in studying religions – and of treating vernacular rather than elite practices as definitive – is the fact that 'myth' and 'ritual' are absent from the contents page (though not the index) of Mark C. Taylor's field-leading *Critical Terms for Religious Studies* (1998). Just as an earlier scholarly interest in 'mysticism' is markedly demoted in favour of a new engagement with 'body', so ritual is reconceived as but one form of religious activity in an article on 'performance'. However, myth is not even mentioned in the book's entries about 'belief' or 'writing' and only in passing, in a few articles, as a phenomenon within some religions. This suggests that 'myth' is just a religious term and not a scholarly one. However, there are plenty of places throughout the book where the telling of stories, the narration of events, the elaboration of ideas, the reification of identities and/or the metaphorical mapping of territory might well have been presented as 'myths'. If this were done, it would further emphasise rather than diminish the performative nature of myth.

The second foundational thinker requests that we constrain any over-enthusiastic adoption of the idea that myth and ritual are inseparable. As important as the whole myth–ritualist debate is, it can conceal the fact that myth and ritual have normally been treated entirely differently. One leading scholar of ritual in Religious Studies, Jonathan Z. Smith, writes:

> The history of the imagination of the categories of myth and ritual was sharply divergent. To say myth was false was to recognize it as having content; to declare ritual to be 'empty' was to deny the same.
>
> (Smith, 1987, p. 101)

Although the myth–ritualist theories discussed by Segal seem positively to value both myth and ritual, Smith argues that:

> The study of myth was conceived, from the beginning, as the study of belief, an enterprise of a 'hermeneutic of recovery' in that the study welcomes the foreign if only to show, by some allegorizing or rationalizing procedure, that it is, in fact, the 'same'.
>
> (Smith, 1987, p. 101)

Just as the Christian ideologues of late antiquity interpreted Greek and Roman myths to find 'truths' (albeit mistaken or at best sub-Christian ones), so Enlightenment sages and Victorian folklorists and anthropologists sought to retrieve the fragments of useful knowledge tangled up in the corrupt myths of the masses or indigenous populations. In contrast, Smith argues that in the study of ritual 'there is no question of beliefs, no problem of the endless subtlety of words, but rather, nonsense' (1987, p. 102). There can be no proper interpretation of ritual because ritual has no meaning. Therefore, the scholar's job is to describe rituals and explain (away) why people persist in performing nonsensical acts until someone teaches them better.

Further consideration of the history of thought about myth and ritual elucidates Smith's argument. Because this is a religious history it will also highlight the value of a Religious Studies approach to these issues. Myth and ritual – which might otherwise be identified as core elements of religion – have both come to be popularly associated with foolishness or obsolescence. Myth, for example, is often used to mean 'false idea' (e.g. the earth is flat) while ritual can denote 'senseless habits' (e.g. kneeling to pray). During the Protestant and Catholic Reformations, Christians distinguished among themselves according to a myth about the authority of the Pope and a ritual centred on the relationship between bread and flesh in the Mass. The question of whether bread is symbolic of flesh or actually transformed into flesh, and the question of what the quotation of the words 'this is my body' in the ritual means and achieves, have implications for the production and interpretation of art, the place of materiality, embodiment and agency in Western culture, and a range of translation problems between different linguistic and cultural domains. The problems of Reformation polemics did not cease with the rise of Enlightenment rationalism. Partly as a response to the wars generated by earlier religious disagreements, Enlightenment ideologues distinguished themselves from religious people by rejecting myths (e.g. the necessity of faith) and rituals (e.g. repetition rather than experimentation). After over five hundred years of such polemics, the negative valuation of the terms 'myth' and 'ritual' seems natural. Even in scholarly debate about mythology it is possible for someone to say 'that is just a myth'. Even in academic conferences about ritual it is possible for someone to insist that 'my gratitude is not merely ritual'. However, as Smith carefully explains, while it is possible to denigrate myth and ritual equally, in academic study they have been treated as different kinds of falsehood. While useful knowledge can be recovered from the misrepresentations and confusions of myth (naming a forest 'sacred' may imply its environmental value), rituals are empty, meaningless repetition that achieves nothing that is empirically demonstrable (blessed bread is still bread; rain dances do not lead to rain).

Smith's own contribution to the study of ritual is to demonstrate that it is a 'mode of paying attention ... a process for marking attention' (Smith, 1987, p. 103). Smith insists that we should continue to understand ritual as 'empty' and should not seek hidden facts requiring the kind of explanatory procedures applied to myth. However, if we treat the *performance* of myths as another mode of 'paying attention', we will see afresh that the act of myth-telling is at least as important as any interpretable content. Attending to the entertainment value of myth-telling may support this claim, not least by highlighting the gap between myths and sermons.

The performativity of myth is stressed here because it coincides with some indigenous perspectives in which not only the characters in myths but the myths themselves, especially when told (rather than dormant and waiting to be told), are active. The remainder of this article engages with myth-telling in several animistic contexts. A brief introduction to animism will aid the more focused engagement with animist/animate myths, trickster tales, animist realism and hunting mimesis.

Animism

Animism is a label for a kind of religion or culture in which people are encouraged to live respectfully as members of local communities made up of humans and other living beings too (Harvey, 2005). Harry Garuba (a Nigerian scholar and poet living and teaching in South Africa) writes:

Perhaps the single, most important characteristic of animist thought – in contrast to the major monotheistic religions – is its almost total refusal to countenance unlocalized, unembodied, unphysicalized gods and spirits.

(Garuba, 2003, p. 267)

It is not that physical objects symbolise spiritual realities, but that material reality is valued as the located, embodied and physical form of beings of vital importance to life. Correlated to this is the trend among animists to value human embodiment and worldly physicality, and to root religious activity in everyday rather than transcendent concerns.

Animism is the understanding that the world is full of persons, only some of whom are human but all of whom deserve respect. In addition to human-persons there are (or might be, depending on which animists one listens to) bear-persons, eagle-persons, salmon-persons and flint-persons. There may also be persons of the kind more commonly treated under the label 'myth'; that is, beings unknown to modern science, such as thunderbirds, elves and communicative rocks. 'Person' in animist discourses, including myths, is an umbrella term covering a range of beings that include humans and other-than-humans. Animists do not all agree on who is a person and what is an object. In the Ojibwa and cognate languages (in North America) stones are grammatically marked as being of the animate gender: they receive the animate plural suffix –iig (Nichols and Nyholm, 1995, p. 238). So, just as one might ask a French speaker 'are all tables female?' because they are grammatically marked as being feminine (*la table*), the American anthropologist Irving Hallowell asked an unnamed Ojibwa old man, 'Are *all* the stones we see about us here alive?' (Hallowell, 1960, p. 24). The man's reply indicated that the question was not quite right. The issue was not about distinguishing between living beings and what Europeans might call 'inanimate objects'. Rather, the vital matter was the question of relationship, and especially the way to enhance good relations. The old man explained a variety of ways in which particular humans acted towards particular stones, and vice versa, that indicated that both these humans and these stones were persons. They were persons not because they possessed souls or consciousness, but because they acted towards one another in ways that indicated relationship. However, not all animists would agree with this Ojibwa version – questions about acting relationally are difficult to translate into taxonomies, especially because relationships (or acts of relating) change.

It is important to note that as a label *animism* is more like the word *monotheism* than it is like *Christianity*. It is a style of religion rather than a specific religion. Just as there are many different kinds of monotheism (Baha'i, Christian, Islamic, Jewish, Zoroastrian and others), so there are different kinds of animism. Animists can be found in many places and do not have a single, global organisation, a defining text or an agreed list of who to include as 'person' and what to identify as 'object'. Animism is itself localised, embodied and physical – it varies from place to place and fluidly resists codification. The difficulty in writing about animism is comparable to the danger Tawhai identifies of writing about traditional knowledges to explain one point and being misunderstood as presenting everything there is to say, thereby fixing what is flexible into a rigid and dead form (Tawhai, 1988, p. 99).

Animist animate myths

Much has been made here of Ojibwa examples of animism because it is not only stones that are considered to be capable of relationship and therefore of definition as persons. Hallowell notes that in the early to mid twentieth century, when he conducted ethnological research among them, the Ojibwa of the Berens River (south-central Canada) distinguished

> two general types of traditional oral narratives. 1. 'News or tidings' (*täbätcamowin*), i.e., anecdotes, or stories, referring to events in the lives of human beings (*änícinábek*). In content, narratives of this class

range from everyday occurrences, through more exceptional experiences, to those which verge on the legendary. ... 2. Myths (*ätíso'kanak*), i.e., sacred stories, which are not only traditional and formalized; their narration is seasonally restricted and is somewhat ritualized. The significant thing about these stories is that the characters in them are regarded as living entities who have existed from time immemorial.

(Hallowell, 1960, pp. 26–7)

Furthermore, and far more interestingly, the *ätíso'kanak* are not spoken about as 'a body of narratives'. Rather, the Ojibwa term refers to the characters who are involved not only as elements in the stories but also as living beings, and thus as participants in the telling of their stories. In support, Hallowell quotes William Jones's note that 'Myths are thought of as conscious beings, with powers of thought and action' (Jones, 1919, p. 574n). 'Myths' here translates a term that refers to the persons of the stories rather than the stories or story-telling. To talk about these *ätíso'kanak* is to involve them, and that makes it likely that they will act in the world. Since some of the most powerful acts of these beings are not necessarily positive for humans it is dangerous to invoke them. Paying too much attention to them at inappropriate times or without appropriate caution is not a good idea. Ojibwa myth-telling is therefore surrounded by careful restrictions, especially that the more powerful of them are only told in winter months when ice covers the lakes and restricts all movement. Myths may be entertaining stories but they are also powerful creators not only of worldviews but, if we listen attentively to Ojibwa tales, of the living (material and social) world.

Another American anthropologist, Barre Toelken, summarised the potentially dangerous effects of myth-telling among the Navajo (of the south-western United States) by saying that 'The Navajos believe that language does not merely describe reality; it creates it' (1990, p. 389). Short snippets of myths can be spoken in rituals to evoke all that is implicit in the whole myth – but this must be done cautiously so as not to invoke or invite the unrestrained presence of those named or narrated. The full rendition of a myth is surrounded by expressions of care even when considerable humour or drama is involved. Here too, some myths are only to be told (about) in the winter, indoors, by particular people, with appropriate verbal and non-verbal signals of respect for those talked about and those addressed. Since myth-telling makes the world a different place it is good to try to make it a better rather than a worse place. Invoking cannibal monsters or maleficent witches is never a good idea unless you first establish a strong defence against them. Often that is done in ritual rather than in myth-telling.

Telling trickster tales

A significant class of myths from places as widely separated as California and Nigeria involves the activities of tricksters. In these, Coyote or Spider (among others) cobble together the reality of the world out of whatever is available or can be begged, robbed or abused (to paraphrase the various assertions about Coyote made by William Bright, 1993). The world is not what humans would make it, and not what we might wish it to be. Neither is it what an entirely good god would make if such a being did not have to work with more tricky collaborators or opponents. In fact, trickster myths suggest that the world in its current state is the product of the combined acts of all beings in the cosmos. A positive spin on such tales might indicate that the acts of tricksters make the world so much more colourful by resisting or wrecking the neat but dull ordering of reality that might otherwise have ensued. There is something delightful, enticing or seductive about tricksters and their stories. No naivety, however, should permit the mistake of thinking it would be good to be part of such a myth. Coyote may make fire available to humans (Toelken, 1990, p. 21). Spider may establish the rules by which men's work and women's work are defined (Pelton, 1980, p. 39). But to do so they steal, lie, abuse and injure. Tellers and hearers of the tale might enjoy these stories and celebrate the results of trickster trickery, but they are unlikely to mistake any part of the myth for an encouragement to imitate or replicate such antisocial and immoral acts.

At the same time, the tales are not told precisely to justify the moralising punchline 'do not act like this'. Myth worlds are more complex than this. Pelton struggles throughout his book about West African trickster tales (1980) to find the right way to say what they do. 'Doubleness' seems helpful in accepting the contradictions of hearing appallingly bad behaviour presented as moral lessons. Pelton writes of Ashanti *anansesem* ('Spider/trickster-myths' and by extension all traditional tales):

> Each begins with the disclaimer, 'We do not really mean, we do not really mean what we say.' ... the stories are told to children as a way of imparting tradition and renewing the present world. But in these stories, the Ashanti are concerned, not so much with the physical shape of the world or with the solemn acts that created it, but with its inner shape – its doubleness, its closeness to and distance from the 'wild,' its absurdity and delightfulness, its renewability. As the children learn this inner shape, they become the source of that renewal.

(Pelton, 1980, p. 69)

Perhaps the kind of satire that presents political and celebrity misdeeds as entertainment serves up a mild version of this doubleness. Trickster tales, as Toelken noted in relation to the alive myths of the Navajo, suggest the more dangerous possibility of the making present and energising of those who only accidentally benefit others.

Trickster tales are not only told by elders to children. Just as they continue to entertain they also carry educative messages worth hearing throughout life. Their ambiguity and polyvalence may explain why trickster myth-telling has become a strand in the creation or reaffirmation of Pagan religions in recent years. The term 'Pagan' was adopted as a self-definition (rather than an accusation levelled against despised others) by people celebrating a range of loosely related spiritualities focused on the celebration of 'nature', broadly and fluidly conceived as the material world and not only as pristine ecosystems remote from human habitation (Harvey, 2007). Already radical (in the context of a modernity derived from Protestantism and the Enlightenment) for celebrating rather than rejecting ritual, making it the primary mode of Pagan religious engagement with the world, Paganism has also elevated oral myth and story-telling above any kind of literature. While Pagans are catered for by a prolific publishing industry, there are no Pagan scriptures. If people do memorise scripts for rituals they treat these as starting points for regular improvisation.

Such tendencies seem most marked among the more eco-activist Pagans. They are particularly likely to act as if deities, elemental beings (earth, air, fire and water) and some or all of the characters of traditional European folklores (e.g. elves, dwarves, boggarts, trolls, elementals, leprechauns, fenodyree and faeries) really matter. The stories Eco-Pagans tell around festival or protest campfires (Letcher, 2001) are likely to be rich in references to classical myths and more recent folklore. Eclectic borrowing habits result in a remarkable range of old stories being brought into play in the making of this old/new religion. Pages could be devoted to the ways in which classical Greek, Roman, Egyptian, Irish and/or Norse myths are retold. We could debate whether or not Pagans are 'true' to the sources they draw on. We could ask whether their myth-telling in celebrations of solstices, equinoxes and so on (or in the proliferating websites containing such material) bear any relation to historical or ancestral practices. However, rather than focus on tales of praiseworthy deities and enviable heroes, the wilder trickster myths are of interest here.

J.R.R. Tolkien released elves from their (temporary) tame and cute existence in Victorian children's books to become noble and aloof denizens of Middle Earth. While some Pagans share the prevalent predilection for romanticism, other myth-tellers are remembering the horror and danger of what were once Northern Europe's arch tricksters. In tales told around Eco-Pagan fires it is remembered that the elves and faeries do not necessarily wish humans well. They are at least ambiguous, always 'other' and often outright hostile. Remembered Anglo-Saxon poetic charms offer aid against the darts shot by elves to wound people. Terry Pratchett's Discworld book, *Lords and Ladies*, evokes this older lore by warning that delightful words can hide more sinister truths:

> Elves are wonderful. They provoke wonder. Elves are marvellous. They cause marvels ... Elves are terrific. They beget terror ... No-one ever said elves are nice. Elves are bad.

> (Pratchett, 1993, pp. 169–70)

The title of Pratchett's book utilises a circumlocution which avoids naming those whose attention is deemed undesirable. Just so, since Irish faeries are not really little they can be named 'the little people' with relative impunity. Here we are in the same mythic landscape as animist hunters who avoid naming prey animals when hunting so as not to draw attention to the planned killing (Willerslev, 2007, pp. 100–1). The Pagan world is not entirely rationalist or mechanical, and myths do not merely or casually describe its 'doubleness' but 'continuously re-enchant' (Garuba, 2003, p. 265) and activate it.

The careful telling of fairy-stories by Eco-Pagans, like the careful reference to Coyote's acts by Navajo myth-tellers, honour the larger-than-humanness of the world. Those who tell such myths may seek health and well-being by resisting the tricksters but they do not imagine a world without contest, transgression, and other openings for possibilities to be imagined. In the careful pleasure of telling trickster tales they do not invite people to imitate tricksters. Nor do they simply say 'do not do this'. Myth is myth rather than sermon or treatise because it is open to multiple tellings and possibilities that only emerge in performance. This may indicate why myth-telling and ritual play the lead roles in Pagan and indigenous religious activities.

Animist realism

The myths of some indigenous people animate significant examples of post-colonial literature. They provide not only romantic local flavour but what Garuba has called 'animist realism' in order to draw attention to structural, thematic and strategic literary devices arising from animist world views (Garuba, 1993 and 2003). The use of mythological and fabulous characters and events as stylistic devices in otherwise realistic novels by Latin American authors (e.g. the Cuban Alejo Carpentier) had already been labelled 'magic realism'. Garuba's interest is in

> Writers from Africa, Latin America, and India [who] constitute the most visible group that has taken advantage of the possibilities of narrative representation inherent in the animist conception of the world.
>
> (Garuba, 2003, p. 271)

While the presence of talking animals, protective trees, mobile rocks, *located* deities and *embodied* spirits as characters in these novels indicates a use of or reference to animism and its myths, it is the pervasive '*materialization* of ideas, this habit of giving a concrete dimension to abstract ideas' that Garuba identifies as specific to animist cultural practice (2003, p. 273). He cites the opening sentence of Wole Soyinka's *The Interpreters* (1970, p. 7) as an illustration of animist rather than merely magical realism. When the character Sagoe complains that 'Metal on concrete jars my drink lobes' Garuba notes that the common animist linguistic and cultural practice of 'materialising ideas' aids understanding. He demonstrates this by drawing a comparison with the wish of his grandmother that whoever planted a calabash (ever thirsty for more wine) in a drunken relative's stomach should not prosper. Similarly, Garuba discusses a tobacco tin full of repressed sorrows and memories lodged in Paul D.'s chest in Toni Morrison's *Beloved* (1987). The metaphorical or poetic idea of a container planted within people is treated as materially present and personally active. Myths may not map or describe the world, but they tempt us to perceive that it is not what it seems.

The popular animism referenced and elaborated in such novels is also the broad context in which the more elaborate myths of religious and cultural traditions occur. The recognition of a river as a goddess or of lightning as an act of a god – and the tales in which river goddesses and lightning gods act – are equally demonstrative of the continuous re-enchantment of the world (Garuba, 2003, p. 265) which is full of persons, not all of whom are human, and of the materialization of ideas that propel further action. But the influences work in reverse too: elite myths feed back into popular culture. Garuba introduces his article with a reference to

> a larger-than-life statue of Sango, the Yoruba god of lightning, clad in his traditional outfit, presiding, as it were, over the offices of the major power generation and distribution corporation of the country.
>
> (Garuba, 2003, p. 261)

Modernity and its rationalist, bureaucratic and disenchanted production of energy to supply consumerist production and markets is displayed by local elites (managers of the national power corporation) by reference to a 'traditional' source of power in Sango's myth. However, this elite act makes available to the dispossessed of colonial and post-colonial cultures a verification of the continuing fecundity of animistic world views and practices. The old myths accommodate, absorb and convert new knowledges in fluid and elastic ways (to paraphrase Soyinka, 1976, pp. 53–4, as cited in Garuba, 2003, p. 263). Sango, god of lightning, becomes patron of electricians and authorises the incorporation of electricity into ancient shrines. Stories can now be told about Sango travelling streets lit by electricity, just as sacrifices can be offered to Ogun (guardian of roads and god of iron) to protect car journeys. Modernity's definitive communication and transportation technologies can be colonised by traditional culture and utilised in ways that contest the alienation and disenchantment that are said to go with them.

None of this is to say that there is no conflict between modernism and animism, or that the accommodative elasticity of animism always cushions the effects of modernity on the dispossessed, and always inspires rumours of enchantment. Post-colonial animist realist novels may evoke myths and mythic themes, but these same myths have been manipulated by local and regional elites for centuries before transnational elites insinuated their own myths ('the American dream' or 'wealth by speculation'). Nonetheless, a powerful contest becomes visible to those exposed to animist realism that seduces readers into entertaining the idea that the world can still be enchanted without romanticism. The story is not yet over, and it is unclear which set of myths (those of modernity, animism or some other) will succeed. Even then, we might hope, it will always be possible to retell the myth to reach a different (perhaps always temporary) conclusion. Just as published myths can be reclaimed for retelling, so there will always be another novel. What Garuba writes about animism may as well be applied to myth:

> [A]nimism presents us with a form of religiosity that is not explicitly tied to an expressed doctrine, a codified set of beliefs, or an elaborated theology. It may be seen, very broadly and fundamentally, as providing avenues for knowing our way around our world and society. In this respect, the animist unconscious is much closer to a kind of social imaginary, following Charles Taylor's use of the term as 'the ways in which people imagine their social existence, how they fit together with others, how things go on between them and their fellows, the expectations that are normally met, and the deeper normative notions and images that underlie these expectations'.
>
> (Garuba, 2003, p. 283, citing Taylor, 2002, p. 106)

Mimetic hunting myths

Perhaps there is little at stake in Pagans retelling old stories, even sinister elf-lore, around their fires out in the woods while waiting for a solstice sunrise. Perhaps the reading of animist realist novels, though undoubtedly evidencing the rewriting of the colonialist and modernist story, can be hijacked as entertainment for global elites. It is possible, however, that in one final example of contemporary myth-telling, success in the real world may be enhanced by paying attention to the enchanted doubleness of the animate world. Among Yukaghir hunters in Siberia, tales convey not only practical information about animals and hunting, but also cultural knowledge and values. Like trickster tales, they rarely end with a punchline such as 'and that is how elk got their antlers' or 'and that is why we hunt elk as we do'. Even when such codas occur, they hardly encapsulate the majority of the preceding myth. Myths may inculcate local values – such as, for Siberian hunters, the requirement that possession entails donation – but they resist becoming sermons, creeds or manifestos, instead evoking the larger-than-human cosmos.

A common theme of literature about indigenous hunting insists that the practice and its whole culture is driven by reciprocity. The 'masters of animals' (mythic beings who control and direct animals) or the prey animals themselves are said to give food (animal bodies) to hunters who offer respectful gifts, including returning specific parts of the slain animals to their donors or kin. Hunters give food to their communities and receive other necessities of life in return. These reciprocal processes are so pervasive and entangled that it is not possible to say which act of giving comes first. When they break down, when hunters fail to receive prey or fail to distribute food, someone has to determine what is needed in order to restart the reciprocal engine of life. Myths that speak of animals willingly meeting hunters, of entranced shamans 'journeying' into the distant reaches of strange otherworlds (perhaps underground, under-ocean or above-land) to negotiate with powerful allies or opponents (Harvey, 2003), and especially of animals and their 'owners' (e.g. *Khoisian* animal-ruler) choosing whether or not to feed humans, are central to the repertoire of myths in animistic hunting cultures.

However, the Danish anthropologist Rane Willerslev learned from the Yukaghir men who taught him to hunt that the above narrative is missing a vital step. Certainly these hunters tell each other stories that require animals to be thought of as self-conscious and autonomous agents. However, myths encourage a less rosy view of animals' willingness to die. Those who set out on hunts and those who have killed animals do not talk about killing or hunting. They talk about almost anything else. Killing is disguised in hunting stories and rituals as someone else's act or as a love affair between humans and animals or their 'owners'. Yukaghir hunters do not naively claim that hunting is a simple matter of meeting up with an animal which then offers itself to a deadly assault. Rather, they refer to a somewhat more dangerous form of reciprocity. Certainly, successful hunters are those who are able to persuade prey animals to come within range of weapons. They often do so by mimicking animal behaviour and appearances. The more that hunters are able to act like animals, the more likely they are to get close to their prey. Acting like animals not only requires accurate (even scientific) knowledge about them but considerable empathy too. In fact, the best hunters are remembered as those who could think like animals and share their perspective on the world. This is where matters become dangerous. If hunters seek to persuade animals to treat them as other animals, and even as kin, rather than as predatory humans, there is a possibility that humans rather than animals might be seduced into changing nature, perhaps permanently. The Yukaghir therefore tell each other tales about hunters who have found themselves living among animals, becoming members of animal families, and losing connections with their human relatives. Usually such species-bending myths are resolved by the hunter-become-animal coming into proximity with (other) humans and remembering being human. Some myths mention animals acting strangely, such as elk or bear wandering into hunting camps without fear, and therefore being recognised as humans with only the slight vestiges of connection with their previous humanity.

These hunting myths, then, do not encourage the romantic notion that animals wish to die and be eaten. They recognise that animals need to be tricked. Even the 'owners' of animals have to be persuaded to send animals to hunters. The principle of the culture Willerslev describes is not entirely founded on an egalitarian reciprocity. More precisely, myths inculcate the pervasive functioning of the rule 'those who possess must give and those who lack must receive'. Elk are given to hunters because it is right for those who have no food to receive it. But if hunters are too successful they are then obligated to give. Sometimes they must give themselves or be taken.

Yukaghir hunting myths, rituals and actual hunting practices are summed up in Willerslev's claim that 'Mimesis is the practical side of the symbolic world of animism – its necessary mode of being-in-the-world' (2007, p. 27). The *partial* imitation of prey is the key. Knowing about animals and partially or temporarily sharing their perspective is necessary. But knowing that one is human, and remembering what it means to be a human (especially that one has kin who need food) is vital. Myths provide such knowledge so that it can be enacted in actual hunts. They warn about what happens to hunters whose seductive and cunning presentation of themselves as 'not me' goes too far and loses touch with what is 'not not me' at the crucial moment (Willerslev, 2007, p. 113): they fall prey to alien others or become seduced into remaining kin with the desired animal. But myths, as myths, never simply and blandly state these putative truths. They invite attention to a larger than everyday perspective on the world.

Conclusion

Myths, in Siberia and elsewhere, entertain hearers but also purvey locally valued ideas about the nature of the world that is not evident in other more empirically founded and descriptive discourses. Animist myths are particularly generated by a thoroughly relational world view in which every event is an act (Pflug, 1992) – knowing whose act it is can be life-saving or, at least, life-enhancing. (If the sun only rises because it wants to rise, it may be good to know how, on the necessary occasion, to persuade it to rise.) The attractive enchantment of myths is intimately related to their power to re-enchant the everyday world, revealing (usually only partially) the 'doubleness' and otherness – certainly the larger-than-humanness – of the world. Myths (in contrast to creeds and manifestos) provide their tellers with the means to emphasise different perspectives on the world and human activity within in. They are replete with redundancy: even when they are introduced or concluded by phrases that appear to encapsulate a main point they do not have a single 'message'. A myth that is ostensibly about a creator, a deity, a hero, a hunter, an animal or a rock is also about many other things. Being able to tell it another way is of the essence. As Tawhai says of his people's *korero tahito* (ancient explanations) and of his use of them to introduce Māori religion:

> Flexibility ... enables them to accommodate the capacity of the narrator to render them more relevant to the issues of the day. It is therefore with misgivings and a sense of danger that I must explain that this telling is only for this time, and that tomorrow I would tell it another way.
>
> (Tawhai, 1988, p. 99)

It is possible that an inherited over-emphasis on knowing the intention of the author or the original meaning of a book (inherited from normative Christian treatments of scripture) has misdirected some interpreters of myth. If myths are not narratives hiding truths in need of interpretation, but entertaining enticements to act in particular ways in the world, they need to be approached differently to scriptures. The redundancy with which myths contain far more than their title or putative point is what makes them myths – what defines them in contrast with other narratives.

The question remains: do people believe myths? If they do, do they believe them all in the same way? For example, did the ancient Greeks believe the myths of Athena *and* the myths of Odysseus equally? It seems unlikely that anyone except philosophers ever asked whether Athena really existed – and even fewer people (if any) proclaimed the necessity of 'believing in' Odysseus. Perhaps there are narratives now identified as myths that might once have been considered history and were therefore believed to be true. (Perhaps our 'history' will one day read like myth.) Rather than start a new debate about the wide range of meanings of 'belief' and 'believe', maybe we could content ourselves with the sweeping statement that it seems unlikely that belief is the appropriate or expected response to myth-telling. Although myths may be told as if they were 'just so' stories – explaining how things came to be as they are – their frequent humour and lewdness, entertainment value and performative impact all arrest our attention and make us take notice of the enchanted world that myth wishes us to actively *make-believe* (Segal, 2006, p. 353). Myth invites its hearers to see the world differently and then to participate in making it different. This is a world in which such 'make-believe' could happen.

References

Bright, W. (ed.) (1993) *A Coyote Reader*, Berkeley, CA, University of California Press.

Garuba, H. (1993) 'Ben Okri: animist realism and the famished genre', *Guardian* (Lagos), 13 March, p. 23.

Garuba, H. (2003) 'Explorations in animist materialism: notes on reading/writing African literature, culture, and society', *Public Culture*, vol. 15, no. 2, pp. 261–85.

Hallowell, A.I. (1960) 'Ojibwa ontology, behavior, and world view' in S. Diamond (ed.) *Culture in History: Essays in Honor of Paul Radin*, New York, Columbia University Press, pp. 19–52. Reprinted in G. Harvey (ed.) (2002), pp. 18–49.

Harvey, G. (ed.) (2002) *Readings in Indigenous Religions*, London, Continuum.

Harvey, G. (ed.) (2003) *Shamanism: A Reader*, London, Routledge.

Harvey, G. (2005) *Animism: Respecting the Living World*, London, C. Hurst & Co.

Harvey, G. (2007) *Listening People, Speaking Earth: Contemporary Paganism* (2nd edn), London, C. Hurst & Co.

Jones, W. (1919) *Ojibwa Texts: Part II*, New York, Publications of the American Ethnological Society.

Letcher, A. (2001) 'The scouring of the shires: fairies, trolls and pixies in eco-protest culture', *Folklore*, vol. 112, no. 2, pp. 147–61.

Morrison, T. (1987) *Beloved: A Novel*, New York, Knopf.

Nagy, G. (2002) 'Can myth be saved?' in G. Schrempp and W. Hansen (eds) *Myth: A New Symposium*, Bloomington, IN, Indiana University Press, pp. 240–8.

Nichols, J.D. and Nyholm, E. (1995) *A Concise Dictionary of Minnesota Ojibwe*, Minneapolis, MN, University of Minnesota Press.

Pelton, R.D. (1980) *The Trickster in West Africa: A Study of Mythic Irony and Sacred Delight*, Berkeley, CA, University of California Press.

Pflug, M.A. (1992) 'Breaking bread: metaphor and ritual in Odawa religious practice', *Religion*, vol. 22, no. 3, pp. 247–58.

Pratchett, T. (1993) *Lords and Ladies*, London, Gollancz.

Segal, R. (ed.) (1998) *The Myth and Ritual Theory*, Oxford, Blackwell.

Segal, R. (2005) 'Myth and ritual' in J.R. Hinnells (ed.) *The Routledge Companion to the Study of Religion*, London, Routledge, pp. 355–78.

Segal, R. (2006) 'Myth' in R. Segal (ed.) *The Blackwell Companion to the Study of Religion*, Oxford, Blackwell.

Segal, R. (2008) 'Myth and ritual' in J. Kreinath, J. Snoek and M. Stausberg (eds) *Theorizing Rituals: Classical Topics, Theoretical Approaches and Analytical Concepts*, Leiden, E.J. Brill, pp. 101–21.

Smith, J.Z. (1987) *To Take Place: Toward Theory in Ritual*, Chicago, IL, Chicago University Press.

Smith, W.R. (1889) *Lectures on the Religion of the Semites* (first series), Edinburgh, Black.

Soyinka, W. (1970) *The Interpreters*, London, Heinemann.

Soyinka, W. (1976) *Myth, Literature and the African World*, Cambridge, Cambridge University Press.

Tawhai, T.P. (1988) 'Māori religion' in S. Sutherland and P. Clarke (eds) *The Study of Religion: Traditional and New Religion*, London, Routledge, pp. 96–105. Reprinted in Graham Harvey (ed.) (2002), pp. 237–49.

Taylor, C. (2002) 'Modern social imaginaries', *Public Culture*, vol. 14, no. 1, p. 106.

Taylor, M.C. (1998) *Critical Terms for Religious Studies*, Chicago, Chicago University Press.

Toelken, B. (1990) 'Life and death in the Navajo Coyote tales', in B. Swann and A. Krupat (eds) *Recovering the Word: Essays on Native American Literature*, Berkeley, CA, University of California Press, pp. 388–401.

Willerslev, R. (2007) *Soul Hunters: Hunting, Animism, and Personhood among the Siberian Yukaghirs*, Berkeley, CA, University of California Press.

Acknowledgements

Grateful acknowledgement is made to the following sources.

Primary Sources

Block 3

Primary Source 3.2: Eley, P. (trans. and ed.) (2001) *Piramus et Tisbé*, The Liverpool Online Series: Critical Editions of French Texts, No. 5, http://www.liv.ac.uk/soclas/los/piramus.pdf. Reprinted with the permission of the Liverpool Online Series Editorial Board.

Primary Source 3.5: Walsh, P.G. (trans. and ed.) (1994) Apuleius: *The Golden Ass*, Oxford, Oxford University Press. Copyright © P.G. Walsh, 1994.

Block 4

Primary Sources 4.1 and 4.5: from *Theogony: Works And Days; Elegies by Hesiod and Theognis*, translated with an introduction by Dorothea Wender (Penguin Classics, 1973). Copyright © Dorothea Wender, 1973. Reproduced by permission of Penguin Books Ltd.

Primary Sources 4.6 and 4.40: Lattimore, R. (trans.) (1951) *The Iliad of Homer*, Chicago and London, University of Chicago Press.

Primary Sources 4.9–4.25 and 4.27–4.32: Waterfield, R. (trans.) (2000) *The First Philosophers: The Presocrates and Sophists*, Oxford, Oxford University Press. Copyright © Robin Waterfield, 2000.

Primary Sources 4.34, 4.36, 4.37 and 4.48: David Gallop (trans.) (1997) *Plato: Defence of Socrates, Euthyphro and Crito*, Oxford, Oxford University Press.

Primary Sources 4.45 and 4.46: Lattimore, R. (trans.) *The Frogs*, in Arrowsmith, W. (ed.) (1971) *Aristophanes: Four Comedies*, Ann Arbor, MI, University of Michigan Press. Copyright © William Arrowsmith, 1961, 1962, 1964, 1967 and 1969.

Primary Source 4.49: Reeve, C.D.C. (trans.) (2004) *Plato: Republic*. Copyright © 2004 by Hackett Publishing Company, Inc. Reprinted by permission of Hackett Publishing Company, Inc. All rights reserved.

Primary Source 4.50: Emlyn-Jones, C. (trans. and ed.) (2004) *Plato: Gorgias*, Penguin Books Ltd.

Secondary Sources

Block 3

Secondary Source 3.1: Feldherr, A. (2002) 'Metamorphosis in the *Metamorphoses*', in Hardie, P. (ed.) *The Cambridge Companion to Ovid*, Cambridge, Cambridge University Press. Copyright © Cambridge University Press, 2002. Reproduced with permission.

Secondary Source 3.2: Csapo, E. (2005) *Theories of Mythology*, Malden, MA and Oxford, Blackwell Publishing Ltd. Copyright © 2005, Eric Csapo. Reproduced with permission of Blackwell Publishing Ltd.

Secondary Source 3.3: Higbie, C. (2007) 'Hellenistic mythographers', in Woodard, R.D. (ed.) *The Cambridge Companion to Greek Mythology*, New York, Cambridge University Press. Copyright © Cambridge University Press, 2007. Reproduced with permission.

Secondary Source 3.4: Hardie, P. (2002) *Ovid's Poetics of Illusion*, Cambridge, Cambridge University Press. Copyright © Philip Hardie, 2002. Reproduced with permission.

Secondary Source 3.5: Winstanley, D. (2004) 'Phaethon: seizing the reins of power', in Gabriel, Y. (ed.) *Myths, Stories and Organizations: Premodern narratives for Our Times*, Oxford, Oxford University Press.

Secondary Source 3.6: Zissos, A. and Gildenhard, I. (1999) 'Problems of time in *Metamorphoses* 2', in Hardie, P., Barchesi, S. and Hinds, S. (eds) *Ovidian Transformations: Essays on the Metamorphoses and its Reception*, Cambridge, Cambridge Philological Society. Copyright © Andrew Zissos and Ingo Gildenhard.

Secondary Sources 3.7, 3.8 and 3.11: Wheeler, S.M. (1999) *A Discourse of Wonders: Audience and Performance in Ovid's* Metamorphoses, Philadelphia, PA, University of Pennsylvania Press. Reprinted with permission of the University of Pennsylvania Press.

Secondary Sources 3.9 and 3.12: Schmitz, T.A. (2007) *Modern Literary Theory and Ancient Texts: An Introduction*, Oxford, Wiley-Blackwell.

Secondary Source 3.10: Higgins, C. (2009) 'If looks could kill ...', *The Guardian*, 21 March. Copyright © Guardian News & Media Ltd, 2009.

Secondary Source 3.13: Feeney, D.C. (1991) *The Gods in Epic: Poets and Critics of the Classical Tradition*, Oxford, Oxford University Press.

Secondary Source 3.14: Barolsky, P. (2007) 'Ovid's protean epic of art', *Arion*, vol. 14, no. 3 (winter). Copyright © Paul Barolsky. By kind permission of the publisher and author.

Secondary Source 3.15: Hardwick, L. (2003) *Reception Studies: New Surveys in the Classics*, Greece & Rome, New Surveys in the Classics, no. 33, Oxford, Oxford University Press.

Secondary Source 3.16: Leach, E.W. (1974) 'Ekphrasis and the theme of artistic failure in Ovid's *Metamorphoses*', *Ramus*, no. 3, Aureal Publications.

Block 4

Secondary Source 4.1: Algra, K. (1999) 'The beginnings of cosmology', in Long, A.A. (ed.) *The Cambridge Companion to Early Greek Philosophy*, Cambridge, Cambridge University Press. Copyright © Cambridge University Press, 1999. Reproduced with permission.

Secondary Source 4.2: Murray, P. (1999) 'What is a *muthos* for Plato?', in Buxton, R. (ed.) *From Myth to Reason? Studies in the Development of Greek Thought*, Oxford, Oxford University Press. Copyright © Oxford University Press.

Secondary Source 4.4: Most, G.W. (1999) 'From logos to mythos', in Buxton, R. (ed.) *From Myth to Reason? Studies in the Development of Greek Thought*, Oxford, Oxford University Press. Copyright © Oxford University Press.